I TIME LINE

SEPTEMBER: Germany invades Poland. Britain and France demand German troops withdraw; Poland surrenders to Germany and USSR. Britain declares war on Germany, announces naval blockade. British Expeditionary Forces move into France.

MAY: Germany invades the Netherlands, Belgium, and Luxembourg. Winston Churchill replaces Chamberlain as British Prime Minister. Army of the Netherlands surrenders. Roosevelt asks Congress for money to modernize US military. Germany invades France. British troops retreat to Dunkirk after the fall of Belgium.

JUNE: Churchill delivers famous "...we shall never surrender" speech before House of Commons. Italy declares war on Britain and France; Italian troops begin massing on French border. France signs armistice with Germany—3/5 of France to be occupied by Germany, French forces to be disarmed. German troops enter Paris.

SEPTEMBER: Germany, Italy, and Japan sign Tripartite Pact; Japanese forces occupy French Indochina. Selective Service Act signed by Roosevelt.

AUGUST: Germany begins Battle of Britain with air strike and naval blockade of British Islands. The "Blitz" is on.

APRIL: Germany invades Norway and Denmark.

MAY 31-JUNE 4: British rescue 200,000 British troops and 140,000 French troops from Dunkirk

FEBRUARY: German General Erwin Rommel arrives in Africa with the first troops of Afrika Korps.

MARCH: Roosevelt signs Lend-Lease Act.

APRIL: German troops enter Greece and Yugoslavia; Greece surrenders. Japan and USSR conclude neutrality agreement.

OCTOBER: Italy invades Greece. First draft numbers are selected in the United States.

NOVEMBER: Roosevelt elected to third term.

JUNE: German troops invade the USSR.

JULY: Stalin orders scorched earth policy so the advancing Nazis will find nothing of use. Roosevelt freezes Japanese assets in US. Britain and USSR sign mutual-aid pact.

AUGUST: Japan asks US to lift trade embargo and proposes negotiation; US and Britain issue the Atlantic Charter denouncing aggression.

SEPTEMBER: Gas chambers are used experimentally at Auschwitz; German begins siege of Leningrad (St. Petersburg), which would last over 900 days.

OCTOBER: US destroyer torpedoed by German U-boat; two weeks later another destroyer, the *Reuben James*, is sunk.

NOVEMBER: Japan offers new proposals to defuse tensions with US; US Secretary of State says Japan must withdraw from Mainland China and reinstate Chinese Government; Japanese task force sets sail for Pearl Harbor.

DECEMBER: Japanese council, in Emperor Hirohito's presence, votes unanimously to begin hostilities against the US; Japanese bomb Pearl Harbor, killing over 2,400 US servicemen. Roosevelt declares Dec. 7th a "date which will live in infamy" and asks congress to declare war. Japan attacks Guam; Japanese forces land in the Philippines. Italy and Germany declare war on the US. British and American Combined Chiefs of Staff agree to give priority to war against Germany. British forces in Hong Kong surrender to Japan.

1940

1941

SEPTEMBER-NOVEMBER: All missionaries evacuated from Europe.

JANUARY: Mormon Battalion monument in San Diego, CA, unveiled and dedicated.

AUGUST: Hollywood movie, *Brigham Young,* produced by Darryl F. Zanuck, premieres in Salt Lake City.

JANUARY: General Sunday School board announces major curriculum change, focusing on well-rounded knowledge of gospel.

MAY: Hugh B. Brown appointed as servicemen's coordinator.

DECEMBER: Church announces membership is 750,000.

OCTOBER: Missionaries evacuated from South Pacific and South Africa.

DECEMBER: First Presidency releases statement to the military that they won't knowingly call young men on missions to have them avoid the draft; Church membership at 862,000.

APRIL: Assistants to the Twelve first appointed. General Conference broadcast via radio for the first time to Idaho and southern California Saints.

AUGUST: Honolulu, Hawaii, Stake Tabernacle dedicated.

DECEMBER: No new missionaries sent to South America; those already there permitted to remain.

Ten millionth endowment for the dead performed.

... annexes ...slovakia.

...ly ...Albania.

...ous ...nd ...e

...T: All ...naries in ...ny to ...o neutral ...es.

...Native ...an set apart as ...i Timbimboo).

...ni-replica of ...ooth at Golden ...nal Expo on ... at San

SAINTS

AT WAR

Published by Covenant Communications, Inc.
American Fork, Utah

Printed in Canada
First Printing: November 2001

08 07 06 05 04 03 02 01   10 9 8 7 6 5 4 3 2 1

ISBN 157734-947-4

SAINTS

AT WAR

EXPERIENCES OF LATTER-DAY SAINTS IN WORLD WAR II

ROBERT C. FREEMAN AND DENNIS A. WRIGHT

ACKNOWLEDGMENTS

While our effort to collect and archive the experiences of Latter-day Saint veterans of World War II began rather simply, it quickly outgrew our limited talents and resources. We found ourselves depending more and more on others as interest in the project grew. It is therefore appropriate that we recognize those who have contributed to the success of the Saints at War project.

We would like to express our appreciation for the patient encouragement and support of the editors and staff at Covenant Communications. Their enthusiasm for the veterans and their accounts made the process of publishing this book a delightful adventure.

As professors we are indebted to the support of Brigham Young University, the College of Religious Education, the Religious Studies Center, the Charles Redd Center for Western Studies, the L. Tom Perry Special Collections of the Harold B. Lee Library, and the Church Archives.

The *Saints at War* project and this present volume could not succeed without the aid of our student research assistants and volunteers. Their energy and creative ideas are an invaluable support. Included in this group are Jenny Jane Anderson, Jorg Bachmann, Sarah Bytheway, Treva Elton Colten, Kory Godfrey, Lindsay Payne Halgren, Anita Harker, Laurel Hogge, Brent Montgomery, Edmar Rocha, Janet Skinner, Devin Williams, and Chris Winters.

So many others have been most helpful. We especially appreciate the inspiration provided by our mentor Professor Don E. Norton, and our colleagues at the University of Utah for their ongoing work in collecting the oral histories of our veterans. Our colleagues in Religious Education have provided names of veterans known to them, as well as many useful suggestions. We are also indebted to our associate, Paul Kelly, whose dedication to presenting the accounts of Latter-day Saint veterans inspired us.

We are grateful for the generous assistance of community and Church newspapers for their help in encouraging the veterans to participate.

Our wives, Ja Neal and Kaye, have spent countless hours reviewing our work, making comments, and suggesting improvements. Their encouragement and faith in our efforts were invaluable and their expertise indispensable.

Finally, we express our heartfelt gratitude for the veterans who participated in the Saints at War project. They are wonderful people who have made this volume possible by their willingness to share their most remarkable accounts of courage and faith.

DEDICATION

After a recent visit to our office, a veteran decided that it was time for him to record his wartime experiences. He and his daughter then had a wonderful time making an audio recording. They prepared a written transcript and shared it with their family. He was pleased that a copy was placed in the *Saints at War* archive. Later a telephone call came from his daughter expressing her appreciation for the opportunity she had of sharing memories with her father. We were saddened to learn that her father had unexpectedly passed away a short time after their visit to our office.

It is not unusual for us to receive notification that a veteran has died. While this is always cause for reflection, it was recently made even more personal when my own father, also a veteran, passed away. As I watched the flag-draped casket enter the chapel, I felt more deeply than ever before what it meant to be a veteran.

Sixty years ago, while in the prime of their youth, these young men and women stepped forward, prepared to sacrifice their lives so that the nightmare of tyranny might end. While some have referred to them as "the greatest generation," they are always quick to decline such praise. After all, they were "just doing their duty."

My mother wept as they folded the flag and handed it to her at the dedication of my father's grave. As she held the flag close she clearly remembered the war years and what it meant to have her husband in grave danger each time his ship left port.

Many years have passed since my parents celebrated the end of the war. They raised their family, completed their life's work, and retired to enjoy missions, Church service, and their grandchildren. While ordinary in many ways, their example of faith and service has influenced a new generation in an extraordinary way.

Saints at War is dedicated to them, and to the thousands of Latter-day Saints like them. Their service and their sacrifices have blessed us all.

DENNIS A. WRIGHT

FOREST A. WRIGHT
1920–2001

*Merchant Marine
1943–1945*

TABLE OF CONTENTS

(Opposite page) James Ralph Jensen, electrician's mate third-class USNR, served on the submarine Bullhead. *The submarine was the last naval vessel "over due and presumed lost" during World War II. The* Bullhead *left for patrol on July 31, 1945, and was not heard from after her departure. A letter sent to next of kin cited a report from the Japanese that one of their planes spotted a submarine off the coast of Bali and attacked it with depth charges, claiming two direct hits. It is presumed that the submarine was the* Bullhead. *The attack occurred on August 6, 1945—the same day that the atomic bomb was dropped on Hiroshima.*

Of the loss of her brother, Georgia Jensen Blosil said, "When one loses a loved one in death, it is truly and always an epochal event. Yet war is a powerful, multi-dimensional context within which to lose someone, a context that sustains one's shock and sorrow within its historical framework. One ponders war from its beginning, and the ponder never ceases after its end. There is a lingering quest for meaning, not only for oneself but for humanity."

Heber Partington standing on a bench at a base in the Philippines. Heber was a technician, 4th grade.

Burial site of Charles Stanley Bascom, Royal Canadian Air Force. He was buried Dec. 4, 1944 at Liuerantu, Via Columbo, Ceylon, Plot 3, Row A-B, Grave #4.

INTRODUCTION

It was a rare Saturday when our childhood play did not involve an old World War II army helmet and sticks representing various types of weapons. Much of our interest in the war came from hearing stories told by family members and neighbors who had served in World War II. While our understanding of their experiences was often influenced by the fantasy of comics and movies, we knew that real people had fought that war.

Recent works by such renowned authors as Stephen Ambrose and Tom Brokaw rekindled our interest in the stories we had heard as children. We recalled the many veterans we had known who played such an important part in our lives. They had been our scoutmasters, bishops, home teachers, schoolteachers, and owners of the hometown businesses. Many of these were faithful Latter-day Saints who, after the war, returned home to build productive lives for themselves and their families.

We determined that we would add to the work of others by focusing our research on the unique experiences of Latter-day Saint veterans. The project, *Saints at War,* was organized, and funding was provided. From humble beginnings, we have seen the project grow beyond our initial expectations.

The chief objective of the *Saints at War* project is to create an archive at the L. Tom Perry Special Collections housed in the Harold B. Lee Library at Brigham Young University. This archive will preserve the personal histories, journals, letters, photographs, and other documents contributed by the veterans and their families. The materials we are collecting will be a valuable contribution in Church history, military history, and family history research. After the materials go through the process of review and cataloging, they will be made available to the public. We, along with many others, have recognized the importance this archive will hold for future generations.

While the *Saints at War* project initially focused on World War I and World War II, we are expanding our efforts to include the other wars of the twentieth century. While the task seems overwhelming at times, the cause is justifiably important. We are concerned that if these efforts are not carried out while the participants of these wars are still alive, many documents and photographs that would be of great value to the public, and especially to members of the Church, will be lost, tucked away in shoeboxes and old family albums.

This book should not be seen as a history of World War II. We hope it will be, however, a valuable glimpse of Latter-day Saints' experiences in that war. This volume is divided into three sections. The first provides a brief discussion of the war's impact on the Church and its members. The second section provides accounts of veterans who served in the European Theater. The final section contains accounts of veterans of the Pacific Theater.

The process of selecting accounts that are included in this volume was painstaking. The veteran accounts have been edited for grammar, punctuation, readability, and length. We, with the help of our skilled editors, have gone to great lengths to preserve the integrity and personality of each account. During the editing process, a decision was made to replace commonly used derogatory terms associated with the enemy. Although we acknowledge that such terms were a significant part of the vocabulary of that era, it seemed wise to avoid misunderstanding in the context of the present day. Further, given the topic of this volume, several accounts include graphic details. Finally, we have attempted to verify many of the details such as dates, names, and places, but in many cases we have deferred to the veteran. After all, they were the ones who were there.

Whether the account is that of a soldier in a foxhole in France, an airman in the cockpit of a B-17 over Germany, or a sailor on the deck of a battleship in the Pacific, these are the stories of Latter-day Saint servicemen and women. It is not our intent to glorify war or to deify those who served. Rather, it is our hope that through these accounts the reader will better understand the horrors of war and the awful price it demands of any society. We are confident that as you read these accounts, you will have a greater appreciation for the Latter-day Saints whose faith sustained them during the difficult years of World War II.

ROBERT C. FREEMAN
DENNIS A. WRIGHT

LDS Group at Naka, Horisha, Japan, April 1946. Howard Norton is the second from the left on the front row. Howard Norton served in the Army and was assigned to Luzon in the Philippines near the close of World War II. As a result of being wounded while assisting a comrade to safety, Private Norton was awarded the Purple Heart. After the war, Howard participated in the occupation of Japan and saw many difficult scenes including the devastation imposed on Hiroshima. On a brighter note, Howard was able to attend the baptism of the Sato family, the first convert family to join the Church in Japan after the war. Additionally, he attended a Church conference in Tokyo in April of 1946 before returning home in August of the same year.

THE CHURCH AND WORLD WAR II

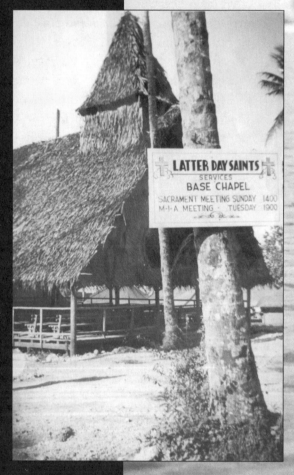

(Opposite page) Convert serviceman baptism in a lagoon off Saipan, early 1945.

(Inset) LDS Base Chapel on New Guinea. LDS serviceman Heber Partington is the contributor of this photo. Each week he would get permission from his Captain to attend the church services which were held in this chapel. On Christmas Day, 1944, he found out he would be leaving for the invasion of the Philippines at Lingayen Gulf. Before leaving, he promised himself if he got home alive, he would do all in his power to keep boys in the Church . . . and he kept that promise.

World War II changed the world—not only during the conflict but forever afterward. Every facet of life, every aspect of human experience was impacted by the war in some way. World War II was not just a pivotal part of a decade, nor of a century, but of all modern recorded history. No war in the history of the world produced more bloodshed and devastation than World War II. By the end of the war many nations lay in ruins. The economic consequences imposed by the war were beyond measure. The greatest cost however, was the toll on humanity. Incalculable numbers of people were scarred both physically and emotionally, and as many as fifty million people died.

Saints at War: Experiences of Latter-day Saints in World War II is about the war's impact upon the Church and its members. World War II was a defining moment for the Church as it offered spiritual leadership both in the United States and abroad. The war also provided a test of the Church's capacity to care for members and nonmembers alike under adverse circumstances. Not only did the Church

have to make adjustments to various programs and policies, it was obligated to provide support to those who experienced the hardships of war both at home and at the battlefront. The Church and its membership contributed in some measure to bring a conclusion to the awful war as priesthood bearers bore arms in a manner reminiscent of the Book of Mormon sons of Helaman.

The interval between World War I and World War II was only twenty years. Those years produced many changes in the Church. An accelerating growth rate in the Church had led to the formation of thirteen new missions, the majority of which were internationally located. Worldwide, there were approximately 800,000 members of the Church at the time of the German invasion of Poland in September 1939.[1] Although the majority of Latter-day Saints still resided in the United States, the international influence of the Church was increasing. Nowhere was the growth pattern more pronounced than in Germany. Consistent growth coupled with a de-emphasis of Church teachings on gathering to America had allowed Church branches in Germany to thrive. At the time of the outbreak of hostilities in Europe, Church membership in Germany was ranked third in the world behind the United States and Canada.[2]

The twenty-year interval between the two world wars meant that those who fought in World War II were the sons of those who fought in World War I. Pictured are Grant M. Turley and his father, Fred Turley, a veteran of World War I.

In 1940, with the threat of war looming over the United States, Congress passed the Selective Service Act, which mandated service for those of military age. The first major group of Latter-day Saint draftees in Utah to take the servicemen's oath did so in November 1940. This was over one year before the events at Pearl Harbor forced the United States to enter the war.[3]

Of course, American Latter-day Saints were not the first to fight in the conflict. Latter-day Saints in Europe, Canada, and other areas were involved from the beginning. While the total number of members outside the United States who participated in the war was a much smaller percentage, it was nonetheless a significant number.[4] Wartime estimates of Church member participation were based on ward and stake reports, which indicated that the number of Latter-day Saints in uniform worldwide steadily increased throughout the war years to a high of approximately 100,000 in 1945.[5]

At the time of the outbreak of hostilities in Europe, Church membership in Germany was ranked third in the world.

According to the 1940 census, members of the Church constituted .5 percent of the population of the United States. At the height of the conflict, however, they comprised approximately 1 percent of the total U.S. military force.[6] According to one estimate, 12 to 15 percent of Latter-day Saints in the western United States were directly involved in the war.[7] In Utah, where the majority of citizens were Latter-day Saints, the state boasted one of the lowest rejection rates for potential inductees of any state in the nation.[8]

In every sense the response of the Church and its members was robust; yet it did not come without clear warnings from key leaders about the hazards of war. David O. McKay, Second Counselor in the First Presidency, proclaimed, "War is incompatible with Christ's teachings. The gospel of Jesus Christ is the gospel of peace. War is its antithesis and produces hate. It is vain to attempt to reconcile war with true Christianity." President McKay continued, "Even though we sense the hellish origin of war, even though we feel confident that war will never end war, yet under existing conditions we find ourselves as a body committed to combat this evil thing. With other loyal citizens we serve our country as bearers of arms, rather than to stand aloof to enjoy a freedom for which others have fought and died."[9] Thus, while the Church taught the futility of war, at the same time it called upon its members to answer the call of the various nations to assist in bringing an end to the conflict.

The contribution of Latter-day Saints to the war was significant—including those who paid the ultimate price for freedom. By the end of the war, approximately five thousand Latter-day Saint servicemen from Allied and Axis nations had died.[10] It was not uncommon for Latter-day Saint families to lose one or more sons in combat. One poignant example of

The Church and the Present War

AN ADDRESS BY

PRESIDENT DAVID O. McKAY

OF THE FIRST PRESIDENCY
of the
CHURCH OF JESUS CHRIST
OF LATTER-DAY SAINTS

April 5, 1942

Throughout the conflict, Church statements regarding war gave direction to members about how to view the tragedy that had engulfed the world, and gave counsel to the Saints both in the military and on the home front.

Weekly Church Edition

The Deseret News

SALT LAKE CITY, UTAH, OCTOBER 3, 1942

Weekly Church Edition

Message Of The First Presidency

THE WAR

We renew the statement made in our message of the last April Conference, that obedient to the direct command of the Lord given to us more than a hundred years ago (directing us to "renounce war and proclaim peace" Doctrine and Covenants 98:16), the Church is and must be against war, for war is of Satan and this Church is the Church of Christ, who taught peace and righteousness and the brotherhood of man.

As those chosen and ordained to stand at the head of the Savior's Church, as followers of the lowly Jesus trying to live His gospel and to obey His commandments, we must call upon the leaders of nations to abandon the fiendishly inspired slaughter of the manhood of the world now carrying on and further planned.

We condemn the outcome which wicked and designing men are now planning, namely: the worldwide establishment and perpetuation of some form of Communism on the one side, or of some form of Nazism or Fascism on the other. Each of these systems destroys liberty, wipes out free institutions, blots out free agency, stifles free press and free speech, crushes out freedom of religion and conscience. Free peoples cannot and do not survive under these systems. Free peoples the world over will view with horror the establishment of either Communism or Nazism as a worldwide system. Each system is fostered by those who deny the right and the ability of the common people to govern themselves. We proclaim that the common people have both this right and this ability.

We renew our declaration that international disputes can and should be settled by peaceful means. This is the way of the Lord.

We call upon the statesmen of the world to assume their rightful control of the affairs of nations and to bring this war to an end, honorable and just to all. Animated and led by the spirit of Christ, they can do it. The weeping mothers, the distraught and impoverished wives, the fatherless children of the world, demand that this be done. In this way only will enduring peace come; it will never be imposed by armed force. Hate-driven militarists and leaders, with murder in their hearts, will, if they go through to the end, bring merely another peace that will be but the beginning of another war.

We call upon the Saints the world over to pray to God constantly in faith, nothing doubting, that He will bring His purposes speedily to pass and restore peace again to the earth to bless His children.

such loss was the Borgstrom family from Garfield County, Utah, who lost four sons within a period of six months.[11] Latter-day Saints truly sacrificed a great deal for freedom, and in the process left a legacy for future generations to remember.

Latter-day Saints served with distinction in the military. Included among those who answered their nation's call were several future members of the Twelve and First Presidency, including Bruce R. McConkie (Army), Thomas S. Monson (Navy), James E. Faust (Army Air Corps), Boyd K. Packer (Army Air Corps), L. Tom Perry (Marine Corps), David B. Haight (Navy), and Neal A. Maxwell (Army). A number of other future General Authorities also served in the military, including several from nations other than the United States. Included in this list are Ted E. Brewerton (Canada), F. Enzio Busche (Germany), Derek A. Cuthbert (England), and Robert E. Sackley (Australia).[12]

(Top) A memorial service for the Borgstrom sons was held in the Garfield Tabernacle and presided over by President George Albert Smith.

(Bottom) President Boyd K. Packer had an unusual opportunity soon after the close of the war to participate in the first baptisms of postwar Japanese converts. Pictured L to R: Boyd K. Packer, Norton Dixon, Tatsui Sato, Yasuo Sato, Elliott Richards, and Chiyo Sato at the time of the baptismal service.

Faithful Latter-day Saints who served in the war typically maintained strong faith and a reliance upon God for protection. Wherever Latter-day Saint servicemen could be found in sufficient numbers, the Church designated group leaders to conduct Church meetings and other activities. These leaders also provided periodic reports to the Church about the strength of its members as conditions permitted. Church services were often held under adverse conditions in places such as pup tents, open fields, and bombed-out buildings. Occasionally circumstances allowed an enterprising group of soldiers to improve the situations under which they worshiped. One group of Latter-day Saint soldiers erected a brick chapel on a small island in the Mediterranean Sea and

Latter-day Saint servicemen visit outside a newly erected chapel on the island of Sardinia in Italy. Chaplain Eldin Ricks dedicated the facility.

(Far Below) Servicemen's conference in India, 1945.

invited a chaplain to dedicate the facility.[13] Half a world away, on the island of Saipan, a young group of marines built another chapel.

Where larger numbers of servicemen could be gathered, such as at military bases and other centers, Latter-day Saint chaplains organized servicemen's conferences.[14] These gatherings provided a spiritual feast for those who attended. At such conferences, participants engaged in a host of activities, including socials, banquets, and Church meetings at which talks were delivered by chaplains and other leaders. The conferences generally concluded with a testimony meeting. Those in attendance considered it a spiritual highlight of their lives. Young Latter-day Saint soldiers who yearned to associate with other members of their faith gladly used furlough time to join in such assemblies.

(Left) Servicemen's conference in Okinawa, 1945.

(Below) Program for servicemen's conference in France, 1945.

(Far Below) Servicemen's conference in Italy, 1945.

PARIS
CONFERENCE
Church of Jesus Christ of Latter-Day Saints

———

APRIL, 8, 1945
HOTEL LOUVOIS
(Metro, Bourse)

PARIS L.D.S. (MORMON) SERVICEMEN'S GROUP
PARIS, FRANCE

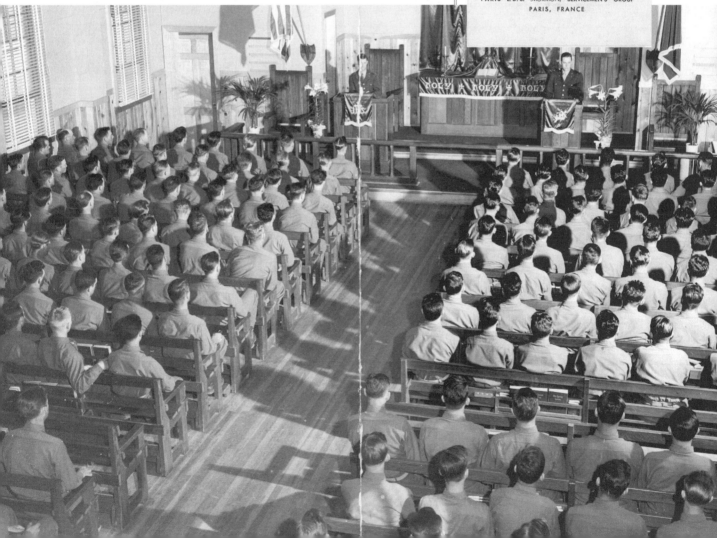

TO THE FOLKS AT HOME:

Dearest Mom;

Here is a sceduel of our confrence meeting. I think I enjoyed it more than any other time in my life. Remember major theo h. burtes our chaplain. He gave a talk on our standards & beliefs. & I got so involved in it. that it made tears come in my eyes.

I think he is the grandest & best leader that any one could hope to have.

I have been enlightened more by his talks. & being under his guidance & supervision sure re-assures a person at a time like this.

With love Lyle.

L.D.S.
CONFERENCE
New Britain

L.D.S. GROUP LEADERS -- NEW BRITAIN

Tank Destroyer-Engineer Sunday School:
                    1st Lt. Rue B. Dastrup
Artillery Sunday School:
                    Captain Andrew Glad
Joint Mutual Improvement Association:
                    Cpl. Emmanuel Ballstaedt

CHAPLAINS

Theo. E. Curtis, Jr.   George R. Woolley
    Headquarters   Headquarters
40th Infantry Division   40th Division Artillery

*   *   *   *   *   *   *

". . . My grace is sufficient for thee: for my strength is made perfect in weakness."
                                    II Cor. 12:9

"There hath no temptation taken you but such as is common to man: but God is faithful, who will not suffer you to be tempted above that ye are able; but will with the temptation also make a way to escape, that ye may be able to bear it."
                                    I Cor. 10:13

"Though he were a Son, yet learned he obedience by the things which he suffered; And being made perfect, he became the author of eternal salvation unto all them that obey him."
                                    Heb. 5:8,9

L.D.S. CONFERENCE
MOUNTAIN VIEW CHAPEL - - NEW BRITAIN
Sunday, 26 November 1944
0900

*   *   *   *   *   *

ORDER OF SERVICE

PRELUDE - - - Frank Nickoley, Gene Wade
HYMN - - "Count Your Blessings" - - No. 218
INVOCATION - - - - Capt. Bromley
SACRAMENTAL HYMN - "How Great the Wisdom" - No. 115
ADMINISTRATION OF THE SACRAMENT
        "Help us, O God, to realize
         The great atoning sacrifice,
         The gift of Thy beloved Son,
         The Prince of Life, the Holy One."
VOCAL SOLO - - - - Capt. Blaine Johnson
         Accompanied by Gene Wade
CONFIRMATION
HYMN - - "We Thank Thee O God for a Prophet" No. 102
VIOLIN SOLO - - - - Frank Nickoley
         Accompanied by Gene Wade
SPEAKERS: - - - W.O. Desmond D. Jensen
                   Captain Andrew Glad
VOCAL SOLO - - - - Capt. Blaine Johnson
SPEAKERS - - - Chaplain Theo. E. Curtis, Jr.
                   Chaplain George R. Woolley
HYMN: - "True to the Faith" - - No. 179
THE BENEDICTION - - Emmanuel H. Ballstaedt
POSTLUDE - - - Frank Nickoley, Gene Wade
    Service conducted by 1st Lt. Rue B. Dastrup
    Chorister - - - Ross Lynch

The role of Church chaplains was not limited to organizing Church meetings and conferences. Latter-day Saint chaplains provided a crucial link between the Church and its members in the service. Whereas in World War I there were only three Latter-day Saint chaplains, by the end of World War II there were forty-six such officers commissioned by the United States military.[15] Like any chaplain, Latter-day Saint chaplains cared for the spiritual needs of any member of the armed forces without regard for religious affiliation. These duties were extensive and included visiting the sick and injured, caring for the despairing, organizing nondenominational church services, conducting marriages, corresponding with soldiers' families, and working side by side with servicemen in combat. They provided official reports to the military branch they represented, and in every way, they sought to lift the morale of the men in uni-

(Above) A program belonging to Lyle G. Stewart who attended a servicemen's conference in New Britain (South Pacific). He wrote a poignant note on the back cover and sent it to his mother.

(Right) Servicemen register for an LDS conference in Kunming, China, 1945.

form. Perhaps the most difficult assignment for Latter-day Saint chaplains was to dedicate the graves of those who died in battle.

Latter-day Saint chaplains not only shouldered these responsibilities, but also assisted the Church in maintaining regular communications with the men in the military. They became a sort of conduit through which messages and literature could be passed to members in uniform. A major challenge for Latter-day Saint chaplains was locating Latter-day Saint servicemen. Young men in the service were often unaware of how to contact a Latter-day Saint chaplain even if one was in the area. In an effort to actively find their own, these chaplains would often employ creative ways to minister to the Latter-day Saint soldiers. One group of especially creative Latter-day Saint "chaps" decorated their jeep with a beehive, an Angel Moroni, and a boldly printed *Deseret*. They then drove among the troops hoping to be recognized by soldiers who were members of the Church.[16] Their resourcefulness paid off as many were located in this way.

One of the stark realities of the war was that it was not unusual for Latter-day Saint servicemen to go many months without meeting even one other person of their faith. For the majority, their time away from home meant prolonged periods without contact with an organized branch of the Church. In large part this was because soldiers, sailors, and airmen were often deployed to remote regions where few units of the Church were organized. This was especially true in the Pacific.

By the end of World War II, there were 46 Latter-day Saint chaplains commissioned by the U.S. military.

(Top) Chaplain Eldin Ricks. Prior to being awarded his commission as an army chaplain, Eldin attended chaplaincy school at Harvard University's Divinity School.

This jeep was decorated by LDS chaplains. On the windshield are images of the Angel Moroni, a beehive, and the word Deseret. *These items were intended to attract the gaze of LDS servicemen in the field. Pictured by the jeep are servicemen Timothy Irons, Vern Cooley, and Claude Burtenshaw.*

On the home front, World War II had a dramatic impact on full-time missionary work. At the outset of the war, the Church evacuated the missionaries from most of Europe. The stories of the missionaries' evacuations are filled with miracles.[17] Remarkably, all escaped without harm. By the end of the war, full-time missionary service had declined dramatically, and those called were sent almost exclusively to missions within the United States.[18]

Recalling American missionaries from Europe and elsewhere left local members alone to administer the programs of the Church, often in nations where there was a limited leadership base. In spite of these challenges, however, local members in Europe persevered, and in the process gained newfound spiritual strength to see them through their trials. At the October 1941 General Conference of the Church, Elder Thomas E. McKay, an Assistant to the Twelve, reported that the headquarters of ten of the twelve European missions remained open. Those missions were located in such places as Belgium, Switzerland, Denmark, England, and Germany. Under the leadership of local mission and district presidents, regular meetings, as well as yearly district conferences, were conducted.[19]

As the events at Pearl Harbor thrust America into the war, the impact of the war on the Church intensified and many of its programs and procedures had to be adjusted. Within weeks of the U.S. declaration of war, the Church issued several policy directives aimed at curtailing the meetings and activities of various auxiliaries.[20] Such moves came in response to travel restrictions imposed by the federal government during the war years.[21] In early 1942, the Tabernacle was closed and as a result, celebrations scheduled in the Tabernacle for the Relief Society's centennial anniversary were canceled. Only General Authorities and selected other priesthood authorities were invited to attend general conferences, which were convened in the Assembly Hall adjacent to the Salt Lake Temple and in the temple itself.[22] The tradition of Christmas lights on Temple Square was suspended until after the war, and the yearly Hill Cumorah pageant was canceled. Additionally, progress on the interior of the Idaho Falls Temple was hindered by the war.

The war's impact was also reflected in the severely diminished numbers of young men attending Church-sponsored institutions of learning. Enrollment at Brigham Young University, for example, decreased from 2,375 full-time day students in 1939 to 884 in 1943.[23] By the close of the war, the ratio of women to men at the university was six to one.[24] Ricks College experienced similar decreases as its enrollment went from 338 in 1940

Liberty Ships

Liberty class ships (LS) carried troops, prisoners, and freight (anything from typewriter ribbons to locomotives) to Allied ports of the world. They were rapidly turned out with techniques similar to assembly lines. The standard LS was 441 feet, 6 inches long; had a beam of 56 feet, 10 3/4 inches; and a gross tonnage of about 7,500. They could carry the same amount of cargo as a freight train with 300 cars, and with a full load could reach speeds of 11 knots. Liberty ships were named only for people who were dead, including regional heroes and pioneers, musicians, philosophers, doctors, politicians, and men killed in action. The USS *Joseph Smith* was purposely sunk when her hull sustained several fractures in a storm in 1944, and the USS *Brigham Young* was renamed after the war, and scrapped in 1973 (*Church News,* Sept. 25, 1983, and Nov. 6, 1983).

to 160 in 1943.[25] Shortages of male students forced the institutions to cancel homecoming, key sports, and many other programs and activities. Young men's Church programs were also greatly affected by the war. Much of the ministering done by the young men's leaders was accomplished through correspondence and other creative means.

During the conflict, the Church emerged as an important beacon for religious values in America. Civic and other leaders regularly sought out Church leaders for advice and counsel. One interesting side note to the war is that two Liberty class merchant ships were named for Latter-day Saint Church Presidents. The USS *Brigham Young* was launched on August 17, 1942, and the USS *Joseph Smith* on May 22, 1943.[26] Local Church members participated in the christening ceremonies as they organized services to accompany the launch of each ship. On both occasions, key local leaders and other dignitaries spoke. In addition, local choirs provided music for each of the celebrations.

In October 1942 the Church organized the General Latter-day Saint Servicemen's Committee and named Church Apostle Harold B. Lee as

The USS Joseph Smith *(May 1943) was the second liberty class ship to be named for a Church President. The first was the USS* Brigham Young *(August 1942). Both were built and launched in California.*

Elder Hugh B. Brown addresses a group of Latter-day Saints in Paris, France, during a conference held shortly after the conclusion of the European war.

(Below) The Church News LDS Service Men's Edition *began distribution in May of 1944.*

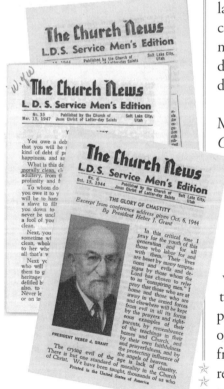

chairman and Hugh B. Brown as servicemen's coordinator.[27] The purpose of the committee was to assist and aid Latter-day Saints in uniform wherever they were stationed. Both leaders traveled extensively to meet, teach, and counsel Latter-day Saint young men. Hugh B. Brown also presided over the British Mission for much of the war. Like so many others, President Brown's life was forever altered by the war when his son, a Royal Air Force pilot also named Hugh Brown, was killed in action in 1942.[28]

President Brown provided valuable reports to Church leaders in Salt Lake City about the welfare of the servicemen as well as local members. One memorable example was his dramatic description written from England of the great number of British citizens "in silent supplication" at the time of the Allied invasion of Normandy on D-Day in June 1944.[29] Two months later, President Brown reported on a series of bombing raids carried out in England, which seriously damaged the British mission home in London.[30] In Britain, as on the continent, damage to Church buildings was yet another example of the destruction associated with the war.

The Servicemen's Committee issued a pocket-sized Book of Mormon and the Church publication entitled *Principles of the Gospel.* Additionally, a small servicemen's edition of the *Church News* was extensively distributed.[31] A servicemen's directory was also made available which included the addresses of Church meetinghouses and mission offices throughout the world.[32] The servicemen's edition of the Book of Mormon in particular provided a great source of strength for servicemen far from home. Many soldiers reported turning to their scriptures whenever a free moment

allowed them to do so. Testimonies of more than a few servicemen were greatly bolstered through such experiences.

In addition to the support efforts initiated at Church headquarters, individual wards and stakes sought to support their servicemen overseas. Many units maintained bulletin boards with soldiers' addresses, and invited members to write to those away from home using V-mail, an economical type of letter used during the war. Such efforts were not without obstacles, however, as many letters sent home from Latter-day Saint servicemen arrived with return addresses that read "somewhere in the Pacific" or some other remote region. The success of wards and stakes in maintaining contact with servicemen varied greatly. A sampling of Latter-day Saint veterans of World War II indicates that many received very little or no mail from local Church units, in part, because of their isolated and constantly

(Top) A group of servicemen involved in scripture study using their servicemen's edition of the scriptures.

(Bottom) The servicemen's edition of the scriptures was pocket-size and thus could be kept with the soldier, airman, or sailor wherever he went. One of the books pictured belonged to Eli Jenkins, and the other to Elder Ezra Taft Benson, who was named to the Quorum of the Twelve Apostles during World War II.

Examples of V-mail, a type of mail used extensively during the war by those in the military to maintain communications with those at home.

changing assignments.[33] Others, however, found great spiritual refreshment in notes from leaders at home or from a care package from their ward.

The challenges of Church members were great, especially in the international setting. Many Saints suffered for want of food, clothing, and shelter. Despite their challenges they persevered, and where they could, they met in homes or bombed-out buildings for Church meetings. In Germany the toll upon the Saints was especially heavy. By the end of the war, 85 percent of German members were rendered homeless.[34] Approximately 550 German members died, most of whom were soldiers. These numbers represent an approximate death rate of 5 percent of Church membership in that nation.[35]

Many German Latter-day Saint soldiers reported careful observance of gospel standards such as the Word of Wisdom. They, too, prayed for protection from injury and death. The experiences of divine intervention in the lives of such Church members were not dissimilar from the experiences of members in the United States.

The war in Europe raged for nearly six years before it finally concluded on May 8, 1945. Ironically, as had happened with World War I, a Church President's death coincided with the end of a terrible world war. President Heber J. Grant died on May 14, six days after V-E Day. Apostle Harold B. Lee commented on the purpose and timing of each leader's death.

Approximately 550 German Latter-day Saints died, most of whom were soldiers.

That President Joseph F. Smith should have died just eight days after the ending of the so-called First World War in Europe, and President Heber J. Grant just seven days following the ending of the Second World War in Europe is not without deep significance. The ending of these great European conflicts apparently means also the beginning of a new era in the work of the Kingdom of God on the earth. Surely the reports of the stewardships of Joseph F. Smith and Heber J. Grant to the councils of heaven have and will make possible even more effective planning for the welfare of the Church of Jesus Christ of Latter-day Saints and its work of righteousness.[36]

Funeral proceedings for President Heber J. Grant, whose death came at the end of the European war. President Grant's administration was the longest of any Church president other than Brigham Young.

Of course, the end of the war in Europe did not mean an end to all of the hostilities. The war in the Pacific continued to rage on. In fact, some of the highest casualty rates of the war came in the summer of 1945. Finally, on August 15, 1945, three months after the end of the war in Europe, the Japanese surrendered after atomic bombs were dropped by the United States on Hiroshima and Nagasaki. Until the bombs were dropped, many had anticipated a full invasion of Japan. Included in the invasion force were many Latter-day Saints who expressed gratitude that their anticipated missions were abruptly aborted.

Following the conclusion of the war in the Pacific, the Tabernacle doors were once again opened and on September

Elder Ezra Taft Benson and Swiss Mission President Max Zimmer with German Latter-day Saint refugees in Langen, Germany, 1946.

4, 1945, a multidenominational thanksgiving service was conducted. The Church soon found itself in a more familiar role as it sought to administer relief to war-torn regions of the world. On November 3, 1945, newly sustained Church President George Albert Smith met with U.S. President Harry S. Truman to make arrangements to dispatch humanitarian relief to starving Latter-day Saints and others in Europe. At the request of the First Presidency, Elder Ezra Taft Benson traveled throughout Europe and assisted in providing aid to Latter-day Saints and others in destitute conditions. From February until December 1946, Elder Benson traveled over 61,000 miles and administered over four million tons of food and supplies to war-ravaged Europeans.[37]

As Elder Benson traveled the missions of Europe and of the British Isles, he was impressed by the resilience of the local members. Devastation was everywhere, but a spirit of faith and hope filled the hearts of the Saints.

Relief came not only from Church headquarters, but from various Church units and individual members. One of the most poignant stories of the postwar period occurred when Saints from the formerly occupied Netherlands sent truckloads of potatoes to assist members in Germany.[38] The healing process was greatly aided by such acts of Christian service and love. In most places in Europe where the Church participated in ministering to the needs of the people, over one-half of the food stuffs and other supplies were allocated for distribution by other relief agencies or churches. Even in the Pacific, Latter-day Saints in Hawaii assisted in aiding Japanese citizens notwithstanding the fact that the Church had very little membership in the island nation. The postwar relief effort of the Church demonstrated the effectiveness of the Church's modern welfare program.

What then is the legacy of World War II for The Church of Jesus Christ of Latter-day Saints and its members? Perhaps

The Church administered over four million tons of food and supplies to war-ravaged Europeans.

Dutch Saints load potatoes onto a truck destined for Germany. Such acts of Christian service by Latter-day Saints after the war demonstrated the forgiving spirit espoused by the gospel.

it is quite simply that the war in some sense defined the Church's role as a healer of hearts in the midst of terrible conditions. Through the war, the Church also had the opportunity to demonstrate both its fierce opposition to war while at the same time signaling that it could be counted on to fight for life's greatest liberties. Finally, the legacy for the Church is found in the contributions of its courageous and faithful members who committed their all to the preservation of freedom during the horrific conflict.

At the dawn of the twentieth century, a century which saw more devastation from war than did the previous nineteen centuries combined, the First Presidency issued a statement, which declared:

> If patriotism and loyalty are qualities manifested in times of peace, by just, temperate, benevolent, industrious and virtuous living; in times of trial, by patience, resistance only by lawful means to real or fancied wrongs, and by final submission to the laws of the land, though involving distress and sorrow; and in time of war, by willingness to fight and battle of the nation—then, unquestionably, are the "Mormon" people patriotic and loyal.[39]

Both current and future generations of Latter-day Saints must hold in sacred remembrance the sacrifices of the faithful Saints who fought in World War II. May the day be hastened in which "nation shall not lift up sword against nation, neither shall they learn war any more" (Isaiah 2:4).

Budget ticket issued to LDS servicemen during World War II. Budget tickets were issued to worthy, butdget-paying members, and served as a "ticket" to various Church activities.

The Church News

L.D.S. Service Men's Edition

No. 7
Nov. 15, 1944

Published by the Church of
Jesus Christ of Latter-day Saints

Salt Lake City,
Utah

Now I pray the Lord to bless you young men in the armed forces of the world, that our Heavenly Father will be with you to sustain you and increase your faith day by day; that you may be preserved in your trials, your hardships, your sufferings, with strength to face the eventualities of each day with the assurance that the Lord, your God, will bring, in His own way and time, everlasting compensations to you for your sacrifices, inasmuch as you walk in His ways and live lives that conform with the priesthood you bear.

I pray for the wives, the children, the mothers and fathers of these men who are serving their countries the world over, that they may be sustained in their waiting, that their anxious fears may be quieted, that comfort and assurance may come into their lives.

I pray for peace; for wisdom, reverence, and humility on the part of the leaders of the nations; for repentance, and a turning to the ways of righteousness on the part of all men (*The Church News: L.D.S. Service Men's Edition,* No. 1, May 15, 1944, 2).

Our hearts, our thoughts, and our prayers go out to those who are in the armed forces. It would appear from all the figures we can gather, that more than one hundred thousand of our young men are in the service of their country, in uniform. We pray for them continually. We pray for the preservation of their lives and for their faithfulness to those things which are dearer than life.

We say to them again to be clean, to keep the commandments of God, to pray, to live righteously; and if you do, peace and understanding will come into your hearts, and our Father in Heaven will comfort you; and will let his presence be felt in the hour of your need.

Young men of Zion, when you return to your homes, return with clean hands and clean hearts—and great will be your happiness, your faith, and your testimony. Your brethren and your loved ones cherish you, pray for you, and await the day of your coming (*The Church News: L.D.S. Service Men's Edition,* No. 7, Nov. 15, 1944, 9).

ENDNOTES

1. *Deseret News 1999-2000 Church Almanac* (Salt Lake City: Deseret News, 1998), 552.

2. Gilbert Scharffs, *Mormonism in Germany: A History of the Church of Jesus Christ of Latter-day Saints in Germany Between 1840 and 1970* (Salt Lake City: Deseret Book, 1970), 222.

3. Joseph F. Boone, "The Roles of The Church of Jesus Christ of Latter-day Saints in Relation to the United States Military 1900-1975" vol. 1 (masters thesis, Brigham Young University, 1975), 332. The present authors are greatly indebted to Joseph F. Boone for his seminal work on Latter-day Saint experiences during the first three-quarters of the twentieth century. This work inspired the authors in their research.

4. Approximately 20-25 percent of Church members lived internationally at this time. Church efforts to track the actual number of Latter-day Saints in the military, at home, and abroad did not begin until the spring of 1942. In the years that followed, however, the Church regularly published its own statistics, which indicated the number of members serving in the military.

5. Heber J. Grant, *Deseret News: Church News Edition*, April 7, 1945, 6.

6. Boone, 337. In June 1946, the First Presidency issued a statement advocating a no-draft policy during peacetime and approximately a year later the number of Latter-day Saints in the armed forces decreased from a wartime high of approximately 100,000 to around 13,000 in May 1947.

7. Ibid., 337.

8. Ibid., 343, 337.

9. David O. McKay, "The Church and the Present War," a general conference address given in the upper room of the Salt Lake Temple and broadcast over KSL radio on April 5, 1942. *Deseret News: Church News Edition*, April 18, 1942, 1, 6. This message was published as a pamphlet and circulated during the war as representing the position of the First Presidency on the war.

10. Boone, 354.

11. Thomas S. Monson, "Becoming Our Best Selves," *Ensign*, November 1999, 18-21. On June 26, 1948, United States General Mark W. Clark presided at a service convened in Garland, Utah, to honor the four young men.

12. For a further discussion about individual contributions of these leaders during the war, see Derin Head Rodriguez, *From Every Nation* (Salt Lake City: Deseret Book, 1990).

13. *Deseret News: Church News Edition*, May 20, 1944, 10.

14. These conferences varied both in size and location. They were held in such locations as the Philippines, the Pacific Isles, Hawaii, the Marianas, Italy, and Britain.

15. The military designation for chaplains was limited to Catholic or Protestant with Latter-day Saint chaplains being grouped with the latter. Individual names of the chaplains are on file with the Military Relations Division of The Church of Jesus Christ of Latter-day Saints, Salt Lake City, Utah. Of the total number of chaplains who served during the war, only a single chaplain, Reed G. Probst, died in combat. A tribute to him was written by a Presbyterian minister and published in the *Deseret News*, July 1, 1944.

16. On one occasion, one group of chaplains decorated the front of their jeep with the symbols of a beehive, an angel Moroni, and the word *Deseret* in hopes that Mormon soldiers would identify themselves to the chaplains. *Deseret News: Church News Edition*, September 2, 1944, 10.

17. For more information see David Boone, "The World-wide Evacuation of Latter-day Saint Missionaries at the Outset of World War II" (masters thesis, Brigham Young University, 1981).

18. *Deseret News 2001-2002 Church Almanac* (Salt Lake City: Deseret News, 2000), 586. According to the Almanac, whereas 1,088 missionaries were set apart in 1939, only 400 were called in 1945.

19. *Deseret News: Church News Edition*, January 17, 1942, 4.

20. *Deseret News: Church News Edition*, February 21, 1942, 1-2.

21. Sheri L. Dew, *Go Forward with Faith* (Salt Lake City: Deseret Book, 1996), 125. The policy was dated January 17, 1942.

22. Ibid., 126.

23. Ernest L. Wilkinson, ed., *Brigham Young University's First One-Hundred Years*, vol. 2 (Provo: Brigham Young University Press, 1975), 388.

24. Ibid., 342.

25. Boone, 338.

26. News of the inauguration of these ships was carried in the *Deseret News: Church News Edition*, August 22, 1942, 1; and May 29, 1943, 2.

27. *Deseret News 1999-2000 Church Almanac* (Salt Lake City: Deseret News, 1998), 136-137. Hugh B. Brown also presided over the British Mission during the last years of the war. One and a half years earlier, in May 1941, Hugh B. Brown was assigned as Latter-day Saint servicemen's coordinator.

28. *Deseret News: Church News Edition*, June 6, 1942, 3.

29. *Deseret News: Church News Edition*, July 8, 1944, 8.

30. *Deseret News: Church News Edition*, August 12, 1944, 12.

31. *Deseret News: Church News Edition*, May 15, 1944, 1.

32. *Deseret News: Church News Edition*, March 27, 1943, 1.

33. In a survey conducted by the authors, approximately 80 percent of Latter-day Saint World War II veterans reported receiving no mail from their local Church units during the time of their military assignments. Statistics in possession of the authors.

34. Scharffs, 117.

35. Ibid., 116.

36. *Deseret News: Church News Edition*, June 30, 1945, 12.

37. Frederick W. Babbel, *On Wings of Faith* (Salt Lake City: Bookcraft, 1972), 168.

38. *Deseret News 1999-2000 Church Almanac* (Salt Lake City: Deseret News, 1998), 138.

39. James R. Clark, *Messages of the First Presidency*, vol. 4 (Salt Lake City: Bookcraft, 1968), 149-150. As cited in Joseph F. Boone, "The Roles of The Church of Jesus Christ of Latter-day Saints in Relation to the United States Military," vol. 1 (masters thesis, Brigham Young University, 1975), 17.

THE EUROPEAN THEATER

World War I did not prove to be the war to end all wars. From its coals flamed an era of increased totalitarianism characterized by ambitious dictators anxious to extend their nation's influence. Nowhere was this more evident than with Hitler's seizure of Austria and Czechoslovakia. When Germany invaded Poland in September 1939, Great Britain and France declared war on Germany. Italy and Japan soon allied themselves with Germany in the Axis pact. German forces then completed the occupation of France in June 1940 and turned their attention to Britain. Through determination and courage, the British were able to maintain control of their skies and avoid a German invasion. Hitler was forced to turn his attention elsewhere.

THE EUROPEAN - AFRICAN - MIDDLE EASTERN (EAME) CAMPAIGN MEDAL was awarded to United States personnel for service within the European-African-Middle Eastern Theater between December 7, 1941, and November 8, 1945, under any of the following conditions:

(1) On permanent assignment.

(2) In a passenger status or on temporary duty for 30 consecutive days or 60 days not consecutive.

(3) In active combat against the enemy and was awarded a combat decoration or furnished a certificate by the commanding general of a corps, higher unit, or independent force that he actually participated in combat.

Following the Battle of Britain, the British Army increased its efforts against German-Italian advances in North Africa and the Middle East. Meanwhile, German forces marched on to Russia while the Japanese prepared for war with the United States. In accordance with a carefully designed plan, the Japanese attacked Pearl Harbor, Sunday, December 7, 1941. In response, the United States declared war on Japan, December 8. Germany and Italy responded by declaring war on the United States, December 11. The United States was now fully at war.

THE EUROPEAN THEATER

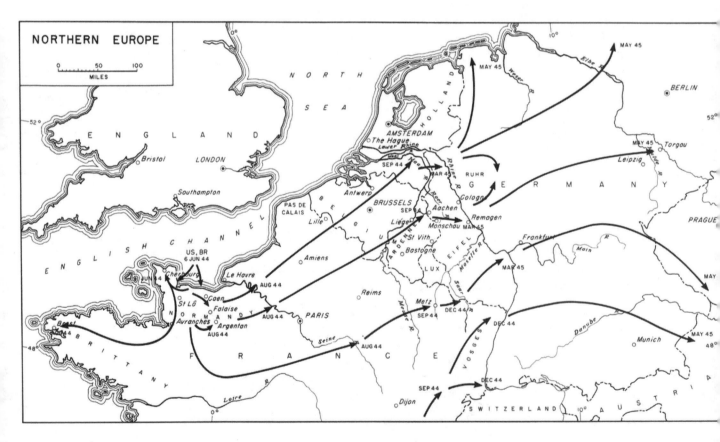

The European-African-Middle Eastern (EAME) Theatre

The western boundary of the EAME Theater was from the North Pole, south along the 75th meridian west longitude to the 77th parallel north latitude, then southeast through Davis Strait to the intersection of the 40th parallel north latitude and the 35th meridian west longitude, then south along the meridian to the 10th parallel north latitude, then southeast to the intersection of the Equator and the 20th meridian west longitude, then along the 20th meridian west longitude to the South Pole. The eastern boundary of the EAME Theater is from the North Pole, south along the 60th meridian east longitude to its intersection with the east boundary of Iran, then south along the Iran boundary to the Gulf of Oman and the intersection of the 60th meridian east longitude, then south along the 60th meridian east longitude to the South Pole. The EAME Theater included Europe, European Russia, Greenland, Iceland, Africa, Iran, Iraq, and Turkey.

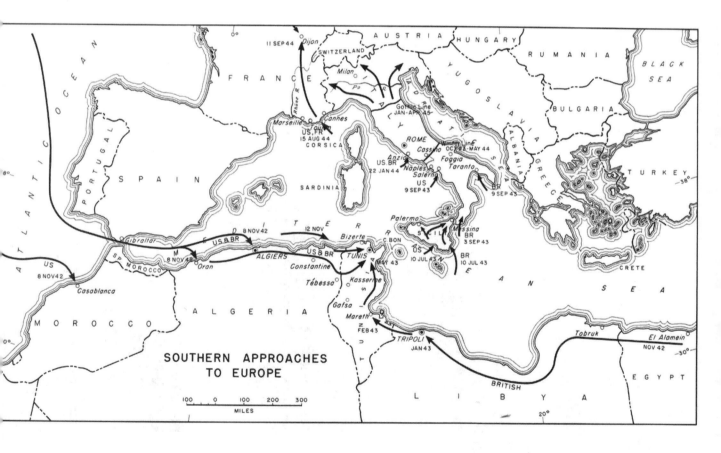

SOUTHERN APPROACHES TO EUROPE

THE AIR WAR

For the first few years of the war, the German Luftwaffe dominated the skies over Europe. Motivated by the devastating bombing raids on Britain, the RAF (Royal Air Force) increased strategic bombing of German targets. This effort escalated when the United States Air Corps joined the RAF Bombing Command in an all-out attack on Germany. A steady procession of Flying Fortress and Liberator bombers from the United States crossed the Atlantic to join RAF Halifax and Lancaster bombers in an effort that would challenge German dominance in the war.

The around-the-clock bombing by Allied planes extracted a terrible toll on Germany's war industries. The Army Air Corps provided precision bombing by day of strategic military targets, while the Royal Air Force mounted massive night campaigns against the industrial cities. Allied losses increased as Germany responded with superb fighter aircraft and an increased number of antiaircraft placements. This resistance only strengthened Allied resolve.

A B-17 bomber on the way home. Note the severe damage to the rear section and tail section of the plane. This plane actually did reach England, where it landed safely.

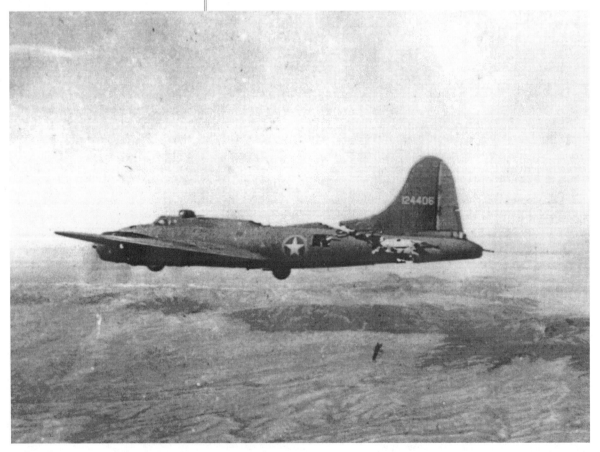

THE INVASION OF ITALY

During the time of increased RAF bombing raids over Germany, the British also faced a difficult desert war in North Africa. The Seventh Army, nicknamed the "Desert Rats," was typical of the brave British troops that challenged the Italian Army in the Libyan Desert. Fearful of an Italian defeat, Hitler reinforced their sagging efforts with General Rommel and the famed Afrika Korps. Rommel used his superior tanks to force the British to give up the vital harbor of Tobruk in June 1942.

By the time the United States received word of the fall of Tobruk, her repeated naval defeats experienced in the Pacific were compounded by the havoc caused by German U-boat attacks on Allied shipping in the Atlantic. At this dark moment in the war, the decision was made to test the newly designed Sherman tanks against Rommel's panzer tanks. The Allies reasoned that the best hope of a successful assault on Europe lay through North Africa and Italy. In the words of Winston Churchill, the Allies would attack

German armbands. Hitler selected the colors red and white as well as the swastika to be the symbols of his Nationalist Party. He described the color red as representing the social ideals of his movement, and the color white as symbolic of his nationalistic ideas. The swastika was to be placed in the center to represent the struggle for the victory of Aryan man.

first the "soft underbelly of the Axis beast." Operation Torch was initiated under the leadership of the British General, Montgomery. American troops joined with their British counterparts to encircle Rommel's forces. The resulting surrender of the Afrika Korps ended Axis domination of North Africa and opened the way for the invasion of Italy.

Allied bombers and naval gunships bombarded the fortress of Pantelleria in preparation for an attack on Sicily. The German forces retreated before the Allied advance, and after thirty-eight days of fighting, Sicily came under Allied control. The fall of Sicily encouraged the anti-Fascist movement in Italy to put an end to the twenty-two-year reign of Mussolini. The provisional government of Italy then surrendered to the Allied command. The German forces occupying Italy had no such plans and organized a stiff defense against the advancing Allied armies.

A well-prepared German defense force met the first troops coming ashore. Only by exercising sheer determination and courage were the Allies able to hold the beachfront. After a week of intense fighting, the Allies began to make their way inland. Relying on the skill of army engineers to rebuild the bridges destroyed by the retreating Germans, the Allied forces spread out and advanced on Rome. German resistance proved difficult, and a plan was devised to open the German line with an invasion of Anzio, Italy, located behind the German lines. Unfortunately, a superior German army trapped the Allied forces in a battle lasting several months. The Allied troops held their position however, giving the Allies an important foothold behind German lines.

The German front was broken in May 1944, and Allied troops joined those from Anzio to force a full German withdrawal. On June 4 the Allied armies entered Rome, setting the stage for the invasion of France.

THE NORMANDY INVASION

The D-Day invasion, formally known as Operation Overload, proved to be the largest single military effort in the history of warfare and the climactic invasion of World War II. It successfully broke open the Atlantic wall of the German defense and allowed the Allied troops to liberate Europe, invade Germany, and force a German surrender. D-Day was a defining moment for the Allied effort in World War II.

Hitler had anticipated an invasion of the French coast and had prepared extensive fortifications. In an attempt to reduce German defensive capability, Allied bombers launched a massive offensive against German positions in France and Germany. It was this extensive air war that ensured the success of the invading ground troops.

When D-Day arrived, the commander of the Allied forces addressed the assembled troops.

> Soldiers, sailors, and airmen of the Allied Expeditionary Forces. You are about to embark upon the Great Crusade, toward which we have striven these many months. The eyes of the world are upon you. The hope and prayers of liberty-loving people everywhere are with you.
>
> GENERAL DWIGHT D. EISENHOWER, JUNE 6, 1944

President Roosevelt then offered a national prayer.

> Almighty God: Our sons, pride of our nation, this day have set upon a mighty endeavor, a struggle to preserve our republic, our religion, and our civilization and to set free a suffering humanity. . . . They will need thy blessings. Their road will be long and hard. The enemy is strong. He may hurl back our forces. Success may not come with rushing grace, but we shall turn again and again; and we know that by thy grace, and by the righteousness of our cause, our sons will triumph. . . .
>
> PRESIDENT FRANKLIN D. ROOSEVELT, JUNE 6, 1944

Soon after 5:00 A.M. on June 6, 1944, naval artillery opened fire on the Normandy coast. D-Day had begun and the first landings would soon follow. At 6:30 A.M., an armada of over 5,000 ships and 10,000 planes combined with 150,000 ground troops to launch the attack. It was to be a costly and difficult battle that raged over several days. The strength of the German beach fortifications made it most difficult to secure the beaches and move the fight inland. By the end of the first day, 2,500 Allied soldiers had lost their lives.

Once the beaches were secure, large landing craft unloaded thousands of troops and vehicles carrying tons of supplies. Overwhelmed by Allied preparation, the German defensive forces gave way, and the Allies moved inland through the hedgerow country of France. The invasion of northern Europe was underway.

Members of an American landing party help rescue other Allies whose landing craft was sunk by enemy action off the coast of France during the D-Day invasion. By using a life raft, these survivors reached Utah Beach near Cherbourg.

THE INVASION OF GERMANY

Following the victory on the beaches of Normandy, the Allied forces pressed on. In an attempt to halt the Allied march, Hitler ordered a massive panzer attack to cut off the Allied advance. The attempt failed; German forces were surrounded and defeated. The remnants of the German Army retreated before the Allies. It was at this time that the famous

Red Ball Express was effective in supplying the rapidly advancing Army. This fleet of supply trucks raced through France with orders to stop for nothing as they delivered their cargo to the front.

In August, 1944, the Allies accepted the formal surrender of the German forces that occupied Paris. But Hitler remained determined and ordered a massive counterattack in the Ardennes. This offensive came to be known as the Battle of the Bulge. Led by the powerful panzer tanks, the Germans pushed through the Allied front. When the American First Army was surrounded by the surging panzers and ordered to surrender, American Brigadier General McAuliffe demonstrated the spirit of the Allied forces by replying, "Nuts!" By so doing, he encouraged his troops to successfully resist the German Army. The overwhelming support power of the Allies soon wore down the Germans and forced them to retreat. The Battle of the Bulge was over, and the Allies were ready to enter Germany.

From three different directions, the Allied forces swept into Germany. Troops fresh from their success in Italy met those marching across France and the Russian Army coming from the east. The German line could not hold against this onslaught. Soon the horrors of the death camps were revealed as Allied soldiers liberated thousands of Jews being held captive by German authorities. Prisoner of war camps were also opened, freeing Allied soldiers after months or even years of captivity.

American and Russian troops finally surrounded Berlin. On April 30, 1945, Hitler committed suicide; one week later on May 7, representatives of the German High Command signed an unconditional surrender. The war in Europe was over. Throughout the world, crowds flocked the streets in celebrations of joy and thanksgiving.

THE LATTER-DAY SAINT VETERAN

The accounts of the Latter-day Saint servicemen and women who fought in the European Theater demonstrate their bravery and willingness to rely on their faith to meet the challenges they faced. Tens of thousands of Latter-day Saint airmen, soldiers, and sailors served in a wide variety of assignments. They fully understood the risks involved and recognized that with each repeated mission, the chances of not returning home unharmed increased. They accepted that they had a job to do and expressed their desire to fulfill that responsibility with honor. Their experiences reflect their appreciation for their country and their reliance on God.

LDS group at Poix, France, 1945. Halbert L. Iverson (second from the left on the front row) served in the U.S. Army Air Forces with his brother, Donald R. Iverson (third from the right on the back row), in the 441st Airborne Troop Carrier Group, which was actively involved in the invasion of Normandy, the Battle of the Bulge, and on to the end of the war in Europe. After the conflict in Europe, Halbert and Donald were held at Poix, France, pending their possible needed involvement in the invasion of Japan or as part of the occupational forces in Austria. While in Poix, Halbert and Donald formed an LDS group with other servicemen in the area. There were approximately eleven members in this group.

During this time, Halbert and Donald heard that the first-ever LDS European Theater Conference would be held in Paris, France, on July 22, 1945, with President Hugh B. Brown conducting. Of course, the two brothers were interested in attending this conference. They were able to obtain a C-47 onto which they loaded a jeep and trailer and flew to Paris with other members of their group. Upon arriving in Paris, they unloaded the jeep and trailer and drove into Paris. The conference was an enjoyable experience for everyone involved, and an uplifting experience for these LDS men and women.

PAUL W. AHLSTROM

In 1944 Paul was assigned to a group that was sent to Russia to assist in the operation of U.S. airbases established by the Teheran Conference. His description of the Russian scene at that time of the war reveals the devastation experienced by these people.

I had wondered what it was like to be on the receiving end of a bombing raid. I found out June 21, 1944. That afternoon a large force of fighters and bombers arrived from England. The planes landed and the crews billeted; we were all raiding the mess hall. High in the clear blue sky we saw a vapor trail, and soon a German reconnaissance plane flew over. Our Russian pilots took off, but they were unable to catch the fast German aircraft.

Six hours after the reconnaissance plane left, the air raid siren blared. In less than a minute I was dressed and outside trying to learn the reason for the alarm. We could hear approaching aircraft. A lone plane dropped parachute flares, lighting up the place. Men poured from every tent, searching for a foxhole. The sky was filled with planes. The Russians fired every ack-ack gun they had. German planes came in so low that I could see the swastikas on their wings. Russian air defense was weak, and the Germans seemed to be enjoying their game of hide and seek with the searchlights.

After the planes left, we saw bursts of light to the east. The following morning we learned that our headquarters at Mirograd had been heavily hit. Out of seventy-two B-17s,

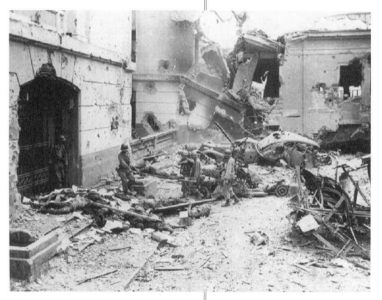

Scene of destruction, somewhere in Europe.

The Teheran Conference

In late November 1943, a conference was convened between the "Three Powers"—U. S. President Roosevelt, British Prime Minister Churchill, and Soviet Premier Stalin. At the conference, held in Teheran, Iran, which at the time was under control of the British Empire, the leaders agreed to assist opposition forces in Yugoslavia; they also agreed that it was in their nations' best interests that Turkey join the Allies. In addition, they determined to coordinate the movements of troops in the European Theater, as it was evident that they could not otherwise defeat the German armies.

only nine could fly. One American officer was killed. At precisely the same hour as the day before, we spotted another reconnaissance plane. We knew the enemy would be back that night. I was placed on guard duty for the night.

When I retired, I put my clothes, gas mask, and helmet next to my cot. I couldn't sleep. It didn't matter much, as at midnight we got word that the Germans were on their way. I dressed in a heartbeat. No need to kid myself, I was scared. As I hit the bottom of my trench, flares began falling; the entire sky above us was full of planes. It was so light I could have read a newspaper. Crouched in the bottom of my foxhole, I watched those bombers circle for three hours as they unloaded. Just before they left, one of our fuel dumps was hit. The sky was red with flames.

MAYS W. ANDERSON

As an army tank commander, Mays found himself in a most difficult situation. During a vicious battle his tank became stuck in mud. It became the target of German tanks nearby. While he escaped with his life, he was captured and endured months of imprisonment as a prisoner of war.

We couldn't even put our heads out or they would be blown off. My own tank was hit and knocked out. A piece of shell went into my face. Mortar and artillery shells were coming in like rain. The shells were coming from both German and American guns. We were in no man's land and a German observer had us zeroed.

* * * * *

On November 22, we were searched, interrogated, and thrown into a damn cold barn. The enemy gave us no breakfast. For dinner we had our first bowl of beet top soup. (Contents: 1 pint of water and three green beet tops.) For supper they gave us one-quarter loaf of German bread. They told us to save it, for we were to march the next day to Bonn, Germany, to a prison camp. We marched about thirty miles with no rest, no

Tank with "duck feet" is being tested in France.

water, and only that small hunk of black bread for food. It rained all day. We were cold, soaking wet, and extremely tired. The Germans would not give us any rest. . . . We reached the stalag at Bonn. I was so tired. We stood outside while [the] Germans very inefficiently searched us again. It was still raining. I didn't dare sit down; I'm sure I couldn't have got onto my feet again (*Provo Herald*, July, 1985).

CHARLES W. ARNETT

After serving a mission, Charles entered the Army Air Corps and trained as a pilot for a B-24 bomber. On this third combat mission his plane was severely damaged, forcing him to crash-land it in a tulip field in The Netherlands. In doing this he saved the lives of his crew. They spent the rest of the war in a German POW camp.

At the time of the Normandy invasion, hundreds of bombers were being sent over to Germany every day. We were proud to be one of the many. I had previously had a two-year missionary experience, so I was delighted when some of the crew asked if I could lead them in prayer under the wing of the aircraft before every mission. As one might expect, the prayers I gave were not long, but definitely to the point. I

Charles Arnett's B-24 bomber crew: "The Boomerang Crew." Charles Arnett, pilot; Lucian Stewart, copilot; Ernie Gavitt, navigator; Charles Vergos, bombardier; Arthur Oakes, nose gunner; Jack Burton, tail gunner; Jim Easley, flight engineer and waist gunner; Bill Lindropp, ball turret gunner; Don Pierce, radio operator; Uriel Robertson, top turret gunner.

asked that we might each perform our assigned tasks well, that we would work harmoniously together to successfully complete our assigned mission, and I then asked for the thing that was uppermost in all our hearts—that we might be protected from harm and return to our home base safely.

As we knelt under the wing of the plane before our third mission, and I said, "return to our home base safely," I suddenly knew that we were not coming back. I was stunned. My knowledge, however, was unmistakably certain. I don't know how I was able to finish the prayer, but I did know that I couldn't tell my crew. . . . I had the crew check everything, hoping to discover a legitimate reason for not going, but we had no such luck.

My thoughts turned to the Lord Jesus Christ and His experience in the Garden of Gethsemane. He knew what was ahead for Him, and He looked, at least temporarily, for an honorable way out as He prayed, "Father, if it be thy will, let this cup pass from me. Nevertheless, not my will, but thine be done." A feeling of peace then settled over me as we crossed the Channel and reached the Netherlands coastline.

We were at seventeen thousand feet and just before reaching the target, our fighter escort had to return home because of fuel restrictions. . . . Suddenly it happened. We estimated about forty ME-109 German fighters made a head-on attack on the outside twelve ships of the 492nd. I recalled Lieutenant Stewart's comment made on our first mission, "Say, this is getting serious! They're using real bullets!" We returned fire, but the rate of closure was fast, and they were only in our range for an instant. . . . We had three engines severely damaged, and the vertical fins and rudders were badly riddled. We left the formation and headed straight home, throwing out everything we could to lighten the aircraft. We let down to a much lower altitude. Then we noticed an American fighter had picked us up and was offering cover on his return to England.

We came to the coast of The Netherlands, and for a moment hope welled up within me. While we might not get back to England, we might come pretty close. Then the oil-splattered engine quit and caught on fire, spinning us around in the direction of the now dead and blazing engine. Lieutenant Stewart and I had considerable trouble getting it straightened out. We were flying very low, and the instability of the aircraft made it certain that the copilot and I would never make it out. Lieutenant Stewart informed the crew that they could bail out immediately, but they elected to stay with us.

We were able to land the plane, but the landing gear was sheared off by the canals and drainage ditches. We slid along on the belly of the plane till we stopped. The German military was there before we could get out of the aircraft. All but one of our crew members were alive. A couple of days later they took us by train to the interrogation center at Frankfurt and from there the officers were sent to Stalag Luft III. The enlisted men went to other camps separately.

German soldiers examine the wreckage of Arnett's bomber plane. This photograph was stolen from the wallet of the dark-haired German in the photo by a Dutch bartender who worked for the resistance.

A tender, memorable experience of my prisoner time was when we were being moved by train from Spremburg to Nuremberg. We were packed fifty to a car that normally carried cattle. It was bitter cold, and food was getting scarce. The train stopped frequently, but we were not allowed to get off. However, at one stop, late at night, a German woman came down the platform with a large basket of fresh baked bread, sharing it with us prisoners of war. I shall never forget the love and compassion I saw in her eyes and felt, as her hand brushed mine in giving me bread.

What have I learned from this terrifying experience of May 19, 1944? I've learned that war is a horrible and terribly destructive thing. I've gained an even deeper feeling of patriotism. I have also learned that good can come even in an evil setting. Most important, I have learned that we must somehow learn to live in peace and harmony on this planet if we are to avoid self-destruction. We must go even beyond "peace" as defined by the "absence of war." We must learn to love one another. This is possible. I've seen it done repeatedly.

JOSEPH BANKS

In September 1944, Joseph's parents received a telegram indicating that he was missing in action. As a crew member of a B-17 bomber that had been shot down, he had become a prisoner of war.

In spite of the danger, my buddies, Lloyd, Bob, Roland, and I decided to attempt an escape. We were successful and had been traveling together several days when we had to go through a town. There was no light anywhere since everyone used blackout curtains. It was late enough that we figured most everyone would be asleep. We crept along slowly with about ten feet between each member of the team. All at once I was startled by a voice in the darkness. As I instinctively turned to look, a door opened from a house on my left side. The light from inside shined on me, and it was such an unexpected contrast from the darkness that it blinded me temporarily. I stood there like deer caught in headlights, unable to move or to do anything. Suddenly a German soldier came striding out of the house straight for me, followed by a woman. Fortunately, the field of light was restricted enough so that they could only see me, giving my three partners a chance to take cover.

As the soldier got closer, his shadow shielded my eyes enough that I could see a huge German tank parked next to the house, and I could see the excited look in his eyes. I just stood there transfixed, unable to move or to even make a sound. I didn't know whether to run, put my hands up, or fall to my knees to beg for mercy, so I just stood there! As he reached me he shouted something unintelligible to me in German. Before I could think of what to do, I was startled beyond words to hear myself respond with a calm, confident, German phrase that obviously was appropriate to what he'd asked me. He then replied to whatever I'd said with an almost cheerful, "Ya, Ya, Ya!" And then he put his arms around the woman, turned his back on me, and went back into the house and closed the door. I was so astonished and frightened that I just stood there with my mouth hanging open.

My buddies had seen and heard the whole thing, and when I didn't move, they came out and grabbed me and pulled me behind a nearby outbuilding where we could hide.

Air view of a B-17 bomber with a wing shot off during a bombing run.

The whole encounter had taken just a few seconds, but it was absolutely unbelievable. The first thing my buddies asked was, "What on earth did he say to you, and what did you say when you talked back to him?" I told them that I had no idea what either he or I said, since I couldn't speak German. I do

Joseph Banks on a training aircraft in Long Beach, California. Joseph received two Distinguished Flying Cross medals—a rare honor. This is the highest honor awarded by the Army Air Forces. Joe received these medals for his heroic efforts in helping to save the lives of his wounded crew members during his "miracle mission," and for his 49th mission when he was shot down.

know that I didn't use any of the few German words that I'd learned in the POW camp, like *hello; yes, sir; or no, sir.* Even if I had, my accent would have been so terrible that a German would have recognized me as a foreigner immediately. Yet, whatever I had said satisfied him. All of us stood there marveling in disbelief at what had just happened. I was standing fully exposed to this soldier with my straggly beard, tattered clothes with no coat, and bright white letters painted on my trousers and shirt indicating that I was a POW; it was just impossible that he didn't recognize me as an escaped prisoner. Instead of shooting me or calling for help, though, he looked straight at me, spoke to me in his native language, listened to my response in a foreign language that I had never spoken before or since, and accepted my answer as legitimate. Even if the guard hadn't figured it out, there was the woman who also stared at me and heard the words that passed between us. Why didn't either of them figure out what was going on?

As all of this settled in my mind, I felt a burning in my heart that told me that I had been blessed once again, and that the Holy Ghost had interpreted what the German had said to me and put the appropriate words in my mouth to respond. In other words, I'd been blessed with the gift of tongues. I don't know what those two Germans saw, but obviously they didn't see the letters on my clothing, even though they would have stood out like a neon sign in the bright light that shone through the door. The Spirit may have also changed what they saw. I think in some unknown way my appearance had been transformed so they did not recognize me.

I've heard it said that for something to be a miracle there can be no logical or earthly way to explain it. If that's true, then in this case I was clearly the beneficiary of a miracle, and it thrilled me to know that God was still watching out for me and that He cared for me.

MELVIN D. BARNEY

Melvin reported for training in November 1942. In March 1944 his unit completed their preparation in England for the D-Day invasion. He boarded his landing craft on June 5 and spent two days aboard the ship before landing on Utah Beach, June 7, 1944. His account provides insight about events of that day. For Melvin, the action began before they landed on the beach.

Not much was said on the boat. It seemed like each man had his own thoughts. Coming in, I never felt so sorry for guys in my life. After we took the first hit, all the men had their heads down, and their eyes were glassy. They were saying very little.

Slightly before the ramp went down, the motors opened wide. Then an armor-piercing shell came right in between the angle irons of the opening. I was in the process of picking up the tripod and cradle, behind the blade of the caterpillar. My rifle was lying on the track of the cat. I couldn't quite decide what to pick up first, the tripod and cradle on my shoulder, or my rifle. So I decided to get the tripod and cradle. I stooped down to pick them up and said to Frank, about two steps away, "Frank, will you hand me my rifle?"

Soldiers jump out of a landing craft and wade ashore during the D-Day invasion.

He said, "Oh geez!" That is all I heard; he took one step over, and the next thing I knew, I was down on the deck. My helmet was blown off. I had blood, flesh, and brains all down my face; my face and hands were bleeding. There was nothing left of Frank from the neck up.

The shell continued on and hit a fellow named William D. Franko, also from Chicago. He was hit in the chest.... The shell tore him completely in two. When the shell hit him, it detonated one of his two hand grenades snapped onto the upper right of the combat pack.

I moved up about two steps to where a jeep was sitting with a trailer behind it. I was kneeling down by the front seat, and another artillery shell came through the side of the boat, through the windshield of the jeep and hit a fellow by the name of Alvin VanZant. . . . He died sometime later. My face around my lips was bleeding from the flying glass of the jeep. By that time the ramp was down.

I stood up and saw in front of us the steel hedgehogs (antisubmarine spigot-mortars). There were men hanging on them, men who had come in on smaller boats but hadn't reached shore. Machine and rifle bullets were hitting all around them and some of them were dead. The water was bloody around them. Some were hollering for help. . . . About twenty men were in the water—some just floating, dead. There were dips in the water where small arms fire was hitting. Men were hollering, "Help! Help!"

Soldiers trapped at hedgehog barriers on beach during D-Day.

After we backed out, I went back to the head to wash all the blood and other things off me. I looked in the mirror and said to myself, "Is that me?" My eyes looked glassy. "You scared sonuvagun, you! Now we've got to go do this again."

So our boat went in again, and the second time we landed. But the fear was greater the second time, because the first time we hadn't known what to expect. We were with the Sixteenth Infantry Regiment of the First Division. They knew what to expect, because they'd been in combat. We were different. We were standing around watching, while they hid up as best they could. They knew what could happen, but we didn't.

The water was from knee to shoulder depth when we got off. The sand on the bottom of the beach was uneven. . . . I was

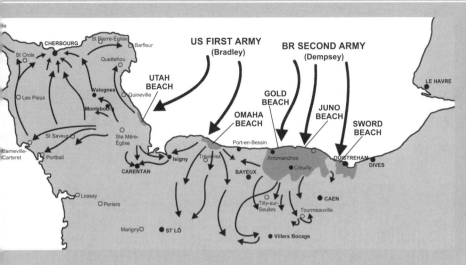

Named to Honor

The U.S. beaches, Utah and Omaha, which were involved in the D-Day invasion, were named after two ships by the same names that were sunk by the Japanese during their attack on Pearl Harbor. See also D-Day Invasion, p. 65.

one of the first men onto the beach. Our captain and some of our guys went in first; they had panels of different fluorescent colors to mark the beach. . . . The markers were hit bad.

The infantry was supposed to go in and clear the beach so we could clear the mines. But the infantry was not able to do that. They needed more help, so when we came in we acted as infantrymen. . . . Most of the casualties were on the beach. Once the infantry got in, it was a lot safer. All the mortars were zeroed in on the beaches, but once we got beyond them, we were a hundred times safer. Everybody wanted to get off that beach. But we were still there, clearing the mines.

MARION F. BARNHILL

During a bombing run over Germany, Marion's plane encountered considerable flak that caused serious damage. His attempt to fly his crippled plane to Switzerland failed by only thirty-five miles. He crash-landed in a lake in the Bavarian Alps. His crew was captured and sent to different POW camps. Marion and several other officers were sent to Stalag Luft III. There he joined a Latter-day Saint group of POWs and managed to have regular church meetings. The group kept detailed minutes.

As Kreigies (prisoners of war) we were assigned to rooms containing several other prisoners. There were sixteen of us in a room that was approximately twelve feet by fourteen feet. The bunks were three feet high and originally had slats. The slats were gradually removed for use in shoring the ground when tunnels were dug.

Sgt. Marion F. Barnhill.

MINUTES OF AN LDS MEETING HELD IN STALAG LUFT III

Beginning in November 1943, minutes were kept of the LDS meetings held in the POW camp. Each week the minutes were faithfully recorded until the camp was liberated April 29, 1945, by the Fourteenth Armored Division. Below are the minutes of their first meeting.

NOVEMBER 7, 1943.

This is the first meeting of the Latter-day Saints in Stalag Luft III, Sagan, Germany, opened with Brother W. E. McKell presiding. We sang, "Come, Come, Ye Saints." Brother B. H. Hinckley was asked to offer the opening prayer. We then sang, "We Thank Thee, O God, for a Prophet."

The gathering was then opened for discussion as to the organization, extent of authority required, and the election of a presiding elder, two counselors, and a secretary. Brother W. E. McKell as presiding elder, Brother B. H. Hinckley as first counselor, and Brother David Ferrell as secretary, were all sustained individually in their capacities by unanimous vote.

The authority and difficulties of a sacrament were discussed and by unanimous vote it was decided to have the sacrament passed every Sunday. It was also decided that Canadian soda crackers were to be used in lieu of white bread. This meeting is to be conducted along the lines adopted in Sunday School. Instead of separating for discussion and teaching, after the sacrament has been passed, a short talk on some fundamentals of the Church or gospel will be given. The meeting will then be opened for discussion in which all members, investigators, and nonmembers are encouraged to participate. There are thirteen of us here, all prisoners of war, all members of the Air Corps. We are searching for more of the truth of the gospel, which we all sincerely believe. Most of us have been out of contact with the Church for over a year. All are eager to live a better life here in camp. We are all vividly aware of the part the Lord has taken in allowing us life. With His help and our labors here, perhaps we can bring to this camp the truth as shown by our prophet, Joseph Smith. We feel deeply this obligation and duty. May God bless this group and help it to prosper and grow. The meeting closed by singing "God Be with You." The closing prayer was offered by Brother Frank K. Watson.

At the first roll call after I arrived at the camp, I heard an announcement about a Latter-day Saint discussion group. I joined in and found that we had quite a number of members there. We met regularly until we were liberated. Knowing the purpose of life helped us to retain a sense of balance. We tried to hold meetings similar to sacrament meetings. We would appoint a member to arrange a program concerning his hometown or other subject. This kept our minds working on something for most of the time. We attempted to interest others in the gospel, but I know of only one convert, Harold W. Porter. We were not sure whether we were authorized to baptize, so we did not.

RAYMON O. BASCOM

Raymon volunteered for service in an airborne unit when he learned that a great need existed because of huge losses sustained by the 101st Airborne. He credits his "guardian angel" for the many times he was protected in combat.

Finding my company, the lieutenant looked at me and asked, "Bascom, do you know how to drive a jeep?"

"Oh, no sir," I replied.

"Well, do you know how to drive a model A Ford?"

"Yes sir," I said.

"They're all the same; get out there. We need a jeep driver to evacuate the wounded."

"Yes sir." I knew that the Germans were all around us. They were up on the little hills and could see anything that moved and would zero in on it. I crawled under the steering wheel, took off my helmet, and said the words my grandfather had said when he was in need of the Lord's help. "Dear Lord, please help me." A calm feeling came over me, and I was ready to try to get the wounded out through town to the aid station. They brought out two men; one was able to sit up, the other could not. They placed him on a door across the back of the jeep. Down through town we went, shells falling all around us.

Unloading them, I went back for more; back through town we went, which was about one-half mile. The third time going through town a big white pig came out of the building just as we passed. I heard an explosion and a squeal. I retraced my route, there was that pig dead.

Raymon Bascom standing on a captured German plane in Austria, 1945.

I went back to the aid station with two more men, only this time the medical lieutenant came out and said, "Will you take them on into Bastogne?" I asked him if we were cut off; he did not know but thought so. Down the road I went. It was a little foggy and when it cleared, I could see there were German soldiers on both sides of the road.

I turned to the fellow in the front with me and said, "Duck." I leaned toward him and he leaned toward me. I stepped on the gas pedal. The windshield was down and just looking over the hood, I could see tracers right in front of me from both directions. We went through that crossfire of machine guns. . . . As we went by, an unseen power took a hold of that steering wheel, turning it one way then the other. We went over a little rise, maybe a half-mile down the road.

The fellow in front said, "Don't you think you'd better slow down?" We were in a jeep that only registered sixty miles, and it was nearly one-half a minute at least before it even registered down to sixty and started dropping. There ahead of us were five of our tanks. I stopped and told the commander about the roadblock. He said he'd been there for two hours trying to break through. That was only one of the many times that I was protected. I received the Bronze Star for this.

101st Airborne Division

The 101st Airborne Division (the "Screaming Eagles"), was one of the most decorated Divisions in U.S. military history. In honor of the stand at Bastogne (the now famous Battle of the Bulge) mentioned here, the Unit was visited by General Dwight D. Eisenhower and awarded the Distinguished Unit Citation (now the Presidential Unit Citation).

ALFRED W. BEELER

At the age of twenty-seven, Alfred left his wife and small son for basic training at Fort Douglas in Salt Lake City, Utah. After completing his training, he left for England. There he was assigned to what was known as a "suicide unit." On D-Day, his Engineer Special Brigades landed on Omaha Beach, Red Dog sector. Below is a first-person adaptation of a report written as part of his family history.

Almost without exception the fighting man has a dual set of emotions. That is especially true when he reaches the battlefront. His heart and mind are turned to home and family while on the other hand death, misery, country, duty, and survival are his immediate concerns. When he comes face-to-face with the enemy he must set aside all thoughts of home and family. Yet it is those thoughts that sustain him through the trial upon him. There is an awesome choice between duty and survival. Even in a situation of supreme demand, the mind flashes to home and family. Words cannot scratch the surface of describing the depth of what a soldier must conquer within himself.

* * * * *

We could see the smoke from the battle on the beach. Battleships were firing big shells over us toward the beach, and the Germans were firing back. We could hear the shells as they passed overhead. Later in the day it was my turn to go. We had redone our packs two or three times to make them lighter. With my squad, I climbed overboard on a rope net and headed for the landing craft far below. It was a real trick to step off the net into the landing craft. As the craft rose on the crest of a wave we had to step into the craft. The next second, the craft would be in the trough of a wave. If men missed the craft and fell into the water, they were lost at sea.

Troop ships were under fire during the unloading into the barges of other ship-to-shore vessels. There were casualties before reaching the shore. Many of the landing craft reaching shore were hung up on underwater barricades anchored in concrete. Once the ramp was lowered on the bow of the craft there was to be no hesitation by anyone in unloading. It mattered not if the water was deep enough that the troops had to swim for shore. Heavy backpacks had to be released or we would drown. That meant that many came ashore without even a weapon or ammunition. Each landing craft had a man assigned to stand at the stern, prepared to shoot anyone who hesitated to disembark immediately.

(Top) Alfred Beeler in combat setting in Europe, 1944.

Alfred, Katherine, and Vernon Beeler (siblings) at the time of their discharge from military service.

I was looking around from inside my foxhole. I saw a man's head above the ground and because of the situation, presumed that the head belonged to an enemy. The light was rather poor, but I took deadly aim at the head and was about to squeeze off a shot when an uncertain feeling came over me, and I delayed. As I observed closely, the soldier in the other foxhole turned to another position, and I recognized him as an American.

HERMAN H. BERGES

As a medic assigned to the 103rd Infantry Division, Herman earned the Silver Star.

Tec-56 Herman H. Berges, 1945, after return home from the war. Displayed on his uniform are: Combat Medic's Badge, Silver Star, Bronze Star, Good Conduct medal, and European Theater Ribbon with two battle stars.

On one occasion I served as a runner or messenger. I was on my way back to battalion when I heard a German rocket launcher go off. . . . The first one hit about thirty yards behind me on the road, and the next one about twenty yards behind me. I kept on walking, fast. The third one hit about ten yards behind, and I decided it was time for me to get out of the way. So I stopped and got off the road, and sure enough, the next one hit just where I would have been. I knew that I had been lucky, or someone was watching over me.

* * * * *

The next day we were walking through a wooded area with a nice hill and a stream when a bombardment of big German shells began to come in. There were some solid bunkers built into the side of the hill, and I ran into one of them. There were other GIs in there too. The bunker had been built by the Germans and was well stocked with medical supplies. I wanted to stay there because it was safe, but almost immediately I heard someone yelling, "Medic." This was the cry I didn't like to hear because it meant I had to leave the safety of the shelter and go out where the shells were. But I went out, first to one wounded soldier, then to another. I patched them up and got them evacuated to the aid station between shell bursts. I finally got back to the bunker myself. By that time, of course, we were ready to move on.

One day the artillery fire was particularly heavy where I was, and I despaired for my life. I was not brought up in the Church, and I did not pray regularly. That day, however, I did pray, in desperation. I told my Heavenly Father, that if my life was spared that day, I would spend the rest of my life serving Him. This was a serious commitment, and I was serious about it.

Several years went by. I went back to college, got married, and graduated as a chemist. During those years I often wondered how I was going to serve God. I remembered the commitment I had made, and I was a little concerned. During this time, we attended a neighborhood church regularly. Our Sunday school class had a program of inviting people from other churches to tell us about their beliefs. One Sunday, a young lady from the Church of Jesus Christ of Latter-day Saints visited and talked about her church. The only thing I remember about her visit is that she told us the Savior had visited the people on this continent after His resurrection. My feeling about this was that if it was true how wonderful that must have been.

Several years later, we met the missionaries. I learned that the Savior had, indeed, visited the people here on this continent. It was true. . . . After a year of investigating, my wife and I were baptized. . . . We learned that the Church is a church of service.

One Sunday I was reading my scriptures, and I came to the book of Mosiah. . . . My eyes stopped at chapter 2, verse 17: "When ye are in the service of your fellow beings ye are only in the service of your God." I suddenly knew how I was going to serve God. All I had to do was to serve those around me. I did not grow up in the Church. I did not carry the priesthood with me into battle. I did not know the purpose of life. I did not serve a mission. I did not have any assurance,

Medics rush to the front line during the German counterattack at the Battle of the Bulge.

except my trust in God that I would come back alive. I did not know how to serve God. However, I did make a commitment, and I am still fulfilling that commitment. . . . I am grateful that my life was spared to fulfill that commitment.

H. REED BLACK

As a member of the 405th Infantry Regiment, Reed was seriously wounded and was expected to die. Although he was facing death, he did not fear it, because he trusted in his patriarchal blessing, which stated he would still have the opportunity to serve the Lord.

On my eighth birthday, January 27, 1930, my mother took me for my patriarchal blessing. The stake patriarch promised two things: one, that if I kept the Lord's commandments and studied hard, I would some day sit on the high councils of the Church, and two, I would serve a mission overseas.

* * * * *

Machine gun nest is captured during maneuvers.

When I entered the Army in 1943, other soldiers said that I was a "mama's boy" because I did not drink or smoke. . . . They told me that when I went on maneuvers and it was cold and I was wet to the skin, I would break down and be as others, starting with coffee in order to get warm. . . . The maneuvers were cold and wet as promised, but I kept the Word of Wisdom. They then said that when I went overseas, I would find the water in the lister bags horrible, and I would start drinking coffee. There were right about the lister-bag water. It was horrible, but I did not break down. Then they said when I went into combat, I would change. After twenty days in combat they gave up on me. I did sin, in that I traded my two cigarettes each day from the K rations for the lemon extract powder they had. The lemon extract powder hid the taste of the water.

* * * * *

Just after dawn, Thanksgiving Day 1944, we climbed out of our foxholes to attack enemy positions. Before we could cross the field to the apple orchard, a sniper shot me in the back. The bullet went through the middle and upper lobes of my right lung and came out between two ribs next to my sternum. . . . About two hours later, four soldiers came up to carry me off the battlefield with a stretcher, but the sniper shot two of the litter bearers.

I should have died for about five reasons. I lost two-thirds of my blood. It was very cold. I went without treatment for about eighteen hours. I was in shock. And I was dropped by the stretcher bearers. By the time we arrived at the battalion aid station, it was about 1:00 A.M. I was shaking all over because of the cold. They offered me a cup of hot coffee, and I was tempted more than at any time in my life to break the Word of Wisdom. I told them no, and then told them that there were about thirty lemon extract packets in my mess kit. I asked if they could make me some hot lemonade. A chaplain told me that they had plenty of hot water and would do so. Lemonade never tasted so good, and it was hot.

Machine gun crew waiting for action in tall grass.

* * * * *

People have asked me if I was afraid that I was going to die when I was on the battlefield. My answer has been no! The Lord, through His patriarch had promised that if I lived His commandants and studied, I would serve on high councils of the Church and serve a mission overseas. I knew that the Lord was bound. I have since served on high councils in Arizona, New Mexico, and Utah. My wife and I served a mission overseas. My patriarchal blessing has been fulfilled completely.

HANS MAX BOETTCHER

Hans was a faithful member of the Church in Germany before the war. He had served a full-time mission and married a young Latter-day Saint woman before being drafted into the German Army. After two years of fighting on the Russian front, he was transferred to fight against the Americans in Italy. There he was captured and placed in an Allied POW camp.

Hans Boettcher in uniform on a clear day in the Italian mountains, 1945.

As POWs we were transferred to Livorno. A double barbed-wire fence surrounded the camp. There were lots of Catholics and Protestants in our camp so I joined the Protestant group because I was the only Mormon there. Soon I let them know of my faith and started to preach the gospel in my tent. It wasn't long before I was asked to give a lecture to the entire Protestant group.

While working as an interpreter one day, an American officer came and talked to us, asking questions, whereby he found out that I was LDS. He then introduced himself to me, reached out his hand and said, "I'm a Mormon too." Occasionally I read the American bulletins to find out where they held their LDS meetings. I prayed and fasted to be able to attend those meetings.

One Sunday morning some fellows from our group showed me a written program about a worship service they had attended in Camp Pisa, where Hans Karl Schade participated as a tenor soloist. . . . I asked the pastor if he could take me to Camp Pisa to see my old friend. He agreed! Hans Karl and I were both overjoyed when we met, the only two Mormons among one hundred thousand German POWs. The first thing we did was find a quiet place where we knelt down and prayed. We poured our hearts out before the Lord for opening the way to see each other.

It was long after Christmas when we met again. Hans Karl had quite a story to tell. He had participated in a Christmas program as he had done often in the past. Royden Braithwaite, a Mormon chaplain near Camp Pisa, had received one of the written invitations. The program had said there would be interreligious participation with the Mormons furnishing Christmas music sung by the one Mormon in that camp, Hans Karl. Brother Braithwaite had decided to visit Hans Karl, who gave him my address about fifteen miles away. Hans Karl told me to expect a visit from him.

One day I was sitting near the door in the mess hall with the others when the door opened suddenly, and one of my tent mates came in with an American officer. I had a hunch as soon as they entered, so I got up with all eyes upon me, and rushed toward the American officer. I extended my hand and said, "You must be Brother Braithwaite!" I forgot my surroundings as we visited with each other while walking through the camp. . . . From that day on, Royden Braithwaite came every Sunday and picked me up for sacrament meeting in town. I did not under-

German POW soldiers washing clothes in the Italian mountains, spring, 1945.

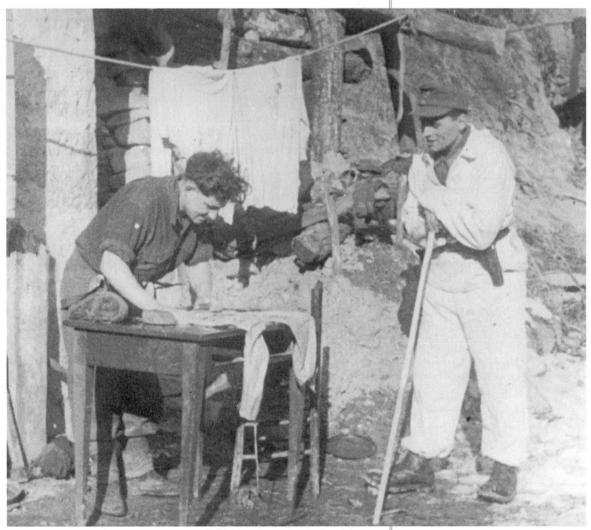

stand everything, but, oh, it felt so good to hear familiar hymns and feel the strong spirit. So my prayers were answered.

HOBART BRIGHT

Hobart began his army service in the Normandy invasion. He then marched with his unit across Europe into Germany, earning four battle stars and a Purple Heart in the process.

Hobart Bright of the 144th Field Artillery. Photos taken in Austria after the war.

On June 7 we went ashore at Omaha Beach. The landing was unforgettable. There were planes as far as the eye could see. We struggled ashore through water chest high, under heavy fire, through mine fields, over abandoned equipment and bodies everywhere—a part here and a part there.

It was our job to secure the beach and rid it of snipers. My assignment in the platoon was a foot messenger. I would go day and night to deliver messages. Sometimes a soldier would halt me, stick his gun in my belly, and ask me for the password before I could go any farther. It was dangerous at night, especially if we were in the woods.

The cliff had been cut down somewhat by the troops ahead of us, and after we scaled to the top, we dug in for the night. During the night, a mortar shell hit beside me, leaving a big hole. We found an underground bunker made from logs, and we were about to throw a grenade inside when French civilians came out.

We kept getting sniper fire, but we couldn't find where it was coming from. There was a church nearby, and it had been searched, but no one was found. We finally learned that the Germans had a tunnel under the pulpit. They would come from the tunnel up through the pulpit, fire, and disappear.

We were tired and hungry, and I longed for a glass of sweet milk. We found what we thought was an abandoned house, but there was a little old French lady there. She took her little bunch of twigs, built a fire in the fireplace, and boiled two eggs for my buddy and me. We could not speak French, but I managed to make her understand that we would love to have some salt; she obliged.

D. CREED BRIMHALL

As a copilot of a B-24 bomber, Creed flew numerous missions into German-held territory. His last mission was to be a run over Munich, Germany. Before reaching target, his plane was shot down, and he was forced to bail out. Captured by German soldiers, he was placed in a POW camp for the remaining years of the war. There he joined with other LDS soldiers to organize a group that regularly worshipped together.

D. Creed Brimhall.

After reaching twenty-six thousand feet and having turned onto the bomb run, I had settled down to flying a good position while trying to keep my window free from ice, which was forming quite rapidly. Since our pilot, Captain Irving Stringham, and I had been taking turns flying first pilot, I was flying first pilot that day. The bomb bay doors had just been opened, and I had just glanced down to check the clock to time the flak which had just begun to appear, when the "hit" came.

The first flak I saw was a single burst and was slightly high. At the same time, I noticed a number of 88-millimeter bursts. The hit, being a complete surprise, did not sound too loud—about like a door slamming—because there was less air at the altitude we were flying and because we were wearing tight helmets. Automatically, Captain Stringham and I tightened up on the control wheels only to find them completely limp and without any pressure at all. That seemed to say that we had been hit squarely and that all of the controls had been shot away. We both instinctively grasped at the release of the flak suits and rose to go to the "bail-out" positions in the bomb bay. At this time the section of the fuselage back to the top turret went into a spin, throwing Captain Stringham and me into the far-right corner of the cockpit. From that time until I found myself out in space, I remember nothing about trying to get out. The action threw me around violently, my headgear was torn off, and I remember flying through a large sheet of flame, which singed my hair and eyebrows.

I immediately reached for and pulled my rip cord, fearing that my chute had been burned off because of the total weightless sensation. Just as the jerk of the chute came, which was like someone shaking me roughly by the shoulders, I floated down through the undercast of clouds. From then until I reached the ground I remember only the sound of flak bursts around me, bombs hitting the ground ahead of me in rural areas, Lieutenant Kipp falling with only three-fourths of a chute and with extensive head wounds, another parachute

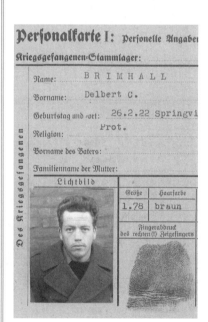

D. Creed Brimhall's German POW camp file.

going down below me, one of our life rafts floating down fully inflated like a leaf, the emergency radio (Gibson Girl) floating down with fully opened orange-colored chute, the catwalk and various pieces of the plane falling down, and parts of the ship burning on the ground.

I landed southwest of what wreckage I had seen in a small, forested area. After sliding down a large pine tree, I gathered up my chute and hid in an outhouse of an unoccupied summerhouse. I rested there for some time trying to get my bearings and to ascertain what injuries I had received. Luckily, all that I found were numerous facial scratches (from the chute opening) and a very sore back.

Creed's B-24 bomber damaged by flak and in a tailspin. Photo was taken by friends in a nearby plane.

DON S. BRIMHALL

Called to serve in 1943, Don was assigned as a tank commander in General Patton's Second Armored Division. During the war he fought in Africa, Sicily, Normandy, and Germany.

Before our tanks could move onto the beach, the Rangers and engineers had to clear minefields in our landing zone.

During this waiting period out in the English Channel, we were like sitting ducks for the large German coastal guns and their fighter-bombers. I shall never forget the loud, fiery destruction from all directions. Landing craft and ships were on fire and sinking, aircraft were being shot out of the sky, dead bodies were floating on the high tides, and much of the oil from sinking craft was burning on the water, creating dense, black smoke and a choking smell.

After several hours we received the signal to land our tanks. Our first tanks drove off the landing crafts and completely disappeared in ten feet of water. All crewmembers lost their lives. The landing crafts had backed on to a large sandbar that had formed along the beach due to high tides. This was a staggering, unexpected military loss. The landing craft commanders had to find another area to unload the military vehicles. After some reconnaissance, they found a more suitable area for landing our vehicles.

By this time the German coastal defenses were really applying the grinding wheel. Our Rangers and infantry were taking an unmerciful beating trying to take their objectives. Wave after wave of American troops lost their lives on the initial landing on Omaha Beach. The Graves Registration Corps was working around the clock gathering dead bodies of American troops, placing them like cordwood in temporary graves in the sand along the beach, and covering them with bulldozers. The heavily fortified ledges and mine fields, together with very few access roads, constituted a real problem for our tanks to operate strategically. After a tremendous loss of personnel and tanks, we maneuvered our tanks out of the beach area to higher ground.

The day had been a nightmare, and I have tried to close it out of my mind. When the day was over, the Allies had suffered some ten thousand to twelve thousand casualties. Thousands of young men sacrificed their lives for the cause of freedom. It would be unpatriotic to say it was a waste of human lives. General Omar Bradley remarked: "Every man who set foot on Omaha Beach that day was a hero." I don't consider myself a hero. I was only doing the job my country required of me that day. And, as with everyone else that day, we were only trying to accomplish our objectives, but at the same time trying to survive and return home in a healthy condition.

It was a great tragedy when some of our close buddies lost their lives in combat. It was a very common occurrence. Our tanks were vulnerable to enemy artillery, fighter-bombers, antitank mines, rocket launchers, enemy tanks, and mortars. Unfortunately, when our tanks were hit on or near one of the two large, one-hundred-gallon gasoline tanks, they would explode and the tanks became a burning inferno. The five-man tank crews had no escape. Their screaming voices would soon fade away. The only remaining evidence of them was their dog tags. We didn't ever see them again in the flesh, but their spirits were always with us.

Omaha Beach

The German forces defended Omaha Beach very aggressively. The "success" of the operation on Omaha Beach had less to do with military might, and more to do with the unstoppable tide of men and equipment coming ashore. Some of the heaviest casualties of the D-Day invasion were on Omaha Beach.

I have always been close to my Father in Heaven. My communications with Him were short but often, and on each occasion throughout my years in combat my prayers were answered. I shall always be grateful for His protection and the blessings He has given me.

Living in a fifty-ton, cast-iron mobile home, with the enemy shooting at us, was not an easy life. During the daylight hours we were kept busy fighting the enemy. At night we would arrange our company of tanks (twenty-three) in a circle called a "Mormon wagon wheel perimeter." For security protection, the 75-millimeter guns and the Browning .30- and .50-caliber machine guns would all be pointing outward. Trip flares were placed around the entire perimeter in case of enemy patrols. During the night on a rotating basis, one of the five-man crewmembers would be stationed in the tank turret as a security gunner. The rest of us would be under the tanks with our clothes on, and in greasy sleeping bags, trying to stay warm and get a wink of sleep. Also during the nighttime hours as the supply trucks caught up, we would resupply our ammunition and refuel each of the tanks.

Personal hygiene was almost nonexistent. Washing our dirty fatigues and having a bath in a steel helmet was a little bit inconvenient. The exhaust manifold of our nine-cylinder radial tank engine provided sufficient heat as a source of hot water.

After months of combat, memories of home including my family, good food, hot showers, clean clothes, and all the conveniences of modern-day living became just a faint recollection. Occasionally my mail would catch up and that was an exciting and happy day. Dawnie's daily letters from home had a great effect on my morale. Quite frequently I would receive seven or eight letters at one time. I was so fortunate to have such a loving and attentive wife.

WALLACE BRUCE

Wallace was drafted on his eighteenth birthday and sent for training at Fort Still, Oklahoma. He was assigned to personnel services because of his typing and office skills. After completing his training, he was sent to Europe for a field assignment.

I was told to sit in a room and someone would eventually come and pick me up. After two hours I wondered if I could desert and no one would ever know. Just then, in walked a sergeant who asked, "Are you a Mormon?" The man was not a member of the Church but grew up in southern Colorado and knew a great deal about the Church. . . . That night I met five active members of the Church who introduced me to the program. On Sunday morning, a Major Van Dam would come in the barracks and pick us up for Church, much to the amazement of the other trainees.

* * * * *

I soon learned how to identify a chaplain's tent or vehicle. Usually there would be a handwritten message that any LDS men who could meet on a specific night would have a sacrament meeting. My first encounter with a non-LDS chaplain was when he told me that he never had to worry about the LDS men finding each other. All he had to do was provide them a place, even if it was his tent.

One Sunday during our sacrament meeting, a medic brought in a soldier in a straight jacket. The medic explained that the man was LDS and had seen most of his unit killed before his eyes and had finally cracked under the strain of what had occurred. However, he had convinced the doctor that if he could get a blessing from a Mormon elder he would be okay. The doctor had given the medic his jeep with orders to find a Mormon. . . . The sacrament meeting was put on

Group of soldiers traveling by train. A common way of moving troops was in boxcars referred to as 40 x 8s—a name which referred to the fact that each car could hold 40 men, or 8 horses. The boxcars were hot and stifling in the summer, and cold and miserable in the winter. Walter Cole is standing on the right in the back row.

hold while several officers ministered to the man. When the medic had brought him in, he looked like a wild man, unshaven, dirty, hair matted, and a wild look in his eyes. After the blessing, he relaxed, gained his composure, and asked if he could remain for the sacrament, and by the time he and the medic headed back to his unit, he was another man.

LDS servicemen's group in England, April 1945, 490th Bomb group.
(L to R) Back Row: Lt. Buckner, Lt. La Chemarinat, Lt. Sutton, Lt. Morris. Front Row: Sgt. Alan Billiter, Sgt. Heider, Cpl. de Mille, Cpl. Rawlins.

E. LAMAR BUCKNER

LaMar served as a pilot of a B-17 bomber. After his training in the States, he sailed aboard the Queen Elizabeth *to his air base in England.*

Our last combat mission (twenty-third) started at 2:00 A.M. and was flown into Aussig, Czechoslovakia. We were leading the entire bomber stream on this day, with Colonel Frank Bostrom in our lead ship. Our ship was flying as the leader of the number two element. Shortly after take off, our navigator, Mel Melkus, told me that we were off course by three degrees. I replied to Mel that I didn't know what I could do about it since we were not allowed to break radio silence and perhaps the colonel had received later instructions as to our flight path. Several times during the morning, as we flew the five hours to the target area, Mel would call in and report to me that we were still off course by three degrees.

In the colonel's crew, the group navigator was a major. I was not in the mood to call the colonel and tell him that Lieutenant Buckner wanted him to know that my second lieutenant navigator, Lieutenant Melkus, thought his major had made a mistake and that we were off course. Who was I to tell the group leaders what to do?

However, we learned a great lesson when we reached the IP (initial point) where we were to begin the start of our bomb run. Instead of being to the right or the left of Aussig, Czechoslovakia, where we should have been, we were right over the city of Aussig. The colonel had to make a decision. He took us on a 270-degree turn to the right, and we then came back

NAME Lt. E. L. Buckner
LEFT NEW YORK HARBOR
DATE January 30, 1945
ARRIVED FIRTH OF CLYDE, SCOTLAND
FEBRUARY 6, 1945

Cunard White Star Liner "QUEEN ELIZABETH"

E. LaMar Buckner served as a B-17 First Pilot with the majority of his missions over Germany during the war. Pictured is the Cunard White Star Liner Queen Elizabeth, *the ship on which he and 22,000 other men crossed the Atlantic Ocean from New York to Firth of Clyde, Scotland. The* Queen Elizabeth *was originally built as an ocean liner to accommodate 2,000–3,000 passengers. LaMar and his crew first saw the* Queen Elizabeth *on January 27, 1945, from the 70th floor of the RCA Building in New York City while on a twelve-hour leave. The ship was camouflaged so it could not be identified, but LaMar reported in his personal history that his crew talked about "how great it would be to travel overseas on a ship as large as the* Queen *instead of a regular troop ship in convoy." When they arrived on board January 30, they quickly learned that it was indeed the* Queen Elizabeth.

All officers on board ship were assigned a cabin on the main deck. These cabins were designed to accommodate two people, but for the transport of troops, the cabins had been equipped with hammocks and could sleep twenty-four men hanging from the wall three and four deep on the sides. The enlisted men slept on the lower decks and often would rotate eight hour shifts on cots during the travel period.

The Queen Elizabeth *wasn't like ordinary troop ships. It didn't travel in a convoy of ships because it could travel faster than convoys were able. As well, the ship had to make a zigzag course across the Atlantic, constantly changing directions every six minutes in order to prevent submarines from lining up on the ship. These changes in direction would be at least ten degrees and became quite monotonous.*

Shortly after arriving on the ship, LaMar learned that there would be an LDS Church service held on Sunday, February 4, at 4:00 P.M. *The chaplain on board the ship gave Buckner the name of another individual, Lieutenant Donald Pickett, who was on board and had also inquired about Church services. They got together and were asked by the chaplain to organize the services for the LDS men on board. Lieutenant Donald Pickett conducted the service and LaMar gave the lesson entitled "Articles of Faith." While at the meeting, LaMar met two of his friends from his home in Ogden, Utah—Russell Thorne and Donald Stegan. On February 6, the* Queen Elizabeth *arrived in Scotland, and from there, his crew was transported by train to their air base in England.*

in over the target on the bomb run. During the time that we were making that turn and returning to the target, we were attacked by Me262s. We lost four ships from the group—one from our own squadron and three in the low squadron, which was just underneath us. They attacked us head-on. We lost more planes that day to enemy aircraft than we had lost at any other time in the history of the 490th Bomb Group.

Instead of trading off every fifteen minutes with Bill, which was the usual practice, I flew for a straight one and a fourth hours steady while we were in the danger zone and in the target area. Our mission lasted nine hours. It was a tough mission and one of the worst we had ever flown. We felt most fortunate to be spared once again. We had learned how easy it would have been to make a simple course correction anywhere along the way, but when we waited until we reached the target city, it became a fatal tragedy for thirty-six of our comrades.

J. ROBERT BULLOCK

Robert commanded a navy LCF (landing craft outfitted with an antiaircraft battery) during the Normandy invasion. He had to sail as close to the beach as he could to look for targets on the shore and to watch for enemy aircraft that might fire on the troops. German gun emplacements that were firing on the troops on the beach were his prime targets. While the troops went ashore, Robert's LCF was patrolling just offshore where he faced the full onslaught of the German artillery.

When we got the word that D-Day was changed from the fifth to the sixth, the convoy was ordered to again set out for France. The weather continued bad, but on the night of the fifth, it seemed to slightly abate, and had improved considerably by the morning of the sixth. When we arrived at what we thought was the transport area and somewhere near Point E marked on the chart, but which in no way was marked on the water, it became light enough to see hundreds of ships of all types and kinds, including battleships, cruisers, landing craft, transports, and jillions of small boats with troops in them, milling about the transports. There was open sea to the west and a long way easterly appeared to be Normandy. We could see gunfire coming in our direction from what appeared to be pill-boxes, so we headed for what we presumed to be Utah Beach. There was no way to tell whether we were in the boat lane, which had been swept of mines. We hoped and prayed we were.

D-Day Invasion

The Allied invasion of Hitler's "Fortress Europe" was a marvel of logistics. Nearly 5,000 ships, 287,000 men, and nearly 10,000 aircraft from the Allied nations were assembled on the island of Great Britain, and were prepared to attack across the English Channel.

First Presidency News Release

The response of the Church to the D-Day invasion was rather subdued. For members it was a time of prayer rather than a time of celebration. Stories that covered the event noted the difference between the national mood and that in Salt Lake City. The June 6, 1944, news release of the First Presidency represented the somber mood of the Saints.

We have been asked for a comment upon the invasion. We feel that this is a day, not for comment, but for prayer for our loved ones who are in the service and for the triumph of righteousness.

Heber J. Grant, J. Reuben Clark Jr., David O. McKay
The First Presidency

A few minutes after 6:30 A.M., we observed a black smoke signal, which meant that our troops were on the beach and firing should cease. But there were still several machine gun nests, which appeared to be continuing their fire, so we continued on our course to the beach in the direction of the nests, shooting our guns, until we could no longer see the fire. German 88-millimeter shells were dropping in our vicinity, but we could not tell exactly where they were coming from. We were as close to the beach as we could get, even with our flat-bottomed ship, although it was still quite a ways. We knew that we were going to be in trouble if we got any closer because several times we had hit the sand and had to back away and move out just a bit farther. From time to time as we made a turn to go along the beach, we fired at what we believed to be machine gun nests. We anchored in the transport area at about 11:30 P.M., having been at general quarters (battle stations) for twenty-three hours. It was quite a long day.

We didn't know how the war was going on Omaha Beach or the British and Canadian beaches, Sword and Juno. They were too far away to see. We did know that the landing of troops and equipment was continuous on Utah Beach almost from the beginning, and things appeared to be going well, although numerous ships, some loaded with troops, struck mines from time to time and sunk. From our standpoint, after the first few days at Utah Beach, mines were much more of a problem than enemy activity.

⭐ ORLAND CALL

Orland entered the Army Air Corps and trained as a navigator for assignment to a B-24 Liberator crew. During his tour of duty he successfully participated in many bombing missions over France and Germany.

Orland Call's B-24 Liberator crew. (L to R) Back Row: Orland Call, Julian Lavon McDonald, Robert M. Looney. Center Row: John C. Watkins, Richard P. Humphrey Jr., Edward P. Hudzinski, Thomas F. Conner. Front Row: Frank C. Vadas.

That night as we were preparing to check the plane out and see if our equipment was working and courses plotted, the pilots started the engines and were running them up to full throttle to check on maximum power. This was standard procedure because it required maximum power to take off. I was busy in the nose of the plane working on my charts and equipment when the radioman, John Dalton, came to check my radio and give me a set of earphones and a throat mike. After he had finished, he quickly lowered himself through the nose wheel compartment on to the ground to return to the radio compartment. That was quicker than crawling on our hands and knees through the tunnel. Very shortly the engines were throttled back and stopped. John Dalton, the radioman, had walked into a turning prop and was killed.

While Dalton was checking out my radio, a voice had told me that I should tell him that the engines were running, but I passed it off because the engines were making so much noise that we could not hear over the sound of the engines. It was difficult to carry on a conversation with anyone. We had to yell into a person's ear if we wanted to talk to him. The tips of the props were only inches away. Only the thin skin of the plane with no insulation was between us and the turning props. I said to myself that everyone knows the engines are running and the props are spinning. . . . The voice came again, and again I passed it off.

I think Dalton had other things on his mind and was just not thinking and walked into the prop. Some of the other crew members who lived with him said that he had told them he would not go into combat and fight, and they thought the accident might have been suicide, but I discount that. He was late getting to the plane for the flight. Some members of the crew said he had been drinking, but I did not detect that. The real story is simply this: I did not listen to the Spirit, or the Holy Ghost. I did not respond to the still small voice.

* * * * *

When flying a mission, a flyer would wear the heaviest clothing he could find— heavy undergarments with heavy shirts and jackets. He then put on a heavy leather jacket and pants that were lined with wool. He would have two or three pairs of socks, a felt shoe, and then heavy, fur-lined boots. Heavy and warm mittens were also provided. The navigator would take his mitten off when he had to record something on his log and chart. The flyer would then put on his Mae West (life jacket), which could be inflated if he parachuted into water. He would then buckle the parachute harness on. The flyer would take his regular heavy shoes and wire them together and carry them to the plane and hang them near his parachute on the side of the plane so that if he had to bail out he could take the shoes with him to use when he got on the ground. During the winter months the temperature would be below zero, and many times as much as fifteen to twenty degrees below zero. The moisture from his oxygen mask would trickle down the front of his outer clothing and freeze.

The pilot and copilot would have backpack parachutes that fit on their backs and fit in the seat with them. The rest

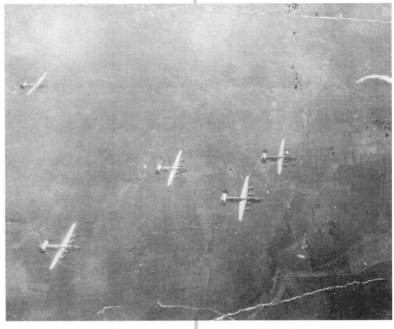

B-24 bombers (464th Bomb Group) in formation over northern Italy, January 8, 1945. Photo taken by the camera ship en route to target.

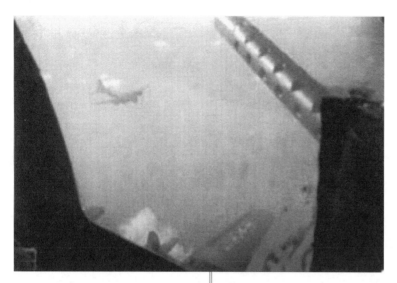

View from the waist gunner position in a B-24 bomber off the coast of England.

of the crew would have to buckle the parachute onto the parachute harness if the plane got into trouble. If the plane was in trouble and we had to bail out, the navigator or front nose turret gunner would pull a lever and the small doors on the compartment of the nosewheel would fall off, and we could dive out of the plane through that hole. It was a very tough job getting out of a bomber spinning down out of the sky. They also provided some metal vests that flyers could wear to protect them from the flak. It was too much of a job with all of the other clothing and equipment, so the crew members just stood on the vests with the idea that the flak would come from under the plane, and they would be protected.

ARTHUR O. CHAPMAN

Arthur's wife saved many of his letters written home during his service in Africa and Italy. He was a technical sergeant who worked in medical labs doing research on the use of DDT to control mosquitoes. He frequently attended Protestant church services held by British servicemen lay preachers. This group recognized his musical talent and invited him to organize a choir.

February 14, 1944.

I suppose it is nice to be able to say, "You are my valentine," but I enjoy it much more when I say, "You are my wife forever." I get a great deal of satisfaction out of thinking about that. . . . It isn't surprising you enter into most thoughts I have about religion.

* * * * *

June 12, 1944.

Just before the service (LDS) started, Bill Allen came in and I motioned for him to take a seat next to me. I just wanted to talk to him about people we knew in Council Bluffs and Salt Lake City rather than sing, but I held myself back and waited until after the service. He was selling knit goods in Council Bluffs when I was there on a mission, and he was very generous in taking us to various places in his car. I have seen him in Salt Lake City a few times since.

During the first song, Chaplain Eldin Ricks came in and sat two rows in front of me. A few minutes later he looked around and saw me, and we shook hands as only old friends can do. He was called on to say a few words in our fine Mother's Day service, and it reminded me of how I have wanted to hear more chaplains like him speak.

I didn't get to talk long with any of them after the service because I had to catch my ride back here; but find that they aren't so far from me, and I may see them outside of the Church. All in all, Dear, it was very good to see them and attend a good old Mormon service again.

* * * * *

Protestant Medical Center Choir. Arthur Chapman (third man from left in second row from the back) was the only LDS member of the choir.

July 25, 1944.

I had a three-day pass and hitchhiked across Italy to the place we were celebrating Pioneer Day. There were about 150 men that joined in the celebration yesterday, and it was the most outstanding Pioneer Day I have spent. If I had come home to spend it with you, it would have been better, but I'll always remember it. Ray Jorgensen, Tim Irons, and Don Hemmingway are new additions to my list of friends I have met over here. Bill Allen and I stayed with Ray last night.

Yesterday morning we had our first meeting, in which we all introduced ourselves. The talks were on the theme. I don't remember the exact words of the theme, but it was about the spirit of '47 as an incentive in our lives in '44. We took our lunches, including some ice cream (boy!) to the beach and had some swimming and eating in the afternoon. Later in the afternoon we had a group leader meeting to coordinate our activities. The out-standing event was a testimony meeting in the evening, and it was certainly a spiritual feast. A fellow, not of our church who was there, said that he marveled that such a large group of men could be found who had such a firm belief, as indicated by the way they expressed themselves, without raising their voices in highly emotional tones. If I remember right, the place of the reunion was Foggia.

* * * * *

Article from the Front Lines *newsletter.*

November 6, 1944.

I mentioned that we are holding LDS group services in a French Protestant chapel. That was the first one I held in France. I had it announced in the *Stars and Stripes* newspaper. Our first meeting was better than I expected. There were six-teen out, and most of them know of others that will come out if they can. I made it a testimony meeting, and it lasted one and a half hours. It was one of the best meetings I've attend-ed. In our second meeting there were thirty-two present, and we organized the group. We held the meetings in the after-noon, as the army Protestant services were held in that church in the morning.

* * * * *

February 25, 1945.

We turned the trio into a quartet about fifteen minutes before time for church today and hit if off pretty well on the song, "I Know That My Redeemer Lives." Captain Larsen was conducting the service and asked us to sing another one a little later in the evening. We then sang "Sweet Is the Work," and hadn't practiced it at all. We went through all four verses of it without a hitch, and they say it sounded very good too. Of course we are glad to take their word for it. This fourth man came in while we were practicing just before the meeting, and Dwight Freeman told me that he bet that man could sing just from the sound of his voice when talking. I asked him, thinking that maybe he could carry the melody, and we could sing the other parts. The melody was too high, and he said he would try the alto. He hit it right off, so we used him. This fourth member of our quartet, name of Richard Holebrook, is too far away to practice during the week with us. The attendance of our meetings is still around twenty-five, with about one-fourth of them being new or irregular attenders.

* * * * *

July 29, 1945.

I went with the Lang family to LDS Church services in a home in Darmstadt. The branch chapel had been destroyed by bombs. Fraternizing restrictions have been lifted, and we are more free to associate with natives. I invited those in attendance to join us in our meetings next Sunday in the Belinda Theater in town. We had separate classes for Sunday School and meetings because not many of them could speak English. It sounded different with them singing in German while we sang in English. I spent some time with the Langs who had a fourteen-year-old son. He and his mother could speak English, and I practiced German with them helping and sang LDS songs with them in that language with Brother Lang at the piano. There was evident hardship among the people whose homes had been destroyed by the war and replaced with shacks made from the ruins.

VICTOR B. CLINE

Victor served in the infantry from 1944 to 1946. He was first assigned to the Sixty-third Division of the Seventh Army and later, he was transferred to the Thirty-fifth Division of Patton's Third Army. Victor kept a personal journal during much of his experience in the infantry as they fought their way across Europe.

Monday, December 25, 1944.

Victor Cline in Germany.

This is one of the most miserable, awful, depressing, and bitter cold Christmases I've ever spent. In fact it is the worst. We were carted away to base camp Christmas Eve, where we spent a miserable night in those ice cold, empty barracks and were wakened at 4:30 A.M. Christmas morn and packed into trucks. (It was awful—even a can of Spam has more breathing space.) We gulped cold K rations, and off we went to Patton's Third Army. Mile after mile across hills of ice and snow we drove. We arrived in the evening chilled to the bone and famished—no food all day. Most other troops were getting big turkey Christmas dinners. After dragging our equipment in and out of the trucks several times, and waiting and waiting, we finally started for the Thirty-fifth Division rest camp four miles away. The captain and lieutenant promised warm, steam-heated barracks, a big dinner, and lots of showers. That news came as a godsend. We could forget our cramped legs, and exhausted and shivery bodies.

But the lieutenant lost his way and led the convoy in the wrong direction. Not until three hours later did we reach our proper destination. The place had no heat whatsoever. Our "big dinner" was C rations eaten in the dark. And hot showers were the biggest laugh. But then we were assigned our jobs in the regiment. . . . Only rifle companies were taking men. . . . It was around 10:00 or 11:00 P.M. when I had to go out to throw up. The trip and rations had made me sick. The CO said as I came in, "We move out at 4:00 A.M. tomorrow morning to engage the enemy in combat."

* * * * *

Monday, January 1, 1945.

I'm standing in my foxhole—it's snowing—we're awaiting the order to "jump off" into the attack. The enemy is all around us, and the shelling is moderately heavy. Last night a direct mortar hit and killed a man in our platoon and injured two others. We made a march up to our jumping off point here (in some woods) with all our heavy equipment. I think it's the most

exhausting thing I have ever done—most of it uphill. I kept saying over and over again to myself, "God just one more step! God just one more step!" I must be weak or my legs awfully wobbly because no one else complained about it. But my cartridge belt restricted my diaphragm, making it extremely difficult to get a full breath. On the way up I saw them putting the American dead in little jeep trailers—stacking them up just like cordwood. All I can say is I'm glad I followed fairly near the straight and narrow and said my prayers and paid my tithing when I was younger.

Victor Cline walking across battle rubble, getting ready to throw a hand grenade.

* * * * *

My eye suddenly caught something moving in the trees thirty yards away—in a white snow cape a Nazi came walking stealthily. It took ten seconds before I fully realized the dangerous situation. I watched him all the time. Then I jumped in the hole and alerted the other men. Then we started picking them off as they came through on either side of us. Both men in the foxhole were hit—one killed (shot through the head). As we fired away we could hear the enemy cry out in pain and others helping the wounded men. But we couldn't see them. The position was too hot so we slithered back through the snow a hundred yards for additional support.

We were wet to the skin, and it was so cold our clothes were beginning to stiffen as the moisture froze. We'd left our overcoats back in the company area so we would be less encumbered. Now we were freezing. I sweat out the night on guard in my foxhole. We had a perimeter defense more or less. They brought up a German tank, which (among other things) shelled and fired on us all night. Some Germans infiltrated to within ten yards of us before they were shot at and discovered. The BAR (Browning automatic rifle) man in our squad (he has five children) was one of the first killed. I still have no sensation of fear (or maybe the real word is panic)—only tension, excitement, and edginess. I have complete faith God will do with me as He wills. I shall try not to worry. Amen.

Victor Cline's unit searching a factory in the industrial Ruhr Valley in Germany.

* * * * *

Monday, January 8, 1945.

Well I'm sure of one thing—either I'm on the Lord's side or He's on mine. I'm still a little shaky from what happened yesterday. The day before, I went out to the woods again (the woods we'd taken from the enemy). We observed enemy movements from our foxholes. It was miserably cold and snowing most of the time. There were three of us to a hole. Mortar and artillery fire kept landing in the woods making it pretty hot.

The next morning they brought us hot chow (prunes and eggs), and there were two of us getting food when a mortar shell exploded two arms' length from me. I was absolutely unhurt though the boy next to me got it—several pieces of steel in the leg. My ears rang for hours afterward, and the stench of burnt powder clung to my clothes. Then finally about 4:00 P.M., in came the good word. We would move back.

Well, we made a grueling two-hour march and finally stopped at a very large dairy. We went up in the hayloft. It was wonderfully warm indoors! Then they brought in supper—fried chicken and pineapple. Several of the boys built a little fire to warm the place up, and I started fixing my bedroll for the night when German artillery fire opened up. Evidently they had spotted the fire through the cracks. It got closer and closer. Then a terrific explosion and part of the roof and a rain of steel descended on our heads. Big six-by-six timbers came toppling down—then silence. Then came the sobs and groans of those wounded. There was complete darkness. I was again unhurt. I gave a little prayer of thanks. . . . I was comforted in prayer. I seemed and felt perfectly safe. We waited for the next explosion that would probably come any second. But a voice or an "influence" seemed to tell me I would be perfectly safe, so I cuddled up in the straw and blankets and went to sleep.

Everyone else quickly deserted the building except the medics who carried broken bodies down an icy (from blood) red ladder. As I can make out seventeen boys got it. . . . I do certainly believe that it is God's will if I am wounded, killed, or untouched. I will certainly not worry about what fate has in store for me. As I looked in the barn this morning I saw stiff bloody blankets and straw. This awful destruction of human bodies is saddening.

* * * * *

All day long we've been cleaning out houses. The families, invariably in the cellars, come out hands up, little children, old, old, women. When we tell them they don't have to keep their hands up, they refuse to take them down. The children especially are sort of shocked by it all, and stare at us dumbly with hands in the air. When they finally learn we are not going to hurt them, their joy and smiles know no bounds. But I feel a little guilty and ashamed when I see old grandmas who are eighty years old, blind, and crippled come out with their feeble hands raised.

In taking men ages seventeen to thirty-five prisoner, we go mainly by looks. In one case the man kissed his wife good-bye. It was heartbreaking to watch her try and hold the tears back. For she thought we might shoot her husband or something terrible would happen.

* * * * *

One of the best fellows I ever knew in high school was killed December 31 in Belgium. This is the first time that the war has really bothered me. It leaves a deep ache in my heart. I've seen many men die with my emotions hardened, but this causes me genuine sorrow. He was a true patriot. He could have easily stayed out of the Army with a physical deformity, but he covered that up so he could get in. It seems the good men always get it first. Someday I'd like to write a tribute to him and my other buddies who have fought for a cause I believe in with all my heart and soul—and who paid the full price.

* * * * *

Roosevelt is dead. . . . It is stunning, unbelievable. . . . We are on the verge of our greatest victory—then terrible news.

We are staying at a little farmhouse. I try to get additional details—shifting the radio dial and tuning in to one wave band after another. In all foreign languages I keep hearing, President Roosevelt, Franklin Delano Roosevelt, and just Roosevelt reechoing hundreds of times. German stations, Spanish, French—in a myriad of tongues the news pours out.

I feel really sad. My heart aches. The man of such great courage, leadership, who in such terrible hours at the beginning of the war gave his country spiritual leadership. Nobody can ever replace him. I believe he was the indispensable man.

* * * * *

In the Army I've kept expecting better things. It's difficult to work up enthusiasm. This sort of thing over and over again crushes me spiritually. It's numbing. It makes me get where I don't want to try anymore. Just give up. The whole atmosphere I'm living in is degenerating and paralyzing. Why should I try to keep being a "good boy?" Why not take advantage of all the physical pleasures which are so easy to get. Everyone I know of lives in this world of satisfying the flesh (with very few exceptions). I'm tired of being alone—and slowly I'm degenerating; it takes more and more will power to say no. What future is there in striving for a goal—upholding these noble ideas of morality? I just get kicked in the face every time. I compromise more and more. God, get me out of Germany. Get me something to occupy my mind, get me something with a goal that will be difficult for me to do. But I'm going to fight this thing to the very end. If I go down, I'll go down fighting. What I need is close contact with my church, with men who think as I do, and my God in heaven. But its tough for one man alone to live as he honestly and sincerely believes he should.

* * * * *

Friday, August 31, 1945.

Victor Cline (left) with a combat buddy.

We land. The 137th Infantry comes home. We pulled in about 8:00 A.M. into the harbor. Coming out to meet us was a pilot boat covered with decorations, a brass band, and a bunch of WACs (Women's Army Corps) singing, clapping, and cheering us in. A navy blimp kept circling us, and the fireboat turned on the works shooting up colored streams of water—red, blue, green and purple. As we came into the harbor proper we were met by a deafening roar of whistles, foghorns, and other noise devices.

And then we finally disembarked. The Red Cross came up with doughnuts and ice-cold milk, which was appreciated very much and tasted wonderful. Everywhere people waved and grinned at us. We hopped right onto a waiting train and took off for Camp Myles Standish. As we passed through the railway yards where scores of locomotives were scattered about, they opened up their whistles and let loose a tremendous welcome. It nearly blew us off the tracks. Grimy workers moved and cheered us in. People in swanky cars stopped at railroad crossings, grinned and waved us on. As we passed through the back of shabby tenement districts, whole families stood on their back porches and welcomed us. Office workers leaned out of windows to wave. Little kids with toy machine guns sprayed us. Women hanging out shabby washings in the backyards of broken down unpainted living quarters cheered us on.

This was the first time anybody had ever made such a fuss about us. It moved us very deeply. People did seem to care about what we did. The fellows who had always been looked down on as infantry—who took the brunt of combat, who endured, and who always caught the dirt—well, it felt good. Lumps came up in our throats. Yes, we were home. But there were some we left behind who would never know the thrill.

WALTER N. COLE

As a member of the infantry assigned to occupy Germany, Walter was very active in seeking out the German Saints. These two letters reflect the results of those efforts.

May 31, 1945.

Elders F. W. Starratt
Clark W. Brimhall
Keith P. Gillen
Walter N. Cole
Elmer Giggey
Noel E. Gold

Dear Brethren:

We are very happy indeed to get your letter of May 14 telling us of the meeting which you had held with some of the Saints in Germany, and particularly happy to get your report that the spirit of the Saints seems to be very fine and that they greeted you so cordially.

We were also most happy to get the report from Sister Muller, which is the first direct report we have received from Germany since we entered the war.

We would be glad to have you say to any groups of Saints with whom you may meet that we send to them our love and our greetings, and that we trust the spirit of the Lord will rest

T-5 Walter Cole when he was in the Army Specialized Training Program (see the patch on his sleeve) before the program was cancelled. The army put soldiers with high test scores into an accelerated college program so they'd have enough officers for 1946-47. The program was cancelled in 1944 because of the immediate need for combat soldiers.

upon them and give them peace and comfort and lead them to live lives of righteousness that shall lead to the blessings promised by the Lord to those who so live.

Again thanking you for your thoughtful kindness in writing to us, and again expressing our appreciation of your spirit and of your expressed determination, we are,

Faithfully yours,
George Albert Smith, J. Reuben Clark, David O. McKay
The First Presidency

* * * * *

East German Mission
District Zwickau

(Below) Receipt of donation made by Wally Cole while his division (89th Infantry Division) was waiting to ship out to Europe.

(Far Below) Group of German members of the Church in Zwickau, Germany, at the very end of the war in front of the LDS Zwikau branch building. It was taken without permission, and against the army's non-fraternization policy. Wally is on the far right.

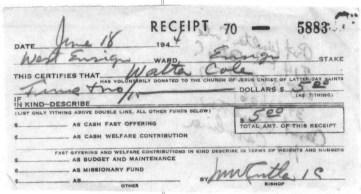

(Below) Wally Cole (on left) with fellow serviceman on the roof where he was billeted on the day the war ended.

(Above) Soldiers serving with Wally Cole (Clement, Frantz, and Dekker) sitting on the "liberated" Olympic flag from the 1936 Berlin Olympics. This building, in Zwickau, Germany, later served as a mission home for the LDS Church. Photo taken the morning after the war ended.

(Right) Meal ticket issued when Wally Cole was on a troopship going to France, 1944.

Dear Brother Grant:

With great joy I can report that under Arnea Garrison, some missionaries and Saints attended our services. For us it was an extraordinary event.

I, Erika Fassmann-Muller, am a missionary and laborer in the mission office since August 4, 1940.

I am the only girl of the mission staff who escaped from Berlin, and now I have the occasion to give you a short report.

Our mission office (Berlin NW 87 Handelallee 6,) was completely destroyed by bombs the night of November 23, 1943. Many documents are lost. Our mission president Herbert Klopfer has been a soldat in the east and has been missing since June 44. His counselors Richard Ranglack and Paol Lang-Heinrich are now presiding in his stead.

The Saints had to suffer many sorrows. Homes and members of the families have been lost; many brothers are killed, many towns destroyed. My father Walther Fassman district president of Zwickau is now responsible for district of Saxony in which are assembled many Saints out of the destroyed areas of Germany.

Under Arnea Garrison we feel free and happy. The food is scarce especially in heavily populated Saxony. But we hope for a change for the better soon.

All Saints look full of confidence toward Zion and would like to reestablish communications with you and the presiding brethren.

In the name of all the Saints I enthusiastically greet you.

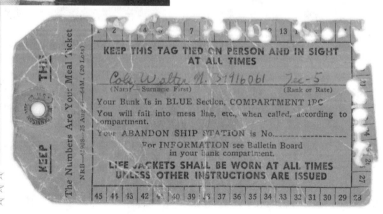

(Left) Rest camp at Schloss Ort, Austria. Wally Cole is the fourth soldier in line smiling at the camera. This was one of the rest camps where soldiers on leave could go and get a shower, watch a movie, and get some food.

(Below) Rest Center pass.

GMUNDEN

REST CENTER PASS

T/5 Walter Cole 39916061

ISSUED Feb22/24 EXPIRED

B	D	S	B	D	S	B	D	S	B	D	S

ONE COUPON ONE COUPON ONE COUPON ONE COUPON ONE COUPON ONE COUPON

Nº PB 740,460

AMERICAN RED CROSS

12 COUPONS

FRANCE : 10 Francs ▪ BELGIUM
HOLLAND : 1 Guilder ▪ LUXEMBURG : 9 Francs
2 ▪ GERMANY : 2 Marks
The number of coupons required for each purchase will be detached at Snack Counter.

ONE COUPON ONE ONE ONE COUPON ONE COUPON ONE COUPON

AMERICAN RED CROSS IN GT. BRITAIN

STAFF BEVERAGE

4197690

(Above) Soldiers in front of a radio truck. Wally Cole was a radioman in the 89th Infantry Division. This photo was taken during their drive across Germany in the last months of the war. An orange marker panel was attached to the radio truck to identify the truck as a "friendly vehicle" to Allied pilots.

(Above and Left) Both during and after the war, rationing continued in Europe. Tickets like these pictured here allowed a serviceman to eat while on leave.

WARREN L. COOPER

As a pilot of a B-17 bomber, Warren flew under the command of General James (Jimmie) Doolittle. Known as the "Hell's Angels," his group flew many successful bombing runs over France and Germany from their base in Nuthampstead, England. Their emblem was a little devil riding a bomb and holding a trident with three small bombs as tines.

Doolittle's Raid

Lt. Col. James (Jimmie) Doolittle led the American raid on Tokyo in April 1942. This was the first American attack on the Japanese mainland. Although it caused very little physical damage, the psychological effects were tremendous—the Japanese wartime leadership had promised the civilian population that Japan could not be attacked. James was promoted to full general in 1985.

Class 44D Perrin Field Air Cadet School, Sherman, TX. Warren Cooper on the right. Photo taken January 27, 1944.

On one of our missions over Merseburg as we approached our target, flak was bursting all around us. Our windshields were made out of Plexiglas, and a piece of flak scooped out a piece of the windshield. It looked like someone had taken an ice cream scoop and dipped it out. At the same time, a chunk of flak entered the plane, flying between the legs of Lieutenant Curtis and myself. It knocked out all the hydraulic and throttle lines. (This is where you find out whether you have a good engineer on board.) Grossman got in back of the copilot's seat, and with a screwdriver chopped a hole in the bulkhead. He reached in with a pair of pliers and pulled the throttle cables out until we could get the throttle settings we wanted. Now we could change the throttle but we couldn't advance it.

After he got us flying and all of our props were synchronized, he went back and took the return line off, which caused pressure problems because it had been cut in two. He put it in place of the pressure line. He then took the webbing out of his helmet and started at the back of the plane, collecting urine from each of us (those of us who had not let it run down our leg during the scare) which he poured in the tank so we would have hydraulics to land. When we got back to our base we had just one chance to land. We could pump the brakes but one time. We radioed for an emergency landing. We landed and finally were able to stop the plane by adding two parachutes opened out to the side of the plane. We ended up against a fence, but we did stop safely.

God bless Grossman. When we got out we counted ninety-six holes in our rear tail section alone. No one was hurt. Needless to say, the urine ruined the hydraulic system in our B-17.

JOHN H. DAHL

John was separated from his wife and family in September 1940, when he was drafted into a German communications unit. He experienced the protection of the Lord throughout his service in the German Army.

The next day I joined the training class, which I passed with the best possible grade. But any expected promotion was not granted. I only found out much later from one of the lieutenants of our regiment the reason why I was not promoted. Here are his own words, as far as I remember them: "Why did you mention in your vita that you are a member of an American church? This made you suspect of being an agent for America. There was no need to mention this, and you would have been promoted at least to the rank of corporal." I was bitterly disappointed, but gave him no answer. My family suffered more under this intolerant decision, for the promotion would have meant a raise in my pay. Ignorance is the enemy of tolerance!

* * * * *

Our company received a certain amount of liquor. Since I did not drink alcohol, one of my comrades asked me if he could have my bottle. "No problem," I said. I gave him the bottle, and he paid me fifty deutsche marks. The deal was fair, and I had forgotten all about it, until one day in a meeting when our company chief asked who among us would sell his bottle of liquor to someone in the company for fifty deutsche marks. I did not answer; neither did anyone else. I was relieved; the matter remained a secret. I got away with it.

While making preparations to leave Charkow our company chief wanted to appoint me to be in charge of a small rear-guard, consisting of six men and a machine gun. I made it very clear that I did not think that I could ever accept that assignment, because I did not know how to handle a machine gun…. No further comments were made on either side. I know it was the influence of the Holy Ghost that gave me strength to act as I did. So I got away with that one too.

* * * * *

Life in Munich was different. While on the front in the Ukraine, we never had any air raids. In Munich, we could expect one each day or night. During one of them, our building was hit. But life still went on as normal. The trolley and busses were running regularly, stores were open, entertainment, opera, theaters and cinemas, museums and galleries were open and sport activities continued. . . . We went to church as often as we did before the war, even on the Sunday afternoon when Munich was taken at the end of the war. We continued to do so after the United States Seventh Army's occupation.

* * * * *

The Thaller's home was near a wide, open field. Heavy flak artillery was placed on one end of the field. One day we had an air raid. Betty, Helga, and baby Rainer were in Karlsruhe. We found shelter in the basement of the Thaller's home, when all of a sudden we heard the shrill sound of an air mine or time bomb coming down over the house. We hurried to one corner of the cellar, for better protection, and prayed. We heard no explosion. Soon it was quiet again. We went upstairs and saw no fire or homes destroyed. The attack, however, did much damage in the inner city.

Some days later we had another air raid. I had to walk to my shift. I went on walking along the trolley tracks, which had been destroyed. Some of them were bent straight upward into the sky. The depot and some big buildings were on fire. While the flak brought more bombers down than the United States Air Force hoped they would be able to do, there were still many of them which made it to their bases in England after they had followed orders to release the rest of their ammunition anywhere possible. It reminded me of Dante's *Inferno*. I made it to my office unharmed.

* * * * *

After staying in Markt Erlbach for nearly four months, the war came to an end, American GIs occupied the city. A messenger of the city came to our house with an order that we had to leave the house immediately so the soldiers could use it as their quarters. Betty and the children left the house. But help came in the form of a lady who was also a member of the LDS Church and whose name escapes Betty's memory. She had told Betty earlier that she and the children could stay in her home whenever needed. Betty took Rainer and Helga and walked to this lady's home. After a short while, the soldiers came with loaded guns to the sister's home. They were looking for a German soldier hiding somewhere. They searched, but found no German soldier anywhere in the house. They were standing in the living room when one of the U.S. soldiers saw a row of pictures on the top of the commode. He asked Betty who those good-looking young men in the pictures were. Betty told him that they were former American missionaries of the Mormon Church who had served a mission in Germany. "Are you a Mormon?" he asked.

Betty said, "Yes I am." The questioner excused himself and left to ask his commander if we could stay in the house with the children. When he returned, he told us that we could stay in the house. In the afternoon he came back to Betty with a pack of cigarettes and offered her a smoke. She thanked him telling him that she had never smoked in all her life.

He patted her on her shoulder, saying, "Now I know that you are a good Mormon."

MARTIN J. DALEBOHT

Martin was wounded September 27, 1943, while fighting in Italy. The medics found him and carried him under heavy fire to an aid station. The doctor was very concerned because of infection and swelling and ordered him to be taken to a field hospital.

It was very late or very early the next day before I had any idea which. They treated me and gave me a big shot of penicillin, dressed my wounds, and prepared to have me flown back to a bigger hospital. One day blended with another; I really didn't care. I just wanted some relief from my problem. The airplane ride was without incident. I was again tended by a doctor. His word was to prepare me for surgery. I was very depressed at the thought of never having any children. I didn't want to go through the operations.

Naturally throughout the whole thing I did a lot of praying. I had never seen or known of a member of the Church there. But the ward boy I was assigned to asked me where I was from. I replied that I was from Utah.

"So am I," he said.

"Are you LDS?" I asked. He said he was. It was a wonderful feeling to finally find someone who was a Mormon. I asked for a blessing before I went into the operating room. His prayer was to protect me from further harm to my body.

Shortly after, three Italians arrived with a gurney to take me to the operating room. They loaded me on the gurney and started down the long hall. I could feel myself slipping just before they dropped me. The pain was terrible. I came completely unglued. I tried to get my hands on them. They stayed clear of me, and I went into shock. They immediately gathered me up and took me back to the aid room and began treating me for shock. It was a blessing in disguise. They put me out and continued treating me with penicillin.

They put the surgery off until the next day. When they came to operate, they gave me an examination and found that the penicillin was working. It helped, but I still insist that it was the blessing of the Lord that took care of me. They did take the bullet out of my leg; I have never had any trouble putting up with my other problem. I now have four lovely children, fifteen grandchildren, and five great-grandchildren. I thank the Lord continually for answering my prayers.

LEE TRUAX DALTON

Lee enlisted in the Navy at age seventeen. Trained to operate sonar submarine detection instruments, he served aboard the USS Instill.

I will never forget the Christmas spent at Argentia, Newfoundland. The German prisoners that were in our care ate in the same mess hall that we all did. They were fed the same food as we ate. We cut a Christmas tree and set it up in the mess hall. We didn't have much to decorate the tree with, but it was much appreciated anyway.

Halfway through our Christmas dinner, the MPs (military police) marched the prisoners into the mess hall and lined them up at the serving tables. They were only a few feet from me as they sat down to eat. I recall thinking, "Hey, these prisoners of war don't look any different than Americans."

Some of the food that day was wrapped in aluminum foil, and I noticed the young U-boat captain was molding his aluminum foil into some kind of image. As the MPs marched the prisoners out of the mess hall, the U-boat captain stopped by the Christmas tree long enough to hang his aluminum creation onto one of the Christmas tree branches.

As soon as the last prisoner left the hall we all ran over to the tree to see what the German skipper had hung on our tree. I fully expected to see a German swastika or some kind of German propaganda. This German POW must have trained as an artist before the war, as the aluminum angel he had hung on our tree was beautiful. Even the wings of the angel were beautifully crafted. No one touched the angel. After Christmas the tree was taken down, and the chaplain took the angel as a souvenir—not of war—a souvenir of peace.

Elder F. Enzio Busche

Elder F. Enzio Busche's involvement in the war was unusual. Enzio was born in Dortmund, Germany, on April 5, 1930. He was named after a comrade of his father who had died in World War I. At age ten, Enzio was required to become a member of the Hitler Youth organization. While not yet fifteen years of age, Enzio was thrust into the conflict as World War II neared its conclusion, but he never fired at the enemy. Soon after his involvement, he and others of his associates were captured and taken to an American prison camp. Fully expecting to be executed, young Enzio was surprised when he and the others were released after promising no further participation in the war. Over a decade after the war, Enzio and his wife Jutta converted to the Church in 1958. His quest for the gospel resulted, in part, from an illness which nearly cost him his life. In 1977, he was called to serve in the First Quorum of the Seventy.

EARL C. DAVIS

Earl enlisted in the Army in 1943. He trained and qualified as a marksman. During his time in France and Germany, he wrote letters home to his family. They later reviewed his letters and organized them into diary-like observations on his wartime experience.

Cpl. June N. (Slim) Davis, younger brother of Earl Davis. Both served in the war.

March 22,1944.

At 5:45 A.M. the 357th Regiment sailed. For most, this was the occasion for the first good-bye to their homeland. As the convoy moved farther out, it grew until finally there were over forty ships of all classes—troop ships, tankers, aircraft carriers, destroyers, and cruisers. The thirteen-day voyage was without particular incident, but many of the landlubbers spent considerable time feeding the fish, and expecting to be sent to the bottom most any day by U-boats.

* * * * *

June 4, 1944.

Final preparations are being made. Most of the men have over two years of hard training under their belts and are in the best physical condition that they have ever been in their lives. . . . On this day the battalions traveled thirty miles to Cardiff, Wales, and embarked on two ships, the USS *Explorer* and the USS *Bienville*.

* * * * *

June 6, 1944.

On our way to France following a route close to the coast of England. . . . During this short voyage across the English Channel, the actions and conversations of the soldiers . . . are worthy of mention. . . . They know that the future holds no picnic and that in a very short time they will be engaged in bloody combat. Most are not worried too much. Things like seeing that equipment is ready and testing life jackets for leaks are important now. Some who are satisfied that everything is in readiness are reading, others just taking it easy. Some of the men are already talking about what they are going to do when they get back home.

* * * * *

May 31, 1944.

When this war is over we will no doubt appreciate the things in America far more than we thought possible a few years ago.

* * * * *

June 20, 1944.

Somewhere in France. I went ashore at Normandy on D-Day plus two. The hedgerows were very difficult to overcome because the Germans were behind them with their artillery and small arms.

* * * * *

June 23, 1944.

Somewhere in France. By the way, if you can get hold of some salted peanuts, send me some; and I'd like to have some of your homemade doughnuts.

* * * * *

June 25, 1944.

Somewhere in France. We are now allowed to mention that we have been in combat. I must confess, that I was somewhat scared the first few times the German guns shelled us, but a person soon becomes used to it and is then not nearly so nervous. And one night we were bombed and strafed by some German planes, and that too is quite a sensation. But we all had good foxholes, and when the shells start coming over, I wouldn't trade my foxhole for the best featherbed in the world.

* * * * *

August 22, 1944.

Somewhere in France. I'm now getting combat infantryman's pay and badge which amounts to ten dollars extra per month.

* * * * *

November 16, 1944.

Somewhere in France. It will soon be Thanksgiving, and it would be swell if we could be home for a big dinner. But even though we are at war, most of us have much to be thankful for.

F. KEITH DAVIS

Keith was ordained an elder before he was inducted into the Army, where he served from June 1943 to December 1945 under General Patton. After landing on Utah Beach during the Normandy invasion, he spent nine months on the front lines in Europe participating in the Battle of the Bulge.

Keith Davis at Auw, Germany, just before Dec. 16, 1944. The famous Battle of the Bulge started just over the ridge behind Davis.

I was present at the liberation of the Ohrdruf concentration camp. That was the first concentration camp liberated by the Allies on the Western Front. It was the camp that Generals Eisenhower, Bradley, and Patton came to view. It was covered in *Life* magazine. There were over three hundred Nazi concentration camps in Germany. We entered the camp, and the Nazis had just machine-gunned many prisoners and had run before we got there. I took some pictures of the people who were gunned down; they did not even bleed. They were so thin from starvation that only a yellow substance drained out of the bullet holes.

There was one young German soldier (about my age of nineteen) hiding in a culvert under the roadway entrance. By that time, hundreds of American soldiers were in the camp, (from all types of military outfits). The American soldiers were so mad at what they saw, they wanted to do away with that German soldier then and there. Someone took him away, I do not know where. He was the only Nazi soldier we saw at Ohrdruf.

Conditions at Ohrdruf were indescribable. I was only there for about three hours, but saw many things. Many barracks had no toilet facilities, and the ones that did had only an outhouse-type hole in the middle of the room with no walls. In the large front yard/courtyard, they had dug a hole that looked like it was sixteen feet square. They had built a bench type seat around this hole, and the inmates were to go to this hole for a toilet. This had no walls or roof—hot in summer and cold in winter and open for all to see. The smell was awful. The people still alive I am sure died very soon. They wore striped pajama-looking clothes. Their faces were sunken in, and their eyes looked large. They were afraid of us at first, because they thought our new uniforms were only more trouble for them.

After leaving the concentration camp at Ohrdruf, we saw many thousands of concentration camp victims on the roads and highways. At first when we saw those people, we offered them our food. We found out too late that our food would kill them, as it was too rich. They needed soup-type food that was not hard on their systems. Many died after they were liberated because they were so weak.

Keith Davis with comrades after discovering a salt mine in Markers, Germany, which contained German gold and valuables.

(Below) Shown in these photos are some of the horrible conditions discovered following the liberation of Ohrdruf Concentration Camp, Germany, in 1945. The Germans tried to burn many of the bodies before the Allies came.

PARLEY W. DESPAIN

Parley was in the Signal Corps. His first assignment was to build and maintain telephone lines in Alaska. He found military life there most difficult but not as challenging as what he found in his next assignment in France. There he found himself part of the second wave of infantry that went ashore at Omaha Beach.

An LST (landing ship tank) was a landing craft used a great deal during World War II in Normandy and some of the South Pacific islands. We were on one of these LSTs. We traveled all night long from southern England to Normandy. We

Scene from infantry camp—laundry time.

landed just off Normandy, at Omaha Beach. It was a real nice clear morning, a beautiful day. An announcement came over the intercom that church services would be held on deck. I figured it would be a Protestant or Catholic service. There weren't enough LDS kids. In fact, I was the only LDS in this crew that was on this boat. When they sent us to Normandy, they had broken up our outfit. They sent part of our outfit on my ship along with part from the quartermaster outfit. So if the ship got hit with a mine or something, it wouldn't decimate a whole outfit. Anyway, they announced that there would be church services. I was sitting in my truck up on deck writing a letter, and an enlisted man came out on the deck.

A lot of men were up there on deck because we didn't know what we were going to run into in Normandy.

Well anyway, they had quite a congregation up there, and this enlisted man got up there and started talking. First he had a prayer, and then he started talking. He hadn't talked but just a little bit when I started listening real close, and I realized that what he was talking was Mormon, only he wasn't saying that.

After he was through, I went up to him and I said, "That sounded like an LDS sermon."

"Yea," he said, "I'm a Mormon; I'm a returned missionary. I asked the captain if it was all right for me to have services and he said yes." I told him I was LDS too.

ALBERT H. DOMAN

The B-17 of which Albert was a crew member was set on fire from enemy fire over France before completing its bombing run. In an attempt to return to base in England, the crew found their situation desperate. Because their bomb-laden plane was over a populated area, the crew chose to stay on the plane and unload the bomb load along the banks of a local river, avoiding harm to the English populace below. The plane exploded soon after the bombs were dropped, killing all but one of the crewmembers. Below is the letter written by the surviving crewman to the Doman family expressing his condolences, and excerpts from a United Press release at the time.

November 26, 1943.

Dear Mr. Doman:

I want to express to you my deepest sympathies upon the death of your son. I was the only survivor of the accident. I shall never know how I managed to get out. I was not as well acquainted with your son as I would have liked to have been. You see, our crew was new and he was flying with us to show us the ropes. I had only met him a week or so before the accident. Your son died doing what he wanted to do. He died true to his God and to his country.

Sincerely,
Alan B. Purdy

B-17 bomber crew. Albert Doman is third from the left on the back row.

* * * * *

Wargrave, Berkshire, November 16, 1943 (UP).

Villagers of Wargrave were convinced that the heroism, self-sacrifice and cool aiming of the airmen saved the village from being wiped out. . . . The local chief of rescue said he was convinced the airmen could have bailed out in plenty of time, as they had previously sent a radio distress call. "In my opinion," he said, "the U.S. flyers deliberately stayed on board to reach the riverside field and unload their bombs before making a crash landing."

KEN O. EARL

After having his mission to West Germany interrupted by the war, Ken finished his mission in the Northern States Mission before enlisting in the Army Air Corps. He trained as an aircraft mechanic, seeing action in North Africa and Italy. He and several other LDS servicemen built the first LDS chapel on the island of Sardinia.

Chaplain Eldin Ricks conducts an LDS servicemen's conference in Italy. Chaplain Ricks served both in Italy and northern Africa. Among the highlights of Ricks' tour of duty was a meeting with Pope Pious II during which he gave the Pope a copy of the Book of Mormon. Eldin later served on the religious faculty at BYU.

Each week everyone was issued cigarette rations, beer rations, and, if available, some candy or other goodies. We usually gave the contra-Word of Wisdom items to friends, but then in January 1944 we had the bright idea of using them to build an LDS chapel down at Decimo where the 319th and 320th were located. We got permission for a particular location, then traded our cigarette and beer rations in return for labor, bricks, mortar, and a tile roof. When the building, which was probably twelve-by-twenty feet in size, was completed in April 1944, I invited LDS Chaplain Eldin Ricks to come over from Naples on one of our B-26s and dedicate the chapel. He did so, and we had a large turnout of LDS servicemen from the three groups for the dedication. We used it for our services from then on until we moved to Corsica.

* * * * *

The following article appeared in *The Church News* May 10, 1944.

Effort - Result: an attractive little brick chapel, the first Mormon edifice ever to be erected on an island of the Mediterranean Sea.

By concerted efforts taken from their hard-earned "liberty" and with funds amassed by practicing a strict abstinence, these earnest American soldiers recently built to their God a tiny shrine. There they might worship in comparative peace "according to the dictates of their conscience."

Built largely of brick and roofed with tile, this miniature house of worship was erected by these Mormon airmen, part of the base personnel at a B-26 Marauder station, with the assistance of Italian bricklayers. It is equipped with a small portable foot-pump organ and rustic benches, fashioned by the men, and will accommodate about thirty men—the number of LDS boys at the base.

The story of their achievement came piecemeal in letters written by Lieutenant Marvel F. Andersen to the LDS Servicemen's Home Office in Salt Lake City as the idea took form and the building grew. Excerpts from those letters follow.

Sardinia, February 14, 1944.

At our meeting last night, we thought we would all put in a few dollars, and build a brick chapel in which to meet. We are checking up on the costs during this week, and will make plans for its erection during the next week. If we make it, it will be the first LDS chapel built in Sardinia, and for the six members here who were at the meeting last night, that won't be so bad for us to do, do you think? When we build our place, we were thinking of getting a few fair-sized pictures of the First Presidency, and of Joseph and Hyrum Smith, and a couple of Deseret songbooks so we can use them. So, if you have a chance to see any of them, and it isn't too much trouble, I would like you to send them to me. There is a need for them to decorate our place. Captain (Ken) Earl has a portable organ, which he takes with him, and we will have it in our meetinghouse, and will be able to use it also to a very good advantage. We will probably have twenty-five to fifty fellows who we can get to come out and join us, and perhaps do a lot of good.

LDS Chaplains: Eldin Ricks, Timothy Irons, Vern Cooley, and Mager Jackson.

Sardinia, February 28, 1944.

Last night we had another good meeting and had a couple more out—that made eight of us. It seems as if each week we get another one or two. We are starting to build our chapel this week. We may have it done by next Sunday. I surely hope so, then we can get a few more out and we will have a nicer time. I'll take a few pictures of it and send them to you when the chapel is completed.

Sardinia, March 10, 1944.

We have our chapel almost finished; however, it won't be ready for use this Sunday. We won't be able to move into it until next week. We will certainly have a nice place to meet in now. At last week's meeting we had twelve fellows out. That wasn't so bad, was it?

REID F. ELLSWORTH

Reid Ellsworth served a mission for the Church from 1939 until 1941. On April 16, 1942, he was inducted in the United States Army as an aviation cadet and received training as a navigator. He was then commissioned as a second lieutenant and assigned to the 346th Bomb Squadron in the Ninety-ninth Bomb Group. Early in his military career he received an impression that his plane would be shot down, and that he would be taken as a POW. He provides a vivid description of his escape from the burning plane as evidence of the Lord's help in a most difficult situation. After parachuting to safety near Milan, Italy, he was helped by sympathetic locals. Eventually he was captured and placed in a German POW camp. He stayed there until being released by Russian troops.

While stationed in Tunisia, a number of Mormon fellows first started meeting together on Sundays after their arrival in the combat area. A pattern was set up with a regular time to meet and the fellows from the different units knew where they could meet to be together for a Sunday meeting. Time passed, and the word was spread from one combat group to another. . . . As the time approached for the invasion of Sicily, the number of Mormon fellows and perhaps non-Mormon friends increased. At this time, we were having meetings in the Second Strategic Air Command auditorium in Tunis, and for a week or two before the invasion of Sicily, the size of the group increased to where we had perhaps two or three hundred fellows meeting on Sunday afternoon. After the invasion, the number dropped considerably back to twenty or thirty of us meeting together.

One morning while walking from my tent up to the mess tent for breakfast, I had a rather complete mental preview almost in the form of a panoramic view of the things that would occur to me thereafter. For example, I knew that in due time the plane in which I was a crew member would be shot down, that I would escape for a time, and that I would be

Reid Ellsworth as an aviation cadet.

captured and sent to a prison camp. I knew also that I would in due time escape and be able to return home. Interestingly this panoramic preview came and was gone just as rapidly and was blotted out of my mind. It caused me no worry or concern, nor did I even think of the matter until each of those things occurred. I believe that this panoramic preview was given to me as a comfort so I would not suffer stress or anxiety over the things that did and would occur in the future.

Later I experienced the fulfillment of my premonition when our plane came under fire, forcing us to bail out. The bombardier tapped me on the shoulder and pointed just as the engineer dropped out of the escape hatch, parachuting to get away from the burning aircraft. . . . By virtue of my location, it was my turn to go next through the nose hatch. I unhooked my oxygen mask from the supply line and headed to the escape hatch. I sat down on the catwalk and reached across the open hatch doorway to grab hold to pull myself off from the catwalk. I expected to drop free. . . . I fell only a few inches. My seat pack had caught on the edge of the escape hatch, and I remained dangling in that position with the fire burning around me.

Reid Ellsworth and fellow soldiers who either evaded capture or escaped from POW camps.

The bombardier was to follow me. . . . When he saw that I was stuck, he had little choice but to try to kick me loose. He knew that if he was to get out alive before the plane blew up, he had to get me out. He kicked me out. I did know enough not to pull the rip cord until I was sure that I had cleared the plane so that the parachute would not get entangled in any way with any part of the aircraft. I waited a few seconds as I fell. When I reached for the D ring of the rip cord, it was not where it should have been. . . . I tried to look to see where the D ring was, but my eyes were watering, and the hose of my oxygen mask was dangling in my line of vision. I tore off the oxygen mask and again tried to locate the D ring. I discovered that it was beyond my reach. By jerking vigorously on the left side of my harness, I was able to pull the D ring and the parachute billowed above me. . . . I figured that I had fallen somewhere between three and four miles with a closed chute before it finally opened.

JAMES E. FAUST

James was assigned to Army intelligence because of his language skills. Following basic training he was married before shipping out for his first assignment in Suez, Egypt. After completing that assignment, he was returned to the States and assigned as an ordnance officer. His assignment was to direct the evaluation of captured German technology.

As I walked around my post, I meditated and pondered the whole miserable, long night through. By morning I had come to some firm conclusions. I was engaged to be married, and knew that I could not support my wife on a private's pay. In a day or two, I filed my application for Officer's Candidate School. Shortly thereafter I was summoned before the board of inquiry.

The questions asked of me at the officer's board of inquiry took a very surprising turn. Nearly all of them centered upon my beliefs. "Do you smoke?" "Do you drink?" "What do you think of others who smoke and drink?" I had no trouble answering these questions.

"Do you pray?" "Do you believe that an officer should pray?" The officer asking these last questions was a hard-bitten career soldier. He did not look like he had prayed very often. I pondered. Would I give him offense if I answered how I truly believed? I wanted to be an officer very much so that I would not have to do all-night guard duty and KP and clean latrines, but mostly so my sweetheart and I could afford to be married.

I decided not to equivocate. I admitted that I did pray and that I felt that officers might seek divine guidance as some truly great generals had done. I told them that I thought that officers should be prepared to lead their men in all appropriate activities, if the occasion requires, including prayer.

More interesting questions came. "In times of war, should not the moral code be relaxed?" "Does not the stress of battle justify men in doing things that they would not do when at home under normal situations?"

I recognized that here was a chance perhaps to make some points and look broad-minded. I suspected that the men who were asking me this question did not live by the standards that I had been taught. The thought flashed through my mind that perhaps I could say that I had my own beliefs, but I did not wish to impose them on others. But there seemed to flash before my mind the faces of the many people to whom I had taught the law of chastity as a missionary. In the end I simply said, "I do not believe there is a double standard of morality."

I left the hearing resigned to the fact that these hard-bitten officers would not like the answers I had given to their questions and would surely score me very low. A few days later when the scores were posted, to my astonishment, I had passed (James E. Faust, "Honesty—A Moral Compass," *Ensign*, November 1996, 42–43).

GLENN FORSYTH

In December 1942 Glenn arrived in North Africa as part of the First Armored Division. He remained in Oran, Algeria, until February 1943 when his tank unit confronted German forces under the command of General Rommel. The superior German panzer tanks destroyed the First Armored Division and took many soldiers captive. Glenn found himself a prisoner of war.

The battle started about 10:00 A.M. I was busy throwing 75-millimeter shells into the chamber with one hand and casting the hot empty brass out the disposal port with the other. Targets were plentiful. Everyone was busy. Our tank commander had the driver pull the tank up close to three big sand banks, one in front and one on the east side. I took a peek out through the disposal port. Tanks were on fire all over the place.

The Desert Fox

Field Marshall Erwin Rommel was one of the most effective and brilliant minds ever to take to the battlefield. He was known as the "Desert Fox" for his cunning and daring maneuvers on the battlefields of northern Africa.

In the late afternoon our tank took a direct hit in the front end. The tank burst into flames. We bailed out of the burning tank. The tank gunner, Gilley, and I started to leave the crippled hunk of steel. We both turned and ran back to the tank and got the wounded driver out. The assistant driver was cut in two. The unused ammunition was starting to explode. Gilley and I started running away from the burning tank. I glanced down and light was flashing between my legs. The light was machine gun tracer slugs. Gil and I both landed belly boost on the ground, and machine gun slugs kicked up the dirt in front of our eyes. Gil was lying on the ground a bit in front of me. I saw his right leg go up and down with a quick movement. He informed me that he had been shot.

He and I crawled up through the bare flat, finally landing in a ditch about a foot deep. I got the feeling that we were behind the Maginot Line. We crawled down a shallow ditch that led into a wash. There I was able to examine his wound. The bullet had passed underneath the large cord that comes down in front of the foot and ankle. No bones were broken. He was fortunate. I was busy administering first aid to Gilley, Sergeant Ellis, our tank commander, and Robertson, the driver. Our tank driver had received what looked like a nasty wound. A piece of shrapnel had sliced a hunk of meat off his backside. The right side of his sit-down looked like a piece of fresh hamburger. We applied sulfa powder and covered the wound with compress bandages.

A German armored car drove up. They demanded that we surrender. I was the only one with a weapon. Somehow, I had come out of the fracas with a .45-automatic pistol. We were not about to take on an enemy armored personnel carrier with a .45 pistol. The Germans hauled Robertson away in a Red Cross vehicle. That was the last time I saw our tank driver.

Drawing by an American POW.

EDWIN B. GAGON

Because Edwin was too young to enlist in the Army, his parents had to give their permission. He knew he had poor eyesight so he drank a lot of carrot juice and was finally accepted into the United States Army Signal Corps. After having his appendix removed he was given a furlough to recuperate. It was during this time that he was ordained an elder, and in that ordination he was told he would return home from the war without a scar. Later he was assigned to the 719th Signal Air Warning Company as their radio repairman and placed on a commando radar team for operations behind enemy lines.

One day while I was recuperating at home, President Elijah Allen, president of the California Mission, stopped in to see my parents. After talking with him for a short time he suggested that I stop in his office in Los Angeles as I returned to camp, and he would ordain me an elder and see that I got a patriarchal blessing prior to my returning to active duty. When he ordained me an elder he told me that I may confront the enemy, but that I would return home without so much as a scar to remind me of my experience. That was a blessing to me, but it also caused me to do several foolish things. I figured that I would be protected. As I was processed for overseas duty at one of the stations, we were asked to sign up for a ten-thousand-dollar life insurance policy. I figured this was a test of my faith so I refused. Not desiring to tell the insurance officer why, he continued to insist that I should sign up for it. Finally to get him off my back I said, "Okay, if it will satisfy you, I will take a five-thousand-dollar policy." I suppose I was the only GI in the service to go overseas without taking out the full amount of life insurance.

* * * * *

Late in the afternoon of June 23, 1943, we loaded onto another troop train and headed for our boat. We had to pull the window shades down so we weren't able to see much; however, some of the fellows from that area told us where we were. We traveled south to New York, got on a ferry, and crossed over the river to the *Queen Mary*. We were among the last of about eighteen thousand troops to load. The next day they made everyone go below deck until we had cleared the harbor. However, I was standing near one of the doors and could look out as we passed the Statue of Liberty. It was a beautiful sight, and I wondered if I would ever see it again.

We were assigned sleeping areas. For the entire trip I slept one night on the forward deck with just a couple of blankets for warmth. Then I moved inside the next night, then back out to the cold-steel deck. Inside the bunk beds were five bunks high, two feet wide, and two feet apart. We really felt like sardines packed in a can. The night that it rained all the people sleeping on deck were permitted to sleep in the hallways.

Because the *Queen Mary* was much faster than most ships, we traveled alone. However, every few minutes we would change course so we would not be detected by German submarines. Except for the night it rained, we had a very pleasant trip.

The day before we landed in Greenock, Scotland, we were all issued enough ammunition to fill our cartridge belt. In my case it was 240 rounds of 30-30 ammunition. That really added weight to my backpack.

* * * * *

When I was near Paris, I obtained the address of an LDS branch that was meeting not too far from the Arc de Triomphe. When I attended this meeting they informed me that the following Sunday July 22, 1945, there would be a servicemen's conference held in Paris at the Hotel Louvois. All LDS servicemen were urged to attend. Elder Hugh B. Brown, coordinator for servicemen and president of the British Mission, would be presiding. It was time for me to return to my unit, but I called my commander and got permission to stay an extra week. There were about 350 servicemen from all over Europe in attendance. I was asked to pass the sacrament before the Sunday morning testimony meeting. Elder Brown was the main speaker in the afternoon session. He had flown over from London, and after the meeting he continued his journey by train to Switzerland for additional meetings. That was the highlight of my Paris trip.

KEN A. GERRARD

On their way to an army base in India, Ken and his unit sailed aboard a ship through the Mediterranean Sea a day after Thanksgiving in 1943. Without warning, German aircraft swooped over the ship and launched a radio-controlled glider bomb that scored a solid hit on the ship.

Here is my army life from start to finish. We left the United States on October 3, 1943. For twenty-three days we saw nothing but water. We had a few scares, but we didn't have any trouble to speak of. We landed in Oran, Algeria, and we stayed there one month and a few days. And then we left Oran on November 23, 1943, on his Majesty's ship the *Rohna* and headed out to sea.

Two days later at 5:00 P.M. the Germans came over. There were thirty in all. I was down in the hole when the fireworks started. I told Morley I was going up on top to take a look. I managed to get to the next deck above where the first sergeant was. I started talking to him when all of our guns started barking, and the men started looking for their helmets. Just then the rocket guns went off. I was sure a bomb had come through the hatch; it sure scared us all. Every time a bomb came close, our boat rocked like a feather on a wave.

Everything started to quiet down except for the guns on the boats next to us. I turned and started for the hole to get my helmet. About ten steps from the hole, I had the most wonderful feeling I have ever had. Something told me to stop, and I did. At that moment an aerial torpedo hit the port side, came through, and exploded out the other side.

The torpedo made a hole big enough to put six trucks in all together. We were all thrown against the wall along with tables, boards, and etc. We were covered up with all kinds of things. It came close enough to burn the hair off my head.

The *Rohna* then caught on fire, and black smoke came rolling in on us. I saw an opening and crawled on my hands and knees to it. I sat in a window for thirty minutes, and those thirty minutes were the worst ones I have ever seen, and never hope to see again. There was a lifeboat filled with wounded fellows being lowered. It came right past me. I was going to get in but didn't. It went a little farther and then the rope broke. They all fell out and drowned. Men were throwing rafts over the side, which were hitting the fellows in the water. It sure was an ungodly sight. It was getting pretty hot about then, and ammunition was going off so I took off my shoes and hit the water.

I was scared then; I thought she might sink and take me with her. But the waves were high, and they took me away. It was like a ghost ship, the flames leaping into the sky. In the light I could see men jumping off, and at a hearing distance I could hear the sickening screams of men calling for help, but there was no help to be had. I came to a raft. It was six-by-six, three inches thick. We couldn't get on it, but we could hold around it, which really helped. We kept collecting fellows as we went along until we had about sixty around the little raft. Some of them were hurt and as the time went by, the group grew smaller. We missed two boats, and then out to sea we went. For about seven hours we stayed in the freezing water. The night was inky black.

The men were all very scared. I prayed and my prayer was answered. I had all the faith in the world, and through that faith I got the men to sing, "Onward Christian Soldiers" and "The Old Rugged Cross." We also repeated the Lord's Prayer. Then a huge light shined on us, and I knew we were safe. In about ten minutes we drifted to the rescue boat. Our raft headed straight into the boat. I managed to get out of the way but two others didn't, and they were killed. There was a rope hanging from the front of the boat; I grabbed hold of it with one hand and the front of the boat with the other. One time the boat went down in a wave and the anchor missed me by inches. I could see a light about halfway back on the boat, also a ladder. The waves were holding me to the boat, along with many fellows who got excited and drowned.

I then swam to the light. I went up on a wave. Two English fellows grabbed me by the wrists and pulled me aboard. I fell to the floor and lay there about five minutes. Then they brought another fellow up. They picked me up and took me downstairs. They took my clothes off and put me in a bed. I woke up about three hours later. I couldn't walk and I was very sick. A fellow I knew had just been picked up and was standing there sneezing. I rolled out of bed and ripped his shorts off and then gave him my blanket and told him to take my bed. I got another blanket and slept on the floor. At dawn we headed for shore and at 9:30 A.M., we landed at Bougie, Algeria.

CHESTER M. GILGEN

Chester served as a radar technician in North Africa. His responsibility was to keep the experimental radar equipment operating properly. He served aboard an aircraft that worked in conjunction with a bomber squadron to find and destroy enemy submarines. His plane, The X-Ray, used radar to locate the submarines. The bombers would then drop depth charges in an attempt to destroy the target. While he did not like flying because of airsickness, he flew missions every other day for twelve to fourteen hours.

When we were not flying, I had plenty of time to myself. I frequented the radar shop and got acquainted with a number of great fellows. I realized early in our tour of duty that there was no LDS group scheduled. So I contacted the chaplain, a Protestant, who accepted my plan to put up a notice inviting any LDS fellows to a group meeting in the base chapel on Sunday morning. And it materialized with an immediate group of about a dozen LDS enlisted men and a couple of officers. They were men who were basically from the western states. They accepted me as the group leader, and we had some very inspirational meetings with hymns, talks, and the sacrament.

* * * * *

I had a wonderful experience of becoming acquainted with a delightful young WAVE (women accepted for volunteer emergency service), who was a nonmember, but I took care of that having just returned from my mission. After baptizing her, we received permission to go to the Salt Lake Temple to be married. And that marriage resulted in an announcement from the Red Cross while I was in North Africa that I was a proud daddy of a son.

* * * * *

I had known that my wife was with child so I looked up a carpenter friend on the base, and together we shaped and put together a beautiful cradle. It was heavy enough to be put into two boxes, which I used to mail to the States at the price of $7.12 postage.

Group of LDS servicemen at a naval base in French Morocco, northwest Africa, April 1944. (L to R) Back Row: Chester M. Gilgen (Ogden, UT), Donald L. Miller (Waterloo, Iowa), Wm W. Blackburn (Pocatello, ID), Russell J. Whittaker (Ogden, UT), Scott McKay (Huntsville, UT). Front Row: Kenneth D. Proctor (Panguitch, UT), Francis A. Webb (Hollywood, CA), James O. Shingleton (Long Beach, CA), Leo B. Lott (Seattle, WA), Revel J. Nielson (Idaho Falls, ID). Not present: Lt. Castleton, Wayne Stewart.

WAYNE B. GOLD

Once the troops left the Normandy beaches, they faced the hedgerow country of France. These obstacles made progress difficult as they blocked cross-country traffic and provided hiding places for enemy soldiers. Getting past the hedgerows demanded determination and special skills learned of necessity by the troops. Wayne served with the Third Army in Normandy.

French nationalists welcome Allied troops into Paris. Such welcomes were typical throughout France as the Allied forces liberated towns and villages.

Our next experience was with the mud. Normandy is all hedgerows, so thick they block the sun and so it rains all the time. We carried everything we owned in our barracks bag. Our belongings consisted of our toilet kit, two regular army blankets, an overcoat, a raincoat, and one-half of a pup tent. We were assigned a buddy that had the other half of the pup tent. We soon learned we couldn't keep warm with that arrangement so we started squeezing three to a pup tent and that allowed us to be warm every third night. This was the arrangement for five months, all through France, Belgium, and Holland. We were allowed one canteen of water a day for drinking and washing. You can imagine what we used the water for. We didn't get a shower for six months. We would occasionally take a sponge bath with a little water in our helmet. But since we all smelled the same, it wasn't really a problem.

Because the Army had by now broken out of the hedgerows, General Patton and his tanks were going like crazy across France. As a result they needed gas and supplies. So for the next four weeks our division drove the Red Ball Express. We picked up supplies at the docks and rushed them to the front. Everything had to give way to the trucks with the red ball painted on the windshield. Most of the towns had narrow streets, and it was quite common to scrape buildings on both sides of the street as we turned the corners. We drove three straight days and nights, one driving, one sleeping, and then we had one day off.

* * * * *

Now I must go back and tell a little love story. . . . This was definitely true love. Lois and I, through at least 180 letters, got to know each other a great deal more than if we had been together, mooning and spooning over each other for those six months. She and Annie, Art's girl, did come to Chicago the day before I got shipped out to Fort Sheridan. So we were able to have one more kiss, and she was left standing on the sidewalk as the truck pulled away. Later this same thing happened with the second chance.

It was while we were in Camp Carson just out of Colorado Springs when we learned were going to be sent overseas to fight in the war in less than a month. Decisions had to be made. Lois and I decided to meet in Chicago for the week furlough that the Army gave before sending men to battle. I went and purchased train tickets for Chicago. The weekend before I had finagled a three-day pass and went home to Salt Lake City to tell Mother and Dad. Well, Mother and I had a long crying talk. I still remember it very clearly. She made it pretty plain that she didn't approve, but said it was my decision. I cried on the bus all the way back to Camp Carson without any change of heart. After lights out, I lay in my bed without sleep and finally decided that if Joseph Smith could go out in the woods and get an answer to his problems, so could I. I got dressed and went out into the grove of trees near the barracks. For the first time in my life I really prayed and poured out my heart to the Lord. I, of course, had said prayers at dinner and evening and in church, but this was different. I really needed to know who my children's mother was going to be. If it wasn't to be Lois, I wanted assurance that things would be all right and that I would meet someone I could love as much or more than her. Well I went to bed with the knowledge that I should call her in the morning. Well the good-byes were taken well and I traded my tickets for? Guess where? Salt Lake City instead of Chicago, and my children received the best mother.

H. LYLE GRANT

H. Lyle Grant served as a member of the 833rd Bomber Squadron as a B-17 turret gunner. His account reveals the difficulties of being a ball turret gunner. During a run over a German manufacturing center, enemy fire crippled his plane, forcing the crew to bail out. Upon landing he was immediately captured by German troops and imprisoned in a POW camp. While in Stalag Luft IV, he was fortunate to meet another Latter-day Saint POW. By his account it was his faith that enabled him to endure the horrors of the camp and a forced march at the end of the war. It was during what he calls the "Black March" that he was able to escape and join approaching British forces. The personal narrative below exhibits his faith as he placed his life in the hands of the Lord.

Before I could enter the turret, I had to move it so the guns were pointing straight down. This brought the trapdoor inside the plane. I took the hand crank from its holding clip and fitted it to the manual shaft to bring the door inside the plane. Opening the trapdoor, I reached inside the turret and clutched in the power operation, then removed the hand crank and returned it to its clip.

Next, I had to remove my GI boots and replace them with the heated boots I would wear in the turret. The ball turret would be about forty to sixty degrees below zero at altitudes of twenty thousand to thirty thousand feet. To keep from freezing to death, it was necessary to wear heated boots and a suit that I could plug into the ship's electrical system.

I put my GI boots in a bag along with the small emergency chest parachute. No large chutes were available for gunners, so I would have to rely on this small one if we had to bail out.

Finally, I hooked on my oxygen mask and descended into the turret. As soon as I was in, I attached my throat microphone and earphones, checked the escape door fastening, and secured my safety belt. Turning on my main power switch, I swung the turret down and around. When the turret was in firing position, I was hunched with my back against the armored door, my knees up toward my chest, and my legs bent and spread. This meant my feet were on resets on each side of the thirteen-inch glass panel. It was through this glass panel, looking down between my legs, that I viewed the outside world.

My face was about thirty inches from the glass, and suspended in front of my eyes was the optical display of the Sperry computing gun sight. Using a pedal under my left foot, I could adjust the red reticles on this glass, and when I had moved them enough so that a target or plane was framed in them, then the firing range and distance were correct.

If one had no qualms about the angle at which the world below was viewed, the turret provided an extraordinary vantage point. That angle, combined with the Sperry computing sight, made the ball turret one of the most effective places to shoot down enemy planes as they passed through our formations. So valuable was the Sperry sight, used in both the upper and the ball turrets on the B-17s, that we were instructed to save the sight if we ever had to jettison the ball turret prior to a belly landing. To work the firing buttons for both guns and move the turret, my arms had to be arched, with my hands above my head. Above the sight, two post handles projected toward the rear of the turret. Flexing those handles worked valves in the self-contained electric-hydraulic system, which made it possible to move the turret.

Imagine the roar that the twin .50-caliber Browning machine guns made when they were fired in such close quarters. Years later, I discovered that the noise from the guns had damaged my ears, leaving me unable to hear high-pitched sounds. . . . At that moment, however, I wasn't as worried about the damage to my hearing as I was with the damage the German flak batteries could cause us. I finished getting in position, with my guns armed; then, all I could do was sit back and wait to reach the target. Our formation of Flying Fortresses arrived at the target area at approximately noon. Immediately the sky turned black with exploding shells from the many big guns on the ground, and our P-51 escort planes became engrossed with the task of trying to outmaneuver German fighter planes. We were in the thick of battle, just waiting for the signal to release our bombs on the target.

Finally, our bombardier's very welcome command, "Bombs away," came over the intercom system. What a relief to know those five 1,000-pound bombs were out of our bomb bay. The bombs were not released any too soon, for within two minutes after releasing them our plane shook violently. An antiaircraft shell had exploded near enough to us that it tore away part of the right-wing engine of our beautiful, new B-17. Suddenly, another shell exploded, crippling a different engine and leaving a gaping hole in the right wing near the gasoline tank.

I was still curled up in the ball turret, swinging around on the belly of the B-17 and keeping two .50-caliber machine guns ready for action against any attack from the German fighter planes. Unfortunately, however, it wasn't the fighter planes causing us trouble; it was that terrifying, exploding flak that I could see all around us. I knew flak had already hit our plane, and that we were in serious trouble. We began to lose altitude and started drifting away from the formation of bombers that were headed back to their bases in England, and safety.

B-17 bomber that was damaged from a life raft that had become wrapped around the tail.

Many times, in our previous eleven missions, we had seen crippled and burning planes drop out of formation, knowing there would be empty bunks in home base that night. Each time we had witnessed such a scene, there had been an unspoken prayer in our hearts that our buddies inside those battered planes would be fortunate enough to bail out before they were engulfed in fire or blown into unidentifiable pieces. Always before, we were the ones to report these missing airmen to our briefing officers as we landed at our home base. As I looked through that thirteen-inch circle of glass, I realized that it was now our turn to be counted as missing in action.

Then, something even more dreaded happened. Our B-17 shuddered and shook from the impact of more exploding shells. It was time for me to move as quickly as possible. I knew that the nearest chest parachute was safely stored in the radio room; but I also knew the ball turret had to be in perfect position before I could open the small trap door, get out, and walk the few steps to the safety of the chute. If any shell exploded near enough to damage the mechanism of the steel ball with Plexiglas windows, it would be impossible for me to move the turret and get the trapdoor open so I could get out.

Quickly, I maneuvered the turret into the proper position, pushed the door open and climbed into the waist section of the plane. It was clouded with acrid-smelling smoke, and I had to grope my way into the radio room where our small, chest parachutes were stored. The waist gunner, radio operator, and engineer gunner had already dropped their flak vests and had their chutes attached to the harnesses that we wore over our heated suits.

I grabbed my chute; and as I wrestled to put it on, the radio operator received the command from the pilot to bail out. "Get out immediately, fire in the right wing!" was his last message.

The waist gunner pulled the safety latch on the escape door, and it went flying through space. Just as I was turning toward the door, I noticed that one chute had not been picked up! I grabbed it off the hook. As the others were jumping, I made my way toward the tail section, yelling at the tail gunner that we were bailing out. Struggling toward me, he noticed that I was holding his chest chute out to him. Instantly, he dropped his flak vest and snapped the chute on his harness.

We both knew that if we wanted to survive, we couldn't waste even a second. Quickly we approached the gaping door, and it wasn't until after I had jumped that I realized I had not changed into my tough GI boots. I still had on the thin, heated ones.

The terrific air stream created as our plane was starting to whirl out of control spun me like a top the second I left the escape hatch. For a few moments, I blacked out completely. Hurtling through the air, I came to and gathered enough presence of mind to determine that it would be best if I tried to get close enough to the ground to recognize cattle or other objects before I pulled the ring that would release my lifesaving parachute. Soon, I became fully aware of the fact that I was fifteen thousand to twenty thousand feet above German territory.

My mind raced through the parachute procedure that had been drilled into us. First, I had to find the ring that, when pulled, would stop my fast fall of about thirty-two feet per second. There it was, on the upper right-hand corner of the chute pack. "But don't yank it yet," I thought, as my fall toward the earth continued.

It was a funny thing how I could control my body while falling at that rate of speed. As a bird in flight, I could turn my body in any direction I desired. At that time, I found I could also turn my thoughts from the fear of the moment to the peace that comes through prayer. As I plummeted toward earth, I whispered a prayer of thanksgiving that my lifesaving chute had been put together properly. What a time to remember that corny old English joke that was so often spoken when we were handed our chutes: "If the blooming thing doesn't work, just bring it back and we'll give you a new one!"

Somehow, I knew my chute would work. I also knew that it was time to open it. Judging from the way the trees and houses looked, I must have been about a mile above the ground, and in a sitting position, when I jerked that ring.

That beautiful, white nylon furled out behind me and slowed my fall. I remembered what we had been taught, and I kept my jaws closed tight so I wouldn't chip my teeth or bite my tongue off when I hit the ground.

I felt like a clay pigeon with no place to hide. Floating above enemy territory, I could count four other chutes out of the eight others in our crew. I knew that because we had jumped out of the plane at different times, and because the wind had blown our chutes in many directions, it wasn't surprising that I couldn't see all of them—or at least that's what I told myself. As I continued to drift downward, I saw our crippled and burning plane dive into the earth with a terrible, fiery explosion.

There's an old saying, "There is no atheist in a bullet-riddled foxhole." I doubt that there were any atheists riding their parachutes into enemy territory this day. For me at least, it was a profoundly spiritual experience, as I looked down at the German territory where I would soon be landing. I realized that this could be the day I would die. With that thought, it seemed as if, for a moment, I was able to see things through different eyes. In fact, it is impossible to relate the fantastic things that were brought to my view while falling through space, and I realized what a marvelous instrument we have in our brain. I saw the final judgment of all things, good and not so good, that had transpired in my life up to that day, and realized that, ultimately, we would be our own judges of our place in eternity as we leave this mortal life here upon the earth.

The ground drew closer, and I knew that there was no one else to turn to but the Lord. I made a solemn promise that I would serve Him and faithfully strive to keep myself worthy to receive the many blessings that I knew I would need from Him.

REX GREENWOOD

As an airman based in Britain, Rex was aware of D-Day prior to the actual invasion. His assignment was to provide bomber support for the infantry coming ashore. Early in the morning, Rex reported seeing thousands of Allied bombers and their fighter escorts filling the skies. He said there was never a time during the day when the skies were not filled with aircraft. The ground shook as planes thundered overhead flying toward Normandy.

We knew of D-Day the day before. We were put on full alert, and we could guess why. . . . The night before the invasion, we didn't go to bed. We all sat out in the fields. . . . In the morning, the invasion was announced on the radio, so then we knew what was going on. I went on duty at daybreak. I'd never heard so much radio contact. In combat, pilots carried radio silence; they didn't talk to each other very much. But that day, radio talk was constant. Some of the pilots were telling us what they were seeing. They were amazed at the number of landing crafts, boats, and people flooding onto the beaches. Strange as it may seem, we didn't lose as many pilots on D-Day as we did on other maximum strike days, even though there were more airplanes in the air. There was very little resistance, only antiaircraft. From D-Day on, I think the Allies had supremacy of the air.

BENNER A. HALL

Benner, a marksman, spent the winter of 1944 stationed in southern France to hold it while others engaged in the Battle of the Bulge. His group camped out in an abandoned home, watching a bridge for German movements. From the window they saw two German soldiers walking through the streets checking to see if the Americans had left the town.

It took about a half hour for the two to reach our house. We sent Paul downstairs to confront the Germans to see if he could get them to surrender while Herman and I remained in the attic to cover them from the window. . . . Paul shouted for them to surrender. . . . One did, the other one didn't. I shot at the fleeing soldier, but I missed. I couldn't believe it.

Later a patrol captured the soldier. They had found him praying. When I met him, I found out he was a Latter-day Saint baptized by one of my friends from our hometown of Mesa, Arizona.

DONALD E. HALL

Donald was ordained an elder just before leaving for military service. He was promised that if he would be true to his religion and live the Word of Wisdom, he would return home from the war. At that time he also received a small copy of the New Testament *and* Principles of the Gospel *that he carried with him during the war. Trained as a communications specialist, he saw action from the Battle of the Bulge to the surrender of Germany.*

Pfc. Donald E. Hall.

We were sent north into Holland. It was still very cold. Sometimes we stopped at abandoned homes; usually the home was destroyed, but the barn was standing. We would take shelter in the barn for the night; we didn't dare have a fire for heat so we would sleep where we could with only our overcoats and blankets for warmth. Being raised on a farm I knew that by burrowing into the hay provided insulation from the cold. I told the men in my platoon to do this, and we slept snug and warm. Others were not so lucky; they didn't know the secrets a farm boy learns while growing up. A lot of the fellows lost their feet and hands because they froze at night.

* * * * *

While in this area, Thell and I went over to an American cemetery; the bodies were stiff and in many different positions. Some still had bandoliers of ammunition, and hand grenades on their bodies.

At night the men of the Eighth Armored drove their tanks and half-tracks around in circles to make a lot of noise to make the Germans think that the next push would come from Holland when in fact it was to come from many miles to the south.

* * * * *

Thell and I were the only two LDS soldiers in our company. We got together whenever we could to bless and partake of the sacrament. This was not always on Sunday because most of the time we didn't know what day of the week it was. We always felt better and comforted after doing this. There were many times that I felt that my life was spared because of the promise contained in my ordination blessing. Being able to pray and know that my prayers were heard was of particular comfort. I felt sorry for the soldiers who felt they had to pray to someone other than the Savior. They had to hope that the person they prayed to would get the message to Jesus Christ on their behalf.

One time in particular I was standing guard near my half-track while the other men in the company went into a bar, when someone behind me said, "Hey buddy, got a light?" When I turned around I found a group of German soldiers who surrendered to me. They could have just as easily cut my throat as ask for a light, but the Lord was watching over me. After their surrender, the German soldiers admitted that they had slipped into town to attack the half-track and its men, but when they got close to me, they decided to surrender instead.

* * * * *

On another occasion, while I was in a foxhole with another soldier at night, our position was attacked. The bullets were kicking dirt into our faces. They were as thick as bees from a hive that has been disturbed. The other soldier was killed and fell across me covering me with blood. I don't know how I was not shot that night.

Jeep patrol in Czechoslovakia hearing of German surrender. Donald E. Hall is holding the field radio.

MORGAN HANKS

Morgan served in the Italian Apennine, Po Valley, and Alpine campaigns as part of the Tenth Mountain Infantry Division. He was responsible for a water-cooled .30-caliber machine gun. During his service, his squad members nick-named him "Old Mormon Hanks" out of respect for his faith.

The trip over was slow, but we were in no hurry. There were around three hundred troops aboard the ship, and the top tier in the hold closest to the superstructure was converted to bunks and had a steam kettle for cooking the C rations which we subsisted on. The first night out they sealed the doors so no light could get out, and most of the men lit up their cigarettes and cigars. With the movement of the ship, up and down, and the smoke, I had to get out on deck. I grabbed my blanket and in order to stay out of the weather, I lay underneath an army truck of which there were several on deck, along with a couple of tanks. The captain in charge of the troops seemed to understand where I was coming from, and allowed me to do as I did the first night. So I crossed the Atlantic, the first night sleeping under a truck and the rest of the time in the back of the truck with my blanket half stretched across the truck bed for shelter. I was given a mattress from the marines who were operating the ship. Others found out what I was doing and joined me, and we were fairly comfortable. For a shower they had a salt water hose on the tail of the ship, and we took our showers there underneath the hose. The troop latrine was a wooden trough encased in a wooden shelter on deck, with a hose running water into it so it was continually flowing, and it drained directly into the ocean.

One day while crossing the Po Valley in northern Italy where there were canals crossing the area, we were assigned to take our machine gun and set up a protective perimeter on the other side of a bridge over a canal which had been blown so that the engineers could repair it, allowing our tanks and supply vehicles to cross. . . . We set up our gun as assigned, facing an orchard and vineyard. We noticed some movement out in the vineyard, and we were about to open fire. I said, "Stop," and told my companion I wanted him to hold off while I made an inspection of the area. I worked myself out into the area using as much cover as I could because I didn't know what was out there. . . . As I got into the area I noted two Italian fellows standing behind a tree. I called to them and said in Italian, "Come here." They came very slowly and reluctantly. I asked them why they had not come quickly when I called.

The one fellow looked at me terrified and said in broken German, "I speak little German."

"Hell," I said, "I am an American." He looked at me, ran to me, threw his arms around me, then turned and called out, "Americano, Americano," and rising out of the vineyards were at least fifty people. Mostly women and kids. If we had opened up, we would have decimated those people.

* * * * *

I was dubbed "Old Mormon Hanks" and didn't really get involved with the extracurricular activities. All the men said they wanted to stand next to "Old Mormon Hanks" because he never got hit. I wanted to find another Mormon who held the priesthood who could administer to me if the occasion arose, but no one surfaced. After the war we had an inspection, and I laid out my brown *Principles of the Gospel* and New Testament books which were given to us by the Church, and the inspecting officer mentioned to me that there was another one of us in the company. I found out that he was an elder, but I never met him.

GEORGE SCOTT HANSEN

As a pilot who flew on D-Day, Scott had orders to bomb coastal targets on the invasion morning. He remembers that it was hard for him to maneuver his plane because of the number of planes in the sky over Normandy. He was expected to drop his bombs between the invasion fleet fifteen hundred yards off-shore and the paratroopers inland. When it was time to drop the bombs, there were Allied aircraft below them. In such a situation his orders were to drop the bombs regardless of the situation with the other aircraft. He was greatly relieved when the planes below cleared away just before the bombs were released.

We took off in the wee hours of the morning and assembled the group together. The release time for the bombs was to be 7:25 A.M. That was pretty early to get that armada of planes assembled and across the Channel. It was very impressive. I am proud to have been a part of the invasion of Europe. They had briefed us that morning that there would be twelve thousand Allied airplanes in the air that day. They set up a course where we would go in a circle and do our bombing. When we came off the target we would swing to the south quite a ways out over the ocean and then fly back to England. That way we stayed out of the stream of airplanes coming from England to the invasion.

There were so many planes, we never knew when there would be a midair collision. The sad part of it was, there was an overcast sky. . . . I didn't ever get to see one ship on the invasion.

DOUGLAS HARDY

Elder Hugh B. Brown set Douglas apart as a Latter-day Saint group leader to serve wherever his military assignments took him. He was able to magnify his calling during his assignment to the Italy campaign, where he was able to organize meetings whenever they were not in a combat situation.

Liberation of Rome

It is interesting to note that the liberation of the Italian capital received very little fanfare amid the chaos that was taking place in Normandy, France.

On June 4 and 5, 1944, we captured the capital of Italy (Rome). . . . In celebration I decided to visit the Vatican and Saint Peter's Cathedral. Exploring the cathedral I noticed a long stairwell, walked up it, and found myself on a balcony that overlooked the Vatican courtyard. A few moments later, along came four costumed servants carrying the Pope in his highly decorated lift. He stepped over the balcony railing, lifted up a microphone there, and spoke in English, then French, then Italian welcoming the American, British, and French soldiers. I was standing about ten feet away, dressed in my combat uniform with my .45-caliber pistol on my belt. I suppose that they might have thought that an American captain had been sent up there to guard the pope.

Raymond W. Harrop in transport truck with other soldiers, Sept. 1944.

RAYMOND W. HARROP

Raymond served much of the war in an administrative field office. He recognizes that it was his typing skill that kept him off the front lines and doing the administrative support work required to manage the war. At the end of the war, Raymond was part of an Allied patrol that visited the Buchenwald concentration camp.

Buchenwald was a concentration camp where the Germans kept Jews and others to work and to experiment on. I was permitted to visit that camp, and they told us what happened to those people. Some were used as human guinea pigs. Small matchboxes infected with typhus had been attached to their wrists for the purpose of finding a cure for typhoid fever. After they were dead, the Germans had peeled off their skin and made gloves and lamp shades. They were made to sleep five or six on a hardboard bed. If they were sick or unable to get up for work, the Germans would take a large hook, forcing it into their bodies and then hang them by the furnace until the next bunch of bodies were thrown into the flames. I saw all of those conditions and the conditions in which they had to wash themselves, go to the toilet, brush their teeth, etc. They were treated like animals. One prisoner I talked to was so thin, I thought if I put my finger to his chest I would punch a hole right through his body.

Scenes from a Nazi prison camp in Austria.

(Left) Raymond W. Harrop receiving a commendation from the commanding officer.

MYRON HATCH

Myron was inducted into military service shortly after returning from his mission. Myron was a platoon sergeant with the Seventh Army, which was the first unit to arrive at the liberation of the concentration camp at Dachau. The following is a letter that Myron sent to the Church News. *It was published in the servicemen's edition of that paper in February, 1945.*

It's Sunday evening in southern France, December 24, 1944, Christmas Eve. I have been reading a dirty, crumpled, well-worn LDS Servicemen's Edition of the *Church News.* It was handed to me by one of the men in the company who had picked it up somewhere and knowing that I was a Latter-day Saint, brought it to me.

I was indeed grateful because it is the only contact that I have had with the Church for a long time. It gave me something I have missed so much. Its message was one of strength, courage, and beauty. The day seems more like a Sabbath and as I read through dimmed eyes, I thank God for this Christmas gift.

Sincerely,
Sergeant Myron Hatch.

Sgt. Myron Hatch, Oct. 5, 1943.

(Below) Myron Hatch and other members of his patrol at Dachau death camp.

FLOYD E. HAUPT

Floyd enlisted in the Army Air Corps on August 17, 1942. He graduated as a navigator in February 1944. His first assignment was as part of a B-24 crew flying out of Italy. He flew over fifty combat missions during his tour of duty.

When I entered basic training at Lincoln, Nebraska, I attended the local LDS Church on Sundays. We could not get off base during the week. . . . I attended church whenever I could get a weekend pass. . . . I did not attend church while in combat. The nearest LDS meeting was in Bari (Italy), forty miles away, and transportation was a problem in Italy. There was a chaplain on our base, but I was not interested. Besides, I had to fly on some Sundays. I heard the chaplain at briefings. I saw much immorality, drinking, etc., but did not join in. I flew two missions with another crew whose pilot gathered the crew under the wing before takeoff and recited the Lord's Prayer.

Back in the United States, I ended up at Smyrna, Tennessee. There was nothing there, so I tried to attend church in nearby Nashville, but there was only one active family there at that time. Once, while there, I was given two weeks TDY (temporary duty yonder) at Columbus, Ohio. I asked the base chaplain for the name and phone number of a local LDS bishop. I called and was invited to Sunday dinner. We

Floyd Haupt's B-24 bomber crew. Floyd is fourth from the left on the bottom row.

were in the middle of it, when we learned I was LDS and he was RLDS. The chaplain didn't know the difference. We were polite with each other, so it was uneventful.

Both K ration boxes and escape kits had four cigarettes in them. Combat men were offered a shot of whiskey after every mission to relax them. I never used any of those items because I had been taught the Word of Wisdom and accepted it. However, I knew drinkers who wasted oxygen supplies trying to get sober before missions, and some who broke down under the strain. Smoking was also a danger. Planes always had a gasoline odor about them. I have seen planes blow up for no apparent reason. I suspect someone lit a cigarette. My own pilot, a smoker, warned crew members not to smoke.

B-24 bomber flying over 464th Bomber Group near Pantanella, Italy.

* * * * *

On one mission to Vienna, Austria, the weather was bad. As we came off the target, we entered a towering cloud. Visibility was so poor we all had to enter into proscribed maneuvers for scattering to avoid collisions. The navigation method available in a cloud was dead reckoning with its inherent uncertainties. The radio compass was useless because the Germans broadcasted false signals. When our plane emerged from the high cloud there was a solid undercast of stratus clouds beneath us. A few miles to our right was another bomber flying parallel to us. The pilot called and asked if we should join him. This was a good question because flying together would give us more protection from fighters. It required faith in my navigation skills to tell him, "No." I said he should fly over Graz, and we would fly just to the left of it. I even predicted he would get flak at a certain time. I was right. At the specified time he was surrounded by shell bursts.

On another mission to Vienna we were badly damaged by flak over the target. The flight controls were so jammed it took the full strength of both pilots working together to move them. We could not fly formation that way so we dropped out. That gave us a sinking feeling in the stomach because fighters were waiting outside the flak area, and they went for cripples first. Sixty fighters hit our group of twenty-four bombers. Depending on who tells the story, between ten and forty of them hit our plane…. The ball turret gunner had his left arm shot off. Three men were badly wounded. Two gun turrets were gone. There was no left aileron, left wheel, or right rudder. They had given us thirteen parachutes for ten men and three of them were shredded. The oxygen bottles were full of holes, the fuel transfer pumps were shot out, the intercom was dead, my navigation instruments were useless, and the plane was vibrating. Our gunners had shot down at least six fighters. The ball turret gunner hadn't felt like counting.

I tried to contact the pilot, but could not, due to the dead intercom. I stuck my head up in the astrodome and looked back at him. He motioned me to join him on the flight deck. Our fighters had driven the enemy off, but now he needed me where we could communicate. So I took some maps and went through the crawl space by the nosewheel.

I had lost dead reckoning with my instruments gone, I lost celestial when I left the forward compartment. And then I had another disaster. I had laid my maps on the desk behind the pilot, but the missing Plexiglas of the top turret caused a suction that plastered my maps around the gunner's seat and some were sucked out of the plane. The vibrations caused the pilot to fear a structure failure so he feathered the engines in rotation to distribute the vibrations in the hope the plane would hold together long enough to get us to the island of Vis in the Adriatic Sea (held by the British). This caused an unbalance of power which made the plane veer off course. The pilot did not want to correct course any more than absolutely necessary because a control cable could have snapped under the strain. We could not touch the outboard tanks with the fuel transfer pumps shot out, and I had to calculate our course to Vis for three paths, with few navigation aids left, so a decision could be made. The vibration caused the levels to jump in the fuel gauges so I could not get accurate readings. Both our flight engineers were wounded. We took the direct path over water despite the risks. I told the pilot we would make it. That took faith.

The island is not much more than one minute of flying time over it, in a north to south direction. We started bailing out as we hit the north coast. The pilot put the plane in a tight right turn to count chutes because he had no communication with men in the rear. Then the pilots jumped, and the plane crashed on the south shore. Vis was nearly three hours from Vienna. Had I been in error by about a minute, we would have died. Our crew received thirty-three medals and ribbons for this mission.

DONALD L. HAYNIE

Donald served as an army staff sergeant during the battle of Rittershoffen, which he referred to as "Hell's capital." He was the leader of a rifle squad assigned to defend the perimeter from enemy advancements.

It was snowing and the ground was frozen. We fell back behind an orchard and dug foxholes for protection during the night. The next morning, my squad fought its way into the very edge of the town, driving some determined German soldiers out of a house and occupying it. Our occupation didn't last long because an 88-millimeter artillery shell from a Tiger tank collapsed the house on top of us. I had been standing giving the company commander a radio message when I was impressed to go to the other side of the room and to hit the floor. I did so, and the artillery shell zoomed right through the spot where I had been standing.

* * * * *

On one patrol we were ordered to recover the bodies of American soldiers who had been killed on other patrols. We had to prepare the bodies for Army Graves Registration Corps, which meant taking their boots, ammunition, and rifles, and leaving their dog tags as identification. A good friend of mine was one of those who had been killed, and it hurt me when I removed his boots.

HAROLD M. HEGYESSY

As a member of the Eighth Air Force, Harold served as a navigator on a B-17. His patriarchal blessing promised him that if he remained faithful to the gospel, he would live to a ripe old age. Before each mission he would pray and upon his safe return he would again seek the Lord. During a mission to Merseburg, Germany, his plane came under fierce fire. They dropped their bombs without too much of a problem and headed home, but during the return trip, German fighters attacked their B-17. His account of the attack reveals how his prayers were answered. The plane limped to Britain where medics waited to take him and fellow airmen to the hospital. For his service he was awarded the Distinguished Flying Cross and a Purple Heart.

Did we pray? Of course we did! I think everyone prayed secretly. I did before, during, and after each combat mission or hazardous flight. The final prayer was to thank my Heavenly Father for preserving my life once again. Perhaps I had an advantage over my non-LDS crewmen. When I was a teenager in southern Utah, an old LDS patriarch laid his hands on my head and gave me a patriarchal blessing. He promised, in part, that if I remained faithful to the gospel, I would live to a ripe old age! There were obviously other things for me to do in this life. Perhaps that protected my comrades, too.

I want to describe a typical mission so that you will understand how terrible combat can be. After the first week of September 1944 the weather improved dramatically over Germany and stayed so for a number of days. We were well rested. On the morning of September 10, our crew was posted on the Alert Board, and we knew that if Eighth Air Force was going to order a maximum effort, we would go. We would find out where at the briefing the next morning.

We went to bed early that evening since we knew that we would probably be awakened about 2:00 A.M. the next morning. At about 8:00 P.M. we heard the great bomb-carrying trucks begin to rumble between the bomb dump and the waiting B-17s. This went on for several hours. We finally fell into a fitful sleep to be awakened at 2:00 A.M. by the dreaded sound of boots on the concrete walk leading to our Quonset hut. The door crashed open. The lights snapped on. The messenger announced: "Garrison, Hegyessy, Lotterman, Grinsted," and so on. "Breakfast at 2:30. Briefing at 3:00. Be on time!"

We wearily swung our feet to the floor with sober thoughts in our minds. The chances were great that we only had five or six hours of life left on this earth. I first put on my expensive gabardine shirt. At least I would have that if I ended up as a POW in some German stalag luft prison camp. Next came heavy socks and my electric flying suit which would be plugged into an electrical outlet in the plane. Then came the full-length nylon zippered jump suit, and then my bulky leather flying boots. With this done, I slung my holstered .45-caliber pistol over my shoulder. No angry German farmer was going to pitchfork me to death as had been known to happen. Lastly came my A-2 leather jacket.

We stumbled sleepily to the mess hall to be greeted by rubber-like, reconstituted eggs, salty bacon, and burned toast. Then we were off to the great briefing room. When everyone was in place, the colonel on the stage who would lead the mission, pulled back the curtain revealing the route and target for the day. As usual, there was a collective groan from the aircrews. Merseburg again! Our bomb load would be six 1,000-pounders. The weather officer briefed that the target would be CAVU, all clear. We were to be at our hardstands at 5:00 A.M. The main briefing over, the pilots, navigators, bombardiers,

Harold Hegyessy's B-17 crew in front of their plane, the Pappy Time, *on August 8, 1944, at Podington Air Station, East Anglia, England. (L to R) Back Row: Harold "Heggie" Hegyessy, Theodore "Ted" Lotterman, Albert "Grinny" Grinsted, William "Bill" Garrison. Front Row: Carlisle "Duke" Dinsmoor, John Paul "Thumper" Tewalt, Austin "Pinky" Pinkham, Ralph "Kobe" Koby, "Tony" Annonio.*

and radiomen went to briefings on their specialties. I learned that another navigator would be riding with us who would complete his twenty-five missions that day and would go home. He was "flak happy" and would be of no use to us. He would spend most of the flight lying on the floor in the nose covered with flak jackets. He was a nervous wreck and showed it. I wondered if that would be my fate.

The gunners had gone ahead of us to prepare our assigned plane for the flight. When the specialty briefings were over, we boarded a truck that would take us to our hardstand. The gunners had done their preflight duties. The guns were loaded. The electric power unit was on and the ship was lighted. The navigation lights on the wing tips and tail were blinking. The bomb bay doors were open and the interior lighted. Grinny climbed up into the bomb bay to make sure that the bomb fuses were properly set. We loaded our gear and made sure that our parachutes were handy. Our own preflights done, we waited for the flares from the tower.

Finally a green flare arched up into the night sky. It was the order to start engines. Bill and Ted started the engines, which coughed and shuddered and then settled down into a low, steady roar. All around the field, the other aircraft were doing the same. After a few moments, a second green flare soared up. Bill eased us out of the hardstand and we took our turn drifting down the taxiways into the fog at the end of the runway. When it was our turn, we wheeled into place. Bill and Ted set the brakes and slowly moved the throttles forward until all four engines were screaming. Finally, the tower cleared us for takeoff. The brakes came off, and we went rocketing down the dark runway.

It was at this point that one of the acute dangers of the mission began. We had three tons of live explosives in back of us in the bomb bay. At forty miles per hour the tail lifted up. We were all praying that Bill and Ted would get this heavy "mother" off the ground before we ran out of runway and ended up in a smoking crater in the English woods. At one hundred and ten miles per hour, the nose lifted up with agonizing slowness, and we were airborne. The landing gear rose up into the wheel wells, and we were chasing the blue exhaust of the plane ahead of us. There were two other First Air Division Bomb Groups taking off from runways not over two miles away from us. As we climbed up through the foggy murk, we could occasionally see dark shadows drifting under us, over us, and on each side. Midair collisions were not uncommon. We broke out into the early morning light at about twenty thousand feet, and raced for our assigned "buncher" (radio beacon) to orbit for squadron and group formation form-up.

Each bomb group had distinctive, painted tail surface markings. The Ninety-second's marking was a large white *B* set in a black triangle embedded in a broad red stripe on the vertical stabilizer. We began the slow process of forming up our squadron combat boxes in the group formation. On this mission our crew was selected to lead the high squadron. At last we were ready and all thirty-six aircraft of the Ninety-second orbited over the buncher until our turn came to enter the Eighth Air Force stream of two thousand B-17 Flying Fortresses and B-24 Liberators at about thirty thousand feet. Along the way, we were joined by our fighter escorts as we crossed the North Sea bound for Germany. Over the sea, the gunners test-fired their machine guns, and we were ready for combat. As we crossed the Belgian coastline, our first relay of P-47 Thunderbolt fighters formed above us. They would leave us at the German border and be replaced by P-51 Mustangs who would take us to the target area. As we crossed the Rhine River just north of Koblenz, we received light but inaccurate antiaircraft cannon fire. That would be important later.

The bomber stream never flew, initially, directly toward the assigned target in Germany so that the enemy would be uncertain what our target would be. Along the way, the B-24s would split off and go in another direction to increase the enemy's confusion. As we turned at our IP (initial point), usually sixty or eighty miles from the target, then the Germans would know. That day we were almost immediately under heavy cannon fire from the some two thousand guns known to be defending the great oil and gas complex at Merseburg. I could see the batteries on the ground winking like lights on a Christmas tree as the shells left the gun barrels. Grinny called out, "Center the PDI," causing the pilots to transfer control of the plane to Grinny who would guide the aircraft from the bombsight. I was leaning over Grinny's shoulder helping him to pick out our exact aiming point in the target complex. The other navigator had covered his head with a flak jacket. Grinny and I did not have that luxury!

The plane was bouncing around due to the terrific anti-aircraft shell explosions all around us. Some clouds interfered but Grinny was "Dead Eye Dick." The crosshairs were directly on the aiming point. The bomb bay doors came open as the two bombsight indices crept together. Zero came and the bombs were away! As usual, Grinny yelled, "Let's get the hell out of here!" Our group wheeled to the left and set a course for home. I never learned if we lost any planes on the bomb run. We were still under fire for another ten minutes, and then we were rejoined by our P-51 escorts.

We did not know it, but the German Luftwaffe had selected the Ninety-second for their morale-shattering attack. Suddenly, diving out of the sun, came about one hundred Me109s and Focke-Wulf fighters to attack our group. Our escorting fighters were overwhelmed and went down in the first pass. Then the German fighters were in among us. It was wild! Again, Duke, Koby, Pinky, and Tony saved our lives. Our B-17 shuddered as the .50-caliber machine guns fired in a constant roar.

Grinny was firing the turret, and I was firing the single gun mounted in a cradle above my desk. Duke got double kills. The attack was devastating! We lost twelve B-17s, mainly from the middle squadron. . . . A few moments later, I saw one of the most welcome sights I have ever seen when a swarm of twin-tailed U.S. P-38s streamed in from the west and pounced on the German fighters like hungry hawks! The attack on the Ninety-second was history. We were home free or so we thought. It wasn't to be. I was now the lead navigator. Remembering that we had received cannon fire on our way in north of Koblenz, I opted to lead the formation south of Koblenz on the way out. What we did not know was that 88-millimeter cannons were mounted on railway cars and had been hauled south when the Germans, by radar, knew our route.

The first shell exploded about a hundred yards to our left. The second one blew ahead of our number-two engine, and jagged hunks of steel came ripping through the nose section. We had already taken off our flak jackets and helmets. On the first round I reached for my helmet and put it on my head. As my right hand was falling away, a piece of steel ripped through my right hand and hit me solidly near my shoulder. If the second shell had exploded more to the right, I would have been a dead man! I was hit twice with the same piece of metal. I can remember seeing white splinters of bone sticking out of my hand. It felt like I had been hit by a baseball bat as I fell violently. I knew that I was hit somewhere, but I didn't know where. I was stunned!

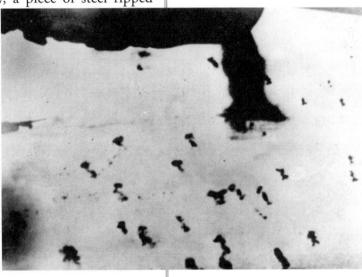

Photo taken from a B-24 bomber showing the flak bursts filling the air.

I was the only one hit. Grinny and the other navigator, lying prone, were looking ahead. With my left hand I grabbed the leg of the spare man lying on the floor between Grinny and me. He yelled at Grinny and used the microphone to tell Bill that there was a wounded man in the nose. I still had my headset on. Bill yelled, "Who?"

I had my microphone button in my left hand and replied, "Navigator." Grinny laid me flat on the floor. Bill sent Duke down from the top turret, and they stripped off my parachute harness. Grinny grabbed a curved knife clipped to the bulkhead for emergencies. He began to slice up my jumpsuit and electric suit. When he started to rip my green gabardine shirt, I swore at him!

Grinny yelled, "Shut up, Heg, you're hit bad!" I was in shock. I had no feelings as yet. I couldn't see that I was bleeding profusely. I didn't know how bad it was. My right arm was partially severed from my shoulder. Although stunned, I didn't believe I was going to die. Many years later in 1990, when our crew was the guest of Fresno City, California, and the movie, *Memphis Belle,* was released, I can remember Grinny grimly telling a reporter, "I wasn't going to let Heggie die!"

Grinny was desperately trying to find a pressure point to stop the flow of blood. He finally applied foot pressure on my shoulder; that and the intense cold slowed it to trickle. Bill asked the spare navigator for the headings for Podington. He didn't know. He had paid no attention at briefing. He was just along for the ride to finish his tour. The guy was useless! I still held the microphone button and, prone from the floor, called the headings from memory. The maps on the desk were destroyed by the shrapnel fragments.

Someone handed Grinny the morphine kit, and he broke off the glass tips of several ampoules and squeezed the contents into the bare flesh of my arm. I was soon woozy! By then, we were over the North Sea and less than an hour from Podington. Apparently, the main artery in my arm was okay. Grinny eased the pressure on my shoulder to let blood flow into my arm periodically. The intense cold on my flesh slowed the seepage. They wrapped my wounded hand to keep the bone splinters intact. It was fortunate that they did. I once told a Pleasant Grove doctor about the bleeding, and he remarked that all bleeding will eventually stop. I replied somewhat cynically, "Yes, when you run out!"

As we approached the Podington landing pattern, the tower was notified that we had wounded aboard, and they signaled that we were number one to land. As we came down the final approach to the runway, Duke was firing red Very pistol flares from the top turret to notify the medics in jeeps at the sides of the runway that we needed assistance. As we slowed to about thirty miles per hour, I was told that one of the medic jeeps, with a flight surgeon standing in the back, came in between our front wing and tail surface. Koby had the rear hatch open and the doctor jumped in from the moving jeep. Seconds later he was in the nose and applying a tourniquet, since, in the warm air, I was bleeding again. As Bill wheeled the B-17 into our hardstand, an ambulance was waiting to take me to the "Mash Unit."

Bill and Ted cut the engines and the doctor, Grinny, and Duke lowered me out of the forward hatch to medics on the ground. I remember standing and grinning up at Bill when I collapsed. An IV was inserted, and I was loaded into the ambulance to be taken to the emergency station.

ROBERT D. HEMINGWAY

As a B-17 pilot, Robert flew thirty-five combat missions over Germany. He was a member of the Thirty-fourth Bomber Group that flew out of Ipswich, England. He kept a log of each mission in which he recorded the significant events.

Robert Hemingway, Lt. Col., Army Air Corps.

Mission twelve, Ludwigshafen, Germany, 7:40 A.M., November 5, 1944.

Today was Sunday, the Sabbath day. We were briefed to go to a spot right on the line of battle as a primary target and Ludwigshaven as a secondary. (This has reference to the battle line between our troops and the Germans, and we never bombed there unless we could see it well, for fear of hitting our own troops.)

It was overcast, so off we went to Ludwigshaven. But before we even took off we had to get a ground spare to fly because we couldn't get our own engines started. We took off late and flew up in a hurry and caught the formation and took off from the coast, as we should have done.

We couldn't bomb the primary and went to the secondary. That was the third time I had been to Ludwigshaven and I didn't like it. When we turned on the bomb run we could see the solid black cloud of flak. There was nothing to do but fly into it in the formation. We flew in and dropped the bombs and were going out when all of a sudden something hit me in the stomach. I didn't know what it was, but I wasn't hurt except my finger hurt on my left hand.

Then it just dawned on me that maybe Johnnie, my copilot, was hit but he looked all right so I gave him the ship and started to look around. The fluorescent light from my control column was hanging down limp. I picked it up, and it was bent all up and all the glass was broken out of it. That was all I saw for a long time.

I was busy flying the ship when the ball turret gunner reported oil streaming from the third engine so I tried to feather it. Then our trouble began. It wouldn't feather, (the engines feathered by oil pressure). It must have gotten a good hard hit in the nose section because it started to run away. It was indicating three thousand RPM and suddenly the indicator dropped to zero. The oil pressure was zero and the engine stopped, but the crankshaft was broken and the prop kept spinning. The spinning prop caused excessive vibration, and I thought the ship was going to fall apart. The control pedestal was jumping around, vibrating an inch each way.

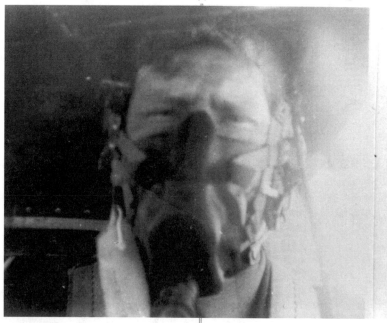

Self-portrait of Robert Hemingway in aircraft cockpit wearing his oxygen mask.

I slowed the ship down to about 135 mph, and it quit vibrating so we headed home. We had to lose the formation, and we called for fighters. The bombardier and navigator had to go to the radio room because I was afraid that the prop might fly off and hit them in the nose of the plane. The copilot also left his seat because that runaway prop was just outside his window. All of the crew was lined up at the door waiting for me to tell them to bail out.

We flew home on as good a course as we could with the navigator in the radio room. Our fighters (P-51s) came up and gave us cover, and they were beautiful. One of them, the *Arkansas Traveler*, stuck with us for a long time. He was a lovely little fellow. We had lost several thousand feet of altitude, and because we were flying so slowly, we were many miles behind the out-group.

Well we got in touch with Air Sea Rescue, and they kept tabs on us all the way home. We came right on over the Channel, letting down and dodging weather. We were down to about seventeen thousand feet in a rain storm, and the prop finally fell off somewhere over the English countryside. I sighed with relief. When the prop came off it hit the side of the ship and put a big hole in it and then swung under the ship and came up on the left and peeled off and dropped to the ground.

Now we had three good engines, and all we had to worry about was weather. We hit the clouds and rain and couldn't find the field. The navigator gave us a heading, and we hit the field and circled it once and came in and landed. On landing the copilot wouldn't let me work the controls so we dropped in and we were down.

We taxied to the hardstand and then got out and looked. It was a hell of a sight—the whole nose section of the third engine was gone, and the cowling was beat right back to the cylinders. No one was hurt, and we got a cluster to our air medals.

When we finally got home we were about an hour late, and most had given us up for lost. My bombardier was a Catholic and the priest had said Rosary for us. That day was a very trying one. I am so grateful to my Heavenly Father for blessing me with the ability to do what was necessary to bring us back safely and for keeping that plane together. I give Him the credit for what I am and what I have been able to accomplish.

Oh yes, the piece of flak that hit me was about two inches long and one-half-inch square. It came in the top of the nose and through the instrument panel and then hit my flak suit with quite a wallop. That was my first real encounter with the stuff, and I don't want another!

(Below) Robert Hemingway boarding a training plane during air cadet school.

(Far Below) Red Cross serving doughnuts to airmen.

CHARLES H. HENRY

As a medical technician, Charles assisted the doctors and other medical personnel with their duties. He served in a field medical station throughout the war assisting the wounded brought in from the front lines. At times there were hundreds of soldiers a day that needed the attention of those working at his station.

For the next four days we traveled southeast across the Atlantic. . . . It was necessary for mine sweepers to travel ahead of the ships to move the seaweed out of the way of the ships' propellers. This was how the convoy lost the enemy submarines. They could not get through the seaweed without help.

During this time of crossing I felt very insecure. I knew that the lives of all of the men under my command were, so to speak, "in my hands." If I gave orders, they had to obey without question. This was the Army and war.

I fasted and prayed that I might have the guidance and help necessary for the accomplishment of our mission and for the health and safety of the men. I remembered the blessing and help that had been given Helaman in the Book of Mormon. I prayed that I might be worthy of and granted such a blessing. I guess it could be said, "I prayed mightily unto the Lord." I even asked Him if I might be granted the blessing of bringing them all home alive. I wept as I prayed. I felt peace and comfort.

* * * * *

The next morning the infantry was to cross the Wurm River. We were all ready. About 9:00 P.M., I called the men for a briefing and suggested that they should relax for the night and told them that we would give them a wake-up call at 6:00 A.M.

I retired for the night. After prayers and pondering I fell asleep. About 1:00 A.M., I heard a voice telling me to arouse the men and move them into the school basement. I ignored the voice, thinking I had been dreaming. I went back to sleep but the voice came again, even more persistently. Again, I ignored the voice and settled back to sleep. At about 1:30 A.M., it seemed that someone grasped my shoulders, shook me awake, and demanded that I get those men up.

I acted immediately and called the first sergeant and required that he order the men to the station area. I also alerted the mess sergeant to have drinks and sandwiches for the company. I wondered what I would do or say to the men when

I had to talk to them as soon as they were assembled. Just as the last man was entering the building, a German artillery barrage blanketed our areas. It knocked out all of the billets, and a lot of shells were bouncing off the walls of the station in the schoolhouse.

When I entered the room to meet the men, I told them of my experience and answer to my prayers for us all. The men were very touched and promised that if I would always follow those promptings they would never complain, nor question any order given them. I told them of my faith in God, and that I knew that this was an answer to my prayers. We had a few tears, and I offered a prayer of thanks.

HORST K. HILBERT

Drafted into the German military in 1939, Horst spent the first year as a construction worker. In 1940 he was assigned to a field unit at the Western Front. He participated in the conquest of France and afterward left with his unit for the invasion of Russia. While retreating from the Russian front he was captured and spent the final days of the war in an Allied POW camp. He went on to become a district president of the Church in occupied Germany before fleeing to the United States.

One early morning, January 6, 1942, I had to stand guard duty with a buddy, Hans Plank. We were standing beside a little shack, the straw roof covered with snow. A Russian machine gun started to shoot at us. I could see the tracers hitting the ground before my feet, then skipping off to the sky. Other rounds hit the straw roof, and I could see the bullets making rows of holes, making the snow coming down like sugar coming out of a bowl.

I was very afraid and since I was forbidden to leave the post, I wanted to pray. I could feel the power of the destroyer. But I could not utter one word of prayer; my tongue felt paralyzed. To think that the first words in my life were prayers on my mother's lap. All I was able to say was that if my mother could pray for me right now, the Lord might hear the prayer of a righteous woman. With that thought, I looked to the east, and felt prompted to look north. When I did that and turned, a bullet passed, and in passing, hit the coat at my stomach. Had I not turned, it would have struck my stomach. After that incident the shooting stopped.

While many young German Latter-day Saints did not always agree with Hitler's cause, they were still required to enter military service. Church members fought through much of the war on both the eastern and western fronts. Pictured above is Jared H. B. Kobs— an 18-year-old member of the Church who was drafted into the German Army and served as a lance corporal. He is shown here in his "show off" uniform in Germany, Nov. 1942.

Some days later I received a letter from my mother. In the letter, she wrote that in the night of January 6 she woke up hearing me calling her "Mama." She also heard the sound of shooting. She got up quickly, woke up my four sisters and said that they needed to pray fast, that I was in mortal danger, and needed their prayer. The five women knelt down, and my mother pleaded with the Lord to keep His protecting hand over me. After the prayer my mother told my sisters to go back to sleep and be of good cheer. I had been in danger, but the Lord helped me.

ROBERT B. HILLIER

The Battle of Normandy did not end at the beaches. As a scout for the Ninety-seventh Infantry Division, Robert found himself at the forefront of the inland battles. His patriarchal blessing had promised him that if he would "conduct himself worthily as an elder in the Church," he would be respected and admired.

Around midnight a German patrol approached in front of our foxholes. I was on watch and was amazed that as the patrol came within close proximity that the patrol was not challenged. I challenged them with a loud, "Halt!" They immediately froze standing up. I asked for the password. They didn't respond. Again I asked. One German soldier spoke in German and charged toward our foxhole pointing his rifle with attached bayonet directly at me. It was a bright moonlit night. At that point, I fired. The German soldier fell, landing within two feet of our foxhole. The rest of the German patrol withdrew. As dawn arrived, there lay the dead German soldier. His one hand still attached to the rifle, his other reaching toward a grenade hanging around his neck. To my knowledge that was my first direct killing. I was sorry it had to happen, but realized that it was either him or me.

* * * * *

One particular night we dug our foxholes on the property line of a big home overlooking the entrance to the city of Werschberg. The homeowners treated us on a friendly basis and offered us a hot cooked meal. As we sat down to the table covered with a white linen cloth and napkins, we were served potatoes, gravy, pork chops, salad, and drink. As I put the glass toward my lips, I had the strangest feeling that all was not right, and I shouldn't drink it. . . . I asked my buddies who had already tasted it what it was, and if it tasted good. They assured me that it was not alcohol, and it was great tasting, but as I again picked the glass up, the same feeling came over me and so I refrained. About an hour later it was evident that the drink had been poisoned because I was the only one in the platoon who was not violently ill. I had to guard alone in a foxhole nearly all night while the others tried to recover from weakness, nausea, and stomachache.

* * * * *

On another night, it was rapidly getting dark. We feared that if we did not get off the knoll soon, the Germans would direct artillery power onto the hill. We persuaded our patrol leader that our only chance of survival was to infiltrate enemy lines. That would be a very dangerous attempt. Chances of success were next to impossible, but this night was a fight for life. To say that we were not afraid would have been lie. This was a time for prayer, even for those who had ridiculed and profaned the name of the Lord and even for those who had claimed atheism. Minutes seemed like hours and then once again, words from my patriarchal blessing came to mind. "I bless you that you will complete your mission here upon the earth; that you shall not be called until the Lord says that it is enough." It was finally dark. We moved out, crawling oh so quietly, each in his own planned area. Each was now on his own. I trembled and sweat as I reached the line of the enemy. It was so quiet except for my pounding heart. Then to my far left I heard gunfire. Someone had been detected. I crawled inch by inch. Again I heard gunshots, but they were behind me. It was then that I realized I had made it. I had crawled, prayed, and sweat my way to freedom, even if only for the night.

✶ M. GLEN JONES
✶
✶

Glen was headed for cadet training in the Air Corps base in Illinois when an army colonel boarded the train and informed Glen and the rest of the men that the train had been redirected to Texas, and they were now in the infantry. After several months of basic training he was shipped to Europe and soon found himself in a railroad boxcar headed to the south flank of the Battle of the Bulge. There he experienced the horrors of hand-to-hand combat.

I was sleeping in the middle of three of us. About 3:00 A.M. the Germans opened up with artillery. They just hammered the whole area. When the shells hit in the trees, the trees went crashing down. I thought, "Oh boy, I hope they stop after while." Then the artillery lifted and went to the rear. I thought, "Maybe they think part of us are down there." About that time a voice said, "Get out of the hole."

I thought to myself, "You didn't hear anything. You're groggy from all these shells exploding and you're half asleep anyway. You didn't hear anything!"

The voice came a second time, "Get out of the hole!" I was still asking myself if I heard something or not. The third time, the voice said, "Get out of the hole, right now!" Just like that. I knew I had been spoken to! I had just dragged myself out of the hole when a German came up to it. He fired a long burst into it with his submachine gun, right where I had been…. Then the German ran directly over to Gitch and Mowack's hole. They must have sensed their impending deaths. I grabbed my rifle in the dark and tried to get the safety off, but he had gunned them down in the back before I could stop him.

Battle of the Bulge

The Battle of the Bulge, which occured in December of 1944, is one of the most famous battles of World War II. Viewed as a desperate last attempt by the Germans to end the war with a cease-fire or truce, it nearly succeeded but for the weather and the quick response of the Allied commanders. Many Latter-day Saints were present at this battle.

✶
✶
✶

H. WENDELL JONES

Wendell credits his faith for helping him survive the horrors of Omaha Beach on D-Day. While he trained for service in a tank unit he was reassigned as a liaison officer between two field colonels leading troops onto Omaha Beach. Wendell was awarded the Distinguished Service Cross and the Bronze Star for extraordinary heroism in action. The following is a first-person adaptation of his personal history.

Each combat team was given a specific landing zone . . . Colonel Charles D. Canham (the one I was assigned to) was assigned to accompany the assault landings on Dog Red (Omaha Beach).

At six-minute intervals from 7:00 A.M. on five assault waves, the main body of troops would begin to land. It was on one of these first waves that I went to shore. From the beginning, the assault on Omaha Beach looked as if it were a disaster. Engineers and naval demolition teams had no chance to function properly. Launching delays prevented half the engineers from hitting the beach at their appointed time, and when they did land, only a third came close to their objectives. The casualties and confusion of the first waves affected every succeeding wave.

All along Omaha Beach the dropping of the ramps seemed to be the signal for renewed, more concentrated machine gun fire. The ramps came down and men stepped out into the water three to six feet deep. They had but one objective in mind, to get through the water, cross two hundred yards of obstacle-strewn beach, climb the gradually rising beach, and then take cover in the dubious shelter of a sea wall. There were big German 155-millimeter antitank guns pointed down at the beach. By the time we went ashore, those guns were really zeroed on things. They were really blasting the devil out of everything that came in there.

Many men froze on the beach. Colonel Canham encouraged his troops inland. I was impressed with his leadership ability. He was an older man and a good soldier as he moved in fast across the two hundred yards of beach to climb the bluffs that rose from the beach. The machine gun bullets were hitting the ground like a sewing machine sewing a row of stitches just a few feet in front. . . . I was intent on just keeping up with the colonel who was moving fast ahead of me. Carrying an 85-pound radio made keeping up with him a real struggle . . . somewhere along the way I was hit in the shoulder with shrapnel, but I ignored the wound in the excitement.

Pictorial Review of Drive That Breached West Wall

Ike Watches—Gen. Eisenhower, from the deck of a warship somewhere in the Channel, watched landing operations in France.

Allies Land in France

Part of World's Greatest Armada—Flying in a Royal Navy Aircraft, a British photographer snapped the best picture of the D-Day Armada. The gigantic fleet of warships, transports, landing craft, supply ships was en route to northern France when the picture was taken.

Leads Yanks—Lt. Gen. Omar N. Bradley, one of America's foremost infantry experts, is leading the U.S. ground forces now assaulting northern France.

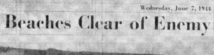

Wednesday, June 7, 1944

Beaches Clear of Enemy

First Picture of Landings in France—American infantrymen wade through the surf to the shore, while to the right are transports from which they disembarked.

Thursday, June 8, 1944

Bayeux 1st City to Fall

Allies Take Over—Bayeux was the first city to fall in France. Bayeux is on the railroad and main highway between Cherbourg and Paris. A street scene of Bayeux is shown here.

U.S. Army Air Force Photo

Blast Bridge—Smoke and bomb bursts mingle in area of wrecked bridge east of Tours, France. The damage was done by Eighth Air Force heavies. Yesterday 2,000 American planes launched another great attack.

Associated Press Photo

Bewildered—German prisoners, displaying every emotion from arrogance to bewilderment, march to waiting trucks and were moved to an undisclosed destination.

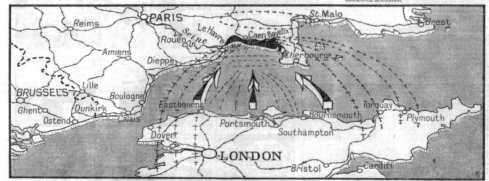

Air View Map of Hitler's Crumbling Wall—Allied armies, supported by more than 4,000 ships, 11,000 warplanes, pierced Hitler's wall in northern France last Tuesday morning. The black area is the coast territory now occupied by the Allies after six days of battling.

Printed in England by The Times Publishing Company, Limited, Printing House Square, London, E.C.4, and Published by the United States Armed Forces—12-6-44.

The enormous amount of confusion is one of the most lasting impressions of the day. Besides the fact that many soldiers had landed in the wrong sectors, a high proportion of company commanders and platoon leaders had been among the first casualties of the day. These problems were further complicated by the loss of so much radio equipment. It seemed that the whole operation could fail.

The next morning I returned to the beach with Colonel Canham. The beach was covered with bodies of dead and wounded soldiers, some whose legs had been blown off but were still alive. Everywhere I looked, I saw bodies of American soldiers. I must have seen hundreds. In fact, there were so many that it was almost impossible to take a step without having to step over someone. The medics were working on getting those still alive back on the LCTs (landing craft tanks). The soldiers themselves had been told not to stop and aid any wounded men. Their job was to neutralize the enemy as quickly as possible and leave the job of caring for the wounded to the medics.

D. REED JORDAN

As an executive officer in the public relations section of the Supreme Headquarters Allied Expeditionary Force (SHAEF), Reed witnessed the surrender of Germany and was responsible for issuing the press release announcing this important event.

I arrived at SHAEF the day before D-Day and was assigned to the communiqué section of the Public Relations Division. Confusion reigned there. Fifty various SHAEF officers were being looked at to see if they would fit into the communiqué section. I was told to head up the newly formed communiqué section for the SHAEF Forward Headquarters, wherever it was to be located, either in London or Paris. We were in business by 6:00 A.M. on D-Day.

We decided to operate like a newspaper editorial section, with legmen reporters in the field where the action was. We depended on telephones to receive our reports. From D-Day until the end of the war we wrote 391 regular communiqués and 8 special communiqués. When the Forward Headquarters was moved to France, I went with it.

One morning, soon after we got to the continent, one of the G-3 officers came from the morning staff briefing, to which I was not then privy, and said, "Beetle wants to see

(Opposite page) Stars and Stripes newspaper, June 12, 1944, depicting the first pictures of the D-Day landings.

you." That was General Walter Bedell Smith, General Eisenhower's chief of staff.

I went to see him; he said, "You had a communiqué this morning. The only thing is, you've got stuff in there we've never heard of."

I had to laugh because I had anticipated this. I said, "Well, I thought you were going to ask about it. I scooped you, and the reason is that the road battalion out there cut you off this morning. You haven't had any telephone communication with the front lines at all, have you?"

He said, "No." As I turned to leave he asked, "Do you have a pass to the war room? All right, from now on you will be at the staff briefings"—that was Eisenhower's briefing—"every morning, with a copy of your communiqué for the day."

Our communiqués were a general guide for the press and radio. They were the first people to receive copies of them every day. They were distributed from the war room and from briefing rooms. They were meant for worldwide distribution. The more the better. It was not just an internal document. We were putting out what happened every day to the men in the air, on the ground, in the artillery, and in the infantry. We obtained our material from the same sources as the G-3 Operations Division of the Army. They had their own report, but theirs was classified. We had no classified information in our releases, but 90 percent of what they had was not classified. We never put out any propaganda; we didn't have time. We had a war on, and it was a tough war. We printed the bad news and the good, the losses, everything.

On my staff was a Frenchman, two or three Englishmen, a Canadian and, of course, several Americans—Army, Navy, Air Force, the whole bunch. I never had more than twenty people working.

Whenever General Eisenhower was at headquarters, I met with him every day. He was a very congenial man, but he wanted the work done properly. If I had something I thought should go to him, I would discuss it with the chief of staff, General Smith. He would usually say, "Write a staff study on it and let the boss see it." From those studies we prepared a one-page summary for "Ike." General Eisenhower was always interested in the men in the field; so if something came across that pertained to them, we made sure he saw it.

* * * * *

One day President Truman came over. He wanted to see his old World War I unit, the Sixty-ninth Division. We were in Frankfurt, Germany, at the time. Ike called a press conference before the president left. A member of his office staff called me and said, "Tell your reporters that if there are any who want to see Truman off at the airport to come." A half-dozen of them showed up, and they talked with the president.

After he was gone, Eisenhower, the reporters, and I were standing on the tarmac. He said to me, "Let's sit down." We sat in the shade of an airplane for an hour and talked. I could see he was letting off steam after having spent a week with the president of the United States. He seemed glad to get that load off his shoulders and be back with people he knew how to talk to.

* * * * *

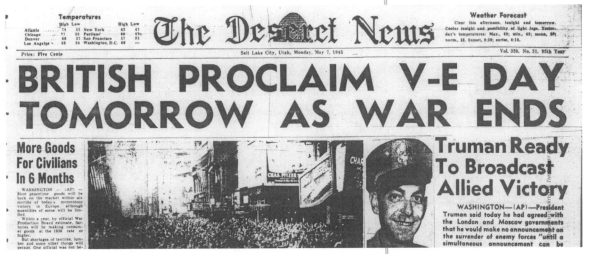

We got word that the Germans were willing to meet our demands for an unconditional surrender shortly after midnight on May 8, 1945. I wrote Special Communiqué Eight, releasing this long-awaited news to the world. I had only a very short time. I realized I would never pass down another document that would mean so much to people worldwide.

General Smith came in while we were setting things up in the war room where the Germans would sign the document and said, "Now you're not going to make a big show of this. I don't want any circus around here. Get those guys in here. They're going to tell us if they accept it—no ifs, ands, or buts—and they'll be out on time."

I was witness to the German signing of World War II surrender documents in the war room in SHAEF Forward Headquarters in Reims, France. It was 2:00 A.M. There were

The Deseret News, May 8, 1945, *declaring V–E (Victory in Europe) Day, celebrating the unconditional surrender of the German troops.*

(Below) Capt. Alan W. Layton.

(Far Below) Capt. Alan W. Layton and Sgt. Edgar R. Alley—both artillery observers plotting for tank and howitzer destroyer units as German troops are driven from the city below—look through the scope at a forward observation post near Brest, France.

no reporters or photographers present. It took only fifteen minutes; there was no messing around. It was a time of joy, but also a time to lament the horrible suffering and loss of life and the appalling destruction of property. It had been a vast calamity. For my part in this ceremony, I was awarded the Bronze Star, a decoration usually reserved for men in combat.

ALAN W. LAYTON

Alan began his military service as an ROTC (Reserve Officers Training Corps) cadet at the University of Utah. Following his schooling he became a gunnery officer and left for the European Theater. He landed on Utah Beach a month after the D-Day invasion and played an active role in the Allied advances across France, ultimately finding himself in the middle of the Battle of the Bulge.

About five or six weeks after the Bulge hit, everything finally collapsed, and the Germans surrendered. We thought this would pretty well finish the war. But as we regrouped and moved eastward, the Germans blew up bridges and fired on us. We kept pursuing them. As we crossed the mountains, we could see great destruction from the minefields and the fighting that had gone on during the Bulge. There were dead cattle, GI soldiers, and German soldiers littering the area, all frozen stiff. It was heartrending to see that the GI boots had been taken off dead American soldiers. Wallets and personal effects were strewn about—including pictures of loved ones. The Graves Registration Corps was out gathering up the frozen bodies of the American soldiers and taking them back to the rear areas and preparing them for burial.

GERALD N. LEAVITT

As an officer in the Army Air Corps, Gerald won five air medals and the Distinguished Flying Cross. As a pilot of a B-17, he made repeated runs over Germany prior to the D-Day invasion.

The last mission I flew was on D-Day; it was my thirtieth mission and frankly, as far as we were concerned, we thought it was a milk run because there wasn't much opposition—there were eleven thousand airplanes in the sky that one day, and the traffic problem was worse than being in downtown Las Vegas.

We flew at twelve thousand feet. It was undercast all the way over Omaha Beach and Utah Beach—we couldn't see a thing. All the planes bombed right in front of the troops who were just landing on the beach. Germany had fortified all the beaches; they had tank traps and all kinds of fortifications. We had to push them off to win. To do this they sent the Navy in to bombard the beaches. The naval guns were the most accurate guns available. Then they sent the Air Force in to bomb the beaches, and they bombed in a pathway, so many yards wide for such and such a distance. They tried not to go outside, just a pathway in progression. When the troops arrived, we were bombing a little farther away than from where they landed. I went over in the middle of the tenth or twelfth wave, somewhere toward the first, but not up front.

It took hours for that many airplanes to get over there through the narrow corridor. There were all kinds of airplanes; we couldn't see the beach—we couldn't see anything. There I

Capt. Gerald N. Leavitt, who was awarded the Distinguished Flying Cross.

The Distinguished Flying Cross

The Distinguished Flying Cross is awarded to any person who, while serving in any capacity with the Armed Forces of the United States, distinguishes himself by heroism or extraordinary achievement while participating in aerial flight. The performance of the act of heroism must be evidenced by voluntary action above and beyond the call of duty. The extraordinary achievement must have resulted in an accomplishment so exceptional and outstanding as to clearly set the individual apart from his comrades or from other persons in similar circumstances. Awards are given to recognize single acts of heroism or extraordinary achievement and are not given in recognition of sustained operational activities against an armed enemy.

was sitting up there, the biggest show on earth, and I wasn't a mile or two miles away from it and couldn't see a thing.

The forming up and getting into a traffic pattern took us about a couple of hours, but from the time we got into the traffic pattern and dropped the bombs, it probably wasn't any more than thirty or thirty-five minutes. Because there were so many airplanes getting back, it took us four and one-half hours. We had to go clear down and over across France almost, then back out to sea to go clear around the traffic coming our way.

A lot of the B-17s only flew one mission. A lot of the lighter planes flew two or three missions during that day, particularly the fighters. They had their own traffic pattern and a lower altitude so they could circle around and get loaded again and come back in. I don't know how many bombs we dropped, but eleven thousand airplanes went over a little corridor, and it took hours and hours to do so, believe it or not, just to get over that little corridor at the right time and the right place. They dropped a series of curtains in front of the troops. Some of them dropped on the troops. Some troops were farther ahead than they were supposed to be, and some pilots didn't bomb properly, killing our own boys.

Capt. Gerald N. Leavitt and crew standing on the wing of the Picadilly Ann, *a B-17 bomber. Gerald is standing on the far left side.*

447 BG 3 M 153 (95-G-3)(10-31-43) CREW 42.

DAVID E. LOFGREN

*While training to become an FBI agent in Washington, D.C., David was draft-
ed into the Army and sent to an engineering school. After training for various
roles, he ended up in the Eighty-sixth Infantry where he served as a jeep driver.*

Sunday at sea, February 25, 1945.

Dear Family:

I had an interesting thing happen today. Thursday I saw our
chaplain about giving us a time and a place to hold LDS services here on board today, and he gave me wholehearted coopera-
tion—even went so far as to give us his office to meet in. I was
expecting four or five at the most, but we ended up with a real
crowd. Ten members and three visitors, standing room only. It
was quite nice though and may lead into something fairly good.
We hope. Well not much else to say except all okay. So I close.

Love,
Dave.

* * * * *

We were going down through Germany, and I was at the
front of the headquarters convoy as jeep reconnaissance. That
was an interesting situation. . . . As soon as we got into combat,
however, we got word one night that the jeep reconnaissance
driver had been killed. He had hit a land mine, and it had wiped
him and his jeep out. There were five or six of us in the room
when the word came. The chaplain pointed at me and said,
"Give it to the damn Mormon. The devil's got so much work for
him still that he'll never get killed!" So I was jeep reconnaissance
for the next five-and-a-half to six months. Interestingly enough,
the prediction that I wouldn't get killed was right. I didn't even
get a flat tire. But the chaplain didn't give me reason to feel that
he had much spiritual guidance in his decision.

* * * * *

Another one of the American soldiers was a guy by the
name of Koocher, who was front line rifle. He said, "Hey,
Lofgren. I can't kill people. I can't shoot back." I had a letter
with one of the messages that Hugh B. Brown had sent the
GIs in which he said that soldiers were not going to be held
accountable for murder if they killed.

I said, "Tell me what happens if you're driving down the street and a guy runs out in front of you and you hit him with your truck and kill him. Is that murder?"

"No," he said, "it's an accident."

"Okay," I said. "Now here's the thing. You can't kill them. You can't murder. But when they start shooting at you, you take a bead on them and yell 'duck,' and if they're stupid, they won't duck when you pull the trigger, and they just committed suicide." He was a very good soldier. He was a loveable character. A guy who shouldn't have been sent into the Army, especially combat, but he was.

ENID MASSEY

Enid's parents had three sons and one daughter serving in World War II. After basic training as a WAVE (Women Accepted for Volunteer Emergency Service), she completed training as a clerk typist and served the duration of the war in an office in San Diego.

I was twenty years old when I came home with papers for Mama to sign saying I had a parent's permission to join the WAVES. I was working with a close girlfriend whose brother was in the Navy, and she thought we should join the women's navy. I said, "No way, I have three brothers who are in the Army, but I don't feel a need to join the WACs," (Women's Army Corps). My mother really didn't want to sign, but finally did with much persuasion.

Women in the Armed Forces

Women were limited in the role they played only in that they were not allowed to enter combat. Many women served as clerks and in other support positions, allowing the men to serve in the forward positions. Women in the Army Air Corps served as pilots, often ferrying the planes from the manufacturing facilities to military airbases in the United States and Europe. Some of the branches women served in were: WAVE (Women Accepted for Volunteer Emergency Service), WAAC (Women's Army Auxiliary Corps) which was later changed to WAC (Women's Army Corps), WASP (Women's Air Service Pilots), WAFS (Women's Auxiliary Ferrying Squadron), and AWS (Aircraft Warning Service).

I can honestly say that the time I spent in the WAVES was a learning experience. Uncle Sam pointed his finger at all of us and told young women to join the military forces and free a man so he could go fight. So we did, and felt we were doing a good thing. We weren't expected to go to the front lines in battle, but we did have our own private battles. . . . Those twenty-two months were a time I shall always remember with gratitude for having served my country as I was called to do.

NORVAL G. MASSEY

As one of three brothers serving in the war, Norval (an infantry sergeant), was part of the force that stormed Omaha Beach during the D-Day invasion. He survived eleven months of combat as the Allied forces moved across Europe toward Germany.

When we landed at Omaha Beach we had to stay on the ship all night as there wasn't enough room to get on the beach. I'm a ground lover and it was hard on me sitting out there like a sitting duck, with planes and shells all around us! The CBs did have their barrage balloons up, but that didn't make me feel too secure. When we did get off the next morning, I felt like kissing the ground. By that time, they had started hauling off the dead in two-ton trucks with racks on them.

The beach had been secured, but going only a short distance from the beach (maybe a mile or so), I knew I was in the war! Up until that time, I had tried to block it out, thinking it might end before I got this far into it. The first thing we did when we landed was to get rid of the stinking, chemically saturated protective clothes we had had on while crossing the English Channel in case the Germans had used gas on us.

Alma L. Keiser took these heads from German machine gun bullets. "The wooden heads are for close distance. They tear larger holes when they go through a body. The others are just normal bullet heads."

ALDEN D. MAYNES

After twenty-five successful bombing missions as a copilot on a B-17, Alden was shot down during a mission over Germany. Upon landing safely, he was captured and spent the remainder of the war in a German POW camp.

At 11:30 A.M. we were over target and had just released our bomb load of six 500-pound bombs. As we turned off target, we were hit by two simultaneous bursts of antiaircraft fire. The plane's tail was shot away throwing the B-17 out of control and into a barrel roll.

As I was making my way to the escape hatch, my parachute caught on something and was pulled open while I was still in the aircraft. I didn't have a chance to get both attaching snaps fastened, but I bailed out anyway. We were at twenty-seven thousand feet and without oxygen when I lost consciousness. When I came back to awareness, the planes were still dropping bombs. The antiaircraft guns were still being fired. Berlin was a mass of fire and destruction underneath me. I tried to pull the collapsed chute to me so that I could fix it, but my attempts were to no avail.

At that point I talked with the Lord and told Him that I had done all that I could and that now I was in His hands.

Photo showing a crash landing of a bomber in England. Bicycles were the typical mode of transportation at the time for the soldiers; thus, the majority of those gathered around the crashed aircraft arrived on bicycle.

Immediately a calm and peaceful feeling settled over me, and I knew whatever happened would be all right.

As I continued to fall, I drifted away from the bombed area. I was gyrating in a twenty- to twenty-five-foot radius. As I came close to a six-story building, the chute caught on the roof of the building then tore loose. I was swinging away from the building at the time; therefore, I never touched the building. The remaining fall was parallel with the building and the parachute caught again, this time on a street lamp, and I came to a stop with my feet just three feet above the sidewalk. I was immediately taken prisoner, and I spent one year in a prisoner of war camp.

BASIL D. McMULLIN

After ten months of what Basil terms "marital bliss," he was drafted into the Army. He trained as an aircraft mechanic before being shipped to North Africa. From there he followed the troops as they moved through Italy toward Germany. On December 9, 1942, he sent his young bride a telegram.

Remembering the happiness and love we have shared other days and Christmas. Million thanks for your love and encouragement. Looking forward to our future happiness. Best Christmas wishes for you, your mother, and the family. Will write as often as possible. God bless you, Darling. All my love to you. Merry Christmas.

Mac.

ARLIN L. MECHAM

Arlin served as a private first class in the Fifty-fifth Armored Infantry Battalion and Ordnance Corps. He found himself in Belgium near the town of Bastogne after a major battle. There was lots of snow on the ground; the cold was biting and when the wind blew down from the north, he described conditions as being wretched.

A wonderful event happened the second day I was in the new company. A soldier who had been in the company a few days longer than I, came to me and asked if I was from Utah and if I was a Mormon. I said I was and he introduced himself and said he was from Mesa, Arizona, and stated that he was also a Mormon. He said he saw my name on the company roster of replacement soldiers.

Arlin Mecham somewhere in Germany on his way home in a WWI box car.

I was very happy to be in a unit with someone who believed as I did, and who had a testimony of the Lord Jesus Christ and His gospel. We hit it off great from the start and got together at every opportunity. We were in different platoons, so our "off times" did not always fall in the same time frame. He told me he was married and had a lovely wife back home in Mesa. That caused me to think of my sweetheart at home, and I hoped and prayed, in my heart and mind, that someday Marilyn would be my wife.

* * * * *

A few days later our battalion, under orders, moved out toward the battle lines and the next confrontation with the Germans. Our direction was southeast through Luxembourg and over the mountains. We traveled in half-tracks, one squad of twelve men and a driver to each vehicle. I saw how the enemy had very carefully camouflaged their pill boxes and gun positions. They had strategically placed them so that they could see us long before we could see them.

Troops involved in the Battle of the Bulge. Arlin Mecham described weather conditions during this battle as being wretched.

Our units got over the mountains without any incident and set up camp just after sundown, in a position that had been occupied previously. Perimeter defenses were established, and I was placed in the outer line, using a foxhole that someone else had dug. The night was pitch black, and I was afraid. It was impossible to see the soldier on either side of me, who was twelve to fifteen feet away.

We were told to, "keep your ears open," and challenge any noise we heard. The effort to keep the enemy from infiltrating our lines during the night was effective, and at first light our unit was ordered to move forward and engage the enemy.

We walked for about one mile and came to the top of a rise where we could see over a valley several miles long and wide. There I saw the first muzzle flashes of artillery and felt the explosive impact of rounds.

Walking down a road, we had to cross a small stream, which was iced over. The bridge had been blown out, so we crossed on the ice. I was assigned to a bazooka (shoulder-fired rocket launcher) team, consisting of two men. The other fellow carried the launcher, and I carried the six rounds. All the soldiers carried a field pack, rifle, full belt of rifle ammunition, and two days of K rations in addition to parts of other light artillery pieces.

I was one of the first to start across the stream, and at mid-stream the ice broke under me, and I went down into the icy water, which was knee deep. The water ran down into my combat boots, thoroughly saturating my socks and felt liners. On we went, advancing in single file down both sides of the road. About half a mile beyond the stream, the road made a sharp right-angle turn, and just beyond the turn I saw the first dead German soldier I was to see. It was such a ghastly sight. He was lying across a ditch bank with his face looking directly at us, mouth open, eyes staring, with his chest laid open from some type of explosion. The look in his eyes haunts me to this day, fifty years later. Whenever I reflect upon this event, I can't do so without crying a little.

ROYAL R. MESERVY

Royal served in the 106th Golden Lion Division. He was captured during the Battle of the Bulge on December 19, 1944, and spent the rest of the war in a POW camp. In the camp he attended Church services and was chosen to be the leader of the group.

In England, my captain had asked me to act as a chaplain if there didn't happen to be one available. I said I would. When we left England, we landed at Le Harve, France. I was in the Battle of Arden where there was no time for any services. Then in Belgium we spent a week in our pup tents on a plowed ground. It rained constantly. I had a New Testament and *Principles of the Gospel* in one shirt pocket and a Book of Mormon in the other shirt pocket. I carried a bottle of consecrated oil in the watch pocket of my trousers.

* * * * *

We were taken to Stalag IX B in Germany. While there, the LDS soldiers obtained permission to hold Sunday services in the chaplain's quarters, not a large room. There were seventeen LDS soldiers who attended those services each Sunday. I was chosen to be the leader of the group. From our meager bread ration we received the night before, we took turns saving a piece about one-half inch wide and three inches long for sacrament bread. We also read and studied the Book of Mormon during the week. We were starved and so weak and tired, but the spirit was strong. . . . In those terrible times, I'd lie and talk to God as I would my father. I told Him if He'd help me so that I could stay alive, go home, get married, and raise a family, I'd do whatever He or His servants asked me to do. Heavenly Father kept His part of the bargain, and I'm trying to keep my part.

OAKLEY MOORE

Oakley was drafted into the United States Army June 11, 1943, at Fort Douglas, Utah, and trained as a field wireman at Camp Roberts, California, and Camp Maxey, Texas, in the 994th Infantry Division. He was supposed to land in France but the harbor at Le Harve, France, was completely blocked with sunken ships. He was diverted to England where he was put on a landing ship type vessel so that he could reach land. He was one of six soldiers assigned to ride on the top of a loaded ammunition truck.

As we proceeded to the front, heavy rain came down. Proceeding through France, the rains turned to snow and the temperature fell. Needless to say we were wet and extremely cold. In order to protect ourselves from the elements, we rearranged the ammunition boxes, making a hole in the center and covered ourselves with our rain ponchos. At midnight we stopped for a rest break, and our cooks had a large pot of coffee, which warmed us physically and mentally. We continued across France and into Belgium, moving higher and experiencing colder temperatures. Finally we reached the area where we would relieve another army unit. We moved temporarily to a side road and prepared to dig in to assume our new positions. The ground was frozen and we ended up sleeping on the road.

While waiting our turn to move up, we busied ourselves trying to keep warm. It was very foggy, and we could have open fires as long as we could see the next village, which was about two miles away. As soon as our fires were out, we froze again. We were not equipped for the cold weather; we did not have galoshes. We had ankle high shoes—not waterproofed—

and canvas leggings, which were frozen solid and very difficult to lace up. It was under those circumstances that we were introduced to German V-1 rockets.

In the fog we couldn't see what we were hearing. As those rockets approached us, they sounded just like a four-motor bomber, but as they passed over us, they sounded like all motors were failing and that they were going to crash. We kept listening but nothing. Later we saw them when the sun was shining. Then we understood. They were cigar shaped with wings and fire from the pulse jet blazing at the rear. We later found out that they were launched from railroad cars and were launched in pairs and flew at treetop height. They had to be launched at ignition speed, utilizing a catapult.

EDMOND MORGAN JR.

After his basic training, Ed elected to join the Army's airborne unit and become a paratrooper. He said that his first jump wasn't so bad, but on the second one, he knew what was coming. In fall 1944, he sailed to Europe on the Queen Mary. *On Christmas Day 1944, his unit entered the war at Reims, France. After considerable ground fighting, his unit was flown over Germany where they parachuted into battle.*

We looked down from the plane and saw a river. As soon as we got across the river, the lieutenant in charge told us to stand up. We stood and checked out our equipment one last time. There was a cable called a static line that ran the full length of the airplane. We hooked onto that cable and stood near the door ready to go. We had a C-46 (airplane) on that jump, which meant we had two rows of men. The plane had two doors, one on each side. Men went out both doors at the same time. . . . It took thirty seconds to put forty-five men

Paratrooper Edmond Morgan, Jr., checks a building for German soldiers.

into the air. You can imagine how fast we poured out of that airplane.

We jumped over Germany near the little town of Wesel in the province of Westphalia…. We saw many farms scattered around on the flat land.

We jumped right on top of them. They could see us in the air and a lot of guys died in the air. It took a bit of doing to clean them out of there. Usually we'd set up a machine gunner or post a rifleman who would pick a point where he figured a German might be and blast away with machine guns, automatic rifles, or mortars. Those mortars were murder. Men couldn't hear them coming; they'd just drop right down their shirt pockets. They were terrible.

We got on big British Churchill tanks and rode them for four or five days and nights. We went racing across Germany. We'd go like crazy until we'd come to a roadblock the Germans had set up. They usually set a couple of cannons on either end and infantry in between; then they'd blast away at our tanks coming up the road. We'd come to one of those, and we'd split and go around to the other end. When we got to the end, we'd pile off the tank and come right down the line killing or capturing Germans—whatever we had to do to clean out the roadblock. Then we would get on the tanks and head down the road again.

QUENTIN C. MURDOCK

Quentin served as a combat infantryman in the First Infantry Division. He served in Africa and Italy, as well as experiencing firsthand the horrors of the D-Day invasion of Normandy.

I had always wondered why I was permitted to live while most of my comrades were killed. One night after about fifteen years of wondering (after the war was over), a very loud and unmistakable voice woke me from a very sound sleep. It bounced me clear out of bed. The voice said, "It was your mother's prayers that saved you." That voice was so real that I no longer wondered how come I was able to survive. I had a very special mother. Since that time, I have tried much harder to be what she wanted me to be.

The War in Africa

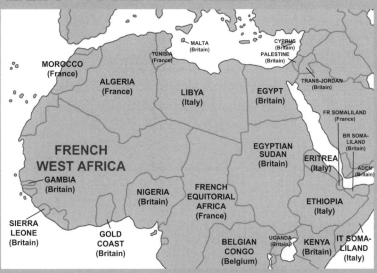

When World War II began, the nations of Europe had vast areas of the globe under colonial rule. France, Italy, and Great Britain controlled most of northern Africa. When France fell to the Germans in 1940, Germany gained control of what is now Algeria, Tunisia, and Morocco. The Allies had to first remove the Germans and Italians from Africa in order to defeat the Axis forces on the continent of Europe.

Lt. Quentin Murdock at the end of the Sicilian Campaign, 1945. Following the defeat of German forces in north Africa, the Allies advanced across the Mediterranean Sea to the islands off the Italian Coast. The capture of Sicily led to the death of Mussolini and the fall of Italy's Fascist government.

REED E. NILSEN

While in college, Reed joined the Navy program for potential officers. After graduating he was assigned to training school where he learned how to command a landing craft tank which carried heavy equipment and troops onto the beach. He participated in the D-Day invasion in this capacity, landing on Omaha Beach.

I was the commanding officer of another officer and a crew of eight men. In my craft was a baily bridge that the Army would use to cross the rivers in France, thirty-six of General Patton's men, and a truck loaded with ammunition. We crossed over to France to Omaha Beach on D-Day. We were about an hour as we moved up to go onto the beach. We couldn't see any of our soldiers alive on the beach. Almost all the soldiers and landing craft had been blown up. Just as we were to go in, the commanding officer on the cruiser *Augustus*, stopped us and sent three destroyers in front of us, and they blasted the entire face of the butte on the beach. We were then sent in, and an 88-millimeter shell landed near us in the water and the concussion knocked all of us flat on the deck. No one was hurt and we continued into the beach. When the tide went out, we had to pull bodies of our soldiers out from under our craft. For almost three days we had to pick up bodies, and they were loaded on trucks and taken to be buried.

Lt. Reed Nilsen.

ARTHUR K. NISHIMOTO

As a lifelong U.S. citizen of Japanese ancestry, Arthur experienced the challenge that faced this group of people during the war years. Yet, in spite of the prejudice and bigotry, he along with many others volunteered for duty. He was assigned to the famous 442nd Regimental Combat Team. This group was composed of Japanese-Americans who fought with honor in the European Theater.

During our training there were the inevitable few American soldiers (white Americans) who screamed to the high heavens about the "damned Japs." As surely as one of them opened his mouth, he found a hard brown fist in it. For the one thing we would not tolerate was to be called "Japs." We lived as Americans, thought as Americans, had traveled thousands of miles to fight for our county, and we asked to be treated as equals.

* * * * *

During the latter part of October and first week of November our "Mormon Boys" decided to take leave to Salt Lake City for a visit since none of us had been there before. We left for our "mission." There were several in our group who wanted to be baptized at the Tabernacle. We were housed by members we had known when they were serving as missionaries in the Hawaiian Islands. We were welcomed and pleasantly surprised by their kind and gracious hospitality. Our short duration for a week or so was filled with interesting, joyous, and spiritual activities.

Roy Tsuya for instance won the "grand prize" when he and Wuta Terazawa, a former missionary who had served in Hawaii, decided to be married only a few hours after they met. It was "love at first sight," according to Roy and Wuta. Without question they knew it was right and were married "for time and for all eternity" in the Salt Lake Temple. He told me, "it was nine days after we met, we were married on Thursday, November 4, 1943, at the Salt Lake Temple by Elder John A. Widtsoe of the Council of Twelve."

I arrived in Salt Lake City a few days after they were married, and they met me at the Union Station with Wuta flashing me her wedding ring. I thought it was a joke because before the boys left, I had made arrangements for all of us to be housed at Wuta's home. Well, I soon found that it was for real. They have now been married for sixty years since that miraculous occasion.

Shortly after the Japanese attacked Pearl Harbor, President Roosevelt signed one of the darkest documents in our nation's history. Executive Order 9066 called for all persons of Japanese heritage living in the United States to be confined to internment camps.

EXECUTIVE ORDER NO. 9066

AUTHORIZING THE SECRETARY OF WAR TO PRESCRIBE MILITARY AREAS Executive Order No. 9066

WHEREAS the successful prosecution of the war requires every possible protection against espionage and against sabotage to national-defense material, national-defense premises, and national-defense utilities as defined in section 4, Act of April 20, 1918, 40 Stat. 533, as amended by the act of November 30, 1940, 54 Stat. 1220, and the Act of August 21, 1941, 55 Stat. 655 (U. S. C., Title 50, Sec. 104):

NOW, THEREFORE, by virtue of the authority vested in me as President of the United States, and Commander in Chief of the Army and Navy, I hereby authorize and direct the Secretary of War, and the Military Commanders whom he may from time to time designate, whenever he or any designated Commander deems such actions necessary or desirable, to prescribe military areas in such places and of such extent as he or the appropriate Military Commanders may determine, from which any or all persons may be excluded, and with such respect to which, the right of any person to enter, remain in, or leave shall be subject to whatever restrictions the Secretary of War or the appropriate Military Commander may impose in his discretion. The Secretary of War is hereby authorized to provide for residents of any such area who are excluded therefrom, such transportation, food, shelter, and other accommodations as may be necessary, in the judgement of the Secretary of War or the said Military Commander, and until other arrangements are made, to accomplish the purpose of this order. The designation of military areas in any region or locality shall supersede designations of prohibited and restricted areas by the Attorney General under the Proclamations of December 7 and 8, 1941, and shall supersede the responsibility and authority of the Attorney General under the said Proclamations in respect of such prohibited and restricted areas.

I hereby further authorize and direct the Secretary of War and the said Military Commanders to take such other steps as he or the appropriate Military Commander may deem advisable to enforce compliance with the restrictions applicable to each Military area hereinabove authorized to be designated, including the use of Federal troops and other Federal Agencies, with authority to accept assistance of state and local agencies.

I hereby further authorize and direct all Executive Departments, independent establishments and other Federal Agencies, to assist the Secretary of War or the said Military Commanders in carrying out this Executive Order, including the furnishing of medical aid, hospitalization, food, clothing, transportation, use of land, shelter, and other supplies, equipment, utilities, facilities and services.

This order shall not be construed as modifying or limiting in any way the authority heretofore granted under Executive Order No. 8972, dated December 12, 1941, nor shall it be construed as limiting or modifying the duty and responsibility of the Federal Bureau of Investigation, with respect to the investigation of alleged acts of sabotage or the duty and responsibility of the Attorney General and the Department of Justice under the Proclamations of December 7 and 8, 1941, prescribing regulations for the conduct and control of alien enemies, except as such duty and responsibility is superseded by the designation of military areas hereunder.

FRANKLIN D. ROOSEVELT
February 19, 1942

Another wonderful spiritual experience we enjoyed was when Tommy Horikami, Ramon Wasano, Tsugio Watanabe, and Tetsuo Yanagida were baptized at the Tabernacle during our short stay there.

I had a most enjoyable and memorable time too. Someone had arranged for me to receive my patriarchal blessing from the Patriarch to the Church, Patriarch Joseph F. Smith. Soon after that, I was ushered into President George Albert Smith's (President of the Quorum of the Twelve) office, who conferred the Melchizedek Priesthood and ordained me to the office of elder. I could not have been a happier young man, for I knew what my immediate future would be. I was going into combat, and I needed the blessings of the priesthood.

While there, several of us were invited to Emma Lucy Gates Bowen's home, wife of Apostle Albert E. Bowen of the Council of Twelve, for brunch. What a lovely and gracious hostess she was. Not only did she feed us well, but she also sang and entertained us with her beautiful voice. She was Utah's beloved songstress and a granddaughter of President Brigham Young.

We all had a most wonderful leave and departed for our camp in Mississippi.

442nd Regimental Combat Team

Perhaps one of the least known but most courageous stories to come out of WW II is that of the 442nd Regimental Combat Team. This unit was made up entirely of Japanese-Americans who had either been interned in camps due to EO 9066, or had family members who were still in the camps while they were out fighting and dying for the very liberties that were denied them. These men served with honor and valor. They felt they had something to prove. They had to be more "American" than the white troops, or they would not earn the respect they deserved. One of the most decorated units in the war, the 442 Regimental Combat Team came to be called "The Purple Heart Battalion," due to the high number of casualties suffered. Their motto was "Go For Broke."

* * * * *

On June 26, 1944, we went into our initial combat. The objective was to overtake the city of Belvedere. We met fierce enemy resistance, but finally were able to gain victory. The battle of Belvedere was an outstanding American victory in the Rome to the Arno River campaign. That was my "baptism by fire." The next battle was among all days on July 4, 1944, for Hill 140, a major German stronghold well entrenched on top of the hill looking down at us. Prior to attacking Hill 140, we were passing through a little village and were resting alongside the road when we heard enemy jeeps approaching us. We could not believe our eyes when we saw three jeeps with approximately a dozen German soldiers coming directly where we were. We immediately hid ourselves alongside the road, and when the first jeep came close to us, Sergeant Fred Ida who was at the head of the column halted them, and the rest of us jumped out on the road with our guns fixed on them.

All three jeeps came to a screeching stop. The soldiers were alarmed that we were there. They perhaps thought the village was not occupied by the Americans. They immediately put their hands up to surrender, but one of them held a machine pistol in his hand as he raised it, and another jumped out of one of the jeeps and tried to make a run for it and that signaled us to open fire. I don't remember how many were killed, but we did take those that were alive as prisoners.

I well remember one of the German soldiers who was shot was wounded severely. It was my first real close encounter with the enemy. Seeing him wounded and suffering, with sympathy in my heart, I thought I would put him out of his misery by one last bullet. My weapon was a .45-caliber submachine gun, and I did not want to use such a heavy weapon, so I asked one of the men to lend me his .30-caliber M1 rifle. I took careful aim standing above him and was about to pull the trigger when all of a sudden a strong feeling came over me with the thought: who am I to judge whether I should put him out of his misery or not. I could not pull the trigger. He soon died. I definitely learned a great lesson.

WAYNE W. OTTLEY

Wayne kept a notebook diary during his experience as a gunner on a B-17 bomber. He recorded the details of each mission and his feelings during those experiences. His entry regarding the one time he had contact with the Church demonstrates his appreciation for that moment in the war.

I took a forty-eight-hour pass and traveled to Birmingham to attend an LDS conference. That was my only contact with the Church during my five months in England. I arrived in the evening and found housing at the YMCA where I met other American and English military members of the Church.

On Saturday morning we played basketball in the rented hall where the conference would be held. An afternoon meeting was held to get acquainted and a dance was held in the evening.

Since there were no General Authorities in the country at that time, the conference was directed by a local English, Russian-born brother, Andre Anastasion. (He and his family immigrated to Utah after the war.)

I found the procedures a little different than I was used to at home, but I was comforted to know that I had at least one opportunity to attend a gathering with other Saints.

Tech. Sgt. Wayne W. Ottley.

Role of Media

Throughout World War II, the role of the media in bringing news of the conflict to those at home was crucial. During the war, overseas war correspondents (which numbered as many as 1,000 persons in Europe alone) were subject to strict censorship by military authorities. Included in the list of censored material were matters considered to be of national security, pictures which too graphically displayed American casualties, incidents of Allied cowardice, or other acts of embarrassment. As advanced technology assisted the media in speed and improved medium, the media found itself playing an even more significant role in the war (John W. Chambers, ed. *The Oxford Companion to American Military History* New York: Oxford University Press, 1999).

HEINZ RAHDE

Heinz was fifteen when he was drafted into the German Army. His whole school class was called up at that time with their teacher appointed as their leader. Below is a personal account of some of his experiences as told to Sandra Stallings in 1986.

From the beginning of the war, I constantly prayed for guidance. I told the Lord that I would do anything I could to be in the right place, but if my foresight was not adequate for the situation I would beg Him to help me. I told Him I would accept the guiding thoughts He would plant in my heart without questioning.

My classmates and I were stationed near Hannover. Every month or so our unit of about three hundred people would get together. Usually there was a unit party, and everyone would be drinking and smoking—except me. I didn't know it at first, but our commander in chief watched me during these parties. One day he called me in and asked me why I didn't smoke or drink. I was a little shy, and I told him that I just didn't believe in it. I think I was the only one who didn't smoke or drink in the whole outfit, and I was the only Latter-day Saint.

"There must be a specific reason why you don't do that," he continued questioning me. I told him it was better for the body to abstain from those things, and I tried to evade the question a little bit. When I was fifteen, it was not so easy when people laughed at me and said I was not a man if I didn't smoke and drink. My fellow soldiers had made fun of me quite often, and my commander had heard that.

"You're a Mormon, aren't you?"

"Yes, I am."

"Why didn't you tell me that?" he asked.

"I'm a little shy," I explained. "You've seen what kind of reaction the others have."

"Well, that might change if you just tell them," he replied. One night we were all sitting at a big table at a party, and everyone was drinking, except me. I think I had a pop that I had bought downtown. My commanding officer was watching me again.

He stood and said, "Rahde, get up." Then he said to the whole group, "I would like to inform you that Rahde is a Mormon. He doesn't drink, and he doesn't smoke. And I would like you to respect that. If I see anybody making fun of him because of that, I will put him in jail."

I was shocked. I turned red because everyone was looking at me. Then he said, "From now on, Rahde, it is your job to take care of these men and see that when they go downtown and have too much to drink they find their way home."

From that minute on I had a lot of groups that wanted me to go with them. They took me to their beer joints and said, "No drinks for Heinz. He doesn't drink, and he has to take us home."

I didn't have to mention anything anymore. I had more friends that way than I would have had any other way. Nothing could have done more good for me than this frankness, as my wise commanding officer had sensed. It was a testimony to me that the others trusted me so much that whenever something came up they always asked me to go with them, and they protected me.

* * * * *

Prayer had been my mainstay. At times it was all I had. I prayed for guidance all the time and received a very peaceful feeling that everything would be all right, and it proved to be true. I don't think a day passed by that I didn't tell the Lord I loved Him. During the war I had feelings of love in my heart. I didn't have feelings of hate. I think for that reason the Lord spared my life. I stayed in tune with Him. I knew that if I kept His commandments and was worthy to receive His guidance, He would protect me. And He did.

Hitler Youth

In mid-1944, Hitler decreed that twenty-five divisions must be ready to counterattack the Allies by November. To facilitate this, Germany scoured the prisons and schools to find men—and often boys—to fill the ranks. This new force was thrust into the thick of the conflicts, including the Battle of the Bulge in December 1944.

FOSTER D. RAPPLEYE

Foster served in the Army Air Corps as a radio operator on a B-17 bomber. During a routine bombing mission, Foster's plane was shot down over Greece. After parachuting to safety, he was cared for by members of the Greek resistance.

We flew down the east coast of Italy along the Adriatic Sea. When we reached the peninsula, commonly referred to as the heel of Italy, I looked out the window on the right and saw the Gulf of Taranto. On the left I saw the Strait of Otranto. I was impressed that the peninsula was so narrow that by flying down the middle I could see clear across it. We soon left it behind and flew over the Ionian Sea to Greece's Peloponnese Peninsula.

The sky was heavily overcast with almost zero visibility. All of a sudden something struck us. It wasn't antiaircraft; we were still one hundred miles from our target. I looked out the window. Number three engine was on fire! I turned and looked at the waist gunner. He looked at me, but neither of us spoke. We couldn't move; it felt as if we were stuck to the floor. I said a little prayer, "Lord, I'm supposed to live through this war, remember?"

He answered, "Yes, but I didn't say you wouldn't get a little adventure." I understood then that my chance to survive was not lost.

Then suddenly the pressure came off, and we were able to move. We both scrambled for the door. I let him go first, but I didn't wait for him to pull the cable to release the door. I saw a big hole where the tail used to be and dove out headfirst. I had no sensation of falling; I just felt a terrific wind in my face. I pulled my rip cord; the chute opened, and I swung into a sitting position under my parachute. "Now for a ride down to the ground," I thought. Then I felt a jolt. I was on the ground, my chute draped over a scrub cedar. I pulled it off, scratched a hole with my fingernails, tore out a piece for a souvenir, and buried the rest as I had been instructed.

I looked around. I had landed on a hillside a hundred yards or so from the top. I thought of climbing to the top to look around. Then I heard someone approaching. It was Ogens, the photographer on my plane. He had talked to the navigator and learned that we were on Mount Erimanthos. I suggested that we go back to the navigator and find out which was the best direction to travel. We started out but we heard someone approaching. We tried to hide—too late. It was Greek people coming to rescue us.

ALDEN P. RIGBY

As a P-51 Mustang pilot, Alden earned a Silver Star for exhibiting a zealous fighting spirit and exceptional bravery. He named his plane Eleen and Jerry *after his wife and daughter waiting at home.*

Sunday was a rather lonesome day for me. I wrote my wife Eleen that it would still be "our day" for special thoughts and an exercise in faith for us. We did have Protestant services available on base, as well as Catholic. But I knew that London would be the only place for an LDS branch. I had not found any members on base, except Wilcox.

We did fly that day. Three of us went up to about fifteen thousand feet and practiced cross-over turns in line abreast formation, as well as real close formation. The close formation would very soon be a part of each flight, and was a necessity because of time, field, and airspace limitations. My landing on the grass field was better than my first flight, and perhaps better than many that followed. Having to use the brakes to stop before the fence and trees would be a new and normal procedure. There were no taxi strips on the field, so getting back to

Alden Rigby with his plane Eleen and Jerry.

the parking ramp was fast and simple. The restricted visibility in a three-point position and the long nose still presented the taxi problem. Taking off with the full fuselage tank on this flight was new to me. Using the fuel from that tank first, down to about thirty gallons would be the routine procedure and would give the plane the best weight balance. Full fuel and ammunition required full throttle to get airborne on that field.

Most of the pilots had their own aircraft assigned. Names were painted on the cowling, which looked fantastic. I knew that it would be quite sometime before I would get my own, but that was something big to look forward to. In the meantime, I flew what was left over. We called them "war weary birds," but they were well maintained.

* * * * *

One of my missions was supposed to have been a long haul, escorting the bombers to Merseburg. The box (a formation of B-17 bombers) we were supposed to escort could not make it through all of the weather so we found another string of B-17s on a shorter run to Cologne. After seeing them safely off the target, we dropped down to twelve thousand feet, but could not draw any enemy fighters up. The weather in the area was good enough to look for ground targets, so we split up for the trip back to England.

The Whole Nine Yards

This saying came into existence during World War II. It is a reference to the ammunition belts that were used in the fighter planes during the early part of the war. The belts were nine yards long, and when pilots were out of ammunition, the saying was that they had used "the whole nine yards." This expression is still in use today.

The events of the next hour taught me a great lesson, but almost too late. By all reasonable standards I should have "bought the farm" twice—the farm phrase, being a polite reference to getting killed. My first near fatal mistake was to strafe a most inviting train target in an open field. My hasty decision was to strafe it lengthwise beginning with the engine. As I lined up, I could see the sides of the boxcars drop down and guns come out. I now knew it was a trap, but I was committed and could not give them a bigger target by turning away. I continued my firing until about halfway down the train when I was hit in the canopy and windshield. I also knew I had taken hits elsewhere. I stayed as low as I could until past the train. Then being in a rather desperate situation, I decided that I needed to get some altitude. In the few seconds it took to get some three thousand feet, I had time to survey some of the damage. The plane responded normally, despite the unnerving hole in my Plexiglas canopy and the shattered windshield. The instruments were still in the green so my immediate thoughts of having to bail out were put on hold. I was hoping that I could get a few miles closer to our front lines before that happened. The two holes in my right wing were less than six inches from my almost-full ammunition bay. I was too preoccupied to realize just how close I had come to being history.

My wing man had broken away from the train in a different direction. He had been hit, but not to the extent I had. As I made my climbing turn to the west, I could see a plane that had to be him, and told him to join up while I continued my turn. I was beginning to relax a little since the engine apparently had not been damaged, and I would soon have a wing man for some added security. My forward visibility was limited because of the shattered glass, but the hole just behind me through the canopy did not pose a problem, except to my shattered nerves.

My next look back to check the position of my wing man brought a scene that I will not forget in this lifetime. The anticipated P-51 turned out to be a German FW 190, some forty to fifty yards behind me, and in perfect firing position. I was still in a shallow turn and presented the perfect target. To say that I was foolish, angry, shocked, and in distress would be the understatement of my fast fading career. To know that the enemy had caught me in such a stupid situation, with two 20-millimeter cannons and two 13-millimeter machine guns at such close range was terrifying to say the least. I can say that there was little time to be afraid or panic. The decision on what I had to do had been made months earlier in training. My only chance for survival was to violently tighten my turn and hope that I could somehow get out of his gun sight. I could no longer worry about the mechanical condition of my plane by keeping reduced power. The response of my aircraft to the abrupt turn surprised me and perhaps even the German pilot. More power and lowering the flaps fifteen degrees made for a very tight turn. After about two complete 360-degree turns, I could see (and feel) that he no longer had the lead necessary (in his gun sight) to shoot me down. After another two turns I was gaining some advantage, and felt it was only a matter of time until I had him in my sights.

The next worry was whether my guns would still function after the hits I had taken earlier. Another problem was the very distorted gun sight on my broken windshield. I did not have the chance to find out on either since the German broke off and headed for the nearby cloud cover. My chances of finding him were almost nil, and at that point I could not take another chance so I again headed west. My guardian angel had been busy, and it was time for both of us to relax a little.

I still had about thirty minutes over enemy territory, which was not the best position to be in alone and in a damaged aircraft. I was very alert to anything behind me, and with the plane running smoothly, I was getting the feeling of possible survival. I had even given the bailing out option less consideration.

It was very soon decision time again. I was now beginning to think that England might be possible. I had crossed the English Channel a couple of times alone before, but this was different. I was thinking that if I landed at an Allied base on the continent, I might be there for days waiting for repairs, or they might declare my older "war weary" P-51 as finished. It was one of a very few left with the camouflaged painting. By the time I reached the coastline, I had radio contact with Bodney, and they reported the weather to be good. My decision to "go for it" may not have been the best, but it proved to be much better than a couple I had made an hour or so earlier. It was only another thirty minutes to the big "grass pasture" that had never looked so good. I felt like celebrating with a low pass, but did not want to press my luck further. The quiet landing ended perhaps my most anxious and terrifying mission. My detailed report to the intelligence officer provided some information on what I thought to be the new long-nosed German FW 190. My friends were glad to see me, but took full advantage of ribbing me about my somewhat innocent and foolish mistakes. My response was, "It could have ruined my whole afternoon." To this day, I do not know why the German pilot did not blast me out of the sky. I do have my own firm conviction as to why I was allowed to live, fly, and fight again.

Perhaps this would be the time to share part of a very important document in my life. This document is my patriarchal blessing, given November 17, 1942. . . . I will quote only one paragraph that had a special meaning during this specific time in my life: "The Lord shall give unto thee a choice daughter of Zion, who shall become the mother of thy *children*, and *they* shall call thee blessed Father because of *their* birth under the covenant, made possible by thy temple marriage." I knew that I had a choice daughter of Zion and a daughter, Jerralyn. Other children were to come, and this of course gave me confidence and great hope for the future. Other promises of the blessing have since become a reality, with others still to come.

I have, at least since marriage, been convinced that each person comes to this life with a mission. This part of my life was perhaps a little difficult to understand as being a part of the plan for me. Looking back, I can see that perhaps the war might even have been a necessary evil in that part of the world. I trust that we will some day better understand wars from the very beginning.

DAVID RIRIE

It was a sad day for David when he left his home to enter the Army Air Corps. His dad said to him, "I sure hate to see you go, but I would have hated it more if you had been unwilling to go." His training prepared him to be a bombardier assigned to the 388th Bomb Group stationed in England. He was shot down on his first mission and spent the rest of the war in a POW camp.

First Lt. David Ririe.

Upon reaching Posen we found it to be covered with clouds so we turned and headed back. The pilot became very angry as the leaders quarreled about which secondary target to bomb. Rostock, a seaport in north Germany on the Baltic, was chosen. As we approached it, we were picked up by antiaircraft batteries, and that time they were uncomfortably accurate. It was a tracing kind in which four shots followed each other in a straight-line pattern. Two shots exploded in front of us, and I held my breath in anticipation of three and four. The third shot raised the tail of our airplane, and as the pieces of metal pierced our fuselage, it sounded like gravel being thrown on a tin roof. The tail gunner reported that the tail was riddled but that he was uninjured. Then we lost an engine, which made it difficult

David Ririe's B-17 crew (L to R) Front Row: Ed Ely, pilot; Fred Pratt, copilot; William Ellis, navigator; David Ririe, bombardier. Back Row: Leo Kornoelly, flight engineer; Constantine Scourbys, gunner; John Russell, radio operator; Vincent Mussaletto, ball turret gunner; Harvey Ringer, waist gunner; Thomas Neal, tail gunner.

for us to maintain our close place in the formation. With relief we dropped our bombs and headed for home base. We flew out over the Baltic Sea. Things were quiet again. The navigator jubilantly announced that our escort was approaching us. Our good feeling was short-lived. One of the enemy planes came up from below us and fired a burst of bullets at us. I saw the plane, but apparently our belly turret gunner, who was the only one who could have fired at the enemy, didn't see him.

The plane started to burn in the radio room. Kornoelly grabbed our extinguisher and tried to put out the fire, but it was a hopeless effort, and we were commanded to bail out! The crew did so as quickly as possible, but the navigator and I were unable to open our escape hatch. A fire also was burning in the rear of our compartment, making it impossible to get to the back of the airplane. We were trapped. When the pilot was notified of our predicament he dived the ship toward the shore, which was some twenty miles distant. As we came over the coastline there was intense activity. Germans quickly took aim and fired at us with small arms. I gave them a burst as we flew over. We reached a low altitude and as the plane leveled out, the escape hatch fell open, but by then it was too late to parachute out. Bill and I were trying to extinguish the fire when Ely landed the plane.

It was a hard belly landing! We bounced around like rubber balls. Sensations of pain told me that my feet and ankles were injured. Actually both of my flying boots were taken off, as my feet were held firm while my body went the other direction. We came to a welcome, but painful stop. In terror Bill Ellis kicked and stomped the object that lay beneath him, which was me. He had panicked because the nose gun handles had come to rest neatly behind his neck and made him feel pinned in. He had a cut on his forehead, and both of us were bruised and scratched.

The copilot arrived and extracted us from the plane. An engine entirely detached from the ship could be seen a few yards from the plane, and the nose was so battered and broken that we stood up and were carried off. We didn't have to leave by a door or a window, as there were none left in our compartment of the plane. As Fred struggled to carry us, one on each arm from the plane, we heard the pilot call for help. Fred went back and pulled him from the window in which he had become stuck. We cleared the plane. One of them said, "We have company." We did all right—an entire troop of enemy soldiers yelling and bristling with guns. We had landed on a military reservation, and so we had no chance to escape.

* * * * *

I wrote a poem about my life in the service.

"ONE MISSION"

I'm a one-mission man
The Germans really did the trick
It must have been a plan
Of, theirs, to end my combat quick

They shot the old plane's engines out
On its first, unlikely trip
In fifteen minutes I found out
How twenty millimeters affect a ship

I spent ten days upon my base
London's lights I failed to see
I'd feel myself a sore disgrace
But for the others with me

I was going to finish twenty-five
Flights, of which to tell
I'll probably finish twenty-five
Months, long months of hell

I'm a one-mission man
Hungry, cold, and damp
It wasn't in my plan
To see a prison camp

LT. D. RIRIE, JULY 1945

* * * * *

On our first Sunday in the POW camp, Rocky and Al Strom and I went to church, which was conducted by a Protestant chaplain who had been captured in North Africa. Rocky was very unimpressed so the next day we went to every room in the compound and located all of the Mormon men. There were several of us: Robert McGregor of Salt Lake City, Blaine Harris of Soda Springs, Idaho, F. W. Betenson of Cedar City, Utah, and W. Rasmussen of Mount Pleasant, Utah, and Rocky and me. We arranged to meet in the room of Blaine Harris who was lucky enough to have been assigned to a double room. His navigator graciously agreed to vacate the room every Sunday for an hour or so, so we could hold Sunday School. Our first meeting was memorable. Rocky and I prepared the sacrament and with difficulty recalled the prayers. It was a task with no Church literature to assist us. Luckily Rocky, Blaine Harris, and I had had some experience, especially Robert Matheson (Rocky) who was a returned missionary. After an opening prayer, the sacrament, and a scripture reading from a library copy of the New Testament, we held a testimony meeting. Each man expressed thanks for his deliverance.

JOHN D. RUSSELL

John volunteered for the Army in February 1943 and was sent to Fort Douglas, Utah. They called for volunteers for the paratroops, and he was one of twelve hundred assigned to the 517th Parachute Regimental Combat Team to complete parachute training in Fort Benning, Georgia.

I was assigned to Headquarters Company, First Battalion of the 517th as a machine gunner. We grew together almost as brothers. After field maneuvers in Tennessee, we were shipped overseas to Naples, Italy, and were shortly introduced into combat at Civitavecchia, Italy. We were under fire for several days and lost several of our buddies. They were either wounded or killed. It was a sad and very scary ordeal.

* * * * *

We fought along side the 442nd Antitank Combat Team (NISEI), a combat team of Americans of Japanese descent, who were very fine and brave soldiers. Our German prisoners, when they saw the 442nd, asked how this could be. We told them Japan had surrendered, and they had joined us to defeat Hitler. They were very shaken by this news.

* * * * *

From that time on we were in combat in France, Belgium, and Germany. We made a combat jump into southern France in August 1944 and were in heavy combat in the Maritime Alps on the French-Italian border for ninety-four days without relief.

In December 1944 we were called to go to the Ardennes, the Battle of the Bulge in Belgium. We boarded trucks that drove us right into combat. We spent the next nine weeks in serious combat conditions. We lost many more men during these times. We went into Germany until the war ended in Europe. I had not missed a single day of combat during that time.

One time during some extremely hard fighting, there was a Sunday where we were free of fighting for part of the day. Two of my buddies from Utah asked me if I would like to go to church services with them. I was dumbfounded that these rough-tough guys would even mention church. Those two men spoke to us with such sincerity and in terms that really shocked me. Then they broke up K ration crackers into pieces and put them in a helmet and blessed them and passed them around; then passed around a canteen cup of water after they had blessed it. Then one by one all of the men there bore their testimonies to each other. I tried, unsuccessfully, to fight back tears. I found out they were Mormons. I knew very little about that religion, but I had in my mind to find out more about it.

*　*　*　*　*

I had gone to school in Council, Idaho, and one of the girls in my class, Betty Jeppson, was LDS. When the war was over, Betty and I dated for a couple of weeks and were soon married. Part of that courtship was again attending a sacrament meeting and feeling the same spirit I had felt before. I joined the Church and later we took our children to the temple to be sealed together as a family. I bear testimony that joining the Church was one of the best decisions I ever made.

A soldier repairing a jeep. The World War II Jeep derived its name from the abbreviation of the term "general-purpose vehicle." It was a well-built and relatively high-powered, all-purpose vehicle that could be mass-produced for the war. Its top speed was 65 mph, and its four-wheel-drive system could carry six persons or a load of half a ton over difficult terrain. The Jeep proved valuable for a wide variety of military purposes.

CALVIN RYNEARSON

Calvin served as a forward observer and radio operator during the European campaign. He landed on Utah Beach on D-Day and marched across Europe, seeing the end of the war in Germany.

We were somewhere in Belgium. We had dug in foxholes and set up our field switchboard in the side of the foxhole and had our phone lines hooked into the switchboard. I was assigned to the switchboard during the day. The fellow who slept in the foxhole by day took over the switchboard at night and relieved me for meals, etc.

One particular day when he came to relieve me for lunch, I told him I wasn't hungry and would skip lunch. As he left I heard a voice say, "Go to lunch." I turned to see who had said that, but only one other fellow was there. I asked him if he had told me to go to lunch. He said he had not said anything. So I turned back to the switchboard. I again heard a voice say, "Go to lunch." I turned around and no one was there, so I hollered to my relief man and told him I guess I had better go eat.

He said, "Make up your mind."

I said, "Yes, I will go eat." I grabbed my mess kit and headed for the kitchen truck, it being across the field and up at the other end. As I got to the truck I heard the whine of an incoming shell. It was the only one we heard so we went about eating our lunch, and then I went back to the switchboard. It was out of business. That shell I had heard landed about two feet from the foxhole and the side of the switchboard, cutting every line coming into it. If I had been sitting at that board as I usually was, I would not be writing this account.

KENNETH W. SCHUBERT

Kenneth, a Canadian, served as a bombardier aboard a Halifax bomber assigned to destroy railroad targets. Like other Canadian and British airmen he flew many missions before the United States entered the war. During his final mission his plane was shot down over Belgium. He was fortunate to be found by local citizens who hid him from German soldiers. They did this at great peril to their own lives. His account demonstrates his appreciation for his fellow airmen and the kindness shown him by his Belgian friends.

As it turned out that night there was no haze and there was the biggest moon I had ever seen. Shortly after the bombing we were attacked by an enemy fighter. Being so low we could take very little evasive action and soon had two engines on fire and fire in the aircraft. At about twelve hundred feet the pilot ordered the crew to bail out. He did not get out and was killed in the crash. In John 15:13 we read that Jesus said, "Greater love hath no man than this, that a man lay down his life for his friends." Our pilot did just that when he saved our six lives and lost his own. When we landed, we were scattered over about twenty miles. The wireless air gunner and I were not captured, but the other four were taken prisoner.

RAF Halifax bomber crew waiting for assignment. No. 431 Squadron, Croft. "Waiting to go was the worst part of it." Serious faces and one forced smile characterize these aircrew members as they await transport to their Halifaxes. (L to R) Sgt. J. Cooke, Sgt. W. Berry, Sgt. C. Bull, Warrant Officer W. J. MacStocker, Flying Officer K. Schubert, Flying Officer H. Pond, Flying Officer D. King, and Warrant Officer A. M. Casey.

When I landed, a Belgian farmer, who had been awakened by the gun battle, came across the field where I was trying to bury my chute. After some conversation in sign language, he took me home. He had a meager house and little food. He had a wife, three daughters, and a son. They took me in as part of their family and shared all they had. They were in constant danger with me there, as the Gestapo was constantly searching for me. These good people would have been shot for harboring me if I had been found. I was with them for four months and came to appreciate and love them dearly. They also were ready to lay down their life for a friend.

To evade the Gestapo I often hid in the attic, where I sat and unstitched my parachute and Mae West (life jacket). The material was stuffed into pillows and after the war was made into dresses for the three daughters.

Kenneth Schubert with the Belgian family that hid him from the German patrols.

One day I was in the backyard and heard the father and mother excitedly speaking in loud tones in the front of the house. I immediately headed for the field to hide, as I could not make it to the attic. I realized it was a wide-open area with no hiding spot available. So I immediately entered the goat shed, a small six-by-seven-foot square room in the work shed, where I squeezed myself in the corner near the door. When I entered, the goat had remained quiet, although she had never been a great friend of mine. Since then I hold all goats in high esteem as she, no doubt, saved me and my family from the Gestapo.

When the Canadian Army came through the area, I was able to contact them and was flown back to Britain. I was eventually returned to Canada. Our squadron had taken heavy losses in 1943 and 1944, having lost 72 Halifax bombers, and out of 490 aircrews, 313 had died in action, 54 were missing, 105 had been taken prisoner, and 18 were returned safely after being shot down. I was one of the lucky ones.

Canadians in the War

It has often been a much-overlooked fact that Canada was actually involved in the war long before the United States committed. Throughout this book, there are many accounts of Canadians who served with courage and honor when their country called.

ARTUR SCHWIERMANN

As a sixteen-year-old member of the Church, Artur was drafted into the German Army and trained to serve in an antiaircraft unit. When the war ended, he was placed in a Soviet prison camp.

It took weeks before we arrived in Brest, a former Polish city occupied by the Russians, which had shifted their boundaries westward. Our camp was located on the outskirts of the city and consisted of a bare field surrounded by a wire fence and four observation towers equipped with searchlights and machine guns. For a place to sleep we dug holes, lined them with cement, and used burlap sacks as a cover. At the onset of winter, we were exposed to snow and ice which caused great misery. The kitchen was very primitive, but since our food did not require much preparation it did not matter. Three times a day we received soup or, in other words, warm water and a slice of bread. If we would have found a mouse in the soup it would have added at least some protein. The bread was handed out in loaves, and it was up to us to cut and divide it. After the bread was sliced, a blindfolded person called out our names while someone else pointed to the bread. That was our way of making sure that no one would be short-changed; still everybody felt he had received the smallest portion and had been cheated. There was no trust among the men, and friend would turn against friend for a crumb of bread. Since the only water in the well was typhoid infested, it was off limits. The Russians used this water only for the laundry. Instead of water, the prisoners received coffee. Not knowing that the Russian people were drinkers, the Americans had shipped enormous amounts of coffee to Russia. To the delight of the prisoners, the coffee was a daily treat except for me. I was determined to adhere to the Word of Wisdom. At night, I filled my canteen with the contaminated water and put my trust in the Lord.

* * * * *

In preparation to ensure the smooth transfer of German spoil, Brest was designated as the point of entry. Prisoners of the war and Russians alike erected a network of rails and loading docks. It was back-breaking work. We moved the earth manually and, regardless of weather conditions, had to be on the job in excess of twelve hours each day. The prisoners were divided in groups of twelve. Each group was called a brigade and headed by a former German sergeant or officer. We were assigned a certain amount of work daily. Only after completing the job were we permitted to return to the camp or, in other words, the designated hole in the ground. The work was very hard, the food just enough to stay alive, and the weather cold. By the middle of September 1945 we saw the first snowfall. Our clothing was insufficient. We were without coats, gloves, or hats. We wrapped paper and burlap sacks around our hands and feet and made masks to protect our faces. We checked each other for frostbite and, if the flesh turned white, rubbed that part of the body with snow.

By December, five hundred of the one thousand prisoners had died. My weight had dropped from 145 to 95 pounds. It was in my favor that I was young, tough, and endowed with a tremendous faith in God. My daily conversations with the Lord gave me great strength. Instead of quarreling as most of the men did and doubting that there was a God in heaven who allowed such inequities, I thought of the Russian men who had spent years in German camps and of their struggle for survival. Each morning at roll call we were asked to report the number of prisoners who had died during the night. If the number was ten, the guards made the comment that it should have been twenty. I thought about my loved ones all the time and wondered if mother and Wilma had survived the war since I did not know if they were alive. Unfortunately, my question was not answered until years later.

RAYMOND J. SHALLBETTER

Raymond entered the Army as a private first class. As a participant in the Battle of the Bulge, he experienced the cold reality of war.

It wasn't that I was afraid to die; I had faced death several times before. I knew that if I should die before this war was through, all was well. I just didn't want to die at that time though. I had a wonderful, loving, eternal companion at home and my firstborn son who wasn't even a year old. I had only held him in my arms a few times. Besides, I wanted more sons and daughters. That was enough of a reason to offer a supplication and plea to be sustained. I just had to survive this night, and the only way was to stay alert. I began to recall all my blessings, my goodly parents, my brothers and sisters, and my wife and baby, to stay awake. I recalled all the good times we had enjoyed and the love we shared. I thought of my mission in California, my companions, and I reviewed the gospel, its fullness, and what it meant to me. I soon felt warm inside and knew things would be all right.

Raymond and George D. Shallbetter, brothers. Raymond is on the left.

BERNELL SHARP

Upon graduating from bomber flight school, Bernell and his fellow airmen "picked up" a new B-17 bomber fresh from the factory. Their responsibilities included checking out the plane and flying the maiden voyage to England via Iceland. As the chief engineer for B-17 bombers, Bernell flew many successful missions before being assigned bombing runs in support of the D-Day invasion.

Bernell Sharp.

Usually they called about four o'clock to go fly. At midnight we knew something was up because it was midnight. In fact I was sitting on the bed with my shoe in my hand. . . . I was just going to bed when he came in and said fly. So we found out it was D-Day. . . . We were eager to fly.

We were scheduled for four missions that day. It was such bad weather we only flew two. . . . We got over the coast and there were hundreds of ships. We could see the beaches. See, I'm emotional about it after fifty years because that day thousands of American, British, and French soldiers died.

As we flew over, it was very cloudy, and we could barely see the beach with the landing infantry and landing tanks pulled up on the beach. We could see the gunfire the battleships were still firing. As we got over our target, which was a little ways in from the beach, behold there was an opening in the clouds right where we were supposed to bomb. Just like the Lord knew where we needed it. So we dropped our bombs and headed back.

LYNN G. SLEIGHT

Lynn piloted a light bomber assigned to an airfield outside of Paris. He flew missions over France and Germany until V-E Day.

I was brought up believing that following LDS standards would someday show to my advantage. This was demonstrated during my fifth month in the United States Army in World War II. I was just getting started in the pipeline to become an army pilot, but I had to pass through the Classification Center in San Antonio, Texas. There were several weeks of aptitude tests, which defined whether my training would be as pilot, navigator, or bombardier. My aim was to go to pilot training. During the days or weeks of waiting, we were kept busy in all kinds of busy work, some of which was not particularly desirable. The conventional wisdom was to get a permanent detail that I liked and stick with it until time for testing.

I had been raised on a farm doing all kinds of repair work, including carpentry, shingling, painting, etc., of houses and barns. When the squadron commander asked for volunteers, I violated the old adage and volunteered. In the captain's interview I must have impressed him in someway, and I was asked to find two others to assist me. He then explained that he wanted a covered bulletin board for the important notices that were the chief notifications for times to go to classification testing.

As I look back on it, in choosing two assistants, I suspected that following LDS standards was a help. Thus, couldn't I just use these same principles in selecting from the diverse group of would-be pilots? I wanted nonsmokers, nondrinkers, nonswearers, nongamblers, and nongoldbricks. My first pick turned out to be a Jensen (we just used last names) from Idaho Falls. I suspected he was LDS. Between us we selected another who was sandy-haired and from California, but met all the LDS criteria. Then we reported to the captain for information on sources of tools and supplies. He put us in his car and drove us to the toolshed and the scrap lumber pile where we could sort out what we needed. His car was always available to us as we scrounged what we needed.

It was a pleasant task, and we worked well together. The framework was soon in place but not all of the finishing materials were available. When we advised the captain, he gave me his car keys and some money and directed us to San Antonio to a hardware store for what was needed. We were somewhat surprised at what he was allowing, but were more shocked at his final words, which I shall never forget, "*You* don't have to be in a hurry to come back to the post."

What trust he had in us three! And needless to say, we did not abuse that trust. The covered bulletin board announced our names as our time came up to go through the testing and on to pilot preflight. Living by our LDS standards had left impressions that had served us well, perhaps better than our combined carpenter ability. The lessons I learned have always remained with me.

Lt. Lynn Sleight in cockpit of A26-A light bomber, April 1945. 643rd Bomb Squadron, 409th Bomb Group, 97th Wing, 9th Air Force. Lynn flew 18 combat missions by the war's end in Europe. In the background is A-20 5I-N, the last A-20 in the unit. It was completely changed over to the A-26 Invader built by Douglas.

HUGH C. SLOAN

As a member of the Royal Canadian Air Force, Hugh served as an air gunner aboard a Halifax bomber. He was awarded the Distinguished Flying Cross for his thirty-nine successful missions. His plane was shot down during his last mission and only he escaped with his life.

Harold Kearl with his Halifax bomber, Willie the Wolf. The Royal Air Force relied on the Lancaster and Halifax heavy bombers for much of World War II. Experts now consider the Halifax as one of the best bombers in the war. For the most part, Halifax crews were assigned the dangerous night-bombing raids over Europe. During the war they flew over 75,000 missions, with some planes completing over 100 missions.

The war was probably one of my most spiritual highs in my life. I had the serviceman's Book of Mormon and *Principles of the Gospel,* which I read often. There were prayers night and morning and on every one of my missions. I had a special place in the airplane where I knelt down and prayed that we would be safe, and I could do my job well. I found the Church several times on leave. While we had chaplains on the squadron, none were LDS. I always felt at peace, even in action.

There's no doubt the Lord helped me a lot; I know that. On one mission, after the bomber had lost its starboard engine, the pilot Victor Stakoff gave the order to bail out. I started forward from my rear gunner position, but on the way a second engine blew, and I actually disobeyed orders and reversed my field, heading back through a sixteen-inch opening into my rear gun turret. I swung it around and went out of the plane to the rear.

As I rolled out, the plane was on its back and went straight down. (I was told later that I was only one thousand feet up.) As I think back, and I have thought back about it many times through the years, I guess I just did what I had to do. I still don't know how I got out.

As I parachuted down, the plane hit and exploded. The concussion of the blast lifted me back up on a cushion of air. That could have been what saved my life.

A. MARION SMITH

Marion served as a veterinarian assigned to the care of the cavalry horses used by officers in the North Africa campaign. He inspected the mounts used by General Eisenhower, General Bradley, and General Patton. He carried out this assignment at the Hampton Roads (Virginia), Port of Embarkation. Here his other duties included the inspection of foodstuffs sent overseas for the troops, training and care for the war and sentry dogs used in the European Theater, and the care of the carrier pigeons used by the Army Signal Corps. While stationed in Virginia, he worked to establish an LDS servicemen's branch.

When I first arrived in Virginia on August 1, 1944, I found that there were no branches of the Church anywhere on the Virginia Peninsula so I had to take the ferry over the Chesapeake Bay each Sunday to the Norfolk Branch to attend meetings in their branch chapel. After about one month of doing that each week, I was set apart, along with three other army officers who were elders in the Church . . . to be LDS coordinators with the authority to conduct services wherever there were no organized branches of the Church.

There was a great need of LDS sacrament meetings for the servicemen and women at Hampton and for the five surrounding army, air, and naval bases. So, I immediately organized a Sunday morning meeting, held each week in the Mariners Hall. . . . I sent out notices of the location and time of our meetings to the surrounding military bases. . . . I then called the district mission president to come and organize it as a dependent branch of the Norfolk Branch Sunday School. He set me apart as the Sunday School superintendent, and I had an army sergeant as one counselor and a civilian elder who worked in the shipyard as the other counselor.

In the two and a half years I was in the service in Virginia, I was able to teach the gospel and baptize six fine people into the Church, including two servicemen, two wives of members, and two teenage daughters of an inactive family. When I was discharged from the Army and left Newport, we had a good stable Sunday School with a number of permanent civilian families and quite a number of permanent military personnel stationed at the various bases.

Capt. A. Marion Smith with his son, David, by their apartment in Newport News, Virginia, after the war.

LOUIS SMITH

Louis belonged to the Utah National Guard 222nd Field Artillery Unit that was activated in 1941. In March 1944 he left for Europe carrying all his hopes and fears in his heart, and all his earthly belongings in a duffel bag. He arrived in France after D-Day and joined the Allied forces marching across France.

Cpl. Louis Smith.

It was in Metz that we ran out of gas. Our supply lines couldn't keep up, and the Third Army ran out of gas. General Patton said it cost the Allies twenty-five thousand lives.

Metz is a city and fort near the French-German border. It has been a fort for two hundred years. . . . At this time the Germans had it and had built the fort almost entirely underground. What was exposed was rounded like half an eggshell. It was built of steel-reinforced concrete. Before we had run out of gas, our tanks and infantry had gone through Metz. But on emergency gas, we had been withdrawn to wait for our supply lines to replenish our gas. This had given the Germans a chance to get reinforcements and supplies into Metz. It wasn't easy to take again.

When we got gas, we tried to take it again. For protection, we pulled our artillery in among the waste of an old mine for a while. We then moved nearer, beside a railroad station. We pounded Metz continually, and we could have written a book on the ways and means the Army used to try to capture Metz. We were told a story of a company of infantry going in, and only eleven survivors coming back.

Finally, they began using Mustang fighters. The P-51s would carry a 500-pound bomb on one wing and a 500-pound container of oil and gas on the other. They flew over in fours several times daily, diving in and dropping the bomb and container together, hoping the bomb would crack the concrete and ignite the gas and oil which would run down into the fort. . . . It was there that I heard from home that my mother had died, October 26, 1944. It was also there that I learned I was a father. My first child, Joy Lynn, was born September 20, 1944.

* * * * *

One night, I walked up to a house where some of the fellows were writing letters. They had the kitchen gas lamp for light and had the windows and doors covered with blankets to keep the light in. They were sitting around reading and writing letters.

I sat down on the floor and took out a pocket edition of the New Testament I had carried across Europe. My wife had given it to me when I left. As I sat reading, I was guided by an unseen hand, and I came to this passage: "He that will lose his life for My sake shall find it." I thought of those words all night, and I made up my mind. "All right, if this is what Jesus wants, this is what I will do." I had been a soldier for four years. If I had to die, I would do it like a soldier and take as many of the enemy with me as possible.

I stepped behind the shed to make final preparations for my mission. My thoughts went home to my family, friends, and loved ones in the land of Rainbow Canyons. For a few moments I dwelt on home and my loved ones. I had such a great longing to see them all again. After a few minutes, I came back to reality and the job I had come to do. I made my rifle ready, stepped out to the gate, took hold of the top board, and prepared to go over and make my assault down the alley and across the street. The Lord, the wonderful, wonderful Lord, kept His promise. He gave me new hope for the future and took away my need for my one-man assault against the German Army. It remains a mystery to me how God performs these miracles.

Damage to a B-17 bomber. It was a fortunate B-17 crew that returned safely to their base in England. The damage to their tail section made it difficult to steer the plane and keep it in the air. Unseen in this picture is the damage to the other parts of the plane. While it was common for bombers to return to base damaged, this one attracted considerable attention.

STANLEY G. SMITH

After graduating from pilot's training in the Army Air Corps, Stanley became a copilot on a B-17 bomber. His assignment took him over Germany where he experienced an attack from the new German jet planes.

I carried my scriptures in the aircraft but did not have a lot of time to read them as the cockpit was a busy place, especially when we were in formation. My most notable form of spiritual support was my patriarchal blessing. At age eighteen, just before leaving for flying school, I visited our stake patriarch, Samuel H. Hurst. In the blessing he said that I would have to pass through dark days, but if I lived righteously I would live to enjoy a family of my own. Indeed, I passed through many dark days, one, when our plane was shattered, on

Bombs falling on Germany. It was common for crewmen to take photos from their position in the bomber. Such pictures, both official and unofficial, show what the bombardier saw as he identified the target and computed the information necessary for accurate bombing.

fire, with large sheets of the aluminum skin peeling off and sailing back in the air. That was a dark day all right. Yet, I remembered thinking of the patriarch's promise and can truly say that I was never afraid during that day or any dark day that followed.

WILLARD D. SMITH

Willard landed on Omaha Beach two weeks after D-Day. He became part of the effort to push through France to Paris. His army unit was responsible for a searchlight antiaircraft artillery battery. He also assisted the unit chaplain.

There was nothing heroic in my two years overseas—six months in England before the invasion and eighteen months on the continent. I did my job, routine as it was. . . . From a personal point of view I have been grateful that I kept my eye on the goal to be personally worthy. So many of my comrades felt released from the restraints of family, home, friends, and community. Immorality was rampant. I kept myself morally clean and felt no temptation to do otherwise for which I shall be eternally grateful. I carried the little book *As a Man Thinketh* by James Allen as a constant shirt-pocket companion. I also read the *Principles of the Gospel* booklet supplied to servicemen by the Church.

* * * * *

In the early days of associating with Chaplain Brown, he asked questions about my religion. I was delighted and anxious to share my religious beliefs. We entered into a number of discussions, and I was so hopeful that he might delve into the treasure chest of Mormonism. I soon discovered, however, that he was merely curious about Mormonism. When I offered him a copy of the Book of Mormon to read, he merely thumbed through it casually a few moments in my presence then set it aside. He preferred simply to read his paperback novels of which he had a supply. In an effort to develop a serious gospel discussion, I asked him one time what he understood would be the lot of the millions who had died without ever having been baptized or hearing about the gospel. He responded indifferently, "They are lost."

I quoted Paul, "Else what shall they do which are baptized for the dead, if the dead rise not at all? Why are they then baptized for the dead?" But the concept did not intrigue him.

On Sundays, in all kinds of weather, we visited the men in the field or in tents, offering Communion to those interested. I participated in the preparation and handling of the sacrament and partook of it myself, but with some misgiving as to whether it was appropriate for me or pleasing to the Lord for me to accept this ordinance administered without proper authority. I resolved it in my mind by repeating quickly in my mind the prayers as given in the Doctrine and Covenants.

GLEN H. STEPHENSON

Drafted in 1942, Glen completed his combat training at Camp Hood, Texas. He drove a jeep that pulled small artillery guns or carried .50-caliber machine guns. He landed at Omaha Beach in an LST (landing ship tank) during the Normandy invasion.

We were let out on top of the ship long enough to see the other ships. There were ships as far as we could see. . . . Our platoon officer told us to go shave because we might not get to shave again for two or three weeks. We were shaving in a bunch of sinks along the one side. Something was hitting the edge of the boat. "What was that?" I asked.

The man said, "That's the artillery from the Germans. The Germans are shelling us." They were hitting pretty close. I finished shaving and got out of there.

There was so much noise, we couldn't even talk or hear ourselves think. The big destroyers were making quite a racket. They were shooting at the big German bunkers.

The infantry and engineers had already cleared Omaha Beach. The engineers had moved all the wreckage so we could move in. I supposed they used heavy equipment. The situation in the water was bad. When the first men went in, the tide was in, and many drowned. There were jeeps and bodies lying all around; they'd had to go through deep water and just had not made it. We saw all that. There was debris all over. The amphibious tanks were still in the water; a lot of them had not made it to the beach.

WALTER STEWART

As the command pilot on a B-24 Liberator named the Utah Man, *Walter flew his first missions in North Africa. He went on to fly low-level missions to the Ploesti oil fields in Rumania.*

We were preparing for a deadly mission. Those chosen to make this raid were a select group. Almost all of the men had impressive combat records. We all knew that our chance of being alive after a month was problematical. I didn't know whether I was going to live or not, so things of the Spirit recorded in the scriptures became more important to me. I suggested we hold MIA. My crew wondered what MIA was, and I told them it was where I went every Tuesday night when I grew up. The first Tuesday we met in my tent. After the first night, the boys, nine of them my crewmembers, decided we'd read the New Testament and talk about it.

We began reading from the book of Matthew. The boys brought their friends, and my tent quickly became too small, so we decided to meet outside. The base at Benghazi had been occupied by the German Luftwaffe until they were driven out by English armies under Field Marshall Montgomery. We found a lot of empty gasoline cans with swastikas on their sides. We circled those cans around an ant bed and got a five-gallon can of gasoline. We borrowed a portable organ from the chaplain, which I could play. When it was dark we dumped the gasoline down the ant bed and took turns reading the Bible by the light of the fire. We would read a passage, then talk about it. Hugh Roper and I took turns conducting.

Briefing preceding one of the Ploesti air raids in Rumania. Germany was very dependent on Ploesti oil. The air raids between June 12, 1942, and August 24, 1944 were not highly successful.

The night we came to the account of Christ's baptism, Sergeant Richard E. Bartlett from Troy, Montana, read: "And Jesus, when he was baptized, went up straightway out of the water" (Matthew 3:16).

At that moment one of the boys asked Sergeant Bartlett, who was a devout Catholic, "How could he come up out of the water? How do you do that when you've just been sprinkled on the head? There's something wrong here."

Another said, "Well, that's because you don't baptize the right way. You're supposed to pour water on them."

To which Bartlett pointed out, "How can he come up out of the water if he poured it on him, that wouldn't be any different."

"Well," said Sergeant Bill Major, "what it was, was the water that came out of his pockets when He came up out of the water. That's a translation problem."

Then Bartlett rejoined, "There you have it, Here's Sergeant William Major from South Bend, Indiana, telling you about Jesus having pockets. Nobody, not the greatest experts that ever lived know all about how Jesus dressed or ever talked about Him having pockets."

Then Bill Major turned to me and said, "Skipper, you tell us what happened."

That was the best opening I've ever had in my whole life to tell how Jesus was baptized. So I explained, "The word baptize means to 'bury in water.' You see, John baptized or buried Jesus in the water, and Jesus came up out of the water."

Bartlett turned to Major and said, "See." It was all spontaneous. No place in the Bible is there a better description of how baptism is to be done. From then on, the guys would ask me about questions that puzzled them.

One night the chaplain came to our meeting. He was a great guy; we all liked him. He was from Springfield, Missouri. The men told him, "Oh, look who's come to our meeting. Padre, you can ask questions, but don't try to answer them. These Mormons have some real good answers that you may never have heard before." Our MIA grew to forty-five guys, and I don't think there was ever an absentee.

* * * * *

The British had hired some Sudanese to guard our aircraft. They were big, tall black men with perfect uniforms who walked at attention. They had feathers in their hats and carried mean looking knives at their sides. But they were very friendly with us, and they'd smile and salute us.

One day their British officer came to me, "I see you hold meetings at night, some of my men would like to come."

"Really?" I said. "I didn't know they understood English."
The officer said, "They don't, but they love your singing."
I replied, "Well they can certainly come."

When it was time for MIA these Sudanese would find me, then salute and say, "You come, you come." They loved to hear us sing. They didn't otherwise join in the meetings, just stood at the edge of the light waiting for our closing hymns. We could see their teeth shining in the firelight as they laughed and sang. After holding MIA three times a week for six or seven weeks we were only to the tenth chapter of Matthew on July 31, 1943, the night before the raid for which we were training.

JOHN S. STRADLING

John was killed in action on January 20, 1944, while serving as a combat engineer near Anzio, Italy. His unit was assigned to carry a roll of telephone wire to establish communications between the various units. They triggered a string of land mines killing John and several others. Following the war his mother collected his letters home and published them in a book she titled Johnny. *Below are three letters: one to his mother about Church services, one to his bishop, and one to his family—the last one before his death.*

John Stradling, killed in action near Anzio, Italy.

Somewhere in North Africa, November 7, 1943.

Dear Mother,

Today is Sunday again and another church pass puts Private Stradling into town and again to church, and the American Red Cross to write. It's surely nice here where it's cool and clean and peaceful, just like writing back in the States. Yeah, the pen even scratches like the rest of them.

Sunday School was nice and here again as usual. The same five of us were here again and this boy was late again. He's sorry for it, too, for they had sacrament this morning. Next week I'll try to get an early pass and get out and catch a ride that much earlier if I can make it. If I do I'll have a lesson on the gathering of Israel to give from my pocketbook. Nice facilities, vest pocket references and vest pocket teacher, but we have a grand time discussing what we do know, anyway. And today being the first Sunday, it saves standing in chow line for a couple of times. Don't forget to finish the day for me by taking care of your end of it. I like to remind you every month, not because you'd forget, but it's more like doing it myself. I guess that's where the real benefit comes anyway, in doing.

Golly, Mom, the things you haven't done for me aren't worth doing. You can sure figure out what's best, maybe because you know me? But, thanks for all of it until I can tell you in a better way. You have a whole warehouse of morale stacked up over here that makes life grand.

And best of all is to know all of you are getting along swell and enjoying life as best you can. That's the constant hope of this boy's heart.

Love,
Johnny.

* * * * *

In Italy, December 16, 1943.

Dear Bishop,

Here's a report on one of your boys, Dad. Something I've wanted to do for a long time. And it is really a pleasure to tell you of one of your boys who you'll be mighty proud of. I told you of meeting Paul Allen on the road the other day and waiting to talk to him. The same night I went to see him (and vice versa), and I met him on the way back so we had a swell talk. I can't exactly describe it, but I think I can come closest by explaining that his spirit is just like that of a returned missionary. His faith and appreciation and understanding as to the importance of the gospel are wonderful. He knows plenty about it, too.

When people are being taught they don't generally show much enthusiasm, and you seldom know how much soaks in. That's especially true in army training, as well as in religious training. But when the trainee is put on his own initiative, everything he ever heard comes back. We can tell you that, even though you already know it. I'm sure lots of people would be surprised if they could see the kids they called men and drafted, and I'm sure they'd be mighty proud of them.

Paul lives his religion in ways that would make you mighty proud of him. It's not hard at all, as long as there's plenty of reason for it. He's a good soldier and a real man. As a matter of fact, if the young gala at home could see him in action they'd be writing about every day to a mighty swell fellow. All in the world we want over here from you people is C rations, a blanket, and plenty of ammunition, and more than all the rest, the knowledge that all of you are at home. We know what else we really want too, and home and church come right up there.

And don't forget the boys in the States. It's just as tough there. We're as satisfied as we've ever been, that's regular. And we get mail once in a month or so, while they get mail call twice a day. You see we don't miss getting mail if the rest don't get it. If there's a mail call we want some; if not, we don't miss it so much, so the boys in the States need that many more. We're used to dehydration.

The other night Paul wanted to have prayer together, so we found a place and it was really inspiring. He knew of another member so we planned a meeting for the next night, but we worked the next two nights so that was out.

It's after dark now and I'm waiting for Paul if he doesn't work tonight. You'll have to go some to beat a three-man meeting in a vacant tent in Italy—GI bread, canteen cup, and all.

I know that the boys would all enjoy a letter from someone representing their Church classes more than to have a feather bed or a real home cooked dinner.

Love to you, Bishop, and best of luck,
Johnny.

* * * * *

Italy, January 16, 1944.

Dear Mom,

Say, are you ever on the beam. You stayed up one Sunday night to write and it came in mighty handy this Sunday night. You're a peach, Jo.

I've got you caught up to the first week of December, and happy to find everything swell. When you do things, you do 'em right.

Tell Lou and Ele thanks for two sets of letters. I'm not stuck up at 'era—they'll be answered at anything 'cept "Vs." Keep the reports rolling in the same, Mom, that's the way we like 'er.

Love,
Johnny.

RAY P. STRATFORD

Ray joined the Army in August 1943. His first assignment was with the 102nd infantry division. He sailed to Europe on the Queen Mary *and entered combat in September, 1944. His particular responsibility was to ensure a functioning phone system between headquarters and the field. Ray served during the march to Berlin. In November 1944, they were taking active defensive measures to maintain pressure along the front of the Allied line. He recounts the story of an intense battle the night before Thanksgiving.*

We had a disastrous operation just before Thanksgiving near a small German village. We went on the attack and were dug in on the back side of a hill. There was a German contingent just over the crest of the hill. They had a pill box (concrete bunker), and were shooting at us. As I passed over the crest of a hill, I passed one fellow that had a hole blown through the calf of his leg and was calling for a medic.

Before we dug in on the hill at night, we were below the crest taking fire. Our first sergeant was hit, and I held him in my arms until a medic came. He was evacuated. We then climbed to the hill and dug in for the night. The Germans were lobbing mortars at us. Mortars had a very high trajectory. They came straight down at us. We didn't hear them coming like an artillery shell. One exploded near my foxhole. As I was ducking down into the foxhole, a piece of shrapnel went right across my upper lip. I felt it on my whiskers. . . . That was a scary night.

The next morning we tried to move over the hill. There were communication trenches that connected the bunkers. I got in one and moved up to the point where I could see the bunker, but then moved back to the crest of the hill. Our battalion commander was trying to direct artillery fire to the bunker where the Germans were. He was hit in the neck by a rifle bullet. The Germans finally withdrew after some heavy artillery fire was directed on them.

We were withdrawn from the front lines that afternoon. I got a ride on a Canadian tank. One of the Canadians asked if this was our Thanksgiving, and I said yes, and that I was very thankful. When we got back, the mess sergeant came to me and said, "I got twenty-four chickens, how shall I cut them up?"

I said to cut them in half. We had returned with only 50 of the 250 men with which we had started.

JACK TAYLOR

Jack served as a pilot for a B-24 Liberator flying bombing missions over France and Germany. While his bomber saw considerable action, it never sustained serious damage and no lives were lost during the many bombing missions he completed.

✯ *(Below) Copilot Jack Taylor in flight suit.*

✯ *(Far below) Jack Taylor's B-24 bomber crew. Jack is the second from the left on the back row.*

We were not only a good crew, we were a lucky crew. Let me give an illustration. A flak burst hit under the airplane and was close enough that we heard the bang above the roar of our own engines. We felt the plane shudder as it was hit. A piece of flak from that burst, a very jagged piece of metal, hit just behind the bomb bay, went along the inside of the plane and out the top of the Plexiglas in the tail turret. On the way out, it went through nine layers of materials of various sorts. One of them was the tail gunner's oxygen hose. It is easy to picture what his reaction was. First he heard the Plexiglas over his head explode, then all of a sudden he couldn't breath at twenty thousand feet. He came tumbling out of there backward, and we got him calmed down.

When we were on the ground, I sighted up through the hole made by the piece of flak and determined that it went through the plane at a high enough velocity that it went through everything in its path. I could sight right though the

422 PL- 25JULY44- 1364B- CREW 253

(Below) Jack Taylor with pilot in the cockpit of a B-24 Liberator bomber. Jack is on the right.

(Far below) Jack Taylor with his crew after painting a new picture on the side of their B-24 bomber.

hole and see where it had traveled in a straight line. Then I had the tail gunner sit in his seat to see where he was when the flak came through the Plexiglas of his turret. We tried and tried every position we could think of and no matter what we tried I could see a piece of him by sighting through the hole. Finally we found one position where the flak would have missed him.

His head was completely down between his legs as if picking something up off the floor. Why he happened to do that at the exact moment the flak flew through his turret we will never know. That was one piece of evidence that we were a lucky crew.

WYNN TINGEY

Wynn served in a field artillery battalion during the march on Berlin. Some of the stress was relieved when Latter-day Saint soldiers could get together. Wynn was fortunate to have five other Latter-day Saint soldiers in his unit. Whenever possible, they got together on Sundays and held sacrament meeting.

The worship services were put together wherever the men could find a place, whether it was a tent or in the great outdoors. For their sacrament, the men shared a canteen and broke bread. . . . We just talked to each other. We kept each other company. It brings tears to my eyes to think of this.

VERNON JOHN TIPTON

Vernon served as a bombardier aboard a B-24 bomber. Flying out of Italy, he took part in the Regensburg and Ploesti raids. Shortly after the Ploesti raid, his bomber was shot down over Toulon, and he became a prisoner of war.

We had been to Regensburg, to Wiener Neustadt, and to Ploesti—about four or five heavily defended targets during that week. Then they woke us up and said, "You're going on a 'mild run' today. It's just up to Toulon."

Our squadron commander was in the lead bomber, and we were second in the formation. Both planes were hit by flak at about the same time. Our plane was on fire and we had to bail out. We were flying at about twenty-two thousand feet, so there was not very much oxygen. The concussion from the bombs down below and the flak all around us caused a lot of turbulence in the air. I was swinging back and forth, and I passed out as I was coming down in the parachute. That was the second time I'd bailed out. Even though I had had the former experience of bailing out, I pulled my rip cord too soon. Instead of free falling for ten thousand feet, I was in the parachute for most of the twenty-two thousand feet. I was supposed to get out of my parachute before I hit the water, but I didn't because I had passed out. So when I hit the water I was still in my parachute, and it was dragging me under. It was then that the Germans came along in the tugboat and pulled me out with some big grappling hooks.

ROY TSUYA

A Church member of Japanese descent, Roy was baptized as a convert in Hawaii on November 16, 1941, just three weeks before Pearl Harbor was bombed. When war was declared, he volunteered for army service and was shipped to fight on the European front.

Roy Tsuya with Chaplain Eldin Ricks in Naples, Italy, 1944.

In January 1943 there were feelings of prejudice toward the people of Japanese descent living in the United States. In many ways we were forced to prove our loyalty. President Roosevelt issued a proclamation for Japanese-American volunteers to form a Nisei combat outfit. During that same time he also signed a bill making it necessary to identify and relocate Japanese-Americans living on the West Coast. These people were forced to leave their homes and many lost everything.

I was asked by Elder Lamont Hunt if I was going to volunteer for the Army. I said, "No, we don't believe in fighting."

"Of course we believe in fighting for our country, you go ahead and sign up," he replied.

I volunteered and was inducted into the military service March 12, 1943, at Hanapepe, Kauai, Hawaii.

* * * * *

It was a wet afternoon after a rainstorm. We were bivouacking in a pine forest in Mississippi. I was cleaning and oiling my rifle when Chaplain Higuchi came to visit me and sat on a stool in front of me, probably because I was the group leader for the Mormon boys. He asked me, "Could I ask you some questions about the Mormon Church?"

I said, "Sure. If I don't know the answer, I'll find out and let you know." I was very young in the Church. It had been less than two years since my baptism. Being in the Army, I hadn't had much contact with the Church. I wish I could have explained to him what I know today.

While we were conversing, I had a burning feeling that I knew what I believed was true, and that I belonged to the true church. I asked him, "Chaplain, may I ask you a question?" And then I said, "Chaplain, do you believe that your church is the true church of God?"

Without looking up for about two or three minutes, he shook his head and said, "No, I don't believe my church is true."

I said, "I know the church I'm a member of is the true church of God."

GRANT TURLEY

Grant was a P-47 Thunderbolt pilot in the Eighty-second Squadron of the Eighth Air Force stationed in Duxford, England. He was Arizona's first ace pilot in WW II, destroying seven enemy fighter planes. He lost his life on March 6, 1944, when his plane went down over Germany.

Diary entry, Thursday, February 10, 1944.

Took off this morning for just an ordinary escort mission, but it turned out Lieutenant Turley, leading second element in Lieutenant Wesson's Red Flight, got two ME 109s. (He shot down two German planes, his first.)

We were bounced at twenty-six thousand feet by these jokers. Well, yours truly and his wing man got on their tails finally and followed them down. I shot short bursts on the way down. When the leader leveled off on the deck, he got a second burst from dead astern. He blew up and went into the deck from three hundred feet. Looked like one big splash of flames when he hit the ground.

I then got on the tail of the second, and he crash-landed in flames. My wing man followed me to the deck where he lost me. There was another P-47 around; I would like to meet the pilot covering my tail.

We then came on home. Saw one Me 109 coming out, but he didn't see us. I was out of ammunition by this time. Boy, was I glad to see England. What a day. Right now it worries me that I have caused the death of one man and probably another. War is hell. I guess I'll get callused. However, it is nicer to say "ships destroyed" and not think of the pilots.

Grant Turley in the cockpit of a P-47 Thunderbolt.

* * * * *

Letter to Kitty, his wife, February 20, 1944.

I am tired, had a mission today and shot down my fifth enemy plane. I am an "ace" so they say. A lot of it has been luck, maybe a little skill. Well, Honey, I have dreamed of being an ace, and now that I have succeeded, it doesn't seem so important any more.

* * * * *

Letter to Kitty, his wife, March 2, 1944 (four days before his death).

Don't worry, for there is not need of it. I carry your picture, a four-leaf clover, and a lock of Comet's mane on every trip. Why, with all that, nothing can happen, so I tell myself. But the thing that gives me assurance is the fact that I know you are asking God to protect me and bring me back.

* * * * *

Years later Kitty wrote about this letter.

It is so tender. God didn't take his life. It was one of those things. And who knows, perhaps his life was spared many times over. There are many "missions" in one's existence, and though we still weep over losing Grant, he was spared some possible heartaches and disillusions that life can bring. Perhaps the effect he has had on our children . . . is as great as if he were here.

Lt. Grant Turley (in cockpit), with his groundcrew.

PIETER VLAM

Pieter was the only member of the Church serving in 1939 as an officer in the Royal Dutch Navy. When the Germans overran The Netherlands, Pieter was on shore leave and not allowed to return to his ship. At that time, he was called to serve as second counselor to the mission president who was busy evacuating missionaries from Germany. During this time German officials arrested Pieter, considering him to be a threat because of his commission in the Dutch Navy. He remained a POW for the rest of the war. This account was written by his daughter.

As second counselor in the mission presidency, Piet wondered often why the Lord had allowed him to be taken away from this important work. One day, he and another officer, Jan Schuitema, were resting outside of the barracks on the ground where there was a little bit of grass. Schuitema, who had worked and traveled with Piet on the *Gelderland* to the West Indies, asked Piet if he could talk with him about spiritual matters. He first talked about Spiritism and asked Piet what he thought of that. Piet told him that Spiritism was real, but that those spirits who came here to manifest themselves through table dancing, etc., were evil spirits; they came to deceive and were in the service of Satan. Piet then told Schuitema of the gospel. Schuitema received a testimony of its truthfulness. When he later was discharged from the prison camp and sent home because of illness, he was baptized in Amsterdam. I witnessed his baptism.

Now many coprisoners came to Piet and wanted to talk to him about Mormonism. They couldn't talk in large groups, for the Germans wouldn't allow it. So Piet took two people at a time, one on each side, and walked with them around the camp every day, for miles and miles. He did this, because inside the barracks the atmosphere was spoiled by cigarette smoke and rough language, which is not conducive to the sweet and pure spirit of the gospel. In this way, Piet talked to almost a thousand officers about Mormonism. He was able to take away many prejudices that existed among them about the Mormons.

After a few months at Langwasser, the prisoners were transferred to Stanislaw, on the Polish-Russian border. Through the Red Cross, the prisoners now received food parcels regularly so life became a little more tolerable. Twice a month now, I received a letter from Piet. They were printed forms consisting of about fifteen lines and a blank answer sheet attached to it with the same amount of lines.

In Stanislaw the gospel talks were continued. Out of the many to whom Piet talked, there remained a small group of permanently interested friends. Piet made up a walk-talk schedule and continued to preach and explain the gospel of Jesus Christ. His shoes had long been worn out, and so he asked if I could send him a pair of wooden shoes. I did, and they served him well.

In Stanislaw, a Catholic priest and a Protestant minister came of their own free will to the camp to live with the prisoners. On Sundays they held church services. Every friend who walked with Piet was noticed by the Protestant minister and afterward was taken aside by him. The minister said that Mr. Vlam might mean well, but he was deceived by his church. He then gave them a little booklet to read about all sorts of sects, including Mormonism. There was not much good said about the Church in that booklet, but the minister got just the opposite effect of what he wanted. For the friends became now even more inquisitive, and they could detect many lies themselves. Now they asked Piet if they could not have church services of their own. Piet consented, but of course this had to be done in secret, for the Germans did not allow extra meetings and services. The friends hunted up an empty barrack in a far-off corner, put a blanket in front of the window, took an old soapbox for a pulpit, and started church. I had sent Piet the standard works of the Church and a songbook. They did not dare to sing for fear of detection, but Piet read the songs to them, prayed, and read the sacrament prayers to them; he explained the sacrament and gave a talk about the gospel. Then they closed again by reading a song and a prayer. One by one they had to leave and take care they were not detected.

One day a certain Mr. Callenbach joined the group. He told Piet he did not want to be converted; he only came to hear the story from Piet because he had read the booklet from the Protestant minister and had found many lies in it. Fast Sunday came along and Piet explained the principle of fasting to the group; they should give the little cup of beans that they would save by fasting to someone else; and if they could not sleep in the night, they should pray to God and ask Him if the things they heard from Mr. Vlam were true or not.

Message of the

FIRST PRESIDENCY

Delivered in the

TABERNACLE

SALT LAKE CITY, UTAH
OCTOBER 3, 1942

Every effort was made to provide Church literature to the troops in the field. This was made difficult by battle conditions. The Church printed the pamphlet pictured here for distribution to the servicemen. Contained in the pamphlet are these words: ". . . We pray in a prayer which daily ascends to our Heavenly Father, that you will live righteously, that you will be preserved, that God will hasten the working out of His purposes among the nations, so that peace may come and you be restored to your loved ones, as clean as the day on which you left them. . . . you brethren in the service have been requested to organize Mutual Improvement groups in your camps, so that both your recreational and spiritual needs may be served. . . ."

The next Sunday they had testimony meeting. Everybody stood up and said a few words of testimony or appreciation. After everyone had taken a turn, they waited a while to give Mr. Callenbach the opportunity to say something. He finally stood up and with tears streaming down his face he said that last night he had been very hungry—for he had fasted—and then he remembered what Piet had said about prayer. So he prayed earnestly to God to let him know if the things that Piet taught were true. He said an indescribable feeling of peace came over him, and he knew that he had heard the truth. Then Mr. Callenbach said he had observed that everybody had something to do to prepare for church, and he also wanted to take part. The men were so impressed that they all wept. Piet assigned Mr. Callenbach to sweep the floor, and he answered that it would be an honor for him to do so. Piet said, "You don't mean that."

But Mr. Callenbach replied, "Yes I mean it, for you enter in this room and with you the holy priesthood." This answer made a deep impression on Piet—to think that this man had recognized the priesthood as a holy gift from God.

Piet told his friends about MIA, so they wanted to have a MIA. They organized it with a president, a teacher, and a secretary. Rob Kirschbaum was president, von Balusek was the teacher and Jan den Butter was the secretary. Piet gave each one a blessing for the work. Jan den Butter told Piet afterward that he wanted to remember every word Piet had said in that blessing, but he forgot it. However, in the night he prayed that he would remember the blessing that was given to him. And it all came back to him. Piet had told him that he would embrace the gospel and become a stalwart member in the Church and that his wife would embrace the gospel, too. That was all fulfilled.

ELMO WALKER

While stationed in Oran, Algeria, Elmo worked to organize a Latter-day Saint branch. His letters and accounts of that experience provide insight to the dedication of the Latter-day Saint servicemen and their efforts to perpetuate the Church in the midst of war.

Letter written to LDS servicemen's group leader, Elmo Walker, from Gordon B. Hinckley, Church Radio Committee.

Through the courtesy of Mr. J. Van Booskirk, director of the American Red Cross Empire Club, a nice room was obtained in which to hold our services. Private Eli Alter of the base post office printed and donated a sign. Our services were advertised in the *Stars and Stripes* August 25-26, 1943, and our first service was held August 29, 1943. There were in attendance three persons.

In this service we prayed that the Lord would bless us so that we would be able to contact the LDS fellows in this area. During the week we sent out a number of church notices. The following Sunday, September 5, 1943, our prayers were surely answered in that we had an attendance of thirty-six. As it was the first Sunday in the month, we decided to have a testimony meeting. It was an inspirational meeting and a number of the brethren expressed thanks for being able to attend LDS meetings once again.

The following Sunday our attendance grew to forty, and the following week to fifty-one. The next Sunday, fifty-two. At our third meeting, September 12, 1943, we decided to formerly organize a branch of the Church. . . . Elder Tom J. Summers from Ririe, Idaho, was chosen and sustained as the presiding elder, and he selected Brother Lloyd M. Sleight and Brother Floyd H. Gibson to serve as his counselors.

Several weeks prior to Easter, the members of our branch of the Church decided to hold a sunset service Easter Day on the crest of a prominent hill near the area. In accordance with the decision, assignments for the program were given, refreshments were obtained through the courtesy of the American Red Cross, and arrangements were made to borrow a portable organ from the chief of chaplains in this section.

Transportation was secured by the several members of the branch who were stationed in nearby units.

When the sun began to settle behind the trees, a spot was selected for the meeting in a secluded wooded grove where many protruding rocks offered themselves for seats.

It was a beautiful afternoon. The evening sun filtered through the trees and flickered on the grass and rocks on the floor of our green chapel. Native plants were blooming profusely, and the blue sky was smiling at us through the boughs over our heads. Above the gentle rustle of the wind could be heard the twittering of the birds.

LDS servicemen's branch in Oran, Africa.

All this loveliness about us seemed to enhance the spirit we enjoyed during the meeting. For the first time, I imagine, the songs of Zion rang through those woods when we began the service by singing "O Ye Mountains High." We had two talks on the resurrection, the reading of "Crossing the Bar" by Tennyson, and a trio sang "The Old Rugged Cross." We closed the service by singing "Come, Come, Ye Saints" because the fellows seem to feel that it applies in a special manner to them, even as it did to those who crossed the plains.

After this service, we all dived into the box of cheese and Spam sandwiches and doughnuts provided by the Red Cross. For thirty minutes we ate sandwiches and made pleasant conversation.

Finally the approaching darkness made us realize we had better start for home so we began the delayed hand shaking and good-byes, so typical of Mormon meetings. After the last farewells, the trucks started for the foot of the hill, bearing three groups of happy and refreshed soldiers back to their tents and narrow beds. I believe all who came will agree that the spiritual refreshment we received on this simple occasion would have amply repaid us for the journey.

Handmade sacrament trays constructed of shell casings.

LAVARR B. WEBB

LaVarr was inducted into the Army at Fort Douglas, Utah, in 1944. LaVarr's good example prompted a nonmember soldier to send a letter to the First Presidency. The First Presidency responded with a letter to the soldier and to LaVarr's parents.

Just prior to boarding the ship that would carry us to Italy, we had mail call. I received a letter from my wife and a small package. In the package were pocket-size editions of the Bible, the Book of Mormon, the Doctrine and Covenants, and the Pearl of Great Price. There was also a form letter from the Church. The contents of that letter are burned on my mind. It said in part:

Under no condition will a member of the Church be involved in the buying and selling of goods on the black market. As you know, the

General Authorities of the Church have spoken strongly against the use of tea, coffee, as well as cigarettes, beer, wine, and other intoxicating liquors. It is just as wrong, moreover, to sell such items to be used by others, particularly through the illegal black markets of Europe and Asia, and other areas where such deplorable enterprises flourish.

In Italy, the black market did more than flourish. It was the channel through which goods flowed from supplier to consumer—from the American soldier, the entrepreneur, the risk taker, to the hungry, the cold, and the destitute Italians. Some soldiers became rich. Some would walk out of camp wearing three shirts, three pairs of pants, and as many shorts and undershirts as they dared pile on, and some came back with very little covering their nakedness.

The soldiers sold anything the Italians found of value—American dollars for liras, clothes for liras, cigarettes for liras, and food for liras. A carton of cigarettes was worth the equivalent of fifty dollars or more, shoes seventy to one hundred, and an American dollar brought five to ten dollars in lira.

I realized how hungry the Italians were for American goods the first time I went to the PX to pick up my rations. The camp was near Caserta. The PX was a tent. Boxes of goods were behind a line of tables. Italian girls, who spoke very little English, collected each man's rations from the boxes and placed them in individual piles on one of the tables.

There was toothpaste and a toothbrush, candy bars and gum, writing materials, razor blades, cigarettes, Coca-Cola, and beer. Each man had to sign for his ration, then a girl would push a pile to him across the table, where he would carefully and greedily place them in his knapsack.

I signed for mine. The girl pushed them across the table. I took the beer and cigarettes from the pile, and pushed them back to the girl.

She said, "No, no, you take," and pushed them back to me.

I said, "No, I don't want them," and tried to put the other rations in my bag.

She insisted on helping me, leaning over the table, her hands fighting my hands in a pushing, dodging battle. She tried to force the beer and cigarettes into my bag, all the while crying, "You take, you take," and all the while trying to make me understand with gestures that I was to meet her outside where she would meet me and buy, or even trade her body for the unwanted items.

A soldier standing in line behind me said, "Hell soldier, take them, and if you don't want them, give them to me."

I, with a red face, and a queasy feeling in my stomach, and wishing that I could escape, muttered, "I can't."

Finally, I was the center of attention. The girl screamed, "Take them, take them."

And the soldiers yelled, "You dumb _____, give them to me."

I grabbed what candy and gum I could, fought off the girl and her clutching hands, turned and walked out of the PX, eyes down, neither looking to the right or the left, but hearing the recriminations.

As I walked away from the tent, a dozen ragged children came running up with their hands out. "Joe, candy Joe," and I gave them what was left of my ration and went back to my tent.

* * * * *

It was April 1945. I was in a replacement department in the Vulturno Valley. There were thousands of men in the valley waiting to be assigned to an outfit, and I didn't know a soul. While I had been in the hospital, all of my buddies from basic training had been scattered, and I was alone.

I hadn't heard from home for months. My wife had been expecting our third child to be born in May. The baby finally arrived in June, and I didn't hear about it until August. But that Sunday in July, I was walking down a street in that vast tent city, worried and homesick, and wishing that I could find a fellow Mormon.

There were radios on every corner blaring music from home— "Don't sit under the apple tree with anyone else but me . . . till I come marching home," and, "When the lights come on again all over the world . . ." Then, as I approached a corner, the music changed, and I heard a never to be forgotten voice say, "We bring you music and the spoken word from the crossroads of the West," and I sat there on the dirt of that corner as hundreds of men milled around me, and the weapons of war rolled by, and I cried as I listened to the songs of the Tabernacle Choir, the music of one of the world's great organs, and the spoken word by Elder Richard L. Evans. For a few moments, I was able to forget my problems.

Shortly after that delightful experience, I was sent to Montecatini, a rest camp, to join a combat engineers outfit. I was still alone, but I thought I might find some LDS soldiers in the camp by contacting the Red Cross.

I found the Red Cross headquarters, walked up to the director's door, knocked, and a big man about fifty years old, in a Red Cross uniform answered. I said, "I am a Mormon, and . . ."

He threw his arms around me, and yelled, "So am I, come on in." He said he hadn't seen a fellow Mormon for more than nine months; then he said, "Now we can hold a sacrament meeting." When two or more Mormons met, on their first Sunday together, they held a sacrament meeting.

I had found out that the Red Cross was serving ice cream, the first ice cream to be served in Italy since the invasion, so I told him that I thought I could round up some other Mormons in that ice cream line, then we could make some plans.

At the assigned time, I joined the line; up ahead, five or six men away, I saw two big ears that looked familiar. I left the line, walked toward the ears, and saw an old friend from high school, Dee Hulse.

We thwacked each other on the back for a few minutes, then went fishing for some more Church members. We figured that ice cream, even though it was made of peanut butter and powdered milk, was an excellent bait.

We pulled thirteen more men out of that line, and rather than a rest camp, it became a reunion camp. For a few short weeks, we were together every day, and the Red Cross director, who was from Layton, Utah, literally turned his facilities over to us.

Elder Bruce R. McConkie

Following a four-year association with the ROTC during his career at the University of Utah, Bruce R. McConkie served in the military for four more years due to the outbreak of World War II. He served in the area of security and intelligence. This future apostle was assigned to the U.S. Army Ninth Service Command, which was headquartered at Fort Douglas, Utah. After the war, Bruce resumed a legal career which had actually started before the war. In 1946, Elder Bruce R. McConkie became the first veteran of World War II to be called as a general authority. He was sustained to the First Council of the Seventy in 1946. In 1972, Elder Bruce R. McConkie was ordained to the Quorum of the Twelve Apostles.

JAY WHEELER

As a member of the Royal Canadian Air Force, Jay served as part of a bomber crew. In November 1943 his plane was shot down, and he was declared missing in action. In reality, he was captured and imprisoned in a German POW camp for the remaining years of the war.

Telegram from Ottawa, 7:43 A.M., November 25, 1943.

N.L. Wheeler
Cardston.

M9802 regret to advise that your son flying officer Jay Edmond Wheeler J two three six four nought is reported missing after air operations overseas November twenty third stop.

RCAF
Casualties officer.

*　*　*　*　*

First letter written to mother of Jay E. Wheeler from RCAF headquarters.

Dear Mrs. Wheeler:

I would like you to know that you and yours are much in my thoughts these days, when you and others live in particular uncertainty and anxiety, because of dear ones. The report that your son, F/O Jay E. Wheeler, J23640, was missing after operations, reached me, and in some measure, all here share your anxiousness.

Our young men are really fine and great: to be associated with them is both privilege and responsibility. Their attitudes, their sheer "gut" and quality of character are inspiring and challenging to all of us.

Proceeding on operations, there are those who do not return. They occupy the thoughts of all who must remain to perform many arduous duties, and more than one silent prayer is offered for our flying comrades.

I hope and pray that your loved one may yet be found to be safe, and that ere long you may receive some good word concerning him.

There remains the possibility that he may be a prisoner of war in the hands of the enemy.

My prayer is that God will sustain you through the long dreary waiting days, and throughout the future, no matter what it may bring.

Yours sincerely,
A.T. Lialewood.

* * * * *

A letter from the government of Canada.

To Mr. and Mrs. Nephi Lincoln Wheeler:

I have learned with deep regret that Jay Edmond Wheeler, RCAF has been reported missing. The government and people of Canada join me in expressing the hope that more favorable news will be forthcoming in the near future.

Charles S. Power,
Minister of National Defense for Air.

W. DEAN WHITAKER

Dean Whitaker served in the Eighth Air Force as a bombardier/navigator on a B-17 bomber. He flew twenty missions over Germany, France, and Holland before being shot down. At the time his plane was hit, he felt the presence of his deceased father helping him escape from the burning aircraft. His account of being trapped aboard the diving plane reflects the Lord's hand in his life. After a miraculous escape, he free fell for twenty-five thousand feet while Germans shot at him. Upon landing, his capture was immediate. Later he learned that when his mother was notified that he was missing in action, she felt the presence of her husband telling her that her son was all right, and that he would return home. After considerable time in a German POW camp, he was finally freed by troops led by General Patton.

Being brought up as a member of the Mormon religion, I had faith in prayer and many times said a short prayer when things got rough. On the mission to Merseburg we were attacked by German fighter planes. We fought off the first wave, but the second wave shot our tail off, killing the tail gunner and sending our plane out of control. Newman, the pilot, gave the order to bail out. I was trying to disconnect all my gear. I found the flak suit would not release, and I struggled with it. I realized that it was not going to come off. It was at this instant I felt my dad's presence. He was telling me to get out of the plane, now! Giving up on the flak suit, I removed my oxygen mask and headed for the escape hatch. Feeling a little groggy, I still felt the presence of my dad urging me to get out.

Dean Whitaker's file from Stalag Luft III, the German POW camp where he was held.

Jumping out of an airplane, with a heavy flak suit on, and a parachute buckled on just one side, was kind of risky. But as soon as I hit the outside slipstream of the plane, the flak suit was ripped off. All I had to do was to fasten the other side of my chute. It was like a bad dream, falling through the air, trying to get it fastened. I guess I had no strength from the lack of oxygen. In fact, I probably passed out for a short time. Upon entering the low cloud bank, I figured it was time to pull the rip cord, parachute fastened or not.

Pulling the rip cord at approximately three thousand feet meant I had had a free fall of twenty-five thousand feet. It was a good thing I did not pull the rip cord sooner because some German civilians were shooting at me as I was coming down. Luckily for me (or with a little help) a German soldier guarding a POW camp ran forward and told them to stop shooting. . . . After my mother was notified that I was missing in action, she related to family members that she had felt my dad's presence and that he had told her that I was okay and would return home.

CURTIS WILLIS

Curtis joined the Army Air Corps in the fall of 1942 and graduated from pilot's training the next year. His assignment was as a photo-reconnaissance pilot flying a P-38. He was shot down on his twenty-fifth mission. What follows is a first-person adaptation of the account of his escape.

I was acting operations officer, fully responsible for flying operations at the base because the operations officer was missing in action. On August 20, 1944, for my twenty-fifth mission, I took up the only plane left to fly, a P-38 that seemed to be jinxed, as it never handled quite correctly. I didn't feel comfortable about sending another flyer up in that plane.

My mission was in the Po Valley in northwestern Italy. I was flying along at about thirty-five thousand feet and had taken several photographs when I glanced up at two o'clock high and saw an Me109 pulling a contrail and heading in my direction.

An unarmed photo plane's only protection was speed so I dropped the belly tanks, but when I hit the throttles on the P-38, it didn't respond, making me an easy prey for the German fighter. My plane was hit, with the entire right wing bursting into flames, and I had to get out! Calling, "Mayday" and giving my identification code name, "Brassnook 26," I slowed the plane to about 150 miles an hour and bailed out. I didn't pull the rip cord on my parachute until I was at a low elevation, so as not to attract German enemy attention. All pilots were briefed about where and how to contact the underground.

Landing in a tree, and finding my only injury was a badly bruised lip, I freed myself and drew my pistol as I saw two men and a boy approaching. They came toward me shouting, "Brave Americano," and with great relief I knew I was lucky and among friendly Italians.

They hurried me around a hill and to a farmhouse, as the Germans were not far away. From the house came fifteen typical partisans. They were heavily armed with guns and grenades and had ammunition strapped all over them. As they had just begun to eat, they made a place for me, but my lip was too sore to eat much. Just as they finished eating, the Germans came. Hiding in a heavy thicket, they trained every gun on the enemy. The Germans didn't stay long, and the partisans went back inside the house and put me in a hayloft above the house to sleep, as they would be traveling that night. Allied lines were about 150 miles from the place I was shot

Photo of Capt. Don E. Packham with his P-38 fighter named Pistol Pack'um, *in France, Nov. 1944. The main responsibility for pilots of the Lockheed P-38 was to serve as bomber escorts. The P-38s were especially suited for this because of their speed, maneuverability, and flying range.*

down. I found myself in Carlo's group of Italian resistance near Ovada, Italy. Carlo had about two hundred men. Italian resistance was amazingly well organized. One of their best sources for recruits was Italian soldiers who had been forced to continue fighting for the Germans after the Italian Armistice. I found the people in the underground very friendly, willing to help escapees, and even risk their lives.

KEITH R. WILLISON

Keith served as a seaman aboard the light cruiser USS Brooklyn *during the invasions of Sicily, Anzio, and southern France. His introduction to the Church came during that time.*

One Sunday I was invited by one of the bluejackets (a man enlisted in the Navy) to go to church and meet the new chaplain. I declined in no uncertain terms. I had heard enough "hell and damnation" preached to me, and I was not going to listen to more. "Okay," he replied, "but it beats KP duty."

Nothing more needed to be said. I went to church. The chaplain, Glen Y. Richards was a Mormon. We became good friends, and he recognized that I had no gospel foundation whatsoever. He gave me my first set of scriptures. The Book of Mormon was a hard copy, and I carried it around with me between my belt and shirt. Whenever I had a spare moment, I was reading the Book of Mormon, and I went to church every Sunday.

One of my mates asked, "Are you one of those nasty old Mormons?"

I told him, "No, but I like what I am reading." His reply was that he was a Mormon, and he would be glad to answer any questions. We became buddies, and when we went ashore we would first look for an LDS meeting and if none were available, we went to the services of another denomination.

With all my reading of the Book of Mormon and the comparisons to other faiths, I had determined that if there was a true church it was the Mormon Church. While at port in New York, I attended church in the Manhattan Ward and told Bishop W. L. Woolf I wanted to be baptized. He told me "No, we want to get to know you and for you to know us."

I informed him I did not have time, as we were going into some heavy fighting, and I didn't know if I would come out alive. He invited me to his home for dinner. As we visited I now realize that he was interviewing me for baptism, but I did not realize it at the time. He gave me a recommend for this sacred ordinance and I was baptized June 7, 1943. There were problems inasmuch as the church was not open, and I had to climb a six-to-eight-foot fence and then had to wait on the steps for the arrival of Elder D. Leon Johnson. The custodian did not have the font filled. We had to run a garden hose through the basement window to fill it. The water was cold, but I was warmed by the feeling of the Spirit. The Lord was with me as I hurried back to my ship. It was pulling out as I hurried aboard. I would have been in deep trouble if I had missed my ship.

* * * * *

My most spiritual moment came later when I was stationed on the searchlights. Eight men manned the four lights, two on each light. One cold night all the men left to go into the radio shack to smoke and get a little warmth. I was alone. I heard my father's voice telling me to look toward port side.

He had been dead since 1941. I looked and detected a submarine periscope, and I immediately called the bridge from my headphone. A destroyer in our convoy was alerted and used depth charges to eliminate the German submarine. My father saved our ship.

FOREST A. WRIGHT

As a merchant marine, Forest signed on for the duration of the war plus six months. It was said that those sailors experienced the greatest risk, as their small transport ships carried troops and supplies across the Atlantic. Often without escort they faced the danger of submarine attacks and the unpredictable North Atlantic weather. His ship, the USAT George W. Gothels, *was one of the thousands of ships anchored off the Normandy beach on D-Day. His responsibility that day was to unload supplies needed by the troops going ashore.*

The chief engineer told my friend and me to completely overhaul an auxiliary diesel motor. It took us about four days to do it, and when we had it put back together we noticed a few extra parts lying around. We checked and double-checked and couldn't find anyplace to put them, so we decided to start the motor and see what would happen. The motor ran as it should and everything checked out fine.

The chief engineer was quite a character and was always pulling jokes on the rest of us, so we got to thinking that he had just tossed in a few extra parts to confuse us. So we decided to throw the parts overboard into the ocean. We didn't say a thing to the chief. For about a month or so he would look at us and at the motor and shake his head. I believe that he was wondering what we did with the extra parts. We never told him.

* * * * *

One time we were in port taking on fuel oil. The second engineer's duty was to direct this process. He began drinking and was soon drunk and did not pay attention to the fuel being pumped into the ship. As a result he filled only the tanks on one side of the ship. This caused the ship to list to one side and threaten to capsize. My friend and I were rousted from our bunks by the drunken engineer and told to fix things. I have never worked so hard in my life. We started the pumps to pump the oil from one side of the ship to the other. After working feverishly the whole night, we finally corrected the

Forest Wright in full uniform at ATS St. Petersburg, Florida. Forest served as an Engine Room officer aboard the USAT George W. Gothels.

problem. Word got around the ship concerning this and as a result, the second engineer was dismissed from our ship.

* * * * *

The sole purpose of the *Gothels* was to carry troops, mail, and supplies to the European Theater during the war. It could carry about three hundred men and supplies. The soldiers we carried were very young and most had never been on a ship before. They were confined to the holds below deck. They slept in hammocks, and they were served their meals in their own mess hall. They were not allowed on deck very much and did not mingle with the ship's crew. While crossing the ocean, most of them became seasick; some were sick the entire trip. By the time we reached our destinations, the ship's hole where they lived smelled really bad. The soldiers were put ashore at the ports where the ship landed or in large rubber rafts when the port was under fire.

When we crossed the Atlantic we would black out our windows at night to avoid detection. Our job below deck was to keep the engines running at peak efficiency to minimize the smoke from our stacks. A smoking stack was a dead giveaway for the German submarines in the area. We had a crew of fifteen in the engine room assigned different four-hour shifts. I was on duty from noon to four in the afternoon and again from midnight to four in the morning. Our only defense was our speed and a small 50-millimeter gun manned by three regular navy sailors. It was never fired in combat during the war. However, we came close when a German submarine surfaced

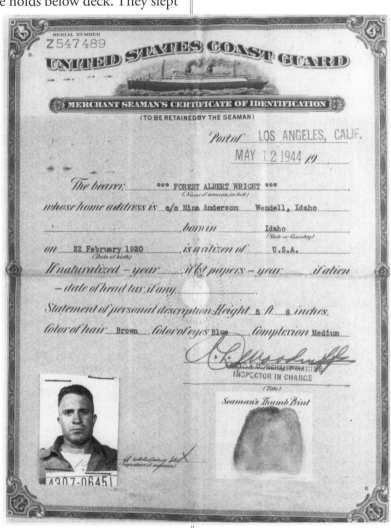

Forest Wright's merchant seaman's identification.

and followed us for quite awhile. I guess he felt we were not worth sinking.

* * * * *

We crossed the English Channel and waited for smaller ships to unload our supplies. We had large cranes on deck that lifted the crates into smaller landing craft. We did not have troops on board on D-Day. In fact we did not know it was D-Day. All we knew was we had to drop off supplies in the Channel. At the time we assumed an attack of some kind was going on, but no one gave us any details. It was just another day in the war.

All the engine room personnel were required to be below deck during battle conditions. The engine room was a very noisy place with furnaces and turbines and all. However, despite the normal engine room noise, we could hear the endless pounding of the artillery and bombs going off around us. It was a very busy time, and I did not get to go on deck to see the action, but I can imagine what it must have been like.

SAM H. WYROUCK

Sam Wyrouck served as the lower ball turret gunner on a B-17 bomber. He was part of the 351st Bomb Group stationed in England. It is clear from his account the risk each mission presented. Like many others, he counted the returning bombers at the end of the day to see how many were missing. With each mission he wondered if it would be his last. His detailed descriptions of his training and missions provide insight to the challenges he faced. Unlike many others, Sam Wyrouck successfully finished his assigned missions and safely returned home.

"Sweating out a mission" has a different meaning to different people at different times. Of course before I enlisted at age seventeen I knew there would be some danger to wartime flying, but as long as there was a war going on and I knew I would have to serve, I wished to have some choice in how I would serve. It looked as if this would be a long war so I would surely be in it. My reading of American losses made me more resolute. Nevertheless, when I thought of the dangers, I felt just a twinge of apprehension.

After I graduated from high school and was called to go into active duty, the day of my departure to basic training camp at Kearns, Utah arrived. Corinne, my sister, and Ernie and Gene came to the Union Pacific train depot in Butte to see me off. The only time in my life I ever saw Ernie cry was when I got on the train to leave. During my training in the States, I kept track of the war news, but still the war was a long way from me.

When Robert Parnell's crew number 5383 arrived at the 351st Bomb Group and we began to experience the urgency of a combat group's business, then the

Sam Wyrouck's B-17 bomber crew. Sam is pictured second from the left on the front row.

war got closer. During the two weeks of training before our first combat mission we really learned how to fly a tight defensive box formation and learned many other things. We were given constant instructions. Pilots were told that instead of the engines being redlined at forty-five inches of mercury for the maximum exhaust manifold pressure, they could push those four Wright Cyclones to fifty inches of mercury. Pilots were also told that if on landing they ever touched down past the first third marker on the nine-thousand-foot runway they would have to pay a five-pound fine (twenty-five dollars).

We had basic lessons in German emphasizing how to get around if we were shot down. We were told to never fly without both dog tags because if we were shot down and captured by the Germans, they would shoot us as spies if they found us without them. We were told to scuff up one pair of our GI shoes and take them when we flew because highly shined shoes were a dead giveaway if we were evading capture. We were told to tie this pair of shoes together tightly and always keep them in the same place in the airplane so we could grab them and snap them onto our parachute harnesses in case we had to bail out, because if walking around in Germany or if captured, we would need a good pair of shoes. Of course when we flew, we wore boots with electrically heated inserts to keep our feet warm at sixty degrees below zero. We were taught how to evade capture and some examples of success. One evader walked all the way across Germany and France pushing a wheelbarrow while looking like a worker. They told us the Army could never make us do anything, but it could make us wish we had.

Also during this precombat time we always walked down to the flight line along with the ground crews when it was time for a mission to return. We counted the B-17s in the group back home. It was easy to subtract the number of bombers returning from the thirty-six sent out that morning to get the losses for the day. Of course there was always the chance that some crews couldn't make it back to the base and landed at another airfield. We saw the battle damage to the bombers and saw the "meat wagons" lined up at the end of the runway ready to haul the wounded to the base hospital. Back at the barracks we saw the supply people clear out the belongings of those crewmembers who were shot down and didn't return that day. We learned to sweat out a mission the way the ground people did. We

Lower ball turret position on a B-17 bomber.

felt bad but still this was far from the gut wrenching of actually being on one of those bombers.

When it came time to fly our first combat mission, we were awakened at 3:00 A.M., which gave us time to wash and shave before going to the mess hall for a combat breakfast. If we didn't fly on a mission, we got what the "groundpounders" got for breakfast, which would be powdered eggs, or "S.O.S.," or mush, or hot cakes and syrup, but flying a mission entitled us to a breakfast of fresh fried eggs, sausage or bacon, hot cakes, and, of course, coffee. For my first couple of missions I had great breakfasts because I knew it might be as late as 10:30 P.M. before I could have another meal, but very soon after a couple of missions, I found that I couldn't eat anything more than black coffee because if I did, it would come back up before we took off.

We soon learned from another gunner from a different crew, Dick Kessner, how to really sweat out a mission. The night before we were scheduled to fly, we constantly stepped outdoors to observe the weather. We had to see for ourselves, because the weather was a military secret, and we weren't privileged to see forecasts. Then we took turns going to operations to see who was flying. Next some of us went to the flight line to see how much gasoline, how much machine-gun ammunition, and how many and what type of bombs were being loaded. We could then put this information together and could better guess what kind of a target and how far.

Dick took this one step further. He checked at operations to see if either of the two West Point graduates was flying because he deduced that they were never sent on missions that were thought to be tough. If neither of them was to fly, Dick would go on sick call before briefing the next morning. If he had waited until after briefing in the morning, when he knew what the target was, then the flight surgeon would turn him away. Our crew flew all the time without any going on sick call. Some crewmembers would go to the flight surgeon after briefing and say that they hadn't slept the night before. The standard remedy was Benzedrine, but the real need was that Benzedrine also calmed nerves and helped a person to control fear. Once we became airborne, my sweating out was over, but the fear would start when the flak barrage began. Fighter attacks didn't cause that fear because a gunner was very busy, but once on the bomb run, no evasive action could be taken to get out of the rack. Flak is the artillery from the ground and even though we flew very high the flak was always with us.

The nearest town to our air base was Polebrook, which had just about one hundred citizens. When we went to their only pub the day after a mission they could always tell us how many we had lost. When the group of thirty-six heavy bombers took off for a mission in the predawn darkness, the whole town would line up on the street and count us out and then later that day, usually after dark, the whole town lined the street again to count us back in. Those wonderful people truly sweated us out. We needed those people and they needed us. At 2:00 A.M. November 25, 1944, the "groundpounders" woke the crews of the 508th Squadron and two other squadrons of our group to fly my ninth mission. We found out the target for the day was the synthetic oil refinery at Merseburg, which was a long way across Germany. We were told how important oil was for the German war machine. We were told that the refinery had been bombed multiple times before and after a brief downtime after each bombing, it was back in operation. The briefing officer said, "This time this group will bomb from eighteen thousand feet so you can't miss destroying the target." It sounded like a good idea, although we were all apprehensive to bomb from such a low and dangerous altitude.

We went to the armament shop and wiped every speck of oil from the machine gun mechanisms. One drop of oil could freeze up a machine gun at a temperature of sixty degrees below zero. We then loaded the guns onto the six-by-six truck and picked up electrically heated clothing rack jackets, parachutes, and Mae Wests (life jackets) and got that all to old "Queenie." When the taxi flare arched over, we took our place in the line of thirty-six bombers and waited to take off. Another flare sent the first down the runway to take off. Each in turn took off in thirty-second intervals. We were supposed to take off in fifteen-second intervals but thirty was about the best we could do. We had a full gas, bomb, and machine gun ammunition load and this was one of the times that Lieutenant Parnell couldn't quite get that "big gassed bird" off that nine-thousand-foot runway without bouncing her a few times to help her out. It seemed like about once per month, one of the planes taking off ran out of runway and crashed at the end it.

We got formed up and the bomber train tried to pick its way so we went around rather than through the rack concentrations. We came to the IP (initial point) of the one-hundred-mile bomb run at eighteen thousand feet, but the cloud cover was up to twenty thousand feet. I'm sure the group leader thought perhaps he should take the group to twenty-two thousand feet. (Most of our missions were flown at thirty thousand and even as high as thirty-four thousand feet.)

While we were in the clouds, it was difficult to maintain a defensive formation. We were lucky to see our wing man, let alone the whole group. The enemy fighters took advantage of this situation and were in and out of the clouds trying to hit us. Closer to the target, the heavy rack took over and the lower altitude was an added advantage for the ground gunners. We couldn't see what was happening, but when we emerged from the clouds after "bombs away" our group was so scattered that we never did form up our own group but formed up with other stragglers from other groups. That was not a good situation because the Germans often flew captured B-17s within an American formation and caused havoc. We gunners had to stay on our toes.

When we got home and landed after dark that evening, we learned that half of the men who lived with us in our barracks had had their belongings picked up by the supply people because they had been shot down. We found out that of the three squadrons that flew that day, we of the 508th Squadron lost five bombers and the other two had losses also. In many ways, this was my worst mission. I just thought to myself, "Whew! That could have been my crew."

CLYDE K. YEATES

Clyde wrote this account for The Deseret News, *December 22, 2000. It tells of his experience as a prisoner of war in Germany during Christmas 1943.*

It was the twenty-fourth day of December, Christmas Eve. We were a group of hungry, cold, lonely soldiers. There were fifty of us jammed into a boxcar. We were being transferred to a new camp, deep in the heart of Germany. We were prisoners of war.

We had been riding in the boxcar two days, not knowing where we were going or when we would get there.

The weather was typical European December weather: snow on the ground, and cold, terribly cold. Ice had formed around the doors from the moisture from our bodies. We had no heat. I was clothed in a British army jacket, without a shirt, the jacket being similar to our Eisenhower jackets, reaching to the waist only. I wore burlap type pants and wooden shoes.

My clothes had been given to me on December 2 when we were called out to take a shower. Our captors took our American uniforms and gave us what we were wearing. We didn't get our shower. They used our clothing to disguise their troops in the resulting Battle of the Bulge. Our new clothes did not keep us warm. It was now some two months since I had been warm, when I left the German hospital in the early part of October.

We were all hungry, very hungry, and so very, very thirsty. Since being taken prisoner some three and a half months before, I could not remember not having hunger pains in my stomach. I had lost some twenty pounds and would lose ten to fifteen more before my hunger would end. We could stand the hunger; we had gradually learned how to cope with it, but the thirst was getting to us. It was two days since we had tasted water. We tried to scrape the frost from the wood, but it didn't help.

That Christmas was my second Christmas away from home. The year before, in the army camp in the States, I had been lonely and homesick, but it seemed so pleasant now, remembering back. We would think of our past Christmases, getting up early, awakening the family, opening the gifts, enjoying the friendship and warmth and food and especially home.

Now, once again it was Christmas Eve. This year, though, we were cold, we were thirsty, oh, so very thirsty, and so lonesome for home and our loved ones. It seemed like a nightmare, that we were here under these conditions, yet the nightmare was real—we could not awaken ourselves and forget.

We forced ourselves into reality. Surely our captors would take us from this cold boxcar, into a warm building, and there feed us and give us water, especially water.

We had been waiting in the train station now for two or three hours. We kept waiting for the guards to open the door and let us out, but it didn't happen. I managed to pry open a small ventilation panel on the side of the boxcar, and then to motion to some German civilians standing nearby for some water. An engineer standing by a neighboring train must have understood, for he came, took the can, filled it with water, and returned it to us. Nine of us had one swallow of water each. It was so good; yet we were still so very thirsty. We motioned for more, but a guard was coming, and the engineer left. We closed the panel.

Finally the train began to move. It was evident that we would not be taken from the train this Christmas Eve.

Eventually we grew more tired and tried to find rest and sleep. We had to lie closely snuggled together to find enough room for all to lie down, and to keep from freezing. It was so very, very cold. After about one-half hour, our upper sides and lower sides grew unbearably cold. Some wanted to turn over; others did not. We practiced our democracy and voted. After the voting, those who lost voiced their disappointment loudly, using every army word that I had ever heard, and even some new ones.

The cars were so narrow that we had to overlap our feet, and those with shoes who didn't remove them caused others to complain. Again the same words were used, but to no avail. I removed my wooden shoes and used them for a pillow. I had put on three pairs of socks, all the clothing I had. My feet were relatively comfortable, while many others ended up with frozen feet.

After approximately one to two hours, when the cold became unbearable, we would have to stand and beat our arms and kick our legs to keep from freezing, and so we spent our Christmas Eve lying down, napping, turning, standing, exercising, and lying down as we had done the two previous nights.

Finally, light began to show through the cracks of the boxcar. Christmas Day had arrived. Christmas! Surely today our captors would take us from these boxcars, and give us warmth and food and water, at least some water. Each time we entered a town, we thought we would surely stop and receive some relief from this unbearable cold and thirst. As noon approached, we had convinced ourselves that we would stop at the next town, in a few minutes, and quench this terrible thirst. Noon passed us by, and afternoon, and as the shadows increased, we started to realize that this Christmas Day was going to end cold and miserable, and we would still be hungry and so very thirsty.

As the shadows deepened, tempers became sharp. Fifty soldiers, crowded together, hungry, cold, haggard from lack of sleep and thirst, realized that this Christmas was to be one that we would not, we could not forget. It was three days now since we had eaten, since we had had any sleep, any restful sleep. Our thirst was almost unbearable. If we bumped a neighbor, he complained; if we said a strong word, others complained; if we talked of home, some complained; and if we did not talk of home, others complained.

The cans we used for latrines were full and overflowing. We had heard aircraft but, thankfully, we had not been attacked as the train behind us had been. We were to later learn that seventy-six of our buddies had died from the attack by our British allies.

The tension grew and magnified until it seemed something must explode. Was this Christmas? Were we to lose our self-control because of our miseries? Had we lost our brotherly love? Were we to lose our minds under the stresses and hardships, under the hunger, the cold, the loneliness, the terrible thirst? It seemed we could bear no more, when someone in the car started to sing, "Silent night, holy night, all is calm, all is bright." This song that originated in this war-torn part of the world seemed to have the inspiration for the occasion.

The angry voices quieted, other started to join in, "Round yon virgin mother and child. Holy infant so tender and mild." The chorus swelled, not in musical harmony, but more important in brotherly harmony and understanding. As the song continued, we were all singing—singing from our hearts as we had never done before: "Sleep in heavenly peace; sleep in heavenly peace." The song ended; the voices again were heard, but were quiet voices, and friendly, and filled with understanding one for another. This Christmas Day we had experienced a warmth and fullness of spirit that we had never experienced before, nor would we or could we forget. Once again we prepared for the night, to lie down, nap, turn over and rise and exercise, and to think of our next Christmas, hoping and praying that it would be a Christmas like others we remembered— a Christmas with joy and peace.

THE CHURCH NEWS

When D-Day dawned last Tuesday and Americans all over the land were awakened by cries of newsboys announcing the beginning of the European invasion, a sobering influence swept over the nation. A pronounced religious note crept into discussions of the great undertaking, radio programs were characterized by appeals to the Almighty . . . and many prayers were said.

The wave of spiritual devotion, which seemed to move from coast to coast, was indeed heartening to all who understand the real meaning of prayer. . . . But it recalled the words of Lincoln in a similar situation when he suggested that just praying was not sufficient, but that living the divine law was quite as necessary. "I am not so concerned," he is quoted as saying, "about whether the Lord is on our side. What does concern me is whether we are on the Lord's side."

The cause of freedom without doubt has the sympathy of the Almighty, but being on his side means far more than a readiness to fight for liberty. It means living from day to day in conformity with his teachings, sustaining religious activity, abstaining from demoralizing practices, worshipping the Author of Liberty in our homes, rearing our children in the fear of God, helping the poor and unfortunate, overcoming selfishness and being kind to others.

To what extent can we say we are on the Lord's side? ("Consistency!" Editorial in *The Church News* published by *The Deseret News,* Salt Lake City, Utah, June 10, 1944).

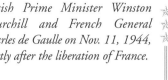

British Prime Minister Winston Churchill and French General Charles de Gaulle on Nov. 11, 1944, shortly after the liberation of France.

Eugene H. Ballard with his B-24 crew. (L to R) Front Row: Eugene H. Ballard, Ronald E. Hall, Stanley W. Richardson. Back Row: Harvey W. Bronsteen, Eugene W. Stout, Charles Kline, William McCabe.

(Right) Medic Eldon F. Lewis, preparing medical reports. Once, while working on medical records in his tent, the Germans attacked. Eldon immediately jumped for cover. When he returned to his desk he noticed a bullet embedded in his journal that he had left on his desk.

(Below) Pfc. Zane S. Taylor (front middle, without a helmet) with comrades in France, Nov. 1944. Zane marched with Patton's 3rd Army throughout much of Europe. In the process his faith grew as he faced difficult combat conditions. He received the nickname "Zack," short for the biblical character Zechariah because of his adherence to gospel standards even in the most difficult situations.

(Right) Lt. Harold Reek (bombardier) sleeping on 500-pound RDX bombs.

(Below) The Mormon Mustang flown by Roland R. Wright. (L to R) Don Roepe, assistant Crew chief; 1st Lt. Roland R. Wright, pilot; Kelley Lloyd, crew chief; Ken Arverson, armorer.

Welcome Home banner in San Francisco at the end of the war.

THE PACIFIC THEATER

For the United States, World War II began and ended in the Pacific. The surprise attack at Pearl Harbor came after months of diplomatic wrangling over deteriorating relations between the United States and Japan. The center of controversy between Tokyo and Washington was Japan's expansionist policies in Asia and the Pacific. Rising tensions coupled with an economic embargo imposed by the United States further intensified Japan's desire to eliminate the only significant obstacle to Japanese dominance in Asia and the Pacific.

(Opposite) A pilot waits in a life raft somewhere in the South Pacific for a rescue plane.

ASIATIC–PACIFIC CAMPAIGN MEDAL was awarded to United States personnel for service within the Asiatic-Pacific Theater between December 7, 1941 and March 2, 1946 under any of the following conditions:

(1) On permanent assignment.

(2) In a passenger status or on temporary duty for 30 consecutive days or 60 days not consecutive.

(3) In active combat against the enemy and was awarded a combat decoration or furnished a certificate by the commanding general of a corps, higher unit, or independent force that he actually participated in combat.

A SLEEPING GIANT AWAKES

On Sunday morning, December 7, 1941, Japan surprised the U.S. Pacific Fleet with an attack on Pearl Harbor. The fleet was severely crippled as nineteen ships were sunk or disabled, including six great battleships at port. The attack took the lives of nearly 2,500 Americans. A nation once divided by the isolation-versus-intervention debate became united over night. America had been attacked.

THE PACIFIC THEATER

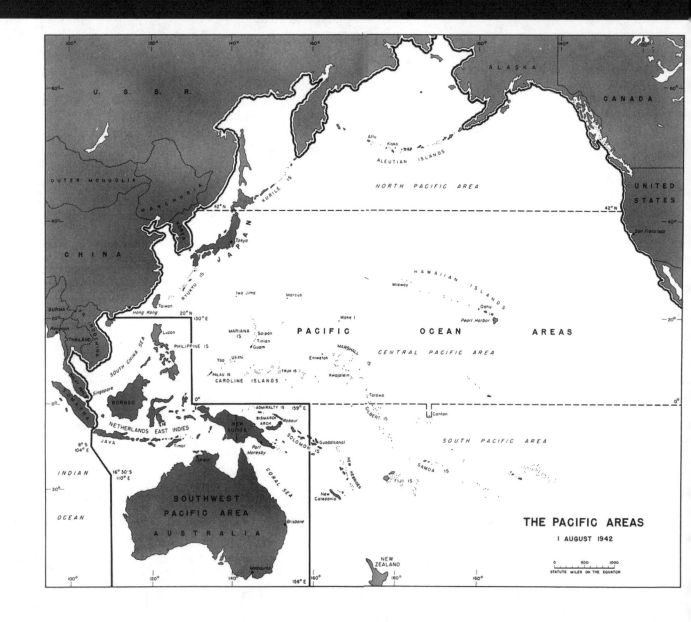

THE PACIFIC AREAS

1 AUGUST 1942

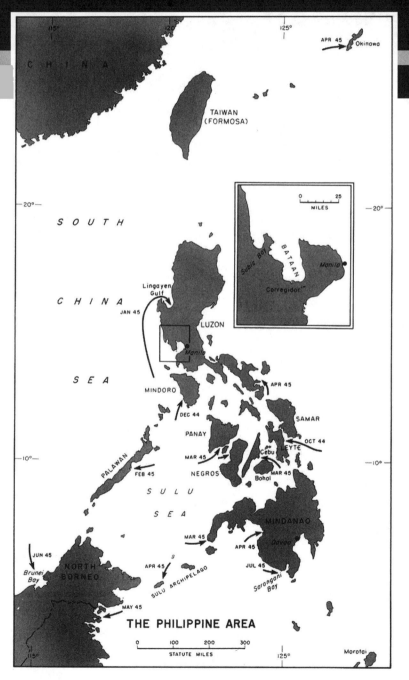

THE PHILIPPINE AREA

The eastern boundary of the Asiatic-Pacific Theater is from the North Pole, south along the 141st meridian west longitude to the east boundary of Alaska, then south and southeast along the Alaska boundary to the Pacific Ocean, then south along the 130th meridian to its intersection with the 30th parallel north latitude, then southeast to the intersection of the Equator and the 100th meridian west longitude, then to the South Pole. The western boundary of the Asiatic-Pacific Theater is from the North Pole south along the 60th meridian east longitude to its intersection with the east boundary of Iran, then south along the Iran boundary to the Gulf of Oman and the intersection of the 60th meridian east longitude, then south along the 60th meridian east longitude to the South Pole. The Asiatic-Pacific Theater included Alaska, Hawaii, the Philippines, Australia, New Zealand, and all of Asia.

ALL THE NEWS ALL THE TIME
LARGEST HOME-DELIVERED CIRCULATION
LARGEST ADVERTISING VOLUME

MAdison 2345
The Times Telephone Number

Los Angeles Times

LIBERTY UNDER THE LAW — TRUE INDUSTRIAL FREEDOM

IN THREE PARTS — 42 PAGES
Part I — GENERAL NEWS — 24 Pages

TIMES OFFICE
202 West First Street

VOL. LXI — CCC — MONDAY MORNING, DECEMBER 8, 1941. — DAILY, FIVE CENTS

JAPS OPEN WAR ON U.S. WITH BOMBING OF HAWAII

City Springs to Attention

Los Angeles, Stunned by Sudden War Start, Turns Wholeheartedly to Defense Task; 'They Started It, We'll Finish It,' Motto

Los Angeles was a city alert yesterday as every man and woman, electrified by the news that Japan had struck at this country 2400 miles westward in the Pacific, took his or her stand solidly for total defense.

Stunned at first, incredulous that Japan actually had bombed Pearl Harbor defenses, the city was set buzzing as the news flashed through the streets.

Traffic lanes jammed, telephones clattered incessantly and the downtown area swarmed with curious citizens.

'WE'LL FINISH IT'

Then came a reaction as truly American as apple pie.

Minutes after news of the Japanese attack was heard, defense and law enforcement agencies began operating. Citizens attached to defense groups mobilized. The city shrugged off its amazement. The word was: "They started it—we'll finish it!"

Soldiers and sailors, their leaves canceled, were ordered to report immediately to their stations. This they did with least confusion. All officers and men in the services were ordered to report for duty forthwith. In uniform. No more audit. It's war.

FAREWELL SCENES

There were farewell scenes in train and bus depots. Mothers, fathers and sweethearts came to wish their loved ones luck. But they were calm, those going and those staying.

Everywhere the import of war was apparent.

From San Diego to the Oregon border fighter planes of the 4th Interceptor Command watched on flight lines—ready to go.

Antiaircraft crews, artillery and machine guns bristling skyward, guarded breathless aircraft factories. All members of the Aircraft Warning Service were ordered to report to their head quarters and all observation posts were directed to be manned at all times.

Complete black-out of the harbor area including San Pedro, Wilmington and a major part of Long Beach was ordered early today by Capt. Richard E. Cliff.

Japanese Aliens Roundup Starts

F.B.I. Hunting Down 300 Subversives and Plans to Hold 3000 Today

NEW YORK, Dec. 8 (AP)—A great man hunt was under way last night in Southern California as the Federal Bureau of Investigation agents sought the alien Japanese suspected of subversive activities.

An exact as war is declared against Japan, judging a certainty today the Department agents, aided by local police and placed to pre tective custody by government agents, The Times learned.

SUSPECTS ROUNDED UP

During the afternoon and night, close to 300 suspicious Japanese were rounded up by police deputy sheriffs and special officers working under the direction of F.B.I. agents.

In West Los Angeles 18 were nabbed, 16 were taken into custody at Terminal police station, 4 at Hollywood, 4 at Wilshire, between 30 and 40 went through the University station, 1 at Pasadena, 1 at Santa Monica, 3 at Hawthorne, 2 at Inglewood, 30 at Hollenbeck station, and on through the list of Los Angeles police stations and outlying cities.

In Santa Ana 15 were taken in custody for questioning, these cameras and 19 guns, finally seized, were confiscated at their homes.

NAMES WITHHELD

The F.B.I. issued orders prohibiting the publication of the names of those held until further orders from Washington.

Raids throughout Los Angeles.

Lindbergh Keeps Silent

WEST TISBURY (Mass.) Dec. 7 (AP)—Charles A. Lindbergh, visiting at Seven Gates farm in this Martha's Vineyard island village, refused tonight to see newspapermen or accept any messages.

F.D.R. Will Ask Congress Action Today

President to Make Plea Personally on Move to Answer Japan Attacks

WASHINGTON, Dec. 8 (Monday.) (AP)—Bombs from Japan made war on the United States today and as death tolls mounted President Roosevelt announced he will deliver in person today a special message to Congress.

In the background as the Commander-in-Chief went before the joint session of the House and Senate was a government report of "heavy" naval and "large" losses to the Army.

ACTION UNCERTAIN

Whether Mr. Roosevelt will ask for a formal declaration of war by the country, to march the action taken in Tokyo, was left uncertain after a hurriedly summoned meeting of his Cabinet.

NEW YORK, Dec. 7 (AP)—A three-major networks — National Broadcasting Co., Columbia Broadcasting System and Mutual Broadcasting System—will carry President Roosevelt's message to Congress at 12:30 p.m. (E.S.T.) 430 a.m. (P.S.T.) tomorrow.

And Congressional leaders of both parties tonight at the White House. Alarm uncertain as to whether the House will take steps toward Japan's Axis allies, Germany and Italy.

It was clear from a statement made by the participants, however, that Congress would be the quickest to adopt a resolution of some nature, and equally clear that it would quickly give its approval. A request for governmental power equivalent to that under a war declaration was expected as a minimum.

WITHOUT WARNING

War came suddenly to the United States early yesterday when "naval operations are progressing at Hawaii with at least one Japanese aircraft carrier in action against Pearl Harbor" the American naval base in the islands.

U.S. ENVOY NOTIFIED

Japanese bombers were declared to have raided Honolulu at 7:35 a.m. Hawaii time (10:05 a.m. Sunday, P.S.T.)

Premier-War Minister Gen. Hideki Tojo held a 20-minute Cabinet session at his official residence at 7 a.m., and shortly that both the United States Ambassador Joseph C. Grew, and the British Ambassador Sir Robert Leslie Craigie, had been summoned by Foreign Minister Shigenori Togo.

The Foreign Minister, Dono said, handed to Grew the Japanese government's formal reply to its own note to Japan by United States Secretary of State Cordell Hull on Nov. 26.

EIGHT HULL'S TERMS

(In the course of the diplomatic negotiations leading up to this day's events, the Domei agency had stated that Japan could not accept the premises of Hull's Nov. 26 note.)

Berlin Shy About Aid to Tokyo

BERLIN, Dec. 8 (Monday.) (AP)—Obligated under the three-power pact to go to Japan's assistance if Japan is "attacked," Germany referred early today to hostilities in the Pacific as "clashes."

A special communique failed to clarify Germany's intentions, but termed President Roosevelt a "war incendiary."

"The stronger Roosevelt has reached his aim," said the Berlin statement.

"Driven by blind hatred against the Reich of Adolf Hitler, he and weapons and materials to British campaign against the Axis and finally gave his Sgt orders to fire on German ships.

"So Roosevelt ran after war like a demon until the Pacific Ocean also is inflamed. Dollar imperialism overcame the good sense of a wide circle of North American people."

Attacks Precede War Declaration

Tokyo Notifies Envoys After Surprise Raid Upon Pearl Harbor Base

TOKYO, Dec. 8 (Monday.) (AP)—Japan went to war against the United States and Great Britain today with air and sea attacks against Hawaii followed by a formal declaration of hostilities.

Japanese Imperial headquarters announced at 6 a.m. (1 p.m. Sunday, P.S.T.) that a state of war existed among these nations in the Western Pacific, as it dawn.

Shortly afterward Domei announced that "naval operations are progressing at Hawaii with at least one Japanese aircraft carrier in action against Pearl Harbor," the American naval base in the islands.

Toll Feared High in Attack Against Isles

Field Near Honolulu Takes Brunt of Bombing; Naval Battle Reported

HONOLULU, Dec. 7. (AP)—War struck suddenly and without warning from the sky and sea today at the Hawaiian Islands. Japanese bombs took a heavy toll in American lives.

Cannonading offshore indicated a naval engagement in progress.

Wave after wave of planes streamed over Oahu in an attack which the Army said started at 830 a.m., Honolulu time, and which ended at around 9:25, an hour and 15 minutes later.

COUNT 50 PLANES

Witnesses said they counted at least 50 planes in the initial attack.

The attack seemed to center on Hickam Field, huge Army air base three miles northwest of Honolulu, and Honolulu where the islands' heaviest fortifications are located.

The planes streamed through the sky from the southwest, their bombs shattering the morning calm. Most of the planes flew high, but a few came low, five down to under a hundred feet elevation in attack Pearl Harbor.

HAWAII HIT

An oil tank there was seen blazing and smoking. An unconcerned report said one ship in the harbor was on its side and four others burning.

Army officials said some Japanese planes had been shot down in the Honolulu area.

Planes which did not bomb Pearl Harbor apparently headed for Hickam Field. But there the attackers apparently did see combat (inadvertently to the heavily fortified areas. From Wahiawa, town of 2900 population about 30 miles northwest of Honolulu, came reports that 10 or more persons were injured where enemy planes poured bullets to the streets.

FROM PLANE CARRIERS

United States destroyers were seen steaming full speed from Pearl Harbor, and spectators reported seeing shell splashes in the ocean, indicating an engagement between United States and Japanese ships.

Several fires were started in the Honolulu area, but all were immediately controlled.

ESTIMATE OF CASUALTIES

There was no immediate statement by military officials here as to whether any servicemen were killed or injured, or as to property damage at military and naval posts.

(Soon after this dispatch was telephoned, a tight censorship was imposed on dispatches from the Hawaiian Islands. It was...)

Fleet Speeds Out to Battle Invader

Tokyo Claims Battleship Sunk and Another Set Afire With Hundreds Killed on Island; Singapore Attacked and Thailand Force Landed

BY THE ASSOCIATED PRESS

Japan assaulted every main United States and British possession in the Central and Western Pacific and invaded Thailand today in a hasty but evidently shrewdly-planned prosecution of a war she began Sunday without warning.

Her formal declaration of war against both the United States and Britain came 2 hours and 55 minutes after Japanese planes spread death and terrific destruction in Honolulu and Pearl Harbor at 7:35 a.m., Hawaiian time (10:05 a.m., P.S.T.) Sunday.

The claimed successes for this fell swoop included the sinking of the United States battleship West Virginia and setting afire the battleship Oklahoma.

WAKE CAPTURED AND GUAM BOMBED

From that moment, each tense tick of the clock brought new and flaming accounts of Japanese aggression in her secretly launched war of conquest or death for the land of the Rising Sun.

As compiled from official and unofficial accounts from all affected countries, including such sources as the Tokyo and Berlin radios, the record of Japan's daring all-or-nothing gamble ran like this:

United States transport Gen. Hugh Scott, carrying lumber, sunk, 1600 miles from Manila;

Liner President Harrison, now a transport, seized or sunk in the Yangtze River near Shanghai;

British colony of Hongkong bombed twice;

Small United States garrison at Tientsin, China, disarmed and presumably captured;

United States island of Guam bombed, surrounded and oil reservoir and hotel set afire. Honolulu bombed a second time;

Shanghai's International Settlement seized; United States gunboat Wake captured there and British gunboat Peterel destroyed;

United States island of Wake captured;

Many points throughout the Philippine Islands bombed;

Northern Malaya and Thailand (Siam) invaded and Singapore and Bangkok bombed.

The first United States official casualty report listed 104 dead and more than 300 injured in the Army at Hickam Field, alone, near Honolulu. An N.B.C. observer in Honolulu reported the death toll at Hickam was 300.

There was heavy damage in Honolulu residential districts and the death list among civilians was large but uncounted.

GERMANS CLAIM SEA BATTLE ON

The German radio reported that a sea battle between the Japanese navy on one side and the British and United States on the other was in progress in the Western Pacific, with a third United States warship hit in addition to the West Virginia and Oklahoma.

The British command at Singapore announced the Japanese invasion and said empire forces are engaging the foe.

There was little news of United States defensive actions, except the report that a number of the attacking planes at Honolulu had been shot down in dogfights over the city;

Latest War Bulletins

NEW YORK, Dec. 8, (AP) N.B.C. said today the United States aircraft carrier Langley was reported unofficially in Manila to have been damaged in action with Japanese forces.

Radio Tokyo, as heard by the N.B.C. listening post in Los Angeles, reported that Japanese bombers had attacked the island of Palawan in the Philippines.

NEW YORK, Dec. 8. (AP)—The British radio today quoted Tokyo broadcasts as saying that Germany probably will declare war on the United States within the next 24 hours.

WASHINGTON, Dec. 7. (AP)—The White House announced tonight that at President Roosevelt's conference with legislative leaders and members of the Cabinet he received word from Gen. Douglas MacArthur that "enemy" planes were over Central Luzon in the Philippines.

N.B.C.'s listening post tonight heard a Tokyo radio report that 63 American soldiers guarding the American concession at Tientsin had been captured and disarmed. The report, quoting the Japanese Army Bureau, did not mention the Consulate staff.

MANAGUA (Nicaragua) Dec. 7. (AP)—Nicaragua tonight declared war on Japan.

NEW YORK, Dec. 7. (AP)—The Berlin radio, heard by the United Press listening post here, said Tokyo had announced a ...

IN THE 'TIMES' TODAY

RADIO. Page 10, Part I.
COMICS. Page 6, Part I.
FASHION. CLUBS, SOCIETY. Pages 1, 2, 3, 4, 5, 6 and 10. Part II.
TOM TREANOR. Page 4, Part I.
WESTBROOK PEGLER. Page 7, Part I.
PUZZLE. Page 20, Part I.
DRAMA. Page 10, Part II.
WEATHER. Page 18, Part I.
DEATH NOTICES. Page 16, Part I.
PICTORIAL PAGES. Pages 8 and 9.
THE SOUTHLAND Southland cities upped civilian defense plans. First class graduated from maritime science at Fort Mac home. Page 22, Part I.
SPORTS. Hollywood Bears bring Columbus Bulls. Page 13, Part I. Conference moguls meet today. Page 13, Part I.

MONDAY DECEMBER 8, 1941

THE CITY. City springs to multitudinous tasks of defense. Page 1, Part I.
F.B.I. roundup of Japanese aliens. Page 1, Part I.
Seven civilian hero and down by motorist. Page 1, Part II.
Welders cancel surface strike situation tomorrow—Page 2, Part I.
County Civilian Defense Committee ordered to be on 24-hour call. Page 6, Part C.
Little Tokyo carries on "business as usual." Page 7, Part I.
British declaration of war on Japan awaited in Parliament moves today. Page C.
Three American warships reported damaged. Page C.
Japanese troops as you can foreign settlement at Shanghai. Page C.
Little news era komma non foreign activity. Page A, Part C.
Japanese attack Thailand as ... Page 8, Part I.

REMEMBER THIS

No nation is free that cannot care in own living.

World Affairs Institute opens session in Riverside. Page 5, Part I.
GENERAL EASTERN Aviation board grants engine and coppers some shop. Page 5, Part I.
THE WAR. United States now held to either pass business war in Hawaii. Page 1, Part C.
Tokyo notifies American and British envoys of war's start. Page 1, Part C.

Air Guards, Attention!

To chief observers: All observation posts—

A.W.S. (Aircraft Warning System) You are directed to activate your observation posts immediately and to see that the post is fully manned at all times.

By order Brig. Gen. William O. Ryan, Commanding Gen., 4th Interceptor Command.

Los Angeles Times, *December 8, 1941. Compilation by* Los Angeles Times.

In the midst of devastation, however, a few things saved the United States Navy from being completely incapacitated. The *Lexington* and *Enterprise*, two aircraft carriers usually based at Pearl Harbor, were at sea. The Japanese failed to destroy most oil facilities and repair yards. Eventually, the United States was able to return most of the damaged battleships to active duty.

Only a few hours after the bombing at Pearl Harbor, the Japanese assault continued with attacks on Hong Kong, Malaya, and the Philippines. The United States Air Corps in the Philippines was dealt a severe blow. Over the course of the next few months, Filipino and American troops fought to hold back the enemy. Ultimately, the troops surrendered at Bataan and Corregidor. The prisoners at Bataan were forced to make a horrific sixty-five-mile march, and thousands died along the way. This Philippine campaign cost 140,000 American and Filipino lives. By contrast, only 4,000 Japanese soldiers were killed.

Meanwhile, other nations became targets of Japanese aggression. With their eyes set on Port Moresby at New Guinea and ultimately on Australia, the Japanese sought for greater control of the Solomon Islands. They planned a surprise carrier attack on the U.S. Pacific Fleet in the Coral Sea. U.S. code-breaking, however, allowed Admiral Chester Nimitz, commander of the Pacific Fleet, to prepare his forces.

The Battle of the Coral Sea in May 1942 was the first naval battle fought completely by carrier aircraft. The United States lost the USS *Lexington*, and the USS *Yorktown* was seriously damaged. The battle, however, became the first strategic defeat for the Japanese. The Imperial Navy abandoned its plan to invade Port Moresby; Japan had lost too many carrier planes. This battle coupled with the surprise air raid over Tokyo one month earlier by "Doolittle's Raiders," under the command of Lieutenant Colonel James Doolittle, conveyed the message that the Japanese forces were not invincible.

Examples of currency used during the period of World War II. (Courtesy of Alexander Baugh III)

THE TIDE BEGINS TO TURN

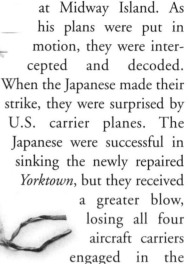

Japanese flag in General Yamashita's possession at the time of his surrender at the end of the war. (Courtesy of Allen Acomb)

The Doolittle Raid removed all internal obstacles to Japanese Admiral Yamamoto's plan to attack an American base at Midway Island. As his plans were put in motion, they were intercepted and decoded. When the Japanese made their strike, they were surprised by U.S. carrier planes. The Japanese were successful in sinking the newly repaired *Yorktown*, but they received a greater blow, losing all four aircraft carriers engaged in the battle. The fighting at Midway turned the tide in the Pacific and put Japan on the defensive.

The United States then initiated an offensive strike as the First Marine Division made a surprise attack on Guadalcanal (Solomon Islands). The prize for this move was a nearly completed and strategically placed landing base, later named Henderson Field. The cost was six months of bloody jungle fighting—the most sustained violence in World War II. Ultimately, the battle was decided at sea, and the United States claimed victory.

Under the direction of General Douglas MacArthur, who commanded forces in the southwest Pacific, American and Australian forces began to advance through the Solomons and along the New Guinea coast. By early fall of 1943, the Allies occupied key territories, which took pressure off of Australia.

During November 1943, the Central Pacific drive began as marine and army forces invaded the Japanese-held Gilbert Islands. The battle at Tarawa, the first strategic battle the United States undertook against a heavily defended island, was short but intense. The Marine Corps suffered three thousand casualties and gained only three square miles of land. The lessons learned at Tarawa, however, paved the way for greater success in the Central Pacific Campaign. By the end of February 1944, Kwajalein and other parts of the Marshall Islands fell into Allied hands, and the invasion date for the Mariana Islands moved forward twenty weeks.

In June, the United States began bombarding the Mariana Islands. The invasion of Saipan (one of the Mariana Islands), provoked a desperate Japanese counterattack. The Battle of the Philippine Sea became the largest carrier battle of World War II, and Japan suffered great losses in the air. By mid-August, Saipan, Tinian, and Guam were under Allied control. In November 1944, B-29 Superfortresses stationed on bases in Guam and Saipan delivered their first strikes against mainland Japan.

THE DRIVE TO VICTORY

The Battle of Leyte Gulf, the largest naval battle in history, began in October 1944. During this battle, the desperate Imperial Fleet employed a new, radical weapon—the kamikaze bomber. The Philippine campaign was a personal war for General MacArthur, who had been soundly beaten in the islands at the beginning of the war. As he marched onto the shores of Leyte, he declared to the people of the Philippines, "I have returned." Leyte was secured in

Gen. Douglas MacArthur (fourth from the left) wades ashore during initial landings at Leyte in the Philippines.

the rear command post and found a bombed-out house. The only thing standing were the walls. But it gave us a little bit of privacy. I scrounged some ammunition boxes and formed a pulpit and sacrament table from those. I found some spent shell casings and some little wild flowers that had survived all the battles, and set them up for a little bit of atmosphere. We had a field organ, which I played. I had to use my knees to pump it to make any music. I waited impatiently to see how many would come.

Then the trucks started coming in. By the time we had our service, there were about fifty Latter-day Saint young men there. They had come directly from combat and their foxholes. They were dirty and unshaven. They had their combat gear, ammunition belts, canteens, steel helmets, and their rifles. They got off those trucks and rather than have them carry their weapons inside the house, we had them stack them outside the walls. They sat on their steel helmets, because that was the only thing they had to sit on. We enjoyed one of the most spiritual services I have ever attended in my life. Some of those men had not been in a Latter-day Saint service since they left home. A number of them had gone astray. I will never forget, as we partook of the sacrament, the priests knelt at the table and could not get through the prayers because they were so emotional about it. I watched some of the men who acted as deacons, tears coursing down their cheeks as they passed the sacrament in our mess gear to the congregation and those receiving it feeling the same spirit, tears in their eyes. After singing some hymns, praying, and partaking of the sacrament, we turned it into a testimony meeting. I do not know when I have heard more fervent testimonies. Men who on the spot repented of things they had done and said, "This is going to change my life just by having this association, singing these songs and feeling this fellowship, and renewing my covenants with the Lord." It was one of those experiences I will never forget. I think that was the highlight of anything that happened to me in the war.

ROSALIE S. BAILEY

Rosalie was a private first class and served in the Women's Reserve Battalion. She was stationed at the Marine Corps Base, Department of the Pacific in San Francisco, California. In the following account, Rosalie describes meeting her future husband and her introduction to the Church.

I was born July 8, 1923, in San Francisco, California. My parents were Jewish and I had a little bit of Jewish training.

When World War II was declared, I had just graduated from high school and felt I wanted to do something for the war effort so I joined the aircraft warning service. I did that for a couple of years until it was disbanded because the danger of Japanese attacks on the West Coast was past. Then I looked for something else to do. I had only one brother who was six years younger than I. I felt it was my duty to help fight this war so I decided to join the Marine Corps. That was difficult. I was not twenty-one yet, and my parents refused to sign the papers for me. When I heard there were only two more groups going to Camp Le Jeune, North Carolina, for boot camp I really put the pressure on my parents, and finally they signed my papers. I tried very hard to fail all the tests for office work, wanting to do something more adventurous. I was an accomplished secretary so it was impossible to fail the typing test, and finally I was assigned as a clerk typist, ending up in the women's reserve battalion office in the Marine Corps Base in San Diego.

I hated it, but finally the reason the Lord put me there came to pass. The girl who had the bunk above mine in the barracks asked me to be her bridesmaid when she married a sailor. They decided to introduce his best man to me by having a blind date. This handsome sailor arrived. His name was Reed Bailey. He was a Mormon, and I had never known a Mormon before. He was from American Fork, Utah. We immediately fell in love and saw each other every night. On the third night he asked me to marry him. I wanted to wait a little longer, so at the end of the week I said, "Yes." We then separated to go to our various hometowns for Christmas leave and to tell our parents what we were about to do. Needless to say, we didn't make them very happy. At the end of the two-week leave, we were again in San Diego and making plans for a wedding. Reed wanted the Mormon bishop to marry us, but he refused saying he couldn't do it because it was wartime and we hadn't known each other long enough and we weren't even the same religion. I didn't mind. I wasn't very impressed by that bishop. So we went to the Marine Corps chaplain and were married in the usual bride-walking-down-the-aisle wedding. My folks were even able to come although they weren't overjoyed, but it didn't take them too long to realize what a wonderful man I had married.

Three months later Reed received orders to return to the South Pacific. He was attached to VJ-9 which was a service unit that did mail, towed targets, ferried VIPs, etc., and he never saw any combat in all his years in the Navy. We had rented a room in Pacific Beach, and we were there together while he was packing his gear to leave. He came to me with a very small book which had been given to all the Mormon servicemen called *Principles of the Gospel*. He said to me, "You know, it would make my mother very happy if you would join the Church. So if you have some time maybe you could read this." And I took it and put it with my things. I knew nothing about the Church at that point.

Rosalie Bailey gazing out through the Golden Gate Bridge while sitting on the beach, wishing for her husband's early return.

He left and I was alone. I moved back to the barracks where I was still alone every evening and felt the best thing to do was get a transfer to San Francisco where I could live with my parents and work for the Department of the Pacific doing my usual and boring office work with the Marine Corps. My transfer came through and I arrived in San Francisco. I was in my old childhood bedroom unpacking my things and came across the little book *Principles of the Gospel* and remembered what Reed had said. I thought, "Well, he said it would make his mother happy if I joined the Church, but I don't really care if it would make her happy, but I wonder if it would make him happy." So I started to read it. Even sitting here writing this, I begin to get the same feeling in my chest that I had when I began to read that book. I certainly didn't know what was happening to me, but I was so excited. I was thrilled by what I was reading. I was completely amazed. That little book had many subjects with scripture references at the end of the subject. Of course, the only scripture in my parent's home was the Old Testament so I used that as a reference. What I was reading filled in the gaps. It brought alive the things I had been taught, and I knew everything was absolutely true. I read every bit of it and knew it was true. My breast burned with excitement, and I tried to share it with my parents but they weren't interested. So I waited until the war was over and Reed came home. He really didn't know very much about the gospel, although he was an elder. So we both waited until we were released from the service and arrived in American Fork.

I started to ask questions. Reed's parents gave me every book they had in their library, and I read them all with great excitement. Then one evening they invited their friend, the stake mission leader, over to dinner. He and I went to a room and had a long talk, and when we came out he said, "This young lady has a great knowledge of the gospel. She doesn't need to have the missionaries. She is ready to be baptized now." And I was. On our first wedding anniversary my husband baptized me in the Alpine Stake Tabernacle.

I know without a shadow of a doubt that the Holy Ghost taught me the gospel. I was prepared to accept it in that way because I would never have listened to the elders. I was truly taught by the Holy Spirit. I had always felt the Spirit near me, although it took me some time to realize what had happened to me. I will never be able to thank the Lord enough for His great gift to me of my wonderful testimony.

W. FRED BANKS

Fred was a first lieutenant in the Army. He received a Bronze Star for his operations against the enemy at Bougainville, Solomon Islands.

As I look back and count the days of the first ninety days we were on the island of Bougainville, I spent something like seventy-two days behind the Japanese lines. I spent more time there than I did in our own area. The airplanes had put together an aerial photograph of the area. It looked like there was a large vegetable garden being grown by the Japanese in the middle of the island. I was given the mission to locate this vegetable garden and see what it was, and if possible destroy it or find out what the Japanese were really doing. I took six men with me on this mission, going through the jungle, traveling at night many times and during the day. We had native guides to help us in the jungles because they had a very delicate sense of smell, and they could locate the Japanese much faster than we could. On this particular patrol we went way back into the island, much farther than ever before to find this place. When we got there, it wasn't a garden, but it was a bunch of other things that they were cultivating. As we started back, the Japanese located us and sent their patrols out after us. Of course, we had no way of retreating fast enough to get away from them.

There was a large swamp that ran most of the length of the island between the beach and the mountains. We were on the mountain side of the swamp and our only retreat was into the swamp, so we went into the swamp where we would be waist deep most of the time in water. There were large banyan trees, much foliage, and many wild papayas. The only solution was to put ourselves in a position where they couldn't find us. We had learned in guerrilla school about a certain reed that grew on the island that was like a hollow tube. I found some of them and we went into the swamp. Each one of us had one of the reeds. We found a banyan tree and at the tree we tied each other together with sound power telephone wire. One person was assigned to stay close to the banyan tree and to come up periodically to see what he could. The rest of us submerged ourselves in the water, breathing through the tubes. We stayed under the water most of the daylight hours, not traveling. At night time, they couldn't find us. At that time, we would take our compasses and travel by night back toward the camp very slowly, moving so that we would make no noise. It took us three days to travel about seven thousand yards; we could never move fast. We could hear the Japanese out trying to find us. They knew we were some place, but they couldn't locate us. We managed to get back to our lines safely and at that time, I was awarded the Bronze Star, because we were able to get back and complete the mission.

*　*　*　*　*

Another time we had the enemy under surveillance. They spotted us, and all of a sudden a shot rang out. I heard a heavy thud on my head, which knocked me down. I thought I had been hit. I shook my head a little bit and a bullet fell down out of my helmet into my hand. I took my helmet off and I found a hole in my helmet, right in the forehead part. The liner had diverted the bullet down. It just ticked my forehead making a little red welt on my forehead and no further injury. It is impossible to explain why the bullet didn't go through my head, because ordinarily even though the helmet was there to protect us, a direct hit into a helmet like that quite often would cause serious injury if not death. I think certainly the Lord's hand was in this again.

*　*　*　*　*

Another time Japanese mortar started to drop around us. All the men dropped for cover. I was trying to see where the fire was coming from. One came, hit into the tree and dropped down and hit just between my legs and exploded. It injured the two men on my right and left, picked me up, and threw me back about five feet. I was stunned, but I had no other injuries of any kind. We were able to grab our two injured men and retreat back to camp without any problems. That was another time that the Lord had reached out and saved me. I was protected because it was not my time to go, I had a mission to perform.

RICHARD W. BARNES ✯✯✯

Gunnery officer aboard the USS Essex, *Richard fought battles in the Mariana Islands, the Philippines, and in Okinawa.*

No other period in my life has been as eventful as April to August 1943. During those five months I became engaged to Dorothy, was baptized into the Mormon Church, graduated from the University of Utah, began active duty as an ensign in the Navy, and in late August returned home to marry Dorothy. Sandwiched in with the other momentous events, my entry into the Church was not a deeply considered or carefully prepared decision. I knew that Dorothy wanted her future husband to be able to take her to the temple, and I had a good disposition toward the Mormons from youthful participation in primary, scouting, and sports activities sponsored by the Church. Also, even though I had had no religious training, knew nothing about the Bible, the Book of Mormon, or doctrines of the Church, there was a thought in the back of my consciousness that before entering the wartime Navy it might be advantageous to have a closer relationship with God.

A phone call to Bishop Wood of the Capitol Hill Ward had set up an appointment for a baptismal interview. . . . No questions were asked concerning my knowledge of Church doctrines, nor if I accepted Joseph Smith as a prophet or even if I had prayed about my decision. Of course my answers to such questions would have "failed" me, but the bishop took it for granted that I knew what I was doing and inquired only about my personal habits. I told him that it was my desire to quit smoking and drinking and that I would try to do so. With that, he issued me a baptismal recommend and scheduled me to attend the next baptismal service at the baptismal font in the Salt Lake Tabernacle. Now even though I had serious reservations about belief in visions, revelations, angelic visitations, etc., as professed by the Church and also about my capability to shed my bad habits, I did not feel hypocritical because I had close association with many inactive Mormons whose thinking was not particularly different from mine. Furthermore, I had no understanding of the importance placed on those concepts by the Mormon Church.

On June 25, 1943, I reported in at the United States Naval Indoctrination School, Fort Schuyler, the Bronx, New York City. My first time in the big city, 2500 miles from home

This worn-looking picture was carried by Richard's daughter, Jody, during the time her father was away at war. The wear and tear was caused by the constant folding and unfolding of the image by young Jody.

and I was tempted to behave like the typical sailor in such circumstances and have a "good time on the town." But something very surprising (to me) occurred. I shared the second-floor bunk room of a large barracks building with some sixty other new officers in training. We were all sleeping in double-decked metal cots, and I had an upper bunk. Unbelievably, in the lower bunk below me was the only other Mormon in the entire barracks. Furthermore, this Mormon was a returned missionary, dedicated and strong in his faith who, after lights out each night, knelt by his cot and said his prayers. He quickly found out about my recent baptism and promptly took me in hand to attend Sunday services with him at the Manhattan Ward.

Richard W. Barnes receiving an award from his superior.

At the conclusion of seven weeks of indoctrination school, I flew home to be with Dorothy, and we got married before my return. Leaving Dorothy in Salt Lake City, I traveled to San Francisco and the Navy flew me to Pearl Harbor to meet the *Essex*.

The Lord, however, made sure that I was not without Church contact. Within my own division in the gunnery department of the *Essex* was a faithful Mormon young man who regularly encouraged me to meet with him and a couple of others who had formed a small study group. While his invitations did not lead to much participation on my part, it still kept me aware that I was now a member of that unique Church that expected special conduct from its adherents. Also, I was beginning to feel a sense of guilt at my inability to live the Word of Wisdom.

At my next assignment on Guam I became friends with those in my Quonset. One day, Lieutenant Cozzens, our supply officer, who lived in the other Quonset just happened to walk by my desk and saw a picture of Dorothy. He recognized the picture as someone he knew and sought me out for further information. Just like my Mormon friend in New York, Moe Cozzens was also a dedicated, faithful, returned missionary and an exemplary model for me. He took an immediate interest in getting me involved with the group. This time I was ready. Moe obtained for me a Doctrine and Covenants, and for the first time I began to learn the doctrines of the Church. The LDS worship services were enjoyable and rewarding, and I found that I could pray and enjoy the support of the Holy Spirit in overcoming my weaknesses. Through reading, study and participation in Church activities on Guam and particularly through the presence of Moe Cozzens, I came home from the war with a testimony of the restored gospel that has grown and blessed me to this day. There is no doubt in my mind that the many "coincidental" experiences which kept me close to the Church in those early years were divinely inspired to meet my particular needs at the time.

* * * * *

While I was aboard the USS *Essex* we had several engagements with the enemy. Most of the time our ship was not affected, and it was just our aircraft in action, miles away from the task force. On one occasion, though, we were called to general quarters to man our battle stations because an enemy plane had been picked up by our radar and was coming in on us. My battle station was a 40-millimeter antiaircraft gun mount on the port side of the flight deck. I was the officer in charge and was responsible for directing the gun.

After just a few minutes on station, we observed antiaircraft activity beyond the stern of our ship. We pointed our gun in that direction and saw a Japanese plane coming in on a low, shallow glide. Unfortunately our gun could not fire (or fortunately, because the target was so low that the firing-safety cutoffs prevented the gun from shooting). Despite the other antiaircraft fire around, the Japanese plane continued toward us. At the last minute, I told my gun-sight operator to get down, and we both dove under the protecting edge of the flight deck. The Japanese plane crashed on the flight deck about seventy-five feet aft of where we were and exploded. Fortunately no one from my gun crew was seriously injured, although a 20-millimeter gun battery located aft of us received many severe casualties.

One of our ship's photographers standing on the flight deck near the island, was able to snap a picture just before the

Japanese plane hit the deck. It showed the Japanese pilot standing up in the cockpit, saluting as his plane crashed. That was our first experience with the Japanese kamikaze pilots that we had been hearing about. As a consequence of a small scratch on the back of my leg, I was awarded the Purple Heart.

* * * * *

At the end of the war I had been overseas for almost twenty months and did not quite qualify for immediate release but my request for leave and reassignment was based on the humanitarian "need" to see my wife and sixteen-month-old daughter.

Since the Christmas holiday season was approaching, I had prepared some gifts for Dorothy and Jody but there was a dilemma. With the vagaries of the mail services back to the States there was a distinct likelihood that my gifts would not arrive for Christmas. If my orders came through for reassignment, I knew that I might be able to be home just before Christmas. Thus I had an incentive to wait and carry my gifts home with me, but if I waited too long for orders that did not arrive in time, my gifts would surely not get there for Christmas.

One evening before retiring to bed, I prayed for help in knowing what to do about my gifts. In retrospect it now seems like a trivial matter with which to bother the Lord, but at the time, I was so desirous after our long separation to make a happy holiday for my little family that it seemed quite logical to pray about it. Having prayed, I went right to sleep and a rather remarkable event happened. I had a dream about my orders. In the dream I saw my orders very clearly. They were dated at the top, November 24, 1945. They were from the commander in chief of the Pacific Fleet, Pearl Harbor, to Lieutenant Richard W. Barnes, USNR, and they stated that I was to be released immediately from present duty and report to the appropriate authority for transportation to the continental United States where I would begin leave.

Although I felt some nervousness as the days passed by, my orders arrived, and the pages were identical to what had appeared in my dream. This together with subsequent reinforcement over the years, assures me that the Lord does indeed answer prayers

ROBERT E. BARTLETT JR.

Robert joined the United States Navy in Salt Lake City, Utah. He was a navy radio and radarman, third class, at the time of the following incident.

Close to the end of November 1943 we heard rumors aboard ship that we were going to invade the Gilbert Islands. I had never heard of them. Then we heard that we would be going in on a landing craft to invade the Gilbert Islands with the third wave of marines. Our island was Tarawa.

We set up a radar station for detecting enemy planes. The station consisted of three semitrailers—one for power, one for radar equipment, and one for supplies. We would have full backpacks for our personal and sleeping needs.

Our transport ship anchored (I am guessing) probably one-third of a mile from shore. We were up very early in the morning, loaded for "bear," as the saying went, and waiting for the marines to go in first. I did not envy them. I thought, "This is nuts, I'm not supposed to be doing this—I'm supposed to be on a ship!"

We watched the marines load up on the landing craft. The waves were big, but manageable. There were initially a few Japanese planes that flew over the island, but they didn't last very long. I remember seeing one of them trailing a plume of black smoke, and going down on the other side of the island.

We heard lots of guns firing, mostly small guns and machine guns. I think it took the marines longer than they had thought it would to secure the area for our radar equipment.

Finally, it was our turn to go for the beach. I still thought it was nuts.

Our landing craft was filled with Argus Unit 16 personnel and equipment. The landing craft hit the beach, and the bow gate was dropped. I was in front of the landing craft, and off the gate I went. The sand that stopped the landing craft was not very wide, and as I went ahead, I walked into what I thought was shallow water. Wrong! The water was over my head and I was carrying a forty-pound pack with carbine and ammuni-

(Top) Robert E. Bartlett, Jr.

(Bottom) Robert's discharge certificate.

Towing an LST (landing ship tank).

tion. I thought, "I'm going to drown!" However, I knew that Lord was watching over me.

A voice or something in my mind said, "Walk out of the water." Since the water was well over my head, simply walking out did not seem logical, but I listened to that command. I held my breath and walked out of the water on to the beach. I said my prayers that night for sure and thanked my Heavenly Father.

FRANCIS H. BAUGH III

Francis served in the 186th Infantry Regiment, Forty-first Division, where he achieved the rank of supply sergeant. He participated in the liberation of the Philippines.

Francis H. Baugh III.

On February 16, 1944, I turned eighteen years old. World War II was at its height. At the end of May we would be drafted into the armed services. We registered as soon as we turned eighteen.

One week in May 1944 we went to Fort Douglas in Salt Lake City for our pre-induction physical. That was just before our high school graduation. I don't remember much about graduation. Within a week after graduating we were on our way into the United States Army.

We went to Fort Walters, Texas, to train as infantrymen. Infantrymen were the backbone of the military forces. So it was there that I learned to shoot to kill, and of course, it's not in one's nature. I began to realize that it was serious business. It never completely struck home until I finished my training just before Christmas 1944. I was able to take a delay en route and be home for Christmas. After the holidays, I reported to Fort Ord, California, for processing for overseas shipment.

The seriousness of the situation began to sink in, and I commenced looking for some answers. I started reading the Book of Mormon in all earnestness. We went on a new ship that was a troop carrier that transported the men to the campaigns, then served as a hospital ship during the campaign. It took thirty days to cross to New Caledonia, Guadalcanal, Hollandia, New Guinea, and up to Leyte Harbor in the Philippines. I was able to read a good deal by that time. While on the ship, I ate a ham that was spoiled and got deathly sick. I remember that it didn't taste good, but when I had entered the service I decided I would learn to like new things and clean my plate.

I was put in the ship's hospital, and I thought I was going to die. I remember only two things. I remember waking up and there were six or seven doctors around my bunk discussing my sickness. I thought, "Oh, I must really be sick. I must be going to die." After waking up, I began to feel better, and the doctors discharged me from the ship's hospital. I was very thankful to be better but I didn't know how long I had been in the hospital. . . .

As I walked out of the hospital onto the deck of the ship, I experienced an unusual feeling. The doctors didn't realize that when they had released me there was a kamikaze attack on the ships in Leyte Harbor. It was February 16, 1945, my birthday. All the ships' hands were at their battle stations. The planes were attacking the ships at the far end of the harbor. The navy men told me to get below the deck with the other 1,300 troops who were on the ship.

(Below) Francis H. Baugh III with LDS group.

(Far Below) Francis H. Baugh III.

What was significant about all that, was that I had a most peaceful feeling, and I was not frightened. The Holy Ghost had confirmed to me very strongly that because of our Savior Jesus Christ, everything would be all right—that there was no need to fear if I believed in Him and kept His commandments. My faith, my scripture study of the Book of Mormon, and my recovery have been great blessings.

ROY C. BEACH

Roy was a pharmacist's mate, second class, in the United States Navy. He enlisted in 1943 when he was seventeen years old.

(Below) Roy C. Beach.

(Far Below) USN Hospital Corps School, San Diego, August 1943.

My first view of Okinawa was from the window of a navy C-54 cargo plane in August 1945. The view I had was very beautiful indeed. At the time, though, I wasn't interested in much of anything except home and my wife. The month since I kissed her good-bye seemed like years, and we had been married just a month before that. Things had happened to me so fast in the three shorts months previous to my arrival at Okinawa, that I wasn't sure whether I was dreaming, drunk, in a daze, or what.

In that short time I had arrived back in the States from an eighteen-month tour of duty in the Pacific, had been granted a thirty-day leave, and had gotten married, which alone is enough to leave any man an emotional wreck. Only two weeks after reporting back to duty, I found myself in an airplane halfway around the world. The fact that I was in the Navy and so far from home didn't bother me. I was used to that, and it seemed natural. What I couldn't account for was the vivid memory of home, love, and a wife that kept me thinking day and night. It all seemed like just another dream.

For two years I had dreamed of home and love and a wife I would get if and when I got home; then for three awfully short months those dreams were real. I lived my dreams, I got my wife and love. Then I found myself back overseas again, still dreaming about the same old things, only now the dreaming was a little more real. There weren't so many blank spots, everything was clear to me. It is no wonder that so many sailors went crazy, even without being in the thick of battle.

FRED G. BEEBE

As part of the occupational forces in Japan, Fred was assigned to manage a field grade officer's hotel where he encountered many of the military's generals. During that time, he became a Latter-day Saint group leader. Once again, his special assignment brought him in contact with a man of authority.

One day one of the members of our group suggested that we come to his place at the Signal Corps, where he had made a shortwave radio voice transmitter and receiver, and we could talk to our folks and wives. Most all of us took him up on that. I had a chance to talk to Kathleene and also to Mother and Dad. . . . It was so good to hear their voices. . . . The ham radio operator in Los Angeles phoned Kathleene and Mother and Dad, and we had a direct connection.

As we were talking to an operator in Sandy, Utah, connecting with one of the men's folks, the operator said, "How would you like to talk to George Smith?"

Being the group leader, I responded by asking, "Do you mean President George Albert Smith?!" He confirmed that was exactly what he meant. He told us to be there the following week at the same time, and he would have President Smith there to talk to us. Needless to say, that week dragged by because of our anticipation of the possibility that we—halfway around the world—could talk to our Prophet. Finally the day arrived. We all gathered around our Signal Corps buddy, waiting. Almost at the exact time specified, the Sandy operator came on and started to introduce President Smith. It was about 10 P.M. in Kyoto and 6 A.M. in Sandy. We could not believe that President Smith would get up so early and go to Sandy just to talk to a few servicemen. Nevertheless his was the next voice we heard.

I introduced our group and told him briefly about us, and then we all introduced ourselves to him and he commented individually. When the last one got through with his introduction, President Smith began to bear his testimony to the "people of the Orient." He bore strong testimony of the truthfulness of the Book of Mormon, and of Joseph Smith, and that the priesthood and the organization Christ had established had been restored in these latter days. He said something to the effect that he hoped the "ether waves" would carry his testimony into the hearts and lives of the people of the Oriental nations. I thought it strange that he would use the term "ether waves." We were just a mite disappointed that he didn't talk more directly to us, but we were all so pleased to be able to talk to him that we commented about it for weeks.

Twins Frank and Fred Beebe. The brothers registered for war while serving as missionaries in Hawaii.

Group of LDS servicemen, including Frank Beebe, in Seoul, Korea, in 1945.

MERVYN S. BENNION

A graduate of the Naval Academy at Annapolis, Mervyn was a distinguished naval officer and captain of the USS West Virginia. *Married to a daughter of President J. Reuben Clark of the First Presidency, Mervyn was one of the earliest American Latter-day Saint casualties of the war. For his heroism at Pearl Harbor, he was posthumously awarded his nation's highest military award, the Medal of Honor. The following is an excerpt from an account written by Mervyn's brother, Howard. This account is based on eyewitness interviews.*

Capt. Mervyn S. Bennion, the first Latter-day Saint to qualify for the Medal of Honor during World War II.

Sunday, December 7, 1941, at a few minutes before eight, Mervyn was in his cabin shaving preparatory to leaving the ship to go to Sunday School and fast meeting in Honolulu when a sailor on watch from the bridge nearby dashed in to report a Japanese air attack approaching at hand. Mervyn instantly gave the commands, "Japanese Air Attack! To your battle stations!" Then he ran to his own—the conning tower on the flag bridge. There he verified the readiness of the several gun crews, the preparations for bringing up ammunition from the holds, the preparedness of the other elements of the ships' crew for their roles in action. In a minute Japanese torpedo planes flew in close from the outside, letting go three torpedoes that struck the *West Virginia* in rapid succession, tearing a great hole in the exposed side. Almost simultaneously Japanese bombers flew overhead, barely clearing the masts and hit the *West Virginia*, once in the region already damaged by the aerial torpedoes and once a deadly blow into the magazine. Fortunately that bomb did not explode; otherwise, the ship would have been blown up as was the *Arizona*, immediately astern the *West Virginia*.

When the first fury of the attack was over, Mervyn, anxious to see better what had happened to his ship and the guns and gun crews before giving orders to meet the developments, stepped out of the door at the rear of the conning tower and started around the lateral walk to the flag bridge. He had scarcely taken two steps when he was hit by a splinter from a bomb, evidently dropped from a high level and exploding on a turret of the battleship *Tennessee* alongside the *West Virginia*. This splinter tore off the top of his stomach and apparently a fragment hit his spine and the left hip, for he lost the use of legs, and the hip appeared to be damaged. He fell to the floor of the walk, got on his back, and with nerves of steel put back in place the entrails that had spilled out.

In a minute or so his plight was observed, and a pharmacist's mate came to place a bandage over the abdomen and to try to ease the pain. It was clear to him and undoubtedly to Mervyn that the wound was beyond any hope of mending, though Mervyn said not a word to indicate he knew he was dying. As soon as the wound was given the simplest dressing, Mervyn sent the man below to work with the wounded and refused to be attended further while there was work to be done. As men and officers came to him he briefly asked what was transpiring and gave orders and instructions to meet conditions as they arose. The well-trained crew knew their duties thoroughly. It was easy for him to exercise control. The ship was well handled to prevent capsizing and to keep damage from fire to a minimum. Admiral Furlong, one of the commanders at Pearl Harbor, gave the *West Virginia's* guns credit for bringing down twenty or thirty Japanese planes. Only two lives were lost from the ship's complement of officers and men—Mervyn and one seaman. The wounded were attended to promptly and evacuated from the ship with dispatch. Mervyn was courageous and cheerful to the last moment of consciousness, and his spirit was

(Below) Capt. Mervyn S. Bennion.

(Left) Poem that appeared on the inside of the memorial service program for Capt. Bennion.

In Memorium

MERVYN SHARP BENNION, *Captain*, United States Navy
Born May 5, 1887, Vernon, Tooele County, Utah.
Died December 7, 1941, Pearl Harbor, Oahu, Hawaii.

He loved peace fervently, and the Prince of Peace;
Born to pastoral pursuits, his soul attuned to song,
His heart to tenderness and sympathy;
In manner modest and retiring, yet calm and resolute;
A citadel of strength and courage among his fellowmen.

Beneath his willing hand, no trivial duty
Could be commonplace, nor task deferred.
His joy in service recognized no bounds.
With each assignment faithfully accomplished,
He volunteered for more, beyond the routine calls.

Thus, as the war-clouds threatened, he would go
To man the spearhead in our battle zone,
To meet the first onslaught of treacherous foe
And prove the best traditions were his own.

The swift attack had found him at his post;
Shell-torn, he stayed, and uttered calm commands,
Directing ship and crew, to save the most
Of what had been entrusted to his hands.

He loved peace fervently, and the Prince of Peace;
Like David's soul in youth, attuned to song;
Of earth's nobility, his life he held in lease,
To serve but Him to whom it doth belong.

God bless his memory, and grant that we
May have the strength sufficient for our day,
That Justice, peace, good faith, and liberty
May be restored. My soul, arise, and seek the way!

MAJOR CLARENCE S. JARVIS.

reflected in the conduct of his crew. When the first attack was over he allowed himself to be placed on a cot and the cot to be moved under a protecting shelter on the deck. There he remained during the second Japanese attack which occurred an hour after the first one. He resisted all efforts to remove him from the bridge with a firmness and vigor that astonished officers who thought they knew him well, but did not realize how much force there lay behind his gentle ways.

He talked only of the ship and the men, how the fight was going, what guns were out of action, how to get them in operation again, casualties in the gun crews and how to replace them, who was wounded, what care the wounded were receiving and provisions for evacuating them from the ship, the fate of other ships, the number of enemy planes shot down, the danger of fire from burning oil drifting around the *West Virginia* from the exploded *Arizona*, satisfaction over the handling of the ship, satisfaction with the effectiveness of the gun crews in shooting down attacking planes, and satisfaction with the conduct under fire of officers and men of the ship. His only expression of regrets were of horror for the treachery of the Japanese and of concern because of this paralyzing loss of warships.

Thus passed an hour and a half. About 9:30 A.M. fire broke out in the kitchen, lockers, and officers' quarters beneath the flag bridge and began to envelop it in stifling black smoke and bursts of flame. This cut off from escape Mervyn, Lieutenant Commander Ricketts, a pharmacist's mate, and Lieutenant Commander White, whom he had per-

Medal of Honor

The Medal of Honor is the highest award for valor in action against an enemy force that can be bestowed upon an individual serving in the Armed Services of the United States. Generally this medal is presented to its recipient by the President of the United States of America in the name of Congress (http://www.cmohs.org/medal.htm, Sept 18, 2001). Here is the citation for Captain Bennion:

BENNION, MERVYN SHARP

Rank and organization: Captain, U.S. Navy. Born: 5 May 1887, Vernon, Utah. Appointed from: Utah.

Citation: For conspicuous devotion to duty, extraordinary courage, and complete disregard of his own life, above and beyond the call of duty, during the attack on the Fleet in Pearl Harbor, by Japanese forces on 7 December 1941. As Commanding Officer of the U.S.S. *West Virginia*, after being mortally wounded, Capt. Bennion evidenced apparent concern only in fighting for and saving his ship, and strongly protested against being carried from the bridge.

mitted to stay with him. Mervyn had grown weaker from continuous loss of blood. The officers tied him on a ladder and twice tried to lower him to the deck below to get him away from the fire. The aft part of the ship was free of fire, but the smoke and flames swept over the forward deck to make it impossible for men to receive him. At this point the smoke and flame on the flag bridge became so terrible that all of the small group concluded their end had come, but just as they

The destroyer, USS Bennion, *in Boston Harbor, January 1944. This ship was named for Capt. Bennion and was launched July 4, 1943.*

were being overpowered by suffocation, a small gust of wind came seemingly out of nowhere and gave them air and vision. Quickly they seized Mervyn and by superhuman effort carried him up a ladder to the navigation bridge to a corner at the rear that seemed to be free from smoke. While being carried up the ladder he had lost consciousness, but as soon as they laid him out flat on the bridge floor, the blood returned to his head, and he told them to leave him and save themselves if that was possible. They made him as comfortable as they could and leaving the pharmacist's mate at his side the two officers spent the next half hour trying unsuccessfully to put out the fire. Twenty minutes after they left Mervyn, the mate reported that Mervyn had slumped over and breathed, "I'm gone."

The Commandant
requests the honour of your presence
at the Launching of the
U. S. S. Bennion
Sponsor, Mrs. Louise Clark Bennion
at the Navy Yard, Boston, Massachusetts
on Sunday, the Fourth of July
nineteen hundred and forty-three
at 12:40 p. m.

No cameras allowed

Invitation to the launch of the USS Bennion.

PEARL HARBOR

Awaking a Sleeping Giant

In mid-1941, the U.S. government banned shipments of scrap metal to Japan after numerous warnings to Japan about its military agressions. In response to the embargo and the resulting fuel shortage, the Japanese military dictatorship, led by Hideki Tojo, conquered the Dutch East Indies and Malaya to secure a source of oil and metals.

In the summer of 1941, the United States had stationed B-17 heavy bombers in the Philippines as a deterrent to the Japanese. The Japanese planned to destroy those bombers while they were on the ground, and secure a supply line to the Dutch East Indies. Admiral Isoroku Yamamoto insisted on an additional attack against the United States. The target was the fleet at Pearl Harbor. They believed that by destroying the U.S. Pacific fleet, Japan would have control of the Pacific.

At this time, sentiment in the United States was divided between those determined to keep America out of the war at all costs, and those supportive of Great Britain and fearful of German and Japanese aggression. In November of 1941, Japan sent Special Envoy Saburo Kurusu and Ambassador Kichisaburo Nomura to the United States to defuse tensions and ease sanctions that had been placed against Japan.

At 2:05 P.M. local time December 7, 1941, Nomura and Kurusu called upon Secretary of State Richard Hull in Washington, D.C., and delivered a document that had been sent from Tokyo. Secretary Hull accepted the document, glanced over it, and said, "In all my fifty years of public service, I have never seen a document that was more crowded with infamous falsehoods and distortions—infamous falsehoods and distortions on a scale so huge that I never imagined that any government on this planet was capable of uttering them." Unbeknownst to the Japanese, Secretary Hull had already read the memo from Tokyo. U.S. intelligence sources had intercepted and translated the memo in record speed. Secretary Hull had already been informed that Pearl Harbor had been attacked.

Early in the morning on December 7, 1941, a Japanese float plane made a high-level aerial reconnaissance of the island of Oahu and radioed back to the Japanese fleet, "Hawaii sleeps." At that moment, pilots on the Japanese carriers began boarding their planes, saying prayers to their Shinto shrines, and preparing for the attack on Pearl Harbor.

Most of the servicemen stationed at the various military bases on Oahu were enjoying a leisurely Sunday morning. At 7:55 A.M., the first wave of the attack struck Pearl Harbor. Japanese fighter planes aimed for the Army airfields—where American aircraft were sitting helplessly on the ground, wingtip to wingtip and unarmed, providing perfect targets for the well-trained Japanese pilots. Japanese bombers aimed for Battleship Row on Ford Island. The USS *West Virginia* was 50 feet from the bow of the *Arizona*. The *West Virginia* absorbed 9 aerial torpedos, and 106 people were killed, including the captain. The USS *Arizona* took a bomb that penetrated the forward magazine, igniting more than a million pounds of ammunition and vaporizing more than 1,000 men. In all, six great battleships were sunk or seriously damaged: *West Virginia, Tennessee, Arizona, Nevada, Oklahoma,* and *California.* Many other ships were also destroyed or damaged, but the two U.S. aircraft carriers *Lexington* and *Enterprise,* were unscathed as they were not in port at the time.

Admiral Nagumo's attack achieved total surprise on American forces, but the Japanese failed to capitalize on their success. The tank farms, holding 9 million gallons of fuel, were left untouched, enabling what was left of the fleet to continue operations in the Pacific, though Oahu itself was virtually defenseless through the end of the year.

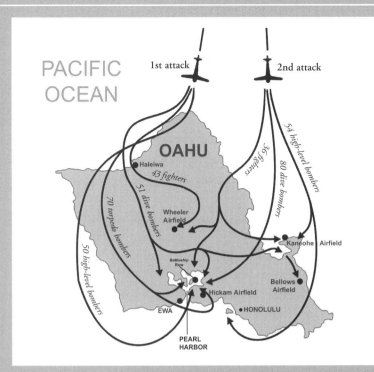

PACIFIC
OCEAN

1st attack   2nd attack

OAHU

Haleiwa
43 fighters

54 high-level bombers
36 fighters
80 dive bombers

Wheeler
Airfield

51 dive bombers
70 torpedo bombers

Kaneohe Airfield

Battleship Row

Bellows
Airfield

50 high-level bombers

Hickam Airfield

EWA
•HONOLULU

PEARL
HARBOR

(Left) Map showing the Japanese attack on Pearl Harbor, which devastated a major part of the U.S. Pacific Fleet. Within 2 hours, 7 U.S. battleships had been sunk or badly damaged; 3 destroyers, 3 cruisers, 2 auxiliary ships, 1 minelayer, 1 target ship, and 188 aircraft had been destroyed; 2,333 American servicemen and women had been killed and 1,347 wounded. The Japanese fleet suffered minor losses: 9 fighters, 15 dive-bombers, 5 torpedo bombers, and 5 midget submarines.

(Below) USS West Virginia, Capt. Bennion's ship, aflame at Pearl Harbor, Hawaii, during the Japanese aerial attack.

VERNON A. BINGHAM

VerNon was a sergeant in the Thirty-seventh Buckeye Infantry Division. He received a Bronze Star and a Purple Heart for his service at the battle of Orion Pass in Luzon, the Philippines.

On June 10, 1945, my outfit reached the front line. The United States forces had steadily pushed north on the island of Luzon and had reached Orion Pass. I remember that morning very vividly. We were marching along the road to relieve soldiers who had run into heavy resistance. I asked a soldier where the front line was. He used his foot to draw a line across the road behind us and said, "You just crossed it." We were ready to move into battle and didn't even know it. That ignorance didn't remain with us for very long. The events that happened the rest of that day and the following day did not in any way resemble what I had known or believed about actual combat.

Our company was to move along the road while another company took the hill to the left and the other took the hill to the right. The heavy-equipment company was on the road with us. Our platoon brought up the rear. Not much time had passed when we started hearing a great deal of gun fire. From farther up the road they were calling for medics and stretchers. A man came running down the road toward us, followed by machine gun fire. He dropped not far from us. A medic reached him and dragged him off of the road so he could dress his wounds. Other wounded men being carried on stretchers passed us. That is when I gained a great deal of respect for the medical corps. We had failed in our attempt to force the enemy to leave their abandoned supply trucks. Because the bridge had been destroyed, trucks loaded with food and other supplies were stranded in the river. There were enemy soldiers all through the hills, determined to defend those supplies. We withdrew far enough to allow our airplanes and artillery to try to destroy their defense.

At 6:00 A.M. the following morning, six men were told to go up the road to try and determine enemy presence. I was one of the six. We found a great deal of evidence that there were lines of communication and that many men had been in the area. We made no enemy contact and so reported. My platoon took over the front position and started up the road. The first two men, who rounded the bend in the road where we had been two hours earlier, were met with enemy fire and both were killed. Mortar shells started falling all around us, and we couldn't move. We were in that position until 2:00

P.M. when two tanks arrived to give us support. I heard my name called to move up front. Because the first scout had refused to go around the bend in the road, the platoon leader told me that I was now the first scout. I had to walk alongside the tank and advise the man with a walkie-talkie if I saw anything, and he would radio the tank to fire in that direction. It sounded very simple.

As I started to walk up the road, my whole life passed through my mind. Who would miss me if I were killed? My widowed mother would cry for me, and my brothers and sister would shed some tears, but other than that, not many would even mourn my loss. I started thinking about things I had never thought of before. I hadn't accomplished anything. I had no family of my own and had not accomplished anything worth remembering. This troubled me and made me desire to live to make some mark in the world. I started thinking about how my older brothers used to use me as a punching bag, repeatedly hitting me on the right shoulder. The thought occurred to me that if I turned my right shoulder toward the hill, which was thick jungle, even if a bullet did hit me, it would bounce off because my muscle was so tough. At the exact moment that I moved, a bullet hit the tank, just missing my head. It took no further warning to have me jump behind the tank. Another LDS man by the name of Bowen, from Idaho, was also behind the tank. There were about three other men, including the lieutenant, taking cover in the ditch alongside the road. Bowen was the BAR (Browning automatic rifle) man, and I was his assistant. He moved to the side of the tank and began firing his BAR. That brought a hail of bullets our way that was incredible. He was hit in the thigh, and I was hit in the arm. My injury was caused by a fragment of a bullet so I was still functional. The bullet fully penetrated the large part of his leg between his hip and his knee. I helped him put a bandage on the wound and told him I would fire the rifle while he crawled back around the bend in the road. We could hear him saying, "I am going home. I am going home." He had a wife and two small children. His wife was expecting a third, but was having difficulty. That is why he was happy about going home.

I managed to hold the enemy down while all of the men ran to safety. The lieutenant ordered me to go next, but because we were out of ammunition and would be running down the road like sitting ducks, I suggested that we each throw a smoke grenade and both of us run at the same time

Purple Heart Certificate and Killed in Action document of George R. Brown. Known to friends and family as "Bobby," George R. Brown died on September 7, 1944, as a result of "friendly fire" when an American submarine sank the ship on which he and approximately 750 prisoners of war were being held. The ship was sunk near the Bay of Zamboanga. George was awarded both the Purple Heart and the Bronze Star posthumously.

with hopes that one of us might make it. We both made it. Because of what happened I received the Purple Heart and the Bronze Star. I had to be taken to the hospital along with the rest of the wounded including Bowen. That was one of many experiences which caused me the greatest of reflections. As I reflect back on that experience, I know that my life was spared because of an inspired quick movement which was provoked by a desire to live and amount to something. This experience was one of the reasons I made the decision to serve a mission after returning home. I also wanted a college degree. It also gave me the desire me to travel miles to attend church whenever it was possible to do so. Sometimes we have to face death to appreciate life.

The Purple Heart

A badge for "Military Merit" that was awarded to personnel who had received a wound that required medical attention. The tradition behind the medal dates back to General George Washington, but the United States did not officially adopt the medal until 1932.

Criteria: The Purple Heart is awarded in the name of the President of the United States to any member of an Armed Force who, while serving with the U.S. Armed Services after 5 April 1917, has been wounded or killed, or who has died or may hereafter die after being wounded; (1) In any action against an enemy of the United States; (2) In any action with an opposing armed force of a foreign country in which the Armed Forces of the United States are or have been engaged; (3) While serving with friendly foreign forces engaged in an armed conflict against an opposing armed force in which the United States is not a belligerent party; (4) As a result of an act of any such enemy of opposing armed forces; (5) As the result of an act of any hostile foreign force; (6) After 28 March 1973, as a result of an international terrorist attack against the United States or a foreign nation friendly to the United States, recognized as such and attack by the Secretary of the department concerned, or jointly by the Secretaries of the department concerned if persons from more than one department are wounded in the attack; or, (7) After 28 March 1973, as a result of military operations, while serving outside the territory of the United States as part of a peacekeeping force; (8) After 7 December 1941, by weapon fire while directly engaged in armed conflict, regardless of the fire causing the wound: (9) While held as a prisoner of war or while being taken captive. A wound for which the award is made must have required treatment by a warranted medical officer.

JACK E. BINKERD

Jack served as a staff sergeant in the United States Army. He spent his entire time in China on outpost duty.

I think my testimony was tempered by what happened to me in the service. I have often wondered what I would have been like if I hadn't had that experience to bring me to a realization of the gospel in all its facets.

I couldn't get good employment. I was twenty-one and had not completed my time in the Selective Service, which

stopped me from getting a meaningful job, so I went to my
local draft board in El Monte, California. I wanted to take
advantage of a tech school education so I opted for gunnery or
sheet metal, but in their wisdom they sent me to school to
become a radio operator/mechanic.

It was on my assignment in Kunming, China, that I found
out the Lord was on my side. I was in the main hostel for a
warm shower when the jing bao (air raid alert) was sounded. I
called the station, and they told me it was a false alarm. I hurried back to the airfield to help. We were short of interpreters,
and I spoke enough Chinese to get by. As I began to cross the
airfield I had the feeling I shouldn't go. I ignored that feeling
and started across. I looked up at the planes coming in, and
they appeared to be three-motored. I ran back, got about ten
feet off the runway and dropped over the edge of the road. . . .
I was so scared, I pulled my .45 and triggered eight shots at the
formation. It wasn't fair, that rear gunner came back with a
machine gun. The bullets hit about eighteen inches from my
head, and kicked dirt all over me. That was scary. They used
smoke tracers; and the air, after they left, looked like ropes
down to the areas they strafed. It happened that day we had an
equal number of aircraft on a bombing mission.

Shortly after that, some B-25s on a sea sweep stopped to
refuel. One of the aircraft was short a waist gunner, and I was
invited to join up for the mission. I was all set to go (I loved
to shoot) and just about got on the aircraft when I had the
feeling I should not go. I didn't, and learned later the plane
had augered into the side of a mountain. I also got amoebic
dysentery which should have killed me, as it did so many.

After three years I was rotated back to the land of the
States. I served the rest of my duty at Gowen Field in Idaho
training aircrews in the use of direction finding equipment. . . .

I feel that my experience in the military, during the war was
something that had to be done. I was scared at times, I felt the
need of being obedient to the things that I had been taught.
After duty we would go into town, order a cake and play
pinochle. There were also "business girls" there. I was well
known for not indulging in liquor, cigarettes or the girls. A new
girl came in. There wasn't a girl sitting by me so she took a seat.
All the other girls told her no, no. Then they said in Chinese
that I was a monk. I was impressed by their opinion of me, I
think it was a reflection of the gospel. As I progressed in my
military career my testimony grew, and it is very strong today.

Grant B. Bitter, 24 years old, March 1946, after the war.

"Ye Ole Three." (L to R) Grant Bitter, Rufus Boldman, John Yates.

GRANT B. BITTER

Grant was a radarman second class in the United States Navy. He was assigned to the USS Gladiator, *an ocean auxiliary minesweeper, and he participated in the invasion of Okinawa.*

We began sweeping operations for the attack on Okinawa on March 24. During that action, Vice Admiral Lee's battleships were lobbing their huge shells over us, softening up the island's defenses. At that time we had no air protection. It was a very tense time. Fortunately we caught the enemy unprepared. The actual invasion started on April 1, 1945. On April 6 our ship came under attack by a Japanese bomber which we shot down with the assistance of four American fighter planes that were on the tail of the enemy plane during its approach. (Another plane was "splashed down" by the ship's weapons six days later. It splashed into the sea on the starboard side.)

This kamikaze did hit the ship and catapulted along the side of the ship, breaking up into pieces; some of the fuselage disintegrated and fell on us, particularly on the bow of the ship where I was acting as gun control operator for our 3-inch gun. Those of us there thought our time had come for sure. Miraculously, the plane did not explode although gasoline was dripping down all around us. (It was customary for suicide planes to drop their bomb loads on one ship and then dive into another ship as they self-destructed.) There were many close calls with death during that time. Another time we were on perimeter patrol (the most dangerous) when we were fired on by our own ships (radio silence was maintained). At the same time we were being bombed by a Japanese bomber. We truly outlived our nine lives.

* * * * *

Rufus Boldman's wife Penny was a member of the Church. Rufus had casually mentioned it when we first met on the *Gladiator*. Soon after my assignment to the ship, I sought permission to hold LDS services aboard. The request was granted. There were several sailors who began attending services each week; among them was Rufus Boldman.

His interest in the Church grew rapidly. He quit smoking and drinking along with other habits not considered consistent with gospel standards. During our escort duties whenever we docked at Guam or Pearl Harbor he attended LDS services with me. Changing attitudes and habits contrary to gospel standards seemed to be no problem for him. Rufus did accept the gospel, and we made arrangements on one of our infrequent visits to Honolulu for his baptism (which I was privileged to perform), in the beautiful stake center there.

We, of course, had long, delightful and serious talks on board ship. One day he told me that he and Penny could never have children. There was a real note of sadness in his voice. Penny had multiple sclerosis. . . . According to medical experts, the condition could be arrested, but not cured.

At the moment that Rufus told me about Penny's condition and that they could never have children, I said, "Rufus if you will accept the gospel of Jesus Christ and live your religion, you and Penny will have children." That statement was quietly electrifying. It startled Rufus and even me, initially. Yet a peaceful and sweet feeling swept over me, and I was assured that the statement was one of prophecy through the power of the Holy Ghost.

After the war was over and Rufus had gone home, I received news that Penny had given birth to a beautiful baby daughter, which was a confirmation of Rufus's obedience to the Lord's promise through the Holy Ghost. The blessings to Rufus and Penny were multiplied many times over with the coming of four other choice children to their home. Their

September servicemen's conference, Guam, 1945. Front Row: second from right is Grant Bitter. Back Row: seventh from right is Rufus Boldman, and fourth from right is William Richan.

posterity has greatly increased, and their descendants are giving outstanding service to others, a trademark of the Boldman family.

(Above) The USS Gladiator *(AM 319), which Grant Bitter served on as a radarman second class.*

(Right) (L to R) Lamar Day, Grant Bitter, and Rufus Boldman on board the USS Gladiator.

WILLIAM B. BLACK

William was drafted into the United States Army and belonged to the First Cavalry Division. His military duties took him to Australia, New Guinea, Leyte, and Luzon.

I had a very close cousin named Frank Raley. We did many things together. He was called into the military service. He was sent to New Guinea, and he fought in the jungle there which consisted of banana groves and heavy plant foliage. He was killed in action. About that time I was called into military service. I was sent to Fort Bliss, Texas, for desert training. I was so upset at the loss of my cousin that I prayed that somehow I would be called to serve in the same area to find out for myself if he had actually been killed or was just missing in action.

First Cavalry Division

The First Cavalry Division was originally assigned to guard the borders of the United States and Mexico. As the name suggests, this was a horse cavalry division until the modernization of the military in the early part of the Second World War. The First Cavalry Division went on to serve with great distinction during the hard-fought campaigns of the Pacific, including the capture of Manila, in the Philippines.

I moved on to California to receive my assignment. We loaded a large troop ship and headed out to—we knew not where. After several days on the ship we crossed the International Date Line, and at that time we received literature telling us we were going to Australia. I continued to pray, hoping somehow that sometime I would get to New Guinea.

After a few weeks, my prayers were answered, and our outfit was transferred there. While there, I was given the opportunity to go to a military cemetery, and I began looking for his grave. I looked for some time. It was an overwhelming task to look through that large cemetery. I prayed for direction, and lo and behold I found it. We were only in New Guinea for a month, and then I was transferred to Japan. My prayers were answered. I had come over eight thousand miles and found his grave!

William B. Black, 1942.

DON C. BLOOMFIELD

Don was stationed at Clark Field and served with MacArthur's forces until the fall of Bataan. He spent the duration of the war as a POW. The following account is provided by his wife, Rosemary.

Prisoners of war taken by the Japanese suffered horrendous treatment at the hands of their captors, and Don was no exception. They had poor food and not enough of it. Their everyday fare was a type of Japanese "radish" made into a watery soup with few nutrients in it, and if they were lucky, an occasional piece of fish. They had little, if any, medical care. Don had malaria several times, plus other health problems. They had inadequate clothing. They worked in extreme cold in a coal yard, shoveling and carrying coal in shoulder pole baskets. As an example of the inhumane treatment they suffered, prisoners on the voyage to Japan were crowded like live-

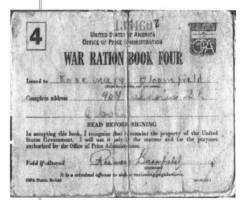

War ration book used by Don Bloomfield's wife, Rosemary, during the war.

Bataan Death March

In March of 1942, General MacArthur left Luzon, in the Philippines, for Australia. One month after he left, the Japanese forces captured Luzon and the Bataan peninsula, taking more than 78,000 Allied personnel prisoner. The prisoners were forced to march to prisoner of war camps under grueling conditions. Many died along the way and those who became ill or had difficulty keeping up were killed. General Wainwright, commander of Allied forces in the Philippines after MacArthur, was captured with the troops and spent the remainder of the war in a POW camp as well.

Don Bloomfield with his wife, Rosemary, after the war.

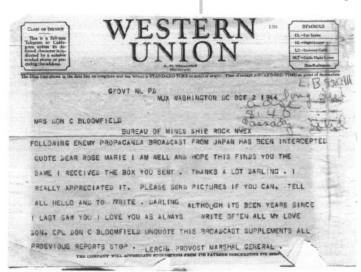

Message sent by Don to his wife, Rosemary, while still a POW in Japan.

stock in the ship's hold without any sanitary facilities, food, or water. Some men kept alive by drinking their own urine.

Upon his return to the United States, Don told of his near death experience. He had malaria and had been put in the "dead tent." (The Japanese had two large tents, one for the sick men and one for the dead ones.) Don said his spirit had left his body and had gone to the other side, where he begged "those in charge" to let him return to life long enough to bring his body back to the States and be able to see his loved ones once more. The next thing he knew, he was walking out of the "dead tent." The Japanese guard said to him, "What are you doing here? You're dead."

He replied, "I'm not dead."

Because of the deprivation and disease, Don's health was ruined, and he died a little over a year after he returned to the States, six weeks before our little daughter, Candace, was born.

Don never lost his testimony of the gospel. In one of his letters he asked that tithing be paid out of his paycheck. In another letter to his parents, he said of me (I was a Baptist at the time), "Someday we'll be married in the temple. My blessing said in time I'd be married in the temple. So I will."

I did eventually join the Church, and Don and I were sealed with Don's brother, Jay, standing in for him.

★ ★ ★

THERON W. BORUP

Theron was a member of the Thirteenth Air Force where he served as a B-24 gunner, an engineer, and a staff sergeant.

At the age of eight when I was baptized and received the Holy Ghost, I was much impressed about being good and able to have the Holy Ghost to be a help throughout my life. I was told the Holy Ghost associated only in good company, and when evil entered my life, he would leave. Not knowing when I would need the promptings and guidance, I tried to live so that I would not lose this gift. On one occasion it saved my life.

During World War II, I was an engineer gunner in a B-24 bomber, fighting in the South Pacific. Before taking off on our combat missions, I had a prayer near our plane. One day the announcement was made that the longest bombing flight ever made would be attempted to knock out the last Japanese oil refinery. It was located in Balikpapan, Borneo. The promptings of the Spirit told me that I would be assigned to that flight, and that I would be shot down, but that I would not be killed. I spent the day before visiting with my friends. At that time I was the president of the LDS group. At 10:00 A.M. the next morning the flight roster was published with my name as the tail gunner with a special crew to fly in the lead plane. We rested in the afternoon as we had to be on the flight line at 11:30 P.M.

Again at the side of the plane under a coconut tree I offered a prayer. The same impression stayed with me that I would be shot down but would not lose my life. Just after midnight we took off. Around 10:00 A.M. we prepared for combat. Being a large man, I left the turret doors open for quick escape. My parachute, life raft, gun, and canteen were laid out for quick use.

The combat was furious as we flew over the Balikpapan oil refinery in Borneo. Our plane was badly damaged by attacking planes. It soon burst into flames, and the pilot told us to prepare to jump. We waited several minutes for word to bail out. Then we noticed one man had jumped from the front. Our airman went to the front and found the pilot and the other five men had already jumped. (The ones in the tail of the plane should have jumped first.) One of the boys with me couldn't find his life raft and so was afraid to jump. I went out last so he could jump between two of us. The Japanese planes shot at us as we floated down. Soon I was in the water struggling to inflate my life jacket and finally got one side to inflate. The life raft would not inflate. . . . Bobbing up and down in the water, I began to drown and passed out. I saw myself dead and being eaten by the fish. My wife was crying; I came to momentarily and cried, "God save me." Again I tried to blow up the life raft and the valve worked. With just enough air in to keep me afloat, I used the last bit of energy and rolled over onto the raft.

Six of us got together, only the bombardier from the group in front was found. He said the others were killed while parachuting down. Then I remembered that the captain should have notified us to jump first. He had but we didn't hear it.

The crew elected me to be the crew captain to keep the matches so no one could smoke as it dried out the throat. I also kept the canteen of water. For three days we floated around in enemy territory with ships all about us and planes

Group of Latter-day Saint servicemen in New Guinea. Theron Borup was the group leader.

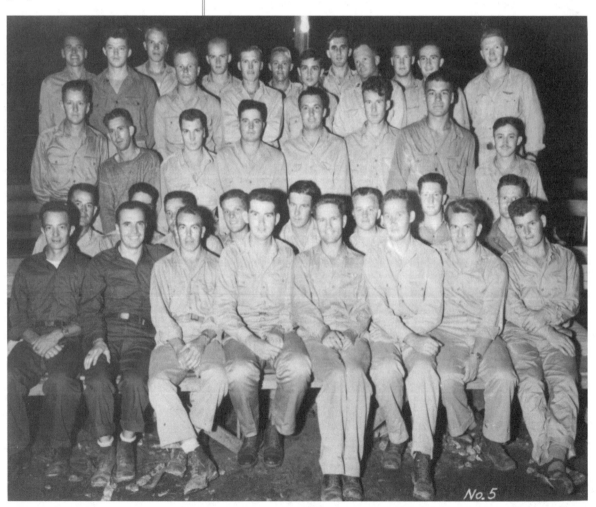

overhead. Why they couldn't see the yellow rafts on the blue sea was a miracle. One night a storm came up and blew us farther from the shore. The waves were very high and our little rafts were nearly torn apart. An officer asked me several times, "Do you pray? Will we be saved?" I said that I prayed regularly and assured him we would be saved. Then he would say, "I wish I had that assurance." The fourth morning the wind calmed down. We were very hungry and thirsty as three days had gone by without food or water.

That evening we saw the submarine that was there to pick us up; we shot up flares, but they passed by without seeing us. The next morning it appeared, but passed us by again; we knew that would be the last day it would be in the area. Then came the prompting of the Holy Spirit, "You have the priesthood, command the submarine to pick you up."

Then to myself I prayed, "In the name of Jesus Christ and by the power of the Melchizedek Priesthood, I command you to turn around and pick us up."

In a few minutes they were alongside us. When on the deck, the captain offered us cigarettes and whiskey which I refused. He took me to his cabin and asked if I would like tea or coffee. I said I would prefer grapefruit juice with sugar in it. His steward brought it. While talking to me about our condition, he said, "I don't know how we ever found you, we were not looking for you." I knew.

How glad I was that somewhere in my growing years, my parents and Church teachers inspired me to so live that I might have the gifts and protection of the Holy Ghost, and to know that God and His Son, Jesus Christ, live.

JOHN W. BOUD

John was the first Latter-day Saint chaplain appointed by the Navy. He recounts the unusual circumstances surrounding a fellow Latter-day Saint chaplain's death.

During my stay in Hawaii a very serious accident took place. Marsden Durham who was an army officer whose family I knew very well at home was injured in action and sent to the island of Oahu for recuperation. He had a shrapnel wound through one of his legs, if I remember correctly. He finally reached a point where he was able to go on several days leave, and we talked it over and decided to take a trip over to the big

Chaplain John W. Boud.

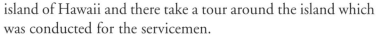

island of Hawaii and there take a tour around the island which was conducted for the servicemen.

We started out from Hilo and went up along the beautiful coastline which extends in the northwesterly direction viewing the sugarcane fields, banana groves, and waterfalls here and there which toppled off the steep cliffs which jutted above the ocean. We finally arrived at a place called Akaka Falls. It is a very beautiful spot of rich tropical vegetation. I suppose there were about nine people who were touring the island together. As we went on the path toward Akaka Falls, I, having been there before, suggested we go down to a lower fall and view it first. A number of us went that direction and another group went over to the highest waterfall in the area.

(Below) John Boud in a sugarcane field north of Wahiawa, Oahu, Sept. 1944.

(Far Below) Akaka Falls, Hawaii, where LDS chaplain L. Marsden Durham fell to his death.

As we stood on the edge of the waterfall that fell down the cliff before us, I stepped across the small stream of water with my Kodak and took several steps upstream to take a picture. Marsden followed me but as he stepped across the small stream of water, he slipped. I suppose he stepped upon a small mossy rock or something. Without a sound he fell over the waterfall, grasping a few strands of grass as he fell. The shock upon my emotional system was terrific. Nobody knew how to get to the bottom of this high cliff, from which the water fell. I finally decided that by going up around and down the brim of the deep canyon for some distance I might be able to make my way down below. This I did. It took me approximately two hours. After I got back through the lush vegetation of the canyon, it was an immense struggle to get through the heavy undergrowth. I was constantly praying that he was all right, continually asking the Lord to bless him that he might have fallen in a little deep pool of water which would have broken the fall and prevented injury.

I finally arrived at the spot at the foot of the falls. There was a pool of water there, but there were also a number of large rocks scattered here and there above the water. I dived in. It was very shallow. I could find no body. I foolishly left my camera on my shoulder, not even thinking to take it off which ruined some of the films I had taken that day. Finally I found some blood on a rock nearby and noticed a place in the vegetation which seemed to have been trampled down. It led upward toward the top of the falls in a much shorter direction than I had come. I followed this path and reached the top of the falls and went over to the area from where he had fallen. There he lay on his back. Several servicemen had come and had followed this other trail down and brought the body up. There were black marks under his eyes. He was not breathing. I placed my hands upon his head and blessed him that he might come to life, but to no avail. His body was finally taken to a mortuary down in Hilo. From there I called Elder Harold B. Lee who was in charge of the servicemen of the Church and told him what had happened. He broke the news to Marsden's parents.

Photo taken of L. Marsden Durham's casket at his funeral.

A few days later a funeral was held in the Waikiki ward on the island of Hawaii. Marsden's brother, Wilby Durham, was able to get permission to fly to Hawaii for the funeral. I was called upon to speak, among others, and it was a very difficult thing which I did.

I have always regretted what happened and wondered just why that happened to Marsden instead of me. He was a very fine young man and very brilliant and had a great future ahead of him, but for some reason the Lord saw fit to take him on this occasion.

* * * * *

The following is an excerpt from a letter written by John.

The men of The Church of Jesus Christ of Latter-day Saints themselves are the finest proof the Church has the true priesthood of God. It is a real thrill to be able to go into a camp and meet with a handful of LDS men, set apart a group leader, two counselors and a secretary, give them their instruc-

(Below) Group of LDS servicemen on Saipan.

tions and tell them to carry on—and then return in a few weeks and behold their accomplishments.

One night we held our first meeting at a certain camp and only three men turned out. One of these was shipping out and so only a group leader, Fred P. Mason, and a first counselor, Floyd E. Lerdahl, were set apart. They were asked to see what they could do by the time of the next meeting. The next week there were twenty-four in attendance, and thirty-four the week following.

This is just an example of what happens when our young men are given a chance to use their priesthood.

(Above) A group of Latter-day Saint servicemen in front of the Honolulu, Hawaii, Stake Tabernacle. During the war, the tabernacle was an important gathering place and refuge for Church members in the armed forces. When the tabernacle was dedicated in 1941, Elder David O. McKay of the Quorum of the Twelve Apostles blessed the edifice that it would be protected from the harms of war. The building had the second tallest steeple in Honolulu and a large light that illuminated it. In spite of its prominent appearance and extensive bombing in the area, the building never sustained damage of any sort from the war ("News of the Church," Ensign, April 1998, 79).

FLOYD BRADFIELD

Floyd was a member of the 222nd Field Artillery of the National Guard. He fought in such places as Negros Island and the Philippines.

On January 9, 1945, we got to the Lingayen Gulf, Luzon Island. We were told that there were about eight hundred ships involved in this landing. There were ships of every kind imaginable. The LST (landing ship tank) that I was on got hit, and we were afraid it was going to sink but three days later we were towed to shore. Then we pursued the Japanese toward Clark Field. The bridges were all knocked out, and we had to use pontoons over most of the streams. When we got to Clark Field in March, we had taken Luzon Island.

Then, using all different kinds of ships, the soldiers, artillery, supplies, and everything were transported to Panay Island. When the LST I was on was making a landing, two bombs from enemy planes came down into the water close to the side of our ship. A few minutes later another bomb landed close to the other side. I helped pass the ammunition to the twin-forty navy gun that shot the planes down. We were very lucky. There were hundreds of ships involved in the

(Below) Floyd Bradfield.

(Far Below) Floyd Bradfield with fellow recruits of B Battery, 222nd Field Artillery, August 28, 1941, in Chehalis, Washington.

campaign with submarines, airplanes, bombs, artillery, and snipers everywhere.

We then landed on Negros Island and pursued the enemy with caterpillars pulling the firing guns, and our planes dropping bombs on the Japanese. It took two and a half months of hard fighting, but we took over the island.

GEORGE E. BROWN

After returning home from a mission in 1939, George enlisted in the Army Air Force and was a B-29 gunner. He suffered many difficulties in Japanese POW camps.

George Brown in front of his parents' home in Pleasant Grove, Utah, before he left for the war.

On December 20, 1944, the call came over the intercom for Captain Campbell's crew to report to operations. Our B-29 was loaded with Christmas goodies for the forward bases in China. We had been selected to fly these goodies (candy, beer, whiskey, etc.) from the rear base in India because we were considered a sober and reliable crew. We made the flight over the hump (Himalaya Mountains) without incident, unloaded, and taxied out to return to India. Before we could take off, the forward base commander came zooming down the runway in a jeep and asked our crew to stick around and fly one more raid against the Japanese.

Early morning on December 21 our plane was on its way to strike an industrial target near Mukden, Manchuria. We never made it to the target. A lucky hit by a fighter plane with a thermite shell set the plane on fire and within minutes our crew had to bail out. Two crewmen were shot by fighter planes while parachuting to the ground. I stayed in the plane until it was in a flat spine. I had difficulty finally bailing out. We were rounded up within forty-five minutes. The Chinese peasants could not help us in any way or they would be tortured by the Japanese. We were taken to Japanese headquarters in Mukden. There we were turned over to be interrogated.

According to the Geneva Convention, a POW was only required to give his name, rank, and serial number. The Japanese had ways and means of making people talk. Our crew members were isolated. Some were badly beaten, others were forced to watch their buddies be tormented. We all talked, told big lies, gave so much wrong information that finally the interrogators grew weary of trying to make sense out of all they were told. We were turned over to the local military police to be taken to local jails. Conditions there were just about as bad as they could get. All the men who could sit up were forced to sit away from the wall. We were not allowed to talk to one another. We were not given enough food or water. Thirst is a most exquisite torture. We waited wondering just when all the "one way tickets to Hell" that had been promised us would be given.

It was Christmas Eve, and we could cut the gloom that engulfed us with a knife. What a way to spend Christmas Eve. One man by the name of Glen Pope was an excellent whistler, and he started to softly whistle "Silent Night." We could see tears in the eyes of some. Bud Harmon began to sing and after the first verse the entire crew joined in. Heads came up, and we looked at one another and as a group sang "Silent Night." The Japanese guards just stood and watched. The atmosphere changed. Some sobbed openly, but we all continued to sing. And as the song ended, each man turned and

(Below) Western Union telegram informing George's parents that their son was missing.

(Far Below) Western Union telegram informing parents that their son was a prisoner of war.

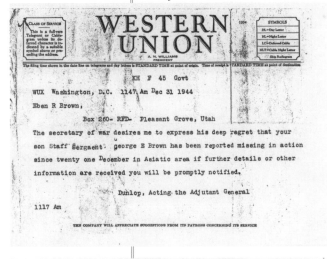

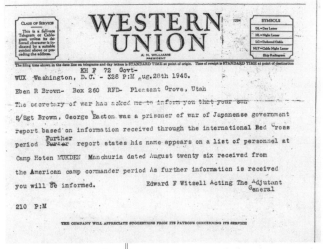

China

It is an often-overlooked fact that the United States had military personnel in China during the war. Many U.S. servicemen spent their entire time in China supplying the armies of China with material and combat assistance. The logistics of keeping these units supplied was one of enormous concern, because the Japanese occupied the Chinese coast from Manchuria to the area of French Indochina. With British bases in India, the Allies were able to fly supplies over what became known as "The Hump." This entailed flying nonpressurized cargo planes over the Himalayan Mountains to the Tibetan Plain, and trucking supplies along primitive roads to the front lines. The existence of the troops on the Chinese mainland prevented the expansion of Japanese control.

wished the others a Merry Christmas. We all stood and joined in a circle, and I was asked to lead in prayer. A humble Mormon prayer that the Lord heard and answered, assured us all that Jesus was the Christ, that He was the Savior of the world and was mindful of a few captured airmen in those cold cells in Manchuria. We all came home to share the memories of Christmas Eve 1944 with our families.

DON E. BUSH

Don was a radioman in the Navy and saw extensive action in the Pacific. He later went on to serve in the Utah House of Representatives. The first story occurred at Leyte, and the second took place somewhere out from Manila.

We were up about 3:00 A.M. to get ready. We ate breakfast. (They always fed everyone as good a meal as they could manage before the battle started, as no one knew when we would get to eat again, and for some men, it would be their last meal.) We also checked gear, radios, carbines, ammunition, rations, clothing, etc., and went over our last-minute instructions. We were always plenty early and had to wait around, but we wouldn't have been sleeping anyway. I don't think we did much sleeping the night before an invasion, with so many things going through our minds. Everyone talked in subdued tones or not at all. We acted nonchalantly like it was just another day, but inside we knew it wasn't, and we found ourselves wondering if everyone would all still be around by the next night.

I remember looking at my teammates and thinking of the different personalities and characteristics each one contributed to our little group, and tried to imagine what it would be like

Don Bush with fellow team members Wally Mastros and Noble Crew on Leyte, October 1944.

without them. I decided I did not want to find out. I had written my last letters, just in case, and had prayed a little longer than usual for my loved ones at home and for the guys I was with. There wasn't any joking or clowning around at this time. I don't remember ever being fearful, as I had placed myself in the Lord's hands, and my testimony was strong enough to know that if it was His will, I would come through all right, and if it wasn't, then I would accept whatever He had in mind for me. I never doubted that our country would win the war, and was confident that each invasion would be successful; which, no doubt, helped me have a positive attitude.

* * * * *

When our convoys were heading for an invasion with troops and supplies aboard, we were screened pretty well by a dozen or more escort ships, including some destroyers. On the way back, however, we could go faster and were leaving the battle zone, so most of the escort ships would stay to help the invasion forces or go on to other assignments. This time was no exception, and so we had only four small patrol craft to protect our group of about thirty ships. As it turned out that wasn't enough.

That night, January 30, 1945, at 1:33 A.M., according to my log, a Japanese submarine sneaked through and picked our lead ship, as usual, to fire its torpedoes at. Our ship was struck by a torpedo near the rear of the ship on the port side.

I was in charge of the midwatch (after being on the beach since dawn), so I was in the radio shack at the time. When the torpedo hit, it felt like some giant had grabbed that huge ship, raised it out of the water, shook it, and slammed it down again. There was a loud rolling explosion as well, and then complete silence and darkness. The radios quit, everything stopped, and it felt as though we were frozen in place. The blackness was so intense we couldn't tell if others were there. No one said a word. It was as though we were all alone in a void. The ship shuddered, at the mercy of the relentless sea, as it gradually lost momentum. Our power source had been ruined, along with our engines, and our ship sat dead in the water, helplessly drifting.

The first thing on everyone's mind was whether the ship was going down, and when the next torpedo would hit. We could easily have been sunk by the tremendous force of the explosion and, as we found out later, we almost were. If our ammunition supply had been hit, it would have been all over. One radioman was very upset, as he didn't have a life jacket on watch with him (we were supposed to), so I told him he could leave to get one, and if he could, to bring me one. He came back with one for himself, but I guess he forgot about me. I didn't need it anyway, as it turned out.

When we were torpedoed, the rest of our convoy just kept going and left us to our fate. They didn't want to risk more of the ships getting the same treatment. What a lonely feeling we experienced as dawn broke, and our convoy was nowhere to be seen. We were just a speck in the middle of the ocean, rolling helplessly as the ship rode up and down on the swells. We felt deserted, but we knew that the ships had to go on to a safe area. We were expendable, if it would save the other ships and their crews.

DOUGLAS R. CAHOON

Doug was a navy lieutenant stationed aboard the carrier USS Essex. *He was killed in action when his fighter plane was shot down during a strafing run over Naha, Okinawa airfield. The following are excerpts from letters he sent to his new bride, Rhoda, prior to his death on March 1, 1945.*

"In Memoriam." Douglas R. Cahoon by Herbert M. Female.

Christmas Eve, December 24, 1944.

My dearest darling:

Tonight was one of the nights I wanted to be with you . . . because it's our first year of marriage. I wanted to be with you to make you laugh, and have it be the happiest Christmas so far in our lives. But I'm not with you, Darling. We are apart the time of our marriage that we should be together. I hope that when our kids get married they will be able to be together; where we were apart—Hmm, gotta quit looking into the future so much! This war has taken a lot apart for a while, and some forever. Yet, in a way it brought us together. The fact that I have you, Twig, will make this Christmas an awful lot better than last Christmas for me. . . . I wish there was some new way of telling you how much you mean to me, Darling. Since we've been apart it has grown a lot deeper and more wonderful. This last couple of weeks I've noticed it more than usual. I know with all my heart, Darling, that our love will endure all.

You are the ideal I've looked for in every respect. Someday we will be together again, and I can tell you and prove to you my love and devotion. Till then, chin-up, my darling.

* * * * *

January 6, 1945.

I'm glad I got a letter from you today, Honey, because I've been sorta low. I've needed you the last few days. We've had a bit of bad luck and it's a little hard on the nerves. We lost our skipper which was the biggest blow. He was hit by AA (anti-aircraft). I sure had a lot of respect for the man. He did a lot for this squadron, and losing him sorta puts a guy off guard! But things are working out all right. I don't want you to worry about me. . . . The letter today helped my morale millions and only a letter from you could do it.

* * * * *

An example of artwork created by Douglas R. Cahoon during the war. Prior to his military service, Douglas studied art at the renowned Art Center *school in Los Angeles, California. Several of his works of art were later published in the* Naval History *magazine (1999), along with a sketch of his life.*

January 17, 1945.

Gosh Darling, I miss you so very much. I wish this damn war would end. I want to be with you every minute forever. We sure are going to have lots of fun together. We'll probably have lots of kids, too. Hope we have a couple of boys and one cute blonde girl.

* * * * *

February 1, 1945.

I'm so thankful that we did get married because I could never love anyone else as much as I love you. Every thought is for you. I only hope I'll be the husband you deserve, forever. These last six and a half months have been a lot easier than I thought they would be. Your letters and pictures have kept you close to me. I was just wondering if I had changed any. A person has an awful tendency to get hard toward things that don't directly pertain to the war. Now and then I find my thoughts being selfish and sometimes rebellious. . . . Being married to you has helped me a lot. Life is a lot more stable with something so tangible as our future. Darling, the time can't pass fast enough. I pray every night that we will be together again soon.

* * * * *

February 27, 1945. (Doug's last letter home.)

I miss you so much, but I know that isn't going to get me home any sooner, so I'm just waiting and loving you more each day. Good night, Angel.

Forever yours,
Doug.

Group of LDS servicemen meeting in the ship library of the USS Essex, *sometime between November 1944 and February 1945. Lt. Douglas Raymond Cahoon (fighter pilot in Air Group Four) is second from the left on the back row.*

LEWIS CALL

Lewis returned home from a mission in March 1944. Two months later, he was drafted into the service. He served as a master sergeant in the United States Army.

We had been on the water about a week and were about a day out of Leyte, a Philippine island. We were to stop there and put off mail and pick up mail to be delivered to the men in Manila, another part of the Philippines. During the morning it began to rain. It really poured. We couldn't even see the other ships in the convoy, and we were in very close formation. I guess it rained for a good half hour and then stopped almost instantly. I got out from under my cover and walked to the side of the ship, and I saw two torpedoes coming at us. One missed the front of our ship, but not by very far. The second one went behind our ship and hit the ship next to us. There was a terrific explosion. It had hit toward the back of the ship were the ammunition was stored. It blew it right apart and the back one hundred feet sunk in less than a minute taking most of the crew with it. The other part of the ship with its supplies and soldiers just floated away. The front part of those ships were built so that they were almost unsinkable. By that time, a destroyer had passed us, putting down a smoke screen. It went down each side and a subchaser was dropping depth charges. It was only a matter of minutes until we couldn't see any ships, the smoke was so thick. One of the protective ships went back and picked up the men off the floating part of the LST (landing ship tank) that had been torpedoed.

I want to bear testimony to anyone who reads this that God does live, and that He does bless those who keep His commandments and serve Him. He certainly protected me, and I thank God for sparing my life.

Lewis Call.

E. JAMES CARLSON

James served in the Corps of Engineers in the United States Army. He saw action in Leyte and Okinawa.

E. James Carlson.

Jennie Elthora Duke, my dear wife, and I were married in the Salt Lake Temple on October 4, 1943, during the time I was in training in the Army in the United States. All during my service overseas we corresponded. I kept her letters and she kept my letters. . . . All the letters sent from me to Jennie were censored before being sent, so any references to our location could be cut out for security reasons. I was very careful to not mention names of cities or countries where our forces were stationed. But while we were on Oahu, Hawaii, I asked Jennie to send my temple recommend. Jennie knew that I was near a temple and very likely in Hawaii. The men who censored did not know what a temple recommend was, so they didn't cut it out. She sent my recommend, and I visited the temple in Laie, Oahu, Hawaii, before leaving there for Leyte.

* * * * *

On October 20, 1944, at dawn, a tremendous bombardment of shells from navy battleships, cruisers, rocket ships, and dive bombers in the Leyte Gulf, started blasting beaches on the east coast of Leyte. At a prearranged time all became quiet. The small LCVP (landing craft vehicle personnel) boats with front ramps, holding about twenty men each or one vehicle, formed into lines and assaulted the beach. The first job was to set up a beachhead, an area near the beach that was secure from enemy small arms fire and an area where additional troops, ammunition, artillery, and equipment could be landed. After clearing the area of enemy troops, our battalion set up a perimeter defense, and the infantry pushed inland. We took a Japanese prisoner, who was very frightened. We built a stockade made from barbed wire to contain him under guard.

Maj. Carlson with amphibious jeep on Leyte, 1944.

On Red Beach, just north of White Beach where we were located, a landing area was secured. General Douglas MacArthur and his staff, including President Osmena of the Philippines, accompanied by General Basilio Valdez, the Philippine Army chief of staff, and General Carlos Romulo who was with General MacArthur on Bataan came ashore. We could see General MacArthur's group from where we were located. A mobile broadcasting unit was set up and this is what MacArthur said:

> People of the Philippines: I have returned. By the grace of Almighty God, our forces stand again on Philippine soil—soil consecrated in the blood of our two peoples. . . . At my side is your President, Sergio Osmena, a worthy successor of the great patriot, Manuel Quezon, with members of his cabinet. The seat of your government is now, therefore, firmly reestablished on Philippine soil.

* * * * *

After we were settled somewhat, and six-man tents were set up to sleep in and keep equipment in, the LDS men in our 170th Engineer Combat Battalion made makeshift benches from palm tree logs, and a cover, made with a tarp on four posts, to protect us from the rain and sun. Sacrament cups were made from .50-caliber shell casings. We held sacrament meetings on Sundays, after the battle for Leyte had settled down, with five to ten attending. I had been set apart as a group leader, and I arranged for and conducted the services. I had the miniature servicemen's combination of the Book of Mormon, the Doctrine and Covenants, the Pearl of Great Price, and *Principles of the Gospel* which also contained a few songs.

The XXIV corps chaplain on Leyte was Lieutenant Colonel Reuben Curtis and his assistant was Chaplain Marsden Durham, both were LDS. They visited our group occasionally, when the war permitted, and gave good LDS support. They could only visit on Sundays and with the many LDS groups we didn't see them very often. They held at least two LDS conferences in our sector of the island before we loaded back on the APA ships.

Maj. Carlson, August 1945, Okinawa —the day Japan surrendered.

A. EARL CATMULL

A marine technical sergeant, Earl was a member of a unit named the Mormon Battalion. This unit was formed in memory of the first Mormon Battalion created during the Mexican-American War in 1846, and was organized at the suggestion of President David O. McKay of the First Presidency.

A. Earl Catmull.

The General Authorities of the Church had recommended that all worthy young men eighteen and older get their endowments before going into the service. Consequently, when I first arrived in Salt Lake City (from my home in Idaho), I called the temple to learn what time the temple opened the next morning. I was informed that it was closing after the last session that evening and would be closed for a time. I said that I was supposed to go to the temple before going into the service so I would call a taxi and try to get there before the last session. When I walked in the temple, someone said, "This must be him now, so we can start." No one can know how impressed I was to know that they had delayed starting the last session for just one person (me). The individual does count.

Inside the temple, as I was heading for the stairs, a man in a white suit came up to me and said, "You are going into the service, I presume. I presume that because you are alone so you're not getting married, and you look too healthy to be going on a mission." (At that time only 4-Fs—inductees declared physically or mentally disqualified—were called on missions.) Then he added, "I would like to promise you that if you stay true to the vows you have taken in this temple this day you will come back from this war without a scratch." I didn't know who that man was, but I believed what he said. I was fully aware that every person was not given that promise, but for some reason I was. Incidentally, my great uncle, who was the patriarch of the Minidoka Stake in Idaho, had given me the same promise just before I left Rupert, Idaho.

What a comfort that was, and what an incentive to live the standards the best I could. It was a great source of hope and of strength during the years I served. I can honestly say that I was never afraid. I wasn't a fool who tried to bounce bullets off his chest to prove a point, but I was never filled with fear. I was, and am always, thankful to the Lord for that assurance I was given.

* * * * *

The first time we went to church on Guam, when the sacrament was passed, the water was passed around in a canteen cup. Each man would rotate it a bit more and take a sip. . . . We did not know how many times that cup rotated before it got to all the men. Chaplain Jackson (Gifford Jackson LDS), happened to be there that Sunday. The next Sunday, the water was passed in little cups set in holes drilled into a board.

Chaplain Jackson also arranged for all LDS servicemen on the island of Guam in all four branches of the service to be excused from regular duties and gather on July 24 for our own Pioneer Day celebration. We had a great time and later learned that others were asking how they could get to be Mormons so they could have a day off for a festive occasion.

* * * * *

We were aboard ship off Iwo Jima waiting for the call to go ashore. Before the invasion began, our battleships started bombarding the island. Our planes had been constantly bombing it. As we looked toward the island, we could see a dark cloud of smoke and dust over the whole island. At night we could see the flame throwers throwing burning flames at selected targets.

Early one morning as I stood looking that direction I saw the Stars and Stripes flying on Mount Suribachi. The rays of the sun were shining on it above the pall of smoke. My whole body tingled, and I choked up momentarily. I then felt like I'm sure Francis Scott Key must have felt as he stood aboard ship and saw Old Glory flying at Fort McHenry during the War of 1812. To this day I tingle at the sound of "The Star-Spangled Banner" and cannot even sing through the first verse without choking up. I shall never forget that moment.

Latter-day Saint servicemen's group, Guam, 1945.

ALLEN C. CHRISTENSEN

"Ace" was stationed in Mindanao, the Philippines, when General Wainwright surrendered all the armed forces in the Philippines. He spent the remainder of the war in Japanese POW camps. It was in one such camp where the following experience occurred.

The Japanese people were not my enemy. Nor was the emperor. The Japanese were just like Americans—some good, some bad. My enemy was an invisible one—the giving up of hope. I had seen others give up. Those who gave up weren't necessarily the sickest among us, but their lack of hope was invariably fatal. We could always recognize them. They would lay in their beds in a semi-fetal position and stare at nothing. By morning they would be dead—starved of hope.

This time it was I who had lost hope. I was so weary from the daily struggle to stay alive that home began to seem more and more like an impossibility. Death began to seem more and more like the only release from the living perdition in which I found myself. Finally, I too entered that wasteland of emotional despair—my spiritual Death Valley. I couldn't take anymore. I put down my sledge hammer and told the guard I would not work any longer. I didn't care what he did to me. I wanted to die. He beat me, and afterward, as I lay in my bed waiting for the end to come, I took out the two precious pieces of paper that I had managed to keep concealed for three years. One was a picture of my parents and the other was my patriarchal blessing.

As I read the blessing, I thought of my grandfather, the patriarch who had given me the blessing, and my dear mother who had patiently taken down every word. The words softened me. Maybe there was a future for me. Then I studied my parents' faces in the picture. I began to recall my childhood, our farm, my brother Max, and the times we'd spent riding our horses.

I didn't know it at the time, but at home in Utah, my grandfather had told my family not to worry. Even though they had had no word from me in three years, he promised them that I would return. I'm sure they were praying for me.

I started to pray. Somehow I began to feel strengthened. I looked at my patriarchal blessing again in my dear mother's handwriting. Helaman's army of two thousand had been strengthened by their mothers' teachings. My mother's last words to me had been while I was still in high school. She knew she was dying so she called my brother and me to her bed. She made us promise that we would always live the Word of Wisdom. She told us that if we did, the Lord would bless us. Weighing only eighty-five pounds at the time, I did not feel like I could run and not be weary. As a matter of fact, my feet felt as though they were encased in very large cement blocks. But maybe I could walk and not faint. That day my spirits lifted. I determined that I would hang on. I had beaten my enemy.

MARVIN M. CLARK

Marvin was from Salt Lake City, Utah, and served as a torpedoman's mate. His ship, which was escorting the carrier USS Enterprise, *should have been in Pearl Harbor at the time of the Japanese attack, but it had been delayed by a storm.*

After a day and a night, now very low on fuel, we went into Pearl Harbor about sunset on December 8. The sight that greeted our eyes was sad, sickening, and shocking. We passed Hickam Field with its burning planes and hangars. In the harbor itself we saw the ships blown up in dry dock. On our right, there were two of our destroyers. To our left, there were sunken and burning battlewagons in Battleship Row, with the *West Virginia* still burning. The *Oklahoma* was capsized, the *California* sunk, as were the others. The *Arizona* was burning fiercely. The cruisers, *Homdil* and *Raleigh*, were hit to the lateral with their sterns underwater. The *Utah*, near our berth, was sunk. That was the spot where the *Enterprise* should have been if we had gotten to the harbor in time. These and other horrible sights were seen as we rounded Ford Island to the nearest berth. The smell of fuel oil on the water and burning ships and flesh was etched in our memory. No one doubted what would have been our fate if we had been there. All of us on board were filled with anger, and we took a silent vow to avenge our dead shipmates while we lived.

REUBEN E. CURTIS

Reuben was a lieutenant colonel and a Latter-day Saint commissioned chaplain. He saw action in several major campaigns in the Pacific including Attu, Kwajalein, Leyte, and Okinawa. He sent many letters to Bishop Marvin O. Ashton of the Presiding Bishopric. These letters gave the Saints back home a glimpse into the lives of Latter-day Saint servicemen.

One day I was holding a service when a large group of natives arrived, having been evacuated from a danger area. They were tattered and torn, dirty and dazed, and had for days been living in holes to escape the terrible bombardment. They seemed a pitiful group as they filed up, men, women, and children with tired faces and dragging feet, each carrying a little ragged bundle containing all the things they had been able to save. As they approached we were singing a hymn and they began to join in, in their native tongue.

As soon as we had finished I was approached by an elderly native who asked if they might have permission to hold a prayer service that night. I replied through an interpreter that there certainly would be no objection, and he invited me to meet with them. He said the Japanese had forbidden them to hold worship services, and they hadn't had any since last June. They busied themselves washing out their clothes, bathing, curling the little girls' hair, and soon were transformed into a pretty respectable looking group. . . . They opened their little bundles that contained all of their earthly possessions and, to my surprise, the things they had saved as being the most precious were the Bible and a number of hymnbooks printed in their native tongue.

During the service I spoke briefly to them, through an interpreter, and then the elderly gentleman who had been to a missionary school preached a powerful sermon. He related the history of their sufferings, telling how the missionaries (Protestant) had come to them more than twenty years before and had taught them about Jesus Christ and the ideals of Christianity. Then he said the Japanese came and the missionaries were forced to leave, but before going they had promised them that some day we would come back and drive the Japanese out. They had been waiting patiently for that day. He said the Japanese had told them that they had driven Christ away and that He would not come back. He said, "They could never drive Christ out of our hearts and we had faith that He would come back. Now," he said, "the Americans have come and driven the Japanese away and brought Christ with them. We are free, again, to worship God. . . ."

When I saw the sincerity and the joy in their hearts as they gathered together in their humble surroundings, after going through perhaps as great an ordeal as human beings have ever been called upon to endure; saw them give thanks to God as they knew Him, for their blessings, my mind went back over the past year to some of the other conditions under which I had joined in worship out under the merciless desert sun with the temperature reaching one hundred and thirty degrees; huddled together on a damp hillside in the bitter cold in the far north; down in the crowded, stifling, hot bowels of a swaying ship; in a tent in an eighty-mile-an-hour gale; out in the rain and mud without any cover or place to sit down; within the thunder of the guns; and now with a group of simple natives who believe that although they had lost every earthly possession they still had everything that really mattered and were thankful.

* * * * *

Kwajalein Miracle

Being a war correspondent, my boat was going in behind the first line of men, and we came upon these two, wounded marines in the water. One, from the stain of red around him we could tell, was wounded badly; the other, wounded too, was holding the other's head above water. We picked them up, midst a hail of shots from shore, then pulled back toward safer retreat to render first aid. The one seemed too far gone to need much help, but the other refused aid until his wounded buddy was attended. But our help seemed insufficient, as we soon realized, and we announced our decision to his comrade. Then it happened.

This young man, the better of the two, bronzed by the tropical sun, clean as a shark's tooth in the South Sea, slowly got to his knees. His one arm was nearly gone, but with the other, he lifted the head of his unconscious pal into his lap, placed his good hand on the other's pale brow and uttered what to us seemed to be incredible words—words which to this moment are emblazoned in unforgettable letters across the doorway of my memory: "In the name of Jesus Christ, and by virtue of the Holy Priesthood which I hold, I command you to remain alive until the necessary help can be obtained to secure the preservation of your life."

Today the three of us are here in Honolulu and he is still alive. In fact we walked down the beach together today, as we convalesce. He is the wonder of the medical unit, for they say he should be dead. Why he isn't they don't know, but we do, for we were there, off the shores of Kwajalein. *This account is from a non-LDS, unidentified field reporter. The story was shared by Elder Ezra Taft Benson in a quarterly conference of the Washington, D.C., stake during the war.*

I'll try to squeeze a little time between air raids to bring you up to date in my travels. I seem to be in on a lot of "firsts." Attu was the first American soil to be recaptured in this war; Kwajalein was the first Japanese soil to be taken; and now I am with the unit that is first in the Philippines. . . .

While holding services last night we were interrupted twice by air raids and had to scatter because of enemy planes. We watched seven enemy planes shot down over our heads and then regathered and finished the service. One learns to do a lot of things out here. I have learned to cuss and pray at the same time.

* * * * *

Now that the battle has somewhat subsided I can tell you something of our activities. We are situated in a beautiful coconut grove right on the beach where we enjoy the salt breeze by night and a daily "dunk" in the ocean. In fact, I went swimming Christmas Day.

I enclose as of possible interest to you a picture of the chapel I just completed (with the help of twenty natives) and of the Christmas Eve candlelight service I held in it.

The chapel was built entirely of native materials, i.e., bamboo, nipa, coconut palm matting, and it was tied together with abaca and rattan. We went out into the swamps for the materials.

The building was quite a bit of fun. The natives had a meager knowledge of English and Spanish. I had a very meager knowledge of Spanish and no knowledge of the Filipino dialect prevalent here. We were both fairly well versed in the language of the hands, so, when we had a difference of opinion on certain architectural features the "Capitat" and I would argue the thing out for an hour in four different languages and finally he would say: "Oh-Kay, Oh-Kay," and then do it his way.

The natives scorned any modern tools and the only tool used in the entire construction was the native "bolo knife." The chapel seats one hundred men and we filled it to overflowing five times Christmas Eve and Christmas Day. We had a twenty-six-voice choir that sang Christmas carols in a way that brought tears to many an eye as old memories came floating by.

Christmas Day I met with two groups of LDS men, led by Brother Don C. Kimball and Brother Wallace Gatrell, both of

Salt Lake. I felt it a privilege to enjoy the fellowship of these splendid men, partake of the sacrament, and sing some of the old familiar hymns of Zion.

We have a number of LDS services started here now. . . . Chaplain Marsden Durham and I visit these groups as often as we can. Most of our boys are preaching the gospel to many souls by the fine example of their lives. There is something about a clean way of life that draws men to it.

Wishing the best for you and yours during the coming year and praying for an early end to the war.

* * * * *

One time when I was in the Philippines, I was the corps chaplain. I put a sign up on the beach "LDS Service will be held here . . . next Sunday." The battle was still going on. The men were going up and down in the jeep and the word would spread. Whenever Sunday came, I always had one hundred to two hundred men waiting there for services. I remember that my assistant who was the Catholic chaplain on base said, "Now, Chaplain so and so up here about twenty miles up the line here is kind of mad at you."

I said, "What is the matter?"

He said, "He says that you can't hold a service there."

I said, "What do you mean I can't hold services?"

"He is not going to let you hold a service."

So I got him on the phone. I said, "Now Chaplain so-and-so, I understand that you are not going to let me hold a service up there."

"Yes," he said, "Your sign on the beach says Church of Jesus Christ. What do you think my church is?" He was a Baptist.

I said, "What is your church?"

"It is a Baptist church."

I said, "Mine is the Church of Jesus Christ. Now what is your complaint?"

"You can't hold it."

I said, "Do you know who you are talking to?"

"Who am I talking to?"

"This is Colonel Curtis, the corps chaplain."

For about ten seconds there was absolute silence and then he began to stutter. "Colonel Curtis, how can I help you? What can I do? Could I advertise this for you? Could you use my chapel? What can I do?" He had pictures of my sending him down to the Christmas Islands and I was already writing out the order. This happened because I was the amateur holy man and in the Mormon Church, which was very unpopular among the other chaplains because they all had theological degrees and we didn't have any. I had a rough time until I got a little authority and then I gave them an equally rough time. I wouldn't be pushed around. I enjoyed it.

* * * * *

I climbed a mountain range and recovered the body of an aviator who had crashed. Unable to get the body down the steep slope, I dug a grave on the hillside, and with uncovered head, sang a hymn and held a simple graveside service. I could see in every direction and all seemed so peaceful and beautiful that I could hardly bring myself to believe the distant roar was anything but thunder and the flashes of fire anything but lightning.

THEODORE E. CURTIS JR.

Theodore was one of forty-six Latter-day Saint chaplains commissioned during World War II. He sent the following letter dated April 19, 1944, to Bishop Marvin O. Ashton, member of the Presiding Bishopric.

Seven Christmas services were held aboard ship in order to accommodate all of the men. Perhaps under present circumstances we were more deeply conscious of the real significance of the day than we ever had been before. More thought was given to the greatest gift of all—that "God so loved the world that He gave His only begotten Son"—and to what that gift means to the serviceman as he faces possible physical destruction.

Sunday morning, following Christmas Day, dawned with a richness of color one rarely beholds. How far removed war seemed as the celestial canvas reflected the color harmony of the Master Artist!

An LDS service was held just after breakfast. It was good to sing our hymns again, and to partake of the sacrament. We closed with the stirring words of the pioneer theme song: "But if our lives are spared again to see the Saints their rest obtain, Oh, how we'll make this chorus swell—All is well! All is well!" It would have done you good to have heard the men sing it.

The country is romantic and beautiful. (Steamship ticket agencies, like chambers of commerce, just can't be wrong.) As you stand enraptured by the lacy silhouette of palm fronds against the silver of a tropical moon, coconuts drop on your head, land crabs crawl up your legs, centipedes get tangled up on your chest, small lizards play tag on your stomach, mosquitoes drill through your toughest callouses. Then you are startled to note that you have sunk waist deep into the mud. A South Sea paradise! All that you ever read about jungles, of a derogatory character, is true.

WILLIAM H. DAVIS

William served in the United States Navy aboard the USS Signet *and was involved in campaigns at Iwo Jima, Okinawa, and Japan.*

The most poignant episode in my navy career occurred at Okinawa. We had been at sea for more than twelve months. The Okinawa campaign was nearing a conclusion. A radio message was received by the operator on the USS *Signet* that an LDS sacrament service was being held on a destroyer nearby. This message was given to me, and Captain Gentry authorized my use of the captain's launch so that I could attend that service.

It was a wonderful service attended by forty (plus or minus) men from nearby ships. The sacrament was administered and passed to each sailor. It was my first sacrament in more than eighteen months. I felt truly blessed. We heard later that that particular destroyer was hit by a suicide plane, and the elder who had led the meeting was killed.

* * * * *

William Hatch Davis.

Our big worry at Okinawa was the Japanese suicide planes. They seldom missed a night flying right near our patrol station on their way to the anchorages. The thing that worried us most, was that they weren't a bit choosy about the size of the ship they crashed. Sometimes we'd see them, and on dark nights we'd hear them, and sometimes we'd just "feel" them going past. On the nights of the big air raids it was really something to stand at our General Quarters stations and see the tracers from the ships streak the sky and now and then, a big flash of flame when a plane was hit.

Kamikaze

Late in the war, the Japanese resorted to suicide missions to prevent Allied forces from achieving victory. One of these was the kamikaze pilot. Literally meaning "Divine Wind" or "Spirit Wind," these pilots were often only given minimal flight training and only enough fuel to make it to their objective. They would fly their planes into the midst of Allied naval convoys and try to take down the largest ship. Many troops were killed by these desperate attacks.

Happy natives of Okinawa after liberation, July 1945.

April 7, 1945, was our big day. Our patrol station was just southwest of the southern tip of Okinawa. There had been several raids earlier in the evening. We were at general quarters when the USS *Staunch* reported a plane heading directly for us. In a few minutes our gun crews could see the exhaust flames of a Japanese Betty (medium bomber) off the port beam. Our port guns opened fire, and we could see our tracers hitting him. As the plane passed low overhead, we could see it just beginning to flame. The starboard guns opened fire, and the plane went down in flames about a thousand yards off the starboard beam. Parts of the plane floated and burned for a few minutes (which seemed like hours), but we could see no survivors, so we returned to our patrol station. The *Signet* had actually shot down an enemy plane. We were all just shaking with patriotism.

ALMA R. DUNFORD

Alma was a sergeant in the Ninety-ninth Ordnance Bomb Disposal Squadron in the United States Army.

That morning on Okinawa our bomb disposal squad had just loaded forty native laborers onto eight Japanese trucks to go into the Japanese munition dump located just outside Youtan airfield in central Okinawa. It was a beautiful clear morning with bright sunshine warming the steamy grass. The happy chatter of the men and boys attested to the pleasure of their anticipation of a busy work day that would enable them to earn enough yen to feed their families for days ahead. We drove into the canyon and roused the United States Army guards who were stationed there.

We had just unloaded the laborers and assigned them to their tasks among the stacks and rows of piled boxes of grenades, shells, and bombs to ready them to stack onto the trucks for transport down to the wharf and thence out to sea to dump into the safety of the deep. All of the sudden a great flash of fire filled the upper part of the canyon where the army guards had started a fire to warm their morning coffee. One foolish guard had tossed a handful of propellant sticks near a stack of munitions. . . . The stack ignited with a gigantic "whoosh." A tremendous bang and then a sustained roar sent us all fleeing as fast as we could run back down the canyon past the trucks and stack after stack of shells and bombs and huge marine torpedoes. As the flaming inferno intensified, huge gobs of burning explosives were thrown helter-skelter from the head of the canyon among the lighter munitions past us and over us, landing on every side and even ahead of us as we ran for our lives, wild-eyed with terror.

One of the Japanese truck drivers had managed to turn his truck around and sped down the canyon, pausing to let us clamber aboard, and he carried us to safety. We who managed to reach the truck were the only ones to escape the inferno. We drove way out into the broad valley below and watched the tremendous conflagration blow the canyon to pieces.

Fourteen laborers, eight truck drivers and ten United States soldiers were killed. It took four days for the fires to burn down so we could enter and begin to count the casualties and begin to clean up the mess. Amazingly, two GIs had fled into an old mine cave and survived the tremendous blasts and concussions. One was a guard who had been horribly burned, and he later died after being treated and flown back to Hawaii for treatment. The other never did recover his hearing and was so shell-shocked that he required much therapy. Thereafter we changed our operating procedure for disposing of munitions dumps—we simply strung fuses and prima cord through the dumps and then withdrew—and just blew them up!

L. MARSDEN DURHAM

Marsden was a commissioned chaplain who received a Bronze Star for his service in Leyte. The following excerpts are from a letter he sent to a member of the General Commission on Army and Navy Chaplains. (See also John Baud account.)

The division to which I am attached participated in the initial landing of the Philippines, and helped make possible General MacArthur's "I have returned." I came in with my unit which comprised part of the assault troops in the fifth wave. In the subsequent thirty-two days on the front lines I learned the nature of war. Sherman was right too, war is hell. I know that my guardian angel kept a constant vigil, and I am grateful to the Lord for the preservation of my life. I have been in several tight spots yet feel that I was blessed to look in the right direction at the proper time. I have said from the beginning, and I repeat it again, that I have as a chaplain the best job the Army has to offer. . . .

In garrison life I learned that a chaplain had a certain worth. In combat I found, however, that worth enhanced and magnified, for in combat a chaplain can be the spark plug and nerve center of an organization. The men rely on him. His very presence on the battle scene is an asset, and a nod to this man, a smile to that, a word of prayer with another, and a comforting arm thrown about still another combine to fortify and replenish the spiritual needs of the men. . . .

Combat has been rough. For nights on end we "slept" in foxholes, in water up to our heads and we were grateful when it rained only two inches a day. I've crawled over rice paddies and bogs with mud shoulder-deep, moving along by placing a stretcher on the surface, crawling its length, and then repeating the process. You can imagine our difficulties with the wounded. But through all the trials, I didn't hear a complaint from the men. The wounded were heroic in the acceptance of their misfortune, and I am all admiration for the pluck and grit of the American soldier.

FRANKLIN T. EAST

A serviceman in the United States Army, Franklin spent over three years as a Japanese prisoner of war. In his account, he describes the days just prior to the fall of Bataan.

We had to get on small boats Christmas Day to go to Bataan. That was where we were going to make a stand against the enemy. Well, they bombed where we were supposed to land. We had our Christmas dinner with us, and when we ran to get away from the air raid we lost our dinner. So, we had no Christmas dinner and nothing to eat until the next evening when we got to Bataan.

They put me with an outfit that was guarding ration trucks to the front line. They had to have a guard on the trucks or else they would never get the rations to the men. Rations were very short. We had a Philippine driver on the truck. One night I had a load of rice to go to the Philippine Army, and I could hear rice running, so I had Joe stop the truck to see where it was running. I found that the driver had a bamboo tube stuck in a sack of rice that ran into a five-gallon gas can in the front seat with him. If he could have gotten the can of rice, he would have received a lot of pesos for it. I could have shot him for it and there would have been no questions asked, but I only told him not to do it anymore. I hope he didn't.

I only met one other Mormon while on Bataan. The Fifth Cavalry had horse meat—not too bad. We ate all the horses up. Some of the fellows shot some monkeys and cooked them up, but I didn't try them. They didn't appeal to me. Just before the surrender, I was taking a load of rations out. The truck was out of gas, so we went to one gas depot, and they were out of gas. I noticed several trucks pull away at the time, so we went to another one down the road. We got our gas and started up the road. They had a bombing raid, and the Japanese bombed the road to the hospital. I noticed some of the trucks were on it. The men who were still in the trucks burned to death. I was blessed that I had to go farther to get gas. We went on our way and delivered the load. We went on without any trouble.

The surrender came, and they set fire to the ammunition dump not far from where we camped. It made a lot of noise. That was April 1942. They told us to put our guns in a stack and wait until the enemy came into camp. I noticed an officer trying to burn something, so I walked over to help him. I noticed that his tears were running freely. He was burning the flags; they were beautiful. I found out that he had been a prisoner of war during the first World War, so he knew what it meant to surrender—that when we lost our flag, we lost our freedom, our right to worship God, to read, to hold meetings, or anything. We were slaves to the Japanese, we did what they told us to do. We didn't know what to expect when the enemy came in. They could have lined us up and shot us, but they didn't. It might have been better for some if they had done that. They wouldn't have had to suffer so much and then die. We had to walk seventy-five miles to San Fernando. Most of the way there were guards along with us to keep us moving along and to see that we didn't stop. They searched us and took anything they wanted. If they found Japanese money on someone, they took him out of the group, and we didn't see him again. One day as we were marching along, I was near the end of the line, and a fellow said, "Let's drop out." We were going through an abandoned Philippine valley, and there wasn't a guard in sight. I had had an attack of malaria the night we left Bataan. I wasn't feeling so hot, so I told him no, that I was going to try and stay with it. He dropped out and started toward a house, and all at once a guard came from nowhere. Three shots rang out, and I knew that he was no more. I only had a handful of cooked rice on the whole march. It is known as the Bataan Death March.

CLYDE L. FAIRBOURN ★★★

Soon after returning home from a mission, Clyde was drafted into the United States Army in July 1944. He served in five campaigns during the war.

We were loaded on another ship and informed that we were on our way to Luzon Island, where we would land on a beachhead. I was aware that this was the real thing, and I was frightened with the realization that I might not return from what lay ahead. It was at this time I felt that I should take my problem to the Lord, as going to the Lord in prayer was not new to me. My petition to the Lord was that if He would protect me and bring me back home safely, that I would do my best to serve Him the rest of my life. The rest of this report is to show that the Lord did hear and answer my prayer.

We did make the beachhead landing in a very military manner. To my surprise we did not find much resistance, as most of the people, including their forces, knew of our coming and had pulled back farther into the mountains. We walked twenty-five miles that day, and I had blisters on my feet from carrying so much weight and from the new heavy shoes I was wearing. The second day, we started to see evidence of the enemy. When we started into higher ground, we started to get some resistance. The battalion commander wanted to bring in some of our artillery for protection, but some objected, as we were in heavy trees and feared it would hit the treetops and explode over us. He ordered two rounds anyway to see if it would work and

Clyde Fairbourn is on the right, holding the weapon.

sure enough we got a tree burst right above where I was lying. My squad leader was lying just ahead of me on the side of the road. The shrapnel was flying through the air, and one piece hit his shoe, right in front of me. I could see that it cut the sole of the shoe right in half. I saw this same shoe about an hour later.

It was late afternoon, and our company was moved to the front of the column, which made us the first to confront the enemy. We were told to dig in and get ready. I started to dig a hole. My assigned companion was next to me. I noticed all of our officers standing about ten to fifteen feet behind us. They were standing in a circle, talking over what should be done that evening. All at once there was a terrific explosion. The concussion was so violent that it blew my companion and me on our faces. My first reaction was to look up, but the air was so cloudy and dark with dirt and flying debris that I could not see. There were several other explosions. When it cleared enough to see, I looked straight ahead. I saw a small tree, and it had a little stream of blood running down its trunk. I then glanced farther up, and there in the crotch of the tree was a pair of human legs hanging, and I knew whom they belonged to. I was looking at the same shoe that had been cut by the shrapnel one hour before when we experienced the tree burst. It was my sergeant in that tree.

Things were now in chaos. The six officers that had made up the circle behind me were gone. Two of them were blown out over the treetop and were found some distance away. There was a hole six feet deep where they had been standing only moments before. The dead and dying were everywhere, and it was then that I experienced my first miracle. My buddy and I were the ones next to the hole and neither one of us was injured at all. I had one piece of shrapnel in my backpack and my companion had none. However, he was out of his head. I held on to him, but he didn't know where he was. That one artillery attack killed about one-half of our entire company. Darkness was now settling in. The enemy could no longer see us, but we couldn't take care of our wounded very well. So many were so badly injured that it has always haunted me. We saw so many arms and legs missing and had no way to help them. Those who could be helped were cared for, and the others died during the night.

All of the leadership, the ones in the circle, were killed, including our radio operator. Someone finally managed to find a way to work the radio, and we contacted headquarters company about two miles behind us. We were told we were cut off from all other units. Everything in back of us was blown up, and since they did not know exactly what our position was, they couldn't give us any fire protection with the big guns. Our best chance to survive was to play dead until morning. Then we were to retreat as fast as we could or make a break for it. We positioned ourselves along a ditch, parallel to the road, with a distance of approximately twenty feet between us. My companion still didn't know where he was. The shock hit him hard and made it mighty scary for me. The long night found me pulling him back to save him from being hit. I thought the enemy would send in ground troops to finish us off. I never quit praying that night. When morning came, the ones that were left and able to move, waited until everyone was ready. Then we made a run for it, as we knew our movements would quickly bring in another attack. Sometimes I thought Abe was the lucky one not to remember that horrible night. I never could quite get it out of my mind.

We spaced ourselves and started as fast as we could back down the road so that we would not be together. This was what we were taught to do in our training. We started on a fast trot back down the road. As we expected, the enemy saw our movement and sent in another barrage of artillery. The last ones of our group looked back and saw the area where we had been suddenly go up in smoke. F Company, behind us, was completely blown out, leaving hardly any survivors. I was completely shocked and saddened as I witnessed the devastation of war. Everywhere I looked was destruction—man-made tools of war and dead bodies.

* * * * *

In July 1945 there were places on the island of Mindanao that still had some heavy resistance from the enemy, even with most of the island secure from the Japanese. We stopped one evening to dig in. We always dug a foxhole to secure ourselves through the night. We made a battalion perimeter, which was very unusual. Most of the time we formed perimeters as a company. I was still handling as my assignment, the mortar weapon. Since it was larger than most of our weapons, we looked for and found a hole that was already partially dug. With a little more work, we made the hole large enough to set up our mortar in the hole with us. We had never before had a spot that was so convenient.

The battalion commander strung a phone line from his hole to ours, so he could call for fire at anytime without getting out of his hole. During the night the enemy had moved in within a few hundred yards of us. As daylight approached, they began to fire at us at fairly close range. We couldn't see too much since we were more or less pinned down. The commander called to me on the phone and told me to send out some mortar rounds to see if we could get it quieted down enough for some of our machine guns to get into action. I sent out twenty rounds and could hear them start to land and explode. Everything went quiet, and I could hear our own men moving into action. The next sound was a terrific explosion right next to my head. I was numb and in shock at the sight of the devastation. It seemed I was bleeding everywhere, and I didn't know how badly I was hit. My first thought was that it was the end of the mortal road for me, and as quickly as that thought moved out, a comforting feeling moved in. I knew that I was not going to die, but would be all right.

GOLDEN L. FENN

Golden enlisted in the Army in March 1941. He was a staff sergeant in the Eighty-second Field Artillery Battalion of the First Cavalry Division.

While stationed at Bilibid prison I was given a dangerous assignment. . . . The water supply station of the Bilibid prison had been guarded by Filipino guerillas (fighting with the Americans). The Japanese had run the guerillas off, and the water supply station had been abandoned. The warrant officer came to me and asked me to select three men with .30-caliber machine guns. We had to go down through the city and back into the jungle to protect the water supply station. In the evening we loaded in the jeep and were driven about three miles out of the city. The four of us were dropped off in the jungle with enemy troops still scattered all around. There was a large metal building housing the water tank. Also a small brick structure sat in front of the metal building. We were all alone in the dark night except for my sub-Thompson .45-caliber machine gun and the other soldiers with carbines and .30-caliber machine guns on tripods. I placed one machine gunner on the right of the brick building and the other on the left in the shadows of the building. There was a brush-covered wash that ran in front of the buildings. The road bisected this wash and opened in front of the brick building. It would have been excellent cover for the enemy to maneuver through the wash. . . . I perused the area checking on each gunner and reported every hour, as instructed, to our commanding officer, Warrant Officer Carter. The metal building with the water tank had an old crank phone, and I would use it to report and let the officers know we were okay and still alive. To the right of the pump station opposite the wash and road was hill with a light on top. This lit up the area and us like sitting ducks. We were there that evening and through the night with no mishap. We could have easily been picked off by enemy troops hiding in the heavy underbrush of the jungle. What a relief it was when the next day the jeep drove up, and we were relieved of our duties.

A. LOUIS FIFE

Louis served in the 382nd Infantry Regiment, Ninety-sixth Infantry Division in the United States Army. The following incident took place on the front at Okinawa.

During one Sunday at the front, we dug a large foxhole and rounded up all the LDS guys to hold a meeting. There were about five or six of us there. We were all LDS except Charles C. Johnson. Gene and I, Chuck, Burg, Dudley, and a couple of others were there. We had a very inspirational meeting. We tried to remember the sacramental prayers, but didn't get them exactly right. Gene wrote them down, and I kept them and gave them to Gene's mother. We used the crackers in the top of our C rations for bread and water from our canteen. I talked on the resurrection. It was truly inspiring and a wonderful meeting. Though muddy and in a foxhole, the Spirit was there more than any other place, other than the temple, that I have ever experienced.

Alexander Louis Fife Jr.

Louis Fife's best friend, Gene Y. Bennett, who was killed on Okinawa June 15, 1945.

LELAND J. FIFE

Leland served in the Third Fleet of the Navy and for a time was an assistant navigator and damage control officer. The following incident occurred while Leland served aboard the aircraft carrier USS Nehenta Bay.

Leland J. and Dove C. Fife, husband and wife. Leland and Dove both served in the war. Dove was a commissioned officer in the Nurse Corps assigned to Nebraska. The two were married in the Salt Lake Temple while on leave. They spent only twenty-nine days together during the first two years of their marriage.

We started refueling at 1:00 P.M. and by 4:00 P.M, the winds came up to about 20 knots, and we had to abandon fueling operations.

The storm continued to increase in velocity. By 6:00 P.M., the winds were over 60 knots. With that much wind it was impossible for the ships to keep in formation. At that point, Admiral Halsey ordered the cessation of formation, and ordered each ship to be on its own and to follow the course and speed that allowed it to take the waves at its most advantageous course and speed. With so many ships in a concentrated area, it became very dangerous. We just barely missed hitting the battleship *New Jersey*. The storm kept increasing in intensity and by 9:00 P.M., it was a full-blown typhoon with winds. The rest of the night was a nightmare. No one could eat or sleep.

The next morning, after all officers had made their inspections of their assigned sections of the ship, it was reported that the ship was still sound and no major damage had been inflicted by the storm. I had the 8:00 A.M. quarterdeck watch that morning, and the anemometer registered winds between 160-165 knots during the entire morning. Luckily we couldn't see any other ships in the area. We couldn't make radio contact with any of them. Winds continued at about the same intensity all that day and all the next night. We changed courses several times, but the storm seemed to change with us.

I shared a stateroom with an engineer by the name of George Mariana. On the morning of the third day of this storm, we both made our respective inspections. He finished his inspection just a minute or so before I completed mine. We were both on our way to the bridge to make our report to the captain. Mariana entered the catwalk. He was halfway across before I entered the catwalk. He stopped at that point and observed the movement of water on the hangar deck. I stopped too, waiting for Mariana to say something. Suddenly, he threw his arms high into the air along with his clipboard and cried out, "This ship is sinking." At that moment my hands froze to the railings on the catwalk. I could not move.

I don't know how long I was frozen to the railings. It seemed like a long, long time. I thought that somehow the water on the hangar deck was associated with a problem in the boiler rooms, and that the ship was really sinking. Then, almost as suddenly, in my mind's eye, I saw my mother get up from her knees, and I knew that she had been praying most of the night. I saw her walk down the hallway of our home in Ammon, Idaho, and into my bedroom. She sat down at my dresser and adjusted a three-way mirror so that I could see her face as I lay in my bed. I caught her eye in the mirror, and she said, "I now know your ship will make it." I was overcome with a warm glow of peace and contentment—more wonderful than I had ever felt before. My body immediately relaxed. I could release my hands, and I could straighten my fingers.

As I continued to the bridge to give my report to the captain, I was astonished at how relaxed I was. I had sure knowledge that our ship would survive the storm. I was so relaxed and confident of what I had learned that when I approached the captain, I saluted smartly and said, "All is well, Captain." At that moment a huge wave broke over the quarterdeck nearly knocking both of us to the deck. As the water poured off his rain gear, he asked, "So all is well, Lieutenant Fife? Look at the anemometer." It registered 164 knots.

At this moment, the captain seemed confused, and I thought maybe he thought I was drunk. He picked up the intercom phone and then put it back on the hook. I thought he was going to call for the ship's police and have me confined to the brig.

He then asked, "What do you know that I don't know?" I then told him that I knew our ship was going to make it. He asked, "Fife, how do you know that?"

I then told him what I had seen in my mind's eye. I said, "My mother lives very close to the Lord, and I know that whatever she says as coming from the Lord will come to pass. She has never been wrong."

The captain looked at me eyeball to eyeball for what seemed a long time. I could feel the Spirit working on him, but I didn't know what he was going to do. Another huge

Leland J. and Dove C. Fife, Oct. 2000.

wave washed over the flight deck and bridge, and for a minute or so we concentrated on just holding on. When the water subsided, the captain again picked up the intercom phone and called to the bosun mate to pipe general quarters. The general quarters' alarm was sounded, and the captain ordered all hands not on watch to report to the midship's mess hall.

The captain then said, "Lieutenant Fife has an important message that I want him to give to you." He then ordered his two orderlies to go with me to the mess hall. He told me to give the message that I had given to him to those who were assembled.

Old-time seamen are usually not fond of spiritual things. But I was sent to do a job, and I told them of the spiritual experience I had had with my mother. That she had received a revelation from the Lord that our ship was going to make it through this typhoon.

I was somewhat surprised at how well they accepted this spiritual revelation. Some of the rough-necked sailors had tears in their eyes, and displayed a sort of awe and amazement toward me. The Spirit really touched those men. Many of them went away with new hope, and some with the assurance that the ship would indeed make it through the terrible storm. By 11:00 A.M. the storm started to recede. By 4:00 P.M. we were in a perfect calm, three days and three nights after it started.

HYRUM FINK

The following excerpt is from a letter that Hyrum sent to his parents. It was later published in the first servicemen's edition of the Church News.

There have been times when we have been so scared we would tremble, but the fear was put out of our minds with prayer, and the thoughts that we knew we were being guided through the waters by the Lord. Dad, I love my religion, and I'm proud that I had someone like you and Mother to teach me to pray. My little Book of Mormon is the greatest help I have. It seems to me that every time I'm worrying about something or fear something, I open the book just at the right place, if you know what I mean. I'd be lost if I'd ever lost it. Then I also know that you are praying for me each morning and night, and sometimes I feel that I can almost hear just about what you would say.

WILFORD A. FISCHER

Wilford was a first lieutenant who served as a forward observer for the Second Marine Division. He participated in battles in Saipan, Tinian, and Okinawa. He was awarded a Silver Star for the following experience on Saipan.

After our battalion was secure on the beach and placed into position and the Second and Fourth Marines had established themselves on the island, we knew as the support battalion, it would be our turn next. The Japanese artillery was giving our troops a bad time and making it almost impossible for the Tenth Marines to fire back at the Japanese artillery and make it safer for the troops on the beach and the amtracks coming in for a landing. From aboard ship we could see the water shoot up into the air as the shells landed near the amtracks headed for the beach. The sound of our battalion commander's voice rang out, "Fall in." The command was given. "Line up to debark," was the next command. The Second Battalion of the Second Regiment of the Second Marine Division started down the rope ladders to the waiting landing crafts. Large swirls of water spouted into the air as the enemy shells dropped into the water nearby. Sometimes the shells dropped so close to our landing craft that

Silver Star medal being awarded to 1st Lt. Wilford A. Fischer for "gallantry in action" on Saipan. The presentation was made by Maj. Gen. Watson of the Second Marine Divison.

Silver Star

The Silver Star is awarded to a person who, while serving in any capacity with the U.S. Army, is cited for gallantry in action against an enemy of the United States while engaged in military operations involving conflict with an opposing foreign force, or while serving with friendly foreign forces engaged in armed conflict against an opposing armed force in which the United States is not a belligerent party. The required gallantry, while of a lesser degree than that required for award of the Distinguished Service Cross, must nevertheless have been performed with marked distinction.

water sprayed us. As we hit the beach, the large ramp was lowered, and the men quickly headed to the beach to take cover from the enemy fire. "Lieutenant Fischer take your team and go to the front lines and knock out those Japanese gun positions, they are causing us all kinds of trouble. It's difficult to advance against their continual firing at our artillery. Their guns are very accurate and make it extremely difficult for our artillery to set up, so we can knock out those enemy guns."

Realizing my responsibility, I knew that without the help of the Lord we were in a dangerous situation. I was assigned a cruiser and a destroyer to accomplish this job. My job was to radio the destroyer and give them directions where to shoot their naval guns. The destroyer was equipped with 5-inch guns. . . . At first we were unable to see where they were shooting from, but as it became dark, I was able to spot the flash of their guns. This made it possible to locate their positions. "*Wintergreen* (the destroyer), look straight ahead and a little to your right about five thousand feet from your position. Watch for the red flash." A huge ball of fire shot into the air as we hit their ammunition dump by the gun position. One by one we knocked out the enemy guns, except for one large 16-inch naval gun that was mounted upon a track. The gun was set in a canyon, making it impossible for the trajectory of our naval shells to clear the ridge of the mountain. They were safe from our naval guns. Their 16-inch shells were causing a great deal of trouble and

Silver Star citation which accompanied the medal awarded to Wilford Fischer.

THE SECRETARY OF THE NAVY
WASHINGTON

The President of the United States takes pleasure in presenting the SILVER STAR MEDAL to

SECOND LIEUTENANT WILFORD A. FISCHER,
UNITED STATES MARINE CORPS RESERVE,

for service as set forth in the following

CITATION:

"For conspicuous gallantry and intrepidity as a Naval Gunfire Spotter, attached to the Second Joint Assault Signal Company, Second Marine Division, in action against enemy Japanese forces on Saipan, Marianas Islands, 16 June 1944. Braving enemy fire during a hostile counterattack, Second Lieutenant Fischer advanced through our lines into Japanese territory to observe an enemy artillery battery which had been firing into our lines inflicting casualties and damaging our supporting artillery. Determining the location of the hostile artillery, he directed two destroyers to a position from which to shell the objective, thereby contributing directly to the silencing of the enemy battery. His courage and devotion to duty reflect the highest credit upon Second Lieutenant Fischer and the United States Naval Service."

For the President,

John L. Sullivan
Secretary of the Navy.

causing many marines to get hurt. Like a flash the thought came to my mind. If we had a destroyer on the north end of the island of Saipan we could fire our shells into the canyon from that position. Immediately I radioed my destroyer, "Relay the following directions to the destroyer on the north end of the island. When you see the flash of the gun which should be to your right and six thousand feet straight from your position, locate this position on your map and relay your directions to the other destroyer. Have them fire all guns up and down the canyon from their position." Soon it was quiet, the enemy gun stopped firing, indicating the gun was knocked out. Peace settled over the island; no more enemy guns could be heard.

Wilford Fischer (center) standing with fellow soldiers.

CHARLES F. FOSTER

Charles was a seaman, first class, with the United States Navy. He served for a time aboard the USS Winged Arrow *where he was able to briefly become acquainted with future General Authority, A. Theodore Tuttle.*

When we were going down to New Guinea we stopped at the Admiralty Islands. . . . We tied up in the harbor of Manus Island. There were many ships in the harbor. The ammunition ship from which I had been unloading forty 2000-pound bombs just three weeks before, blew up in the harbor. It killed more than a thousand men. It killed people on ships all around it. We were anchored at least a mile or maybe more from that ship. I was down about second or third deck on the ship. It felt like it was going to tear my eardrums up when it blew up. . . . We went running up on deck to see what happened. Pieces of the ship were falling everywhere. Shortly after, planes started circling all around this smoke. They were searching for the Japanese. They thought the enemy had come in and set the ammunition off, and I'm pretty sure they did.

I think what they did was to get aboard that ship disguised as our men. Losing their lives was nothing to them. They were dedicated to kill at least ten men before they lost their own lives. Those people were hard to fight.

We had one kamikaze guy in our navy on our aircraft carrier. His name was Collin P. Kelly. He ran out of fuel and couldn't get back to his ship. He had a bomb so he was determined he was going to take a Japanese ship to the bottom with him. He put his plane in a dive and went down the smokestack. It took the ship down. They named a ship after him.

Domain of Neptunus Rex
Charles F. Foster
KNOW YE, that on the 2nd day of November, 1944, aboard the U.S.S. WINGED ARROW Latitude 00.00. Longitude, appeared into Our Royal Domain, and having been inspected and found worthy by My Royal Staff, was initiated into the Solemn Mysteries of the Ancient Order of the Deep. I command my subjects to honor and respect the bearer of this certificate as One Of Our Trusty Shellbacks.

Davy Jones
His Royal Scribe

Neptunus Rex
Ruler of the Raging Main

Charles F. Foster (see arrow) with his crew aboard the USS Winged Arrow.

★
★
★

(Above) The USS Winged Arrow *was a merchantman class ship.*

(Right) Charles Foster's navy training course certificate.

H. RONALD FROGLEY

Ronald enlisted in the Marine Corps and served as a pharmacist's mate, third class. He earned a Silver Star in connection with the invasion of Okinawa.

On April 1, 1945, while assigned with the First Marine Division First Battalion, as a front line corpsman, we hit the beachhead at Okinawa. We expected and had been prepared to receive heavy Japanese gunfire, but found only token resistance. We quickly cut the island into two halves, north and south and then turned north to secure that part of the island which was our assignment. We did it quickly and were overjoyed to find the opposing army absent. It was not long, however, until we received news that the army which had been assigned the south half of the island had found the Japanese and were in serious trouble. They were in danger of being overrun by the opposing forces. Our marine forces were assigned to spearhead and attack from the middle of the island driving south into the Japanese Army.

I had been working in the field hospital again as a surgical technician. I was assigned as instrument nurse for the lead surgeon. He had been called to Guam for some special surgery, and I had stayed behind. The first sergeant came to me and asked if I would go up on the front lines for just a few days while the doctor was gone. I said I would and soon found out that all of the other hospital corpsmen had been killed. I was all that was left in the entire company. I was gone thirty-three days and was missing in action most of the time, because no one knew where I was. I had several exciting times facing Japanese banzai charges, having the heel of my shoe shot off by a sniper, and rescuing several wounded marines under fire.

On one occasion we had been making a sweep down a particular valley, chasing the enemy. We came out on a hill and looking over a small valley saw the Japanese soldiers running up the other side. Suddenly a cry for corpsmen echoed up the slope. A small canal ran through the bottom of the valley and a marine had been shot and was floating in the water. The marines looked at me as if to say, "Well what are you going to do?" I buckled my helmet and ran into a hail of fire. I could see bullets digging into the earth and could hear bullets cutting corn stalks down around me. I got stuck in the mud after jumping off a three-foot embankment but wiggled out, ran some more and made the canal. I went into the water which was up

H. Ronald Frogley.

to my chest, grabbed the marine and found out he was still alive but had a serious head wound.

The three or four marines that had made up the advance party were all pinned down, but they were not making any effort to escape. I called out for a smoke grenade. One marine had one, and I told him to throw it. We tried to run out under the cover of the smoke, but found the smoke had followed the canal. We were completely exposed as we ran out of the water. I had the wounded man over my shoulder and moved rather slowly. All but one of the marines escaped. I was left with the wounded man and the remaining marine. The heavy enemy fire pinned us down again.

As we lay there, I prayed for wisdom and help in surviving and getting the marine to safety. I finally picked him up again and ran to cover. My only weapon was a

UNITED STATES MARINE CORPS

HEADQUARTERS
FLEET MARINE FORCE, PACIFIC
C/O FLEET POST OFFICE, SAN FRANCISCO

In the name of the President of the United States, the Commanding General, Fleet Marine Force, Pacific, takes pleasure in awarding the SILVER STAR MEDAL to

HOSPITAL APPRENTICE FIRST CLASS HENRY R. FROGLEY,
UNITED STATES NAVAL RESERVE

for service as set forth in the following

CITATION:

"For conspicuous gallantry and intrepidity in action against the enemy while serving as a hospital corpsman with a Marine rifle company on OKINAWA SHIMA, RYUKYU ISLANDS, on 5 June, 1945. When the company to which he was attached was held up in its attack by three enemy machine guns which completely covered its front and one Marine was severely wounded while crossing a field that was covered by the grazing fire of the enemy's automatic weapons and could not be evacuated because of his hazardous position, Hospital Apprentice First Class FROGLEY, voluntarily and with complete disregard for his own safety, ran out into the hail of enemy bullets and dragged the wounded man to a position in defilade where he administered first aid and blood plasma. His heroic actions were an inspiration to all who witnessed them and were in keeping with the highest traditions of the United States Naval Service."

ROY S. GEIGER,
Lieutenant General,
U. S. Marine Corps.

Temporary Citation

H. Ronald Frogley's Silver Star citation.

.45 automatic, but it had been underwater for over an hour, and I didn't even know if it would shoot. We entered a farmhouse and found it full of civilians, or at least we thought they were civilians. I knew we had to get out of there so I pulled my .45, and in the best western style threatened to shoot if anyone moved. They didn't want any part of my gun and we left.

We went around the house following a path that led to a little barn. Just as we got by the barn, a sniper shot the heel of my boot off and spun me around into a big ditch. I thought I had lost my foot, but not finding any blood, I gathered up the poor wounded man. I followed the ditch which I later found to be the sewer until I found our forward lines. I warned the advanced marines of the sniper and told them where he was, and then I headed for the field hospital. I got the wounded man returned, tended to his wounds again and sent him out for better care.

I had just fixed and eaten a can of rations when a marine messenger came into the tent. He inquired if anyone had heard from me or knew where I was. I identified myself, and he told me I was needed badly, that the company was under heavy fire. It was very dark and raining. We ran in the rain until it was just getting light when we came up to the company. They told me the company commander was across a wide open space and had been calling for help. He had been shot. Again I buckled my helmet and ran out into the path of a machine gun that was holding up the company's advance. I will never know why I wasn't killed that day except for the protection of the Spirit. I could see the ground being torn up all around me by the machine gun bullets, but I ran on unharmed. I got to the commander and took care of his wounds. I have always been grateful for the protection granted me on that occasion as I have been protected all my life as I tried to be obedient to the teachings of the gospel.

H. Ronald Frogley (on the right) with a fellow serviceman.

The Invasion of Japan

The United States invaded the Japanese island of Okinawa on Easter Sunday, April 1, 1945. The battle lasted until June 21. The island lies only 325 miles from Japan, and was a key strategic position for the Allies, who at the time were planning the final assault on the Japanese home islands.

When the battle finally ended, some 110,000 Japanese soldiers had been killed or had taken their own lives, while the U.S. Navy reported casualties of 9,731, of whom 4,907 were dead. Of the U.S. Tenth Army, 7,613 were killed, including the commander, General Buckner, and some 52,000 were wounded or missing.

HERBERT H. FROST

Herbert served as master sergeant in the Army. An unusual note about Herbert is that he collected insect and bird specimens throughout his tour of duty and dutifully preserved them and sent them to the BYU Zoology Department.

Many times it has been said that actions speak louder than words. During my time at Salinas, California, this was forcefully brought to my attention. By this time our unit had been together for almost a year and so everyone knew quite a bit about everyone else. My behavior was watched more closely than I was aware. The men knew I was a Mormon and had some habits that were not the general run-of-the-mill activities of those in the service. One Sunday morning I picked up my mess kit and headed for the mess hall. I hadn't got out of the barracks when one of my good friends, Earl Dabin said, "Hey, Jack, where are you going?"

I responded, "Over to get some chow."

His reply I'm sure I will never forget. He said, "Have you forgotten that this is the first Sunday in the month?"

I turned around, returned to my bunk, and thanked him for reminding me it was fast Sunday.

GLEN J. GARR

Glen served in the Seventy-first Naval Construction Battalion. The first incident took place at Bougainville, and the second on Okinawa.

One morning while our field kitchen was still at the landing area and our cooks were feeding all personnel in the area, about five hundred men were ahead of me in the chow line. When Japanese planes appeared over the area, everyone scattered and made a run for shelter. I happened to see our planes intercept the Japanese and start to drive them from the area. I made a run for the head of the chow line and got my breakfast. Then sitting under a tree eating, a 155-millimeter howitzer fired right behind me. I threw my mess kit and breakfast and lit on my face, until I realized that it was our artillery and not their artillery. We were all jumpy.

* * * * *

On April 6, 1945, the Japanese made their first big kamikaze strike against our ships off Okinawa. The world's

Glen J. Garr, Williamsburg, VA, 1943.

largest battleship, the *Yamamoto,* had sailed from Japan with just enough fuel to reach Okinawa with the intention of sinking as many of our ships as possible. However, our planes attacked and sank the *Yamamoto* before it ever reached Okinawa. They also sent hundreds of kamikaze planes, most were shot down by our air cover but some got through. I remember seeing three planes falling in flames at one time. One of our LSTs (landing ship tank) was hit and was burning on the beach. The enemy also used what they called a "cherry blossom." We called it a "baka bomb" meaning fool bomb. It was a small aircraft carried under a Japanese Betty bomber and released when in range of a target. The baka bomb was about twenty feet long with a wingspan of about eighteen feet. There were twin tails with three rockets in the end of the fuselage, and in the nose was a thousand-pound charge of explosives. The cockpit had a joy stick, a rudder control, and a plastic canopy; there were no instruments, and the plane had no landing gear. It was a one-way ride for the pilot.

CB (Construction Battalion) moving day, Okinawa, 1945.

ARVIN S. GIBSON

Arvin served as a staff sergeant in the United States Army. He arrived at Iwo Jima twenty-three days after D-Day and was there for approximately one year.

For the entire time that I was on Iwo Jima, I remember attending religious services only once. That was on Easter, and it was held on Mount Suribachi. People were still dying, so everyone attended. Although I did not consider myself religious, I did pray. Especially when I felt my life threatened, which was fairly often during the first few months. And I was not alone in such prayer. It had the effect of freeing us from overwhelming fear. My prayers restored in me a sense of calm and peace—in the midst of chaos and non-peace—so that I could properly function. At times I even found myself reassuring others, sometimes individuals older than my twenty years. On one cataclysmic occasion, for instance, during a rather prolonged air raid when the entire sky seemed to be alight with explosions and fire, I found myself hugging a soldier who was sobbing like a child.

* * * * *

This Saturday Evening Post *cover depicts a scene similar to that which Arvin Gibson describes in his account.*

We had just recovered from a storm, and on the afternoon of May 21, Rademacher came to the Quonset hut, where a number of us were gathered, with exciting news.

"I was down by Suribachi, and the Seabees have set up a giant movie screen. They're going to have a movie tonight, and anyone can go who wants to."

We looked at Lieutenant Brown. "What about it, Lieutenant Brown, can we take the truck so most of us can go?"

He grinned, "I don't see why not. Take your helmets and some carbines, just in case." We piled in the truck at about six so we could get there early and get a good seat. We took our helmets, a few carbines, and our ponchos, since it often rained in the evening. We had everything we needed to stay through the movie, no matter what. Nothing was going to interrupt our first chance at a movie since landing on Iwo Jima. We hoped it was a cowboy show, maybe something with John Wayne.

The screen was a large canvas stretched over a metal frame located at the bottom of a hill. Hundreds of troops were already seated on the hill. We found a good place about halfway up, and waited for it to get dark. Finally the movie began. It was a good one with Spencer Tracy and Katherine Hepburn.

The movie had been running about an hour, and we were deep into it when the air raid sirens began to blow. The movie screen went dark, and the announcer said, "Air raid alarm; movie is terminated for tonight. Troops find shelter, and return to your own area."

We frequently had practice air raid alarms, and Rademacher was furious. "Of all the stupid times to have a practice. I'll bet the dumb brass knew about the movie and dreamed up this air raid just to make us squirm. Anytime a GI has anything good happen they . . . "

"Aw, quit your gripin' Rademacher, it doesn't help anything," Baker chastised him in a resigned way. "Come on, let's go back to our area."

We trudged down the hill with the other troops. We got in our truck and started back. The sirens kept sounding, which was a little unusual for a practice alert, but we didn't think anything of it. As we drove along, several searchlights went on and began probing the sky.

"Looks like they're going to put on a show for us tonight," Tank observed.

We kept driving, but began to watch the sky as several antiaircraft outfits began shooting. The tracers were always fun to watch as they arched up into the night, as if in imitation of some berserk meteorite.

Soon, many hundreds of antiaircraft guns were shooting skyward. Even machine guns were adding their barks to the cacophony of sound. Tracers were everywhere, and they appeared to be shooting at us, although we knew they weren't. Nevertheless, Johnny yelled at Rademacher, "Stop the truck, Ed, so we can get in a ditch. It's a real air raid!"

"You're nuts, Johnny, the Japanese aren't that stupid," Ed shouted back, but he stopped the truck just in case.

We jumped out and lay in a ditch watching the show. There were explosions and noise all over the island, and it was impossible to tell what was going on. After awhile, the searchlights locked onto a bright spot high in the sky that was descending. Many tracers were targeted on the spot.

"They've hit an enemy plane," Baker shouted.

"That's just a flare for them to practice on. There aren't any Japanese planes here," Rademacher responded.

After about a half hour, the shooting stopped and the all clear sounded. We got in our truck and returned to our area. When we got there, we discovered that it had, in fact, been an air raid, and Charles L. Russell of our company had been killed by a bomb while running for cover. Two others were killed and eleven were wounded in the raid. Two Japanese planes were shot down by fire from antiaircraft batteries.

GEORGE E. GOLDING

George flew as the navigator for thirty-six bombing missions over Japan. He served as first lieutenant in the Army Air Force.

George E. Golding.

En route to Tachikawa, we flew over Mount Fujiyama. Bombing the Hitachi aircraft plant near Tachikawa was rough, and that is putting it mildly. We went in at thirteen thousand feet and were under constant fighter attack all the way in and out. The flak was heavy and accurate. We had one 90-millimeter go through our wing and explode above us. We had shrapnel hit both wings and both horizontal stabilizers. One piece of flak went through the plane, missing me by a few feet. Normally I would have been at the position where the flak went through.

Just after we shook the fighters, Captain Wilcox had to feather the third engine, because the governor had been shot out. The B-29 flew okay with three engines, but only at low altitude. We had to return at one thousand feet. It was tough to navigate, and the ground speed was slower. It took two hours longer to return. Our radio communication system had been destroyed. Before we got back to the field, we were given up for lost. Our buddies shouted for joy when they saw us coming in on a wing and a prayer. However, they hurried back to the hut and draped our area in black and put an empty whiskey bottle on Wilcox's bunk.

We were very lucky. I know God was on our side. I was mighty happy to get my feet on old terra firma.

MELVIN C. GRAHAM

Melvin was a technical sergeant in the Army Air Force who flew supplies over The Hump. This was a difficult, but crucial flight path over the Himalayan Mountains.

I believe my spiritual and religious feelings were enhanced during my time in the service. I had some LDS tracts with me and my standard works. They were nice to have. I read them whenever possible. Prayer was not only a morning and evening practice, but many in between times when circumstances warranted it, such as air raids and strafing missions and some physical ailments at times.

My health was generally good, give or take some dysentery and dobhi itch and prickly heat. My nerves took a beating at times and that wasn't pleasant. I had a slight case of malaria, but it was cured before it got out of hand. The malaria-carrying mosquito was the one to watch for. Other bugs came and went, but we survived their nuisance.

We used mosquito netting over our wood and hemp beds. Rats and mice often scampered up the net, over the top, and out into the night.

One time our mess personnel messed up and used light machine oil for cooking instead of peanut oil. That kept us all on the run for days. In all of my forty-seven months in the service, I received eighty-four medical shots. I must say, they were easier to deal with than lead shots.

(Top) Registering for servicemen's conference in Kunming, China, 1945.

(Bottom) On maneuvers, Oscoda, Michigan, 1942.

WAYNE GUYMON

Wayne was a master technical sergeant in the United States Marines. He served as a communications chief for the First Marine Aircraft Wing.

We flew from New Caledonia to Guadalcanal on DC-3 airplanes. That was a hazardous trip as we did not have fighter cover, and we were within range of the enemy. However, we made the trip okay. As we emerged from the plane, it was easy to see we were in the war zone.

The tops of the coconut trees were all shot away, there were wrecked planes and other vehicles along the runway, and bomb craters were everywhere.

There was one object that really impressed me. It was a large United States battle flag. The flag was flying from a coconut tree; it was very impressive. A unique feature of that flag was the shrapnel holes in it. Obviously it had had been flying when the airfield had been under attack from the Japanese. I guess maybe that flag was what the war was all about. We were there to see the flag, and many like it, fly wherever free men so wished.

We got our gear out of the plane and caught a ride on a truck. We got the driver to take us to our area, and I checked in with our communications officer, Major Robert A. Black.

There was no ceremony in the combat zone—just find a tent with an empty cot, open our seabags, and call the place home.

"Oh, and by the way," the officer said, "make sure there is a vacant foxhole near your bed. If not dig one—you will need it sooner than you think." In the next three months or so I got well acquainted with the bottom of foxholes.

* * * * *

The chaplains usually had Catholic, Jewish, and Protestant services each Sunday. Except for the guys who were Catholic or Jewish, almost everyone else went to the Protestant services.

I usually attended church on Sunday when my duty assignments permitted. I carried a Book of Mormon in my gear all the time as well as a pocket-sized New Testament. The New Testament had a steel cover on the front and many of us kept that book in our left shirt pockets. The chaplain preached a sermon usually based on the scriptures. Hymns were sung at the opening and closing of the services.

The chaplain on Espiritu Santo formed a choir for his services. A number of us participated with him for several months and got pretty good on some of the more familiar hymns. Later on, he had us practice some songs like "The Old Oaken Bucket," "Down by the Old Mill Stream," "Carolina Moon," etc., and we sang those once in awhile when the squadron had an evening of entertainment.

My Book of Mormon suffered from mildew as a result of the damp climate in the Pacific. I still have it, and the mildew stains are prominent on its pages and cover.

Wayne Guyman with his telephone crew laying field wire along a highway in New Hebrides, 1943.

VARD L. HADLEY

Vard was a corporal in the United States Marine Corps. The following is his account of D-Day on Iwo Jima.

Our convoy of troop transports carrying men and supplies from the Third, Fourth, and Fifth Marine Divisions, and dozens of supporting ships arrived at Iwo Jima during the night of February 18, 1945. . . . It was important because it was about halfway along the B-29s' fifteen hundred-mile route from the Mariana Islands (Guam, Saipan, and Tinian) to Japan. The Iwo Jima radar would spot the B-29s and alert the Japanese fighter forces hours before the B-29s arrived. In

Vard L. Hadley..

American hands, not only would this early warning voice be stilled, but Iwo Jima airfields would allow our bombers fighter escort, cutting their losses; and crews of crippled bombers would be able to make emergency landings on the airfields.

Iwo Jima had been bombed almost daily since December 1944, and beginning about 6:30 A.M., February 19, 1945, the Navy began an intense bombardment. There were eight battleships, fifteen heavy cruisers, many destroyers and several aircraft carriers. After the shelling stopped, nearly seventy carrier-based planes dropped bombs, fired rockets, and strafed the beaches for another thirty minutes. We wondered how anything or anyone could survive. It didn't take the first few waves of marines long to find out that the shelling had done very little damage, and there were very few Japanese casualties. This island had belonged to the Japanese before the war so they spent years honeycombing Mount Suribachi and the high plateau ground around the airfields with miles of tunnels, caves, spider holes, machine gun nests, and thick-walled pillboxes that were almost impossible to hit.

D-Day began about 3:00 A.M., February 19, when blaring loud speakers with, "Reveille! Reveille!" roused us from our bunks on our troop transport. Since this was the first time many of us had been in combat, very few had been able to sleep, and it was a relief to have the day finally arrive. We had been aboard ship since leaving Hilo, Hawaii, the last week in

December 1944. After sandwiches and coffee and a short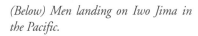
briefing, several members of our team went over the side of
the ship and down the rope ladder into a waiting Higgins
boat. The swells were really large (sometimes ten to twenty
feet high), which presented a real challenge, especially with all
the gear we had to carry. I had the usual backpack which contained a blanket, poncho, a change of clothes, a couple days'
worth of K rations, and a shovel. I also had two bandoliers of
ammunition, my rifle, a cartridge belt with additional ammunition, a bayonet, a canteen, and a radio transmitter strapped
to my chest. I felt like I weighed three hundred pounds. If I
had fallen overboard, I'm certain I would have drowned! I was
with the Fifth JASCO (Joint Assault Signal Company), whose
primary responsibility was keeping the lines of communication open between the front lines, the beach area, and the supply ships and other supporting ships.

(Below) Men landing on Iwo Jima in the Pacific.

Iwo Jima

The importance of the tiny volcanic island of Iwo Jima was its proximity to the main islands
of Japan. Just 660 miles from Tokyo, it had two airfields, one of which would support the
American B-29, the large bomber that was used to drop ordnance on the Japanese industrial
centers almost daily. The battle for the tiny eight-square-mile island began on February 19, 1945,
with more than 450 ships of the U.S. Fifth Fleet ready to attack. After a barrage of heavy naval
bombardment and air force bombing, the Americans attacked at just after 9:00 A.M.

The battle lasted more than a month, and at the end, more than 6,800 U. S. marines had
been killed and 24 Medals of Honor were earned. The battle took 72 days of air bombardment,
a three-day naval pounding, and 36 days of infantry battle. Of the original 23,000 Japanese
defenders, only 1,083 badly wounded were taken prisoner.

The first Marine
assault troops were scheduled to land at 9:00 A.M. on
the beach at the narrow
end of the island with
Mount Suribachi looming
in the foreground. Our
Higgins boat had taken us
to a small communication
ship about five hundred
yards offshore where we
helped coordinate the
assault troops landing. We

Joe Rosenthal, the Associated Press photographer who took this famous photograph, was on a promotional tour in the 1980s in Sunnyvale, California, and signed this photo for Vard.

To Vard Hadley—a real marine who sure was "there" when we needed him—best wishes from Joe Rosenthal

with respect and admiration for the men who fought for our country—

*Joe Rosenthal
AP photographer
Iwo Jima
1945*

were able to watch the first few waves of marines pass our ship. They were hunkered down below the top of their landing boats for protection from Japanese shelling, and I'm certain they were wondering what was in store for them the next few days. The shelling from our ships was still going on, and we could hear the shells whistle through the air. Around noon the captain decided it was time for us to go ashore, too. A Higgins boat returned, and we loaded everything and started for shore. With the mess on the beach, and shelling from the Japanese splashing all around us, the coxswain had a difficult time finding a place to land. After making three attempts to land, the time finally arrived. The ramp was dropped and it was our time to hit the beach. In some ways it felt good to be on land again. However, we didn't have much time to reflect on this. By that time, the beach area was a mess—equipment of all kinds, jeeps, trucks, artillery pieces— were either stuck in the sand or blown apart. Dead and wounded marines were lying on the ground or on stretchers. The dead were covered with a poncho or blanket. The Naval Medical Corpsmen were the most needed people on the beach. The call, "Corpsmen, Corpsmen," was heard all day. They were the unsung heroes. Since there had been so much shelling and bombardment there was nothing green in sight—no trees, grass or weeds—just barren black volcanic sand landscape. The beach area was steep, almost straight down and the undertow from the ocean was so strong that anything stuck near the water's edge would be sucked into the ocean. That included marines, dead or alive.

Walking in ankle-deep volcanic sand was very difficult, especially with all the gear I was carrying. I quickly found a shell hole, took all my gear off, and I got ready for action. Our beach area was about eight hundred yards from the base of Mount Suribachi. The Japanese shelling was intense and accurate. I kept moving from shell hole to shell hole helping to keep the lines of communication operational—radio and telephone. Since the first few waves of marines hadn't been able to advance very far, our own artillery and naval shelling continued to bomb and strafe a few hundred yards in front of us.

With all of the shelling—ours and theirs—the ground shook, and the noise was indescribable. As night came we were given the password and told to dig in and stay put and prepare for the expected counterattack. It was easy to dig in the soft volcanic sand, but the hole kept caving in. However, by the time it was dark, I was settled in my foxhole with my rifle and extra ammunition. I thought I was one tough marine! As the shelling continued from both sides, and I was alone in that foxhole, I became one frightened eighteen-year-old. Those huge glossy posters saying, "The Marines Need Good Tough Men," didn't say anything about what it was like in actual combat.

The destroyers moved close to shore and fired parachute flares to illuminate the area, making it an eerie sight at times. The light from the flares silhouetted the area, and several times my imagination ran away from reality, and I was certain the Japanese were moving all around me. I was too scared to sleep. I said several prayers to keep alert and safe and for daylight to arrive quickly. The only real scare I had during the night was when a shell exploded nearby, and a piece of shrapnel flew into my foxhole, hitting me in the leg. Fortunately, the sand around my foxhole slowed the shrapnel, and I had my leggings on so it didn't break my skin. I picked up the shrapnel. It burned my hand it was so hot. It was a great relief when it was light enough to find the rest of my team members had survived the night too. There was no time for socializing as we prepared ourselves for another day of doing our job and hopefully staying alive.

DAVID B. HAIGHT

As a young husband and father in his mid-thirties, David left his regular employment and accepted an officer's commission in the Navy where he served for the duration of the war. Decades later, he was called as a member of the Quorum of the Twelve Apostles. The following incident took place on a troop airplane flying to Hawaii.

I believe that people have their roads to Damascus in different ways. That night on that plane was my road. I was assigned to attend an important conference at Admiral Chester Nimitz's headquarters at Pearl Harbor.

Commendation issued to Lt. Com. David B. Haight at the end of the war. The citation bears the signature of Admiral Nimitz.

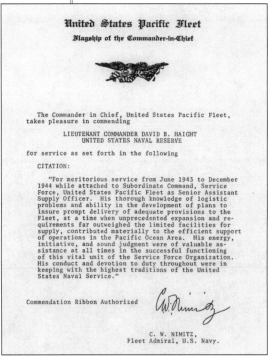

United States Pacific Fleet
Flagship of the Commander-in-Chief

The Commander in Chief, United States Pacific Fleet, takes pleasure in commending

LIEUTENANT COMMANDER DAVID B. HAIGHT
UNITED STATES NAVAL RESERVE

for service as set forth in the following

CITATION:

"For meritorious service from June 1943 to December 1944 while attached to Subordinate Command, Service Force, United States Pacific Fleet as Senior Assistant Supply Officer. His thorough knowledge of logistic problems and ability in the development of plans to insure prompt delivery of adequate provisions to the Fleet, at a time when unprecedented expansion and requirements far outweighed the limited facilities for supply, contributed materially to the efficient support of operations in the Pacific Ocean Area. His energy, initiative, and sound judgment were of valuable assistance at all times in the successful functioning of this vital unit of the Service Force Organization. His conduct and devotion to duty throughout were in keeping with the highest traditions of the United States Naval Service."

Commendation Ribbon Authorized

C. W. NIMITZ,
Fleet Admiral, U.S. Navy.

My family took me to Treasure Island where I bid them good-bye and boarded an old Boeing Clipper for the flight to Hawaii.

San Francisco was under blackout and as we flew over the Golden Gate, I had some concern whether I'd be back to be with my family. The plane was filled with senior medical officers, assigned to the Pacific because of upcoming invasions. The bunks and seats were assigned to the senior officers, with the other officers taking what was available.

As a lieutenant commander I was considerably down the ladder in rank so I and others were given sleeping bags, and we slept in the tail of the plane.

I was where I could see the starboard engine of the plane through the window. It was spewing out so much fire that I thought it was on fire, which caused me some concern.

I wondered about my own commitment to the Lord. I had been involved in the corporate world and had spent a great deal of time working for success on business.

I wondered about my family—whether I would see them again.

As I lay awake through the night and prayed, I made a commitment to the Lord that if I got out of the war alive and back with my family that the Church would always come first in my life.

I shall always remember that long, sleepless night. Before then, it seemed to me that I didn't have my priorities in proper order. That night I reappraised my life, and I recommitted myself to the Lord.

David B. Haight with executives of the General Electric Company with the first postwar washing machine, Sept. 1945, San Francisco. (L to R) Lt. Commander David Haight; Raymond M. Avord, commercial Vice-Pres., GE Co., San Francisco; Capt. Hesser; C. M. Le Caunt, Consultant to Federal Marine Section, G.E. Co., San Francisco.

LEONARD L. HANCOCK

Leonard was a staff sergeant and a member of the famed "Flying Tigers." He joined the Church in response to a prompting he received while attending a funeral of a fallen comrade.

August 21, 1943.

Leonard Hancock singing.

What a day! Fourteen B-24s of the 374th and 375th loaded with 500-pound bombs, flew to Hankow, including six new crews. Far in the distance as we approached Hankow, we could see its twin city Wuchang adjacent to the Yangtze River. Hankow is the launching pad to drive deep into China.

The spies at our American bases had evidently told the enemy we were coming! They were waiting, probably knew our direction and altitude ahead of time. Estimates of up to a hundred Zeros from the Thirty-third Sentai shot down two B-24s and broke up the 374th lead bomber over the target at 12:55 P.M. Major Beat, the commanding officer of the 374th, was in the lead plane. Just before his plane exploded, one crew member bailed out, but the enemy shot him as he floated down. The flak was heavy; black puffs of smoke were everywhere.

Flying Tigers

Shortly after the Japanese attacked the U. S. Pacific Fleet at Pearl Harbor, and before the United States began the counterattack, many Americans volunteered to fight against the Japanese by joining the AVG (American Volunteer Group). This group of pilots fought with the Chinese against the Japanese occupation in southeast Asia. Never numbering more than 100, they fought with great honor and distinction. The "Flying Tigers," as they came to be known, helped develop the air combat tactics that enabled the Allies to gain superiority over the Axis pilots.

Major Brady, our commanding officer, followed up with superb bombing, destroying warehouses, fuel dumps, etc. We were in his formation. I got credit for one and a half Zeros. I had used almost all of my ammunition. I shot at one Japanese as he dived through our formation and hit him. Butler said that as a Japanese soldier started to climb out of the cockpit, he shot him! Another one flew out of range and parallel to us. I fired a few bursts so that he could see the tracers and stay out there. He looped and turned right with us. I was so excited that my legs were jumping up and down, completely out of control; but my mind was clear and I handled the turret well. One gun jammed momentarily, I think. Grover said that when Butler got his first enemy soldier, he stood up and banged his chest and let out a roar.

GORDON W. M. INNIS

Gordon was a private in an Australian infantry battalion. He served in Australia, Papua, Bougainville, and Rabaul.

Gordon W. M. Innis.

Tommy Bluett and I were the signalers for B Company. We reeled out our telephone wire as we moved through the jungle. Suddenly, my companion ran back, calling out, "Stretcher bearers!" A sniper had got him in the foot. As I think about it now, I wonder why the sniper did not get me too, after all, we were almost side by side. Once again, I put it down to the protection being given me by the Lord.

As the battle progressed, Captain Gilleland called out to B Company to get moving. A few minutes later the captain heard movement ahead, and threw his two hand grenades. A little later, he heard movement to our flank and asked if he could have one of my grenades. He threw it; four seconds went by with no explosion.

"What's the matter with your grenades? Do you have another one?"

"I don't know, here's my other one." Four seconds went by and again no explosion. I remembered that Captain Gilleland, himself, on a previous occasion advised me to dismantle my hand grenades, breaking the wax seal. My equipment had been in water one night so the fuses were all wet. Later, I heard that two of our hand grenades had fallen among our own men, and had not exploded. I would suggest that I was being looked after by some power greater than my own.

(Above) Gordon with his brothers during the only leave that the three of them took at the same time during the war. (L to R) Gordon "Mac," Croyle, and Alwyn.

(Left) Private Innis, after one week in the army, age 19.

BLAINE H. JOHNSON

Blaine was a captain in the 640th Tank Destroyer Battalion in the United States Army. He had four brothers who also served in the war—Roland, Ray, Reed, and Glen.

Blaine H. Johnson pictured with four brothers who also served during the war.

CAPT. BLAINE H. JOHNSON

LT. ROLAND JOHNSON

Pvt. GLEN JOHNSON

S/Sgt. REED M. JOHNSON

S/Sgt. RAY E. JOHNSON

Johnsons Proud of Five Sons Who Are Serving Our Country

Mr. and Mrs. William M. Johnson of Spanish Fork are the proud parents of five sons serving in the armed forces of our country.

Three of the boys are serving in the Army in the Pacific area, one is attending school at the University of Kansas, and the fifth is in the Air Corps in Santa Ana, California.

Captain Blaine H. Johnson served 3½ years in the Utah National Guard, and was inducted into the army in March, 1941. He received his commission at San Louis Obispo, Cal. in the summer of 1941; was promoted to 1st Lieutenant a few months later, and to Captain in March of 1943. He is now serving in the Tank Destroyer battalion in the Hawaiian Islands.

About a week and a half after the beachhead landing on Lingayen Gulf, we were at Tarloc on a routine advance down the main highway toward San Fernando, a main dividing junction between Bataan and Manila. I was in command of C Company from which one platoon of tanks was detached to support the 108th Infantry Battalion. As far as I can remember now, this battle unit was about twenty to twenty-five miles up ahead of the main task force. About 2:30 P.M., I received a message that one of our tanks was stuck on a bypass of a blown-up bridge. I dispatched the wrecker with a .50-caliber machine gun jeep to pull the tank out.

There had been little action up to then, but the Japanese kept infiltrating back through our lines and perimeters, so we really didn't know who was where. At any rate, about 6:00 P.M. a radio message came through that the tank was freed, but the wrecker was hopelessly stuck. I immediately called for the battalion wrecker tank, and with two men (one was the driver), we went out to free this wrecker crew, organize a small protective perimeter, and return to our own command post. By the time we arrived at the site of the stuck wrecker, it was almost dark. We hooked on and poured on the juice with both machines and promptly broke the cables and sheered off the pin in the winch.

There was only one solution—someone had to walk back to the command post. We radioed for help, but couldn't make contact. The jeep I had ridden down in was mounted with a .30-caliber machine gun, so it had to stay for security. I could not ask any of those men to walk back, and we could only spare one. So I opted to go.

I often wonder why I was preserved that night during the Luzon campaign. For over nine hours, I expected at any second to be fired at, hit by a booby trap, or a noise trap, in one of our own perimeters. In any case, my chances would have been mighty slim. Never will I forget the clumps of trees with every little branch lit up with fire-flies. It was a marvelous sight. Nor will I forget how pitch black the night. There were no stars since we had had a high overcast all day. It was difficult to stay in the road in such blackness.

It took until after daylight the next morning to make the trip. I have never been so tired. I have never been quite so frightened. There was no way to sneak past any Japanese group or past one of our own units. I just had to keep going, guided by fireflies, whistling or singing or praying to keep up my courage. I knew I wouldn't be preserved because I prayed, unless it was meant to be. For some reason I was never challenged, met no one, or heard no one in that entire hike of twenty-five miles. Not once did I stop to rest, but kept a steady walk the whole time.

Blaine H. Johnson with inseparable friend J. Frank Dolley of Cedar City, Utah. These two men served together for over 38 months in the South Pacific.

* * * * *

It was a shock to arrive home that wintry day and see a white-haired man that I realized was my father greeting us. It came to me . . . that he deeply loved his family, and that the strain of having loved ones in mortal danger for over three years had taken a terrible toll upon him and upon my mother. Each showed in every line of their features the awesome worry that had beset them both.

JACK R. JONES

Jack served as a first lieutenant in the United State Marine Corps. The following citation was for a Silver Star Medal he received for action on Iwo Jima. During the Korean War, Jack received the Navy Cross, a Silver Star, and a Bronze Star.

For conspicuous gallantry and intrepidity as executive officer of Company D, Second Battalion, Twenty-sixth Marines, Fifth Marine Division, in action against enemy Japanese forces on Iwo Jima, Volcano Islands, 22 and 23 February 1945. When intense hostile mortar and machine-gun fire inflicted extensive casualties in his company during an advance against a strongly defended enemy-held ridge, First Lieutenant Jones courageously led and supervised the evacuation of the wounded and, as it was impossible to use stretcher bearers, personally carried several of the casualties to positions of safety. Later, he covered the evacuation of other casualties with well-aimed hand grenades, thereby aiding materially in rescuing approximately fifteen wounded men. Painfully wounded during an attack on 23 February, he continued to perform his duties until ordered to the aid station by his commanding officer. By his courageous fighting spirit and devotion to duty, First Lieutenant Jones upheld the highest traditions of the United States Naval Service.

JOHN A. LARSEN

John served in the United States Coast Guard and saw action in Saipan, Leyte, Manila, and Okinawa. He served aboard the USS Cambria.

On our way to the Saipan invasion, I was set apart as a group leader to preside, organize, and conduct church meetings whenever I was in the South Pacific where there was not already an organized group. I had been holding meetings with the ten or twelve LDS boys aboard ship, and knowledge of this came to the attention of the LDS chaplain for the South Pacific.

Brother Marvin Curtis brought me aboard the flagship of the fleet and set me apart as a group leader, so when the Ninety-sixth Troop came aboard, and we had church call, we would have fifty to eighty in attendance. We were getting more soldiers to church than the ship's chaplain was getting for Protestant or Catholic services. We usually held service on

John A. Larsen, seated on front row, second from the left, during a sacrament meeting held on the fantail of the USS Cambria, *1944.*

the fantail under the shadow of a big 7-inch gun. . . . We had some choice spiritual meetings with those men, some of whom we knew would never come back.

* * * * *

While in the military service most of my time was spent in the South Pacific and in and around the equator. During the day, it would get so hot that most of us suffered with prickly heat, some of us even getting big, draining sores on our arms and legs. Then at night it would cool off and get so cold that when we went up on watch, we had to wear all of our warmest clothing and heaviest jackets.

There was a tradition in the Navy; the first time a man crossed over the equator, he was initiated into King Neptune's Court. Some of us even entered Davy Jones's locker (ocean). That was a day when many of the old "Salts" really had a heyday at the expense of us novices. Someday I'm going to initiate someone else, just to get even!

* * * * *

One of the great testimony builders for me was during a battle in the Philippines. We were being bombed on a daily basis. I can still hear the whump, whump, whump of the bombs as they came closer and closer. One day word came that a squadron of bombers and kamikaze fighter planes was coming in, and orders were given to evacuate the area. Our ship, the USS *Cambria* was already gone, so we gathered up our gear and headed for the beach, hoping to get a lift out to one of the departing ships.

There were just four of us left, and a landing craft came in and picked us up. The man piloting the craft said he would try to get us to the last ship leaving the bay. The landing craft raced out alongside the ship, and we hailed the men on board. They said, "We will throw down some ropes. Climb up if you can." They wouldn't stop or put down a ladder or anything, and I can understand. If they were to survive, they had to get out of there.

With a 6-10 radio strapped to my back, I grabbed one of the ropes, and the landing craft pulled away, heading for some safety. There I was hanging at the end of a forty-foot rope, at the side of a ship headed out to sea, and the closest land was six miles away—straight down to the bottom of the ocean floor. I began pulling myself up hand-over-hand, knowing that if I didn't make it, it was good-bye world. About one-third of the way up I felt like my arms were pulling out of the sockets, and my grip was getting weak. Being as heavy as I was at that time (about 250 pounds), I wondered if I would make it.

Just about the time I felt I had no more strength left, I cried unto the Lord in my heart and told Him I needed help. I didn't want to die, and I told Him I had always kept the Word of Wisdom and needed the blessing of keeping it now. I had always tried to live a good, clean life. As I finished my prayer, I can testify that I felt a surge of strength flow through my body like nothing I've ever experienced before or since. I went up hand-over-hand to the deck of that ship, fairly flying. When I reached the deck I wasn't even breathing hard! I have thanked my Heavenly Father again and again for that blessing.

DORAN C. LEWIS

The following is an account of Doran, a tail gunner who completed thirty-three combat missions over sixteen Japanese cities. He and his brother, Oren, had the unusual opportunity of being gunners on the same B-29 crew. Doran was a master sergeant in the Army Air Corps.

The first raid of the "Fire Blitz" began on March 9. We took off in the early evening so as to arrive over Tokyo at midnight. Our crew, all eleven of us, was to drop a load of demolition bombs, then circle over the city at twenty-one thousand feet for one hour sending radio signals to incoming aircraft who were bombing at seven thousand to eight thousand feet. We were called the "Pathfinder" or "Homing Pigeon," but we felt like a sitting duck. The only advantages we had were that it was a dark night, and the Japanese didn't have any radar-equipped night fighters. They did send up some flak to us, but when things got hot down below we were left alone.

As it turned out, that was the last mission my brother Oren and I flew with our original crew. . . . After a day of rest, our crew was scheduled to go again. The target was Nagoya and this time we wouldn't be the "Pathfinder," but would go in with the main force at low altitude. Lieutenant Thompson, our aircraft commander, came to our Quonset hut and said, "We are on the mission tonight and we are only taking a tail gunner." Since I was the tail gunner on the crew, he looked at me and said, "Doran, you have one mission more than the

Doran C. and Oren C. Lewis standing in front of their plane.

other gunners so you stand down." Looking at the others he said, "You three draw cards to see who goes." I had an extra mission because I had flown one mission with another crew whose tail gunner was in the hospital. So the other three gunners, Oren, Don Goldsberry and Arnold Graham drew cards, high man went. The result was that Don Goldsberry went.

Oren wanted to catch up to me so offered Don ten dollars if he would let him go in his place, but Don refused.

The reason that they were only taking one tail gunner was that General Curtis E. LeMay decided that since the enemy didn't have night fighters, all of the guns and ammunition could be taken out, except for the tail guns, to cut down on gross weight. That made it so more bombs could be loaded in the bomb bays.

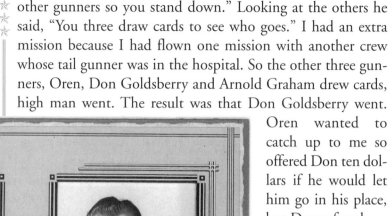

(Below) Oren C. Lewis on the left, and Doran C. Lewis on the right.

(Above) Oren C. Lewis's dog tag, worn from 1943-1945.

That evening we went up to the dispersal area to see them off. Little did we know that it would be the last time we would ever see them. We watched the aircraft lift off the runway and everything seemed to be all right, but the next morning we learned that they had ditched in the ocean about fifteen miles off the island, and no one got out before the aircraft sank. They were flying in V Square 45, and being fully loaded with bombs and fuel, the plane sank almost immediately.

I couldn't believe it. It didn't seem real for two or three days. It became real that they weren't coming back when the squadron adjutant called us in and assigned Oren and me to box up all their personal belongings to send home to their next of kin. Arnold Graham, the other gunner of our original crew was assigned to another crew after we lost our crew, and within two weeks, he and his crew went down over the target. That meant that Oren and I were the only survivors of our original crew.

LOYD A. and BOYD A. LEWIS

Loyd and his twin brother, Boyd, joined the Marines together. They fought together, side-by-side at Iwo Jima. The following account is condensed from an award-winning article written by journalist Jared Thayne. It is a poignant story which underscores the personal loss that often comes from war.

For three days Boyd and Loyd Lewis joined their fellow marines in gaining what little ground they could. Morning blurred evening and night never came. Then, after four days, shrapnel burned its way into Loyd Lewis's upper-left hip. Still able to walk, Loyd Lewis left his twin brother to get medical attention. "They looked at it and cleaned it out a little with some iodine and crap and said, 'you can walk and you're not so bad, go on over to the doc down there and we'll send you over to the hospital ship.'"

"Instead, I went back up to the line," Lewis said. "I wasn't gonna leave my brother."

With a dressing wrapped around his midsection, Loyd Lewis made his way back to a brother who knew only that he'd been hit. On the way, he passed a shadowy pyramid of dead marines.

"They spray the bodies with a gas," Lewis said. "It petrifies it so hard that bugs and insects can't eat 'em. And then they just threw them up on a pile because they didn't have time to bury 'em."

Between the short intervals of sleep that night, Loyd Lewis changed the dressing on his own wound twice. By dawn it had coagulated but a fresh pain brewed.

Something that morning prompted Boyd Lewis to turn to his duplicate and say, "Loyd, I'm gonna leave you."

I said, "What-daya mean you're gonna leave me?" recalls Loyd. "He says, 'I'm gonna get killed.'"

But because he hadn't experienced the same feeling, Loyd Lewis told his brother to forget about it, that maybe he was just "catchin' cold." Only later would he remember he too foresaw the day, when, as a twelve-year-old, a dream of the very moment had thrown him out of bed.

"It was five o'clock in the evening. We'd fought all day," recalls Loyd. "We was sittin' there kinda in this hole, but there was a little piece of dirt between us. Our arms was overlappin'."

(Top) Twins Boyd and Loyd Lewis as boys.

(Bottom) Boyd and Loyd Lewis in uniform. Even during the war, the two were inseparable.

The twins soon looked up to see a pair of identical mortars—Whistlin' Willies, as they'd come to be known—locked in the sky on an uninterrupted path to the sand on which they lay.

"We folded up our arms to cover our eyes," Loyd said. "The next thing I knew, I was airborne . . . and then on the ground with my nose, my eyes, my ears bleedin' . . . bleedin' from the mouth. It was so close, I couldn't imagine what happened.

"Then I tried to tune him in . . . I felt no pain," Loyd said. "I looked over in the hole and couldn't see nobody. I thought, well, he got out, but why couldn't I tune him in? Why? Where are you?"

Devoid of answers, Loyd Lewis lay on the ground battling a muddied mind for what was an indeterminable amount of time. When he regained his bearings, he cleared his eyes of blood and began to focus on a soldier's helmet.

"Something told me," he sobbed.

In the helmet was the face that mirrored his—dog tags that, but for one letter, matched his own.

"I crawled back to the hole . . . I got parts of his legs . . . parts of his arms. I sat in that foxhole . . . I pulled his flesh off my body."

"I knew I had to take care of him," Loyd said, "so I gathered him up and got permission to take him back to the hospital. I went back to the hospital and I was carryin' him in my poncho . . . just wrapped up in a poncho."

At the field hospital, a doctor asked Loyd Lewis what he needed. The only words he could muster were, "I've got my brother." Again the doctor queried. Again the words, "I've got my brother."

No doubt weary himself the doctor shouted words that still ring in Loyd Lewis's ears, "Now look! We're busy. What have you got there?"

With no energy left, Loyd Lewis dumped the poncho on the ground and cried, "There's my brother." He then asked for some water to clean his twin's remains.

"I cleaned him up the best I could, wrapped him back up in that poncho . . . they sprayed him with gas . . . I asked if I couldn't go out to the cemetery." Loyd said.

And there, on Iwo Jima, under the glow of gunfire and flare light, Loyd Lewis dug a grave for which he knew all too well the dimensions.

JACK MARSHALL

Jack was a machinist's mate in the United States Navy. He was stationed aboard the USS Tuglagi, *an escort carrier.*

Some of the Zeros came in low, about twenty-five feet above the water to escape radar detection. They headed for the carrier's stern (rear) where aircraft fire would be at a minimum.

As the fleet formation was moving from the Sulu Sea toward the Mindoro Straits, a twin-engine suicide bomber penetrated radar screens undetected and headed for the escort carrier *Ommaney Bay*, which was sailing just behind the *Tuglagi*. One of the reasons for their inability to spot the plane was the nearness of the Cayo and Panay Islands which blocked their radar. The battleship *New Mexico* was the only ship to open fire on the bomber.

The carrier's first warning that she was the intended victim came from the plane's strafing as it speedily approached. Seconds later, the bomber's wing sideswiped the carrier's superstructure as it crashed the flight deck and exploded, setting off a series of explosions among the fully gassed planes on the hangar deck.

As the torpedo warheads threatened to go off at anytime, Captain Howard Young, facing the moment that gives real meaning to the loneliness of command, sent the order out to abandon ship. The order was conveyed by hoisting the flag to the screen, by word of mouth, and by a sound-powered phone to the men below.

The second bomb passed through the hangar deck, rupturing the fire main on the next deck and starting an oil fire in the forward engine room which produced volumes of heavy smoke which soon permeated the ship. Water pressure in the forward part of the ship was lost immediately, along with

Easter Sunday, April 1, 1945. Several servicemen hold a meeting in the library of their ship for prayer and scripture study. Jack Marshall is sitting in the corner between two officers.

power and bridge communication. The men struggled with the terrific blazes on the hangar deck, but had to abandon their efforts because of the heavy smoke from the burning planes and the ricocheting .50-caliber bullets.

All efforts of the nearby destroyer to get near enough to apply hoses and lend power to the fight were frustrated by the intense heat, heavy smoke, and exploding ammunition. The carrier gradually lost headway, and the entire topside area became a fireball not capable of being contained.

About a half hour after the attack, the most seriously wounded were strapped into cots, covered with kapok life jackets and lowered into the water, with two able swimmers to assist with each float.

From below decks the men stumbled through passageways and clumsily climbed up ladders to the hangar deck to leave the ship. No abandon-ship was ever like this, a mass of confusion where many usual procedures were ignored or forgotten.

A steady stream of men, over eight hundred, were discarding shoes, shirts, and hats and pouring down the side of the ship. The captain, waiting to play out the old tradition of being the last to leave the ship, inflated his jacket, and climbed down a rope ladder into the sea, feeling sure he was the last man off his beloved carrier. Six minutes later the torpedo warheads exploded in the aft hangar deck, sending flying debris into the air, killing two members of the destroyer escort *Eichenberger* which was nearby recovering survivors.

A torpedo shot from the destroyer *Burns*, as ordered by Admiral Oldendorf, sank the burning and exploding *Ommaney Bay*, and she went down twelve hundred feet to the bottom of the Sulu Sea.

For over an hour the air was filled with enemy planes attacking from below deck level and swooping down from the sky like giant birds. Some gun crews were firing into the water just below an oncoming Zero, creating spouts that slapped down the low-flying plane with tons of water. They kept firing even after the plane had hit the water in a ball of fire.

A sinking ship is sad to look at and to hear. As the *Ommaney Bay* took in water, its bow or stern rose higher and higher until it stood up straight out of the water. Some of us could hear the squeaks and groans and tearing sounds of its steel plates separating. Loud banging and crashing noises came from cargo tearing loose and falling through the compartments. Finally, there was an earsplitting roar followed by shock waves as cold water touched the ship's boilers and they exploded. Then there was nothing to be seen except some ripples and floating wreckage. There were ninety-three men either killed or missing and sixty-five men wounded. The escort carrier *Ommaney Bay* was lost forever.

The gunners on our ship yelled like wild men, "Banzai! Banzai!" giving vent to their pent-up fears and excitement as they fired continuously at the approaching suicide planes. It was terrifying the way a kamikaze kept coming at us, hanging in there despite all efforts to bring him down. The noise, clouds of smoke, and the tracer bullets crisscrossed in a crazy pattern that was bewildering. Then there was the sickening feeling when the big cannon on the fantail began to roar, making the entire ship shake and quiver.

The captain frequently called the engine room and the pilothouse, ordering changes in speed and direction to avoid contact with the diving planes. We executed sixteen emergency turns within just fifty-eight minutes.

While the battle was raging above, deep inside the ship, we, in the engine room, waited, listened, and sweat it out. Although the captain kept us well informed of all the action taking place, not being able to take any action was, in many ways, harder to bear than being topside. We had thoughts of a kamikaze plane bursting through our thin metal hull, flooding compartments, causing explosions, and maybe trapping us deep in the bottom of the ship.

It was during this time of intense action that I began wondering what a twenty-one-year-old farm boy from Hunter, Utah, was doing out in the middle of a battle. I was so far from home, so far from those I loved. I missed my sweetheart so much. I was just a kid, fresh from high school, who had exchanged his individuality for a service number, a few shots in the arm, and a seabag full of weird-looking clothes. I had traded freedom for confinement and a highly disciplined routine that allowed no escape. For the duration of the war, my life would be controlled by people bent on snuffing out my young life.

Neal A. Maxwell.

NEAL A. MAXWELL

This future apostle served as an infantryman in the United States Army. He fought in the battle of Okinawa and was part of the occupation force in Japan after the war.

When I was in action in the spring of 1945, as a not-too-effective and very frightened young infantryman in Okinawa, I sometimes sent home what were called "V-mails"—tiny little sheets of paper. They were really not much more than a postcard, but they were the best we could manage in foxholes. My father kindly saved all my letters from the service and all my letters from the mission field.

On one of those V-mails I noted recently that I had "blessed my own sacrament in a foxhole. . . . I certainly felt better. . . . I try to look at the big picture of life and everything seems OK."

In another V-mail, "Please don't worry, I'll be OK. I am in Good Hands."

In another little V-mail, "Today is Sunday. I have tried to make it a point to know so I can bless my sacrament, otherwise it is just another day." In another, "I had a C-ration biscuit and rainwater for my sacrament. That proves it is not the ingredients, but the Spirit. It was wonderful. The mud is terrible here. . . . Many things have so strengthened my faith, but I can hardly wait to go on a mission."

* * * * *

My only surviving aunt said that sometime in May of 1945, she doesn't remember the day, Mother had told her the next day that she and Dad had prayed their usual vocal prayer and included me, of course, and my sisters. Then they got into bed and began to go to sleep, and Mother said, "Clarence, we've got to get out and pray again; Neal is in grave danger." And so they got out of bed and prayed again for me. I don't know which day that was, but I rather imagine, given time zones and all of that, it would have probably been when Japanese artillery shelling occurred at its worst stage. The phrase that comes to mind from the Book of Mormon is about some other young men who went off to war and [what] they [said] was, "We do not doubt our mothers knew it." I don't have any doubt that my mother knew intuitively that they needed to pray. Such parenting . . . is what I hope our young men and women experience, because they will be at times in great danger, too.

LLOYD MILLER

Lloyd joined the Marines soon after completing his mission in 1942. He was committed to continuing his missionary efforts among his associates and was soon dubbed "the Reverend" by members of his platoon.

One Sunday, I decided I wouldn't go to church but just stay in my tent and read the Book of Mormon. Then I would go back to sleep and rest up. Well, I couldn't go to sleep so I figured if I got up and went down and took a shower that I could come back and read and then maybe sleep. I took the shower, but couldn't concentrate. Something kept saying, "Get up and go over to the church and attend church!" Well, I got out of bed and dressed and went out and stood by the side of the road to get a ride.

I stood there fifteen minutes. Then it was thirty minutes and a fellow picked me up. I asked him where he was going, and he said to the Island Command. I suggested that he let me off at the intersection so I could head for the opposite side of the island to the chapel. When I got off I had to wait for twenty minutes more before anyone would pick me up. I knew that now I was going to do whatever I had to do to see this thing through. A jeep with two navy men picked me up. I thanked them and started a conversation. I asked them where they were from and if their ship was in the bay. They told me and said they were just going around the island while their ship was being fueled. I told them my brother was on an LSM (landing ship medium) and somewhere in the Pacific. I asked them what kind of a ship they were on and one said, "An LSM."

I blurted in and said, "Is Number 449 in the harbor?"

The fellow looked me straight in the eye and said, "You bet, right next to ours." With that I told them to stop the jeep and let me off. I jumped off before they could stop. I held out my hand for a ride and someone stopped almost immediately. I asked him where he was going, and he said to the Island Command area. I told him I had some business in the same place and would he please hurry as fast as he could. When I got to the desk, the officer said the last boat of the day was get-

Lloyd L. Miller singing a solo at the dedication of an LDS chapel built by servicemen in Saipan.

ting ready to leave to deliver people to the different ships in the bay. I coaxed him to hold the boat until I could get on. When we finally got to the LSM-449, the officer on deck asked me to state my business and show him my ID card. I did that, and he told me to come aboard. I then asked him to take me to the quarters of Captain Robert B. Miller, as he was my brother. He acted surprised, but said he would do it. I also asked him to just knock on the door and when it was opened or when he was asked to come in, to say to Bob, "Sir, there is a marine out here that wants to knock your socks off." He did that, and I could see Bob sitting at his desk with a paper in one hand a pen in the other.

"Well," said Bob, "send the silly boy in. We just as well finish it right here." I stepped in, and he looked up and then down at the desktop and just froze in that position. There was great joy in seeing each other there in the wide Pacific. We visited and caught up on a few things, and then he told me he wanted to go back to camp to see how I lived and ate. Bob had one of his men lower a boat, and he took us to shore. We thumbed our way back to my quarters. We got in line for chow and to visit with my company. Bob told me afterward that he had never seen a group of men so tough and rough looking. He said, "Boy, they look like they would just as soon kill you as eat." He thanked me for following the still small voice and being able to meet in the Pacific. Yes, that was something special that just didn't happen every day.

* * * * *

I decided that I would make a short list of a number of islands and by each island I would put a name of a popular song like "I Love You Truly," "Hawaiian Love Song," and "Let Me Call You Sweetheart." I would put a number by the song next to the name of the island. My list was inside my serviceman's Book of Mormon, and I sent a copy to my mom. In my letters I would say, "Have you heard the song . . . lately?" She would know where I was in the island groups by checking the list. Otherwise, the letters would be censored and cut up if they contained any information that might be useful to the Japanese.

* * * * *

In New Caledonia, I met a first lieutenant, and we decided we would hold our own sacrament meeting together away from the rest of the people. We sat down on a big fallen log where it was quiet. We had a discussion on religion as well as having the sacrament, which was a lemon drink (the servicemen called it "battery acid"), and cookies that came in our K-rations. We read the prayer from the Doctrine and Covenants, Section 20. We felt the spirit very strongly.

* * * * *

At the dedication of the Latter-day Saint chapel on Saipan, I sang a song accompanied by a fellow name Brower from Chicago. We associated with the island chaplain who

was not LDS. He was a speaker at the dedication of the chapel. The remarks I remember were, "You men were the last ones to come on the island, but the first to build a chapel. So, the first shall be last and the last shall be first."

(Top) A portion of the dedication program for the Latter-day Saint chapel on Saipan. Note the chorister's name.

(Bottom) Group of servicemen in front of the Saipan chapel. These men assisted in building the edifice.

PAUL A. MILLET

Paul left his home in Mesa, Arizona, to serve in the Army's Seventh Infantry Division. The following story took place in Okinawa.

Lyneer Smith and Paul Millet, both Latter-day Saints from Mesa, Arizona. Okinawa, Japan, 1945.

Paul A. Millet with fellow soldiers during sacrament meeting in Seoul, Korea, 1945. Fellow serviceman, John J. Glenn, is the chorister.

One of the soldiers I knew while in Seattle was a man by the name of Pittman. He was a rough character and although married, bragged of his immoral escapades and was in the habit of using abusive and extremely foul language. He had made several derogatory remarks to me about my membership in the Church and the standards I tried my best to live.

Pittman crossed my path again in Okinawa.

We both ended up in the same weapons platoon and were pinned down together in a rice paddy by machine gun fire. Every time we tried to raise our heads out of that small ditch of water, we were sprayed with bullets, and the situation seemed hopeless. I prayed continually in my heart and never really got panicky; I just tried to stay cool and have patience. Private Pittman then surprised me and said in a very frightened voice, "You be my witness, if I get out of here alive, I promise the Lord that I will change my ways." Minutes later we were able to get up and walk out of that paddy safely to join the rest of our company up on the ridge above us. As we moved south on the island, the Japanese resistance intensified and after several days of fighting, we were sent to the rear for a few days of rest. Sadly, while back in the rest area, Pittman again turned on me with the foulest language he could manage. I really wanted to strike him and had to restrain myself because he was so offensive.

A few days later we were called back to the front line and into combat. Pittman was assigned to another machine gun squad, and they were ordered to the left of us. When he was about twenty-five feet from me, he stepped on a land mine and was instantly killed. I shall not judge the man, but I have often felt that he lost his protection because of his broken promise to the Lord. We should keep the promises and covenants we make with the Lord and take them seriously and appreciate it when He has stood as our shield against harm.

(Above) LDS servicemen's group, Seoul, Korea, 1945–1946.

(Left) LDS basketball team, Seoul, Korea, 1945–1946. (L to R) Back Row: Lewis W. Duncan (Salt Lake City, UT); Rulon Nelson (Spanish Fork, UT); Kenneth Thomson (Salt Lake City, UT); Glen Sorensen (Shoshone, ID); Paul Millet (Mesa, AZ); Col. Slaughter. Front Row: John Overdynn (Salt Lake City, UT); Lyman Bruce (Smoot, WY); Glen Skousen (Mesa, AZ); Duard Millet (Springdale, UT); William Owens; John Glenn (Salt Lake City, UT); Dan Stitt.

RICHARD S. MILLS

During his career in the service, Richard attained the rank of technical sergeant in the Army. In the following account, Richard describes conditions as he attended Church services in the Philippines soon after the war.

October 7, 1945. (Near Manila)

My dear wife:

I was captivated by the church services today. We had a wonderful crowd and as it was fast Sunday, we had a testimony meeting. Perhaps I can catch some of that mood in words. I'll try.

As you approach the chapel the eye is met by skeletons of once proud structures . . . here, a mansion which once housed a proud and peace-loving Filipino—there, a public school whose corridors no longer resound with the patter of footsteps. Instead, emptiness and loneliness surround what remains of the structures. How have little hearts and minds responded to this sudden upheaval in their upward climb?. . . The tragic time lost in shaping their minds (those children who escaped) is wasted and cannot be regained! The buildings someday will be rebuilt, but, again, what of the tiny souls!

The deep, drawn-eyed stony youth greets you with, "Veectory Joe!" As you get closer to the church you are amazed at the lack of damage it has sustained. In front of the pastorate stands a nice, shiny black Lincoln car, its interior and exterior spotless. A question comes to mind—how did the car escape the Japanese as they took or destroyed everything of value? But with a shrug of your shoulders you pass on, letting the mysteries take care of themselves. You have become hardened to the ways of this world, you know that there could be many answers—courage, ingenuity, collaboration, luck—call it what you may. Each individual reacts differently. Perhaps this car, this chapel, this spot were passed by; who knows, God, Himself may have intervened.

As the sun is boiling hot and you have traveled over dusty roads in open trucks to attend church, you hurry inside. The coolness and sudden relief from the heat is felt immediately. Actually it seems cooler than it is. You with your shirt and face looking as if you had just emerged from a morning shower, see the cool green banana leaves through the cracks of the windows and give a sigh of relief. As the service starts you scan the wave of faces—soldiers, sailors, WACs—in hope that another Mormon of your locality has arrived in this seemingly godforsaken place so far from home. Soon your cares and troubles are forgotten. The mellow tones of the organ peel forth strains so familiar and behold, a white woman, a civilian member of the Church! You are brought closer to home. The music stirs long cherished memories of those many hours of church back home. Amidst the chords which pluck at your heartstrings, comes a new sound. Birds have flown in the shell hole which mars one corner of the roof and chirp away merrily as an unseen choir is singing the enchanting music. The sacrament is passed. The music is intermingled with chimes from bells at the proper intervals penetrating the air like concentric waves caused by a stone thrown in water.

THOMAS S. MONSON

Thomas joined the United States Naval Reserve and within a few weeks time, the war ended in Europe. A few months later the war also saw an end in the Pacific. Though important, his time in the service was short, being less than a year from the beginning of active duty.

"You hold the Melchizedek Priesthood, Tom. Give me a blessing, please." At the San Diego Naval Training Station, Thomas S. Monson knelt by the side of his suffering shipmate and heard his plea. Tom had been ordained an elder at eighteen, just before he left to serve his country in the Navy during World War II. In great humility he laid his hands on the young man's head, and with two hundred sleepy-eyed recruits looking on he gave him a blessing. The next day the young man was able to go about his normal duties.

Browning Automatic Rifles

Latter-day Saint John M. Browning is known as one of the best firearm inventors of all time. The M1918 Browning Automatic Rifle (BAR) was used extensively in World War I and still saw use in World War II (redesigned in 1943 with slight modifications). In addition, the M1917A1 Browning .30-caliber heavy machine gun was adopted by the Army with only slight modifications after a demonstration of its use by Browning himself. It was the standard ground gun until after WWII. The M1919A4 was a .50-caliber redesign of the M1917A1. In 1933 (after Browning's death in 1926), the gun was redesigned as an air-cooled (rather than water-cooled) model that could be mounted on tanks and aircraft. This later model played a major role in Allied air victories. Browning is credited with 128 gun patents. The Browning automatic shotgun that he first made in 1902 is still made today (www.media.utah.edu, 10-1-01; history.utah.org, 10-1-01; www.raven.cc.ukans.edu/~kansite/ww_one/comment/huachuca/HI1-04.htm, 10-8-01).

J. HEBER MOULTON

Heber served as a quartermaster in the Sixth Infantry Division of the United States Army. He recorded many memorable war experiences and participated in battles in such places as New Guinea and Luzon.

I became acquainted with a Sergeant Johnson. One Sunday morning I asked him to go to church with me. That little building was hot and crowded and noisy. They came and asked me to assist in blessing the sacrament. That was one of the special days of my life. When I blessed the sacrament, as sometimes happens, a quiet peaceful feeling came over me. After church, Johnson was really anxious to get me alone. He was a big man. He grabbed me by the shoulder and said, "Moulton, where did you get that prayer? You didn't make it up." I tried to explain how we got the prayer and what it means to us. Seldom do I hear the prayer, but what I think of Sergeant Johnson.

* * * * *

Officers of the Latter-day Saint branch at APO 179 Sansapor, New Guinea, December, 1944. One week later, most of these men were shipped out for the invasion of Luzon, the Phillipines. (L to R) Herbert Frost–2nd coun. & clerk; Clifford N. Barrow–presiding elder; Ralph R. Hafen–chorister; Melvin T. Woolf–1st coun.; R. J. Swain–1st coun. MIA; Joseph R. Rich–sec. MIA; Grant G. Fredrickson–pres. MIA; Grant N. Carpenter–2nd coun. MIA.

On Sundays, I met with about sixteen or twenty other LDS fellows. We had our sacrament services and testimony meetings. One such occasion was just before we left for the Philippines. It remains fresh in my mind today. I recall two people, especially, bearing their testimonies. One of them was Sergeant Grant Fredrickson. . . . He was a returned missionary. He was preceded in his testimony by Lieutenant Woolf, also from Salt Lake City. Lieutenant Woolf made the statement that he had prayed and had been given the assurance that he would return home safely. That was quite a remarkable assurance. Lieutenant Woolf was a forward observer with the division artillery. That was one of the most dangerous jobs in an infantry division. Sergeant Fredrickson then spoke, claiming no such assurance.

"I had a patriarchal blessing before my mission. It said nothing about having a family. So, just before going into the service, I asked for an added blessing. Again, the patriarch said nothing about my having a family. I was going off to war—and this concerned me. After that meeting I used to go, alone, out in the black night and pray. I asked for the same assurance that Lieutenant Woolf had been given. I received no such answer."

Latter-day Saint branch at APO 179 Sansapor, New Guinea, December, 1944. (L to R) Front Row: George M. Carpenter, Robert G. Reynolds, Phil N. Eliason, Lynn M. Dewey, Walter T. Wilson, Robert J. Evans, Lenn Jones, Denven L. Bundy, Glenn E. Childs, unknown. Middle Row: Herbert Frost, Grant Frederickson, J. Heber Moulton, Melvin T. Woolf, Robert B. Litster, Arnold F. Skinner, Ralph R. Hafen, Andy F. Hobbs, Lorin N. Rogers, unknown. Back Row: Robert G. Burton, William H. Bills, Walter N. Wilson, Coey B. Richards, Lee F. Newman, Ronald J. Harvey, Omni G. Carbright, R. J. Swain, Joseph E. Rich, Harold P. Strumpfer, Clifford N. Barrow.

* * * * *

The division held a mock invasion. There was some question whether to hold it because the water was wild. The waves were high, and it was a very difficult situation. General Patrick decided to go ahead with the practice. He thought it would be valuable experience and that the actual invasion might go better because of the experience.

The infantry boys had loaded onto big ships the night before. That morning they were transferred to small landing craft to make their "invasion." The men were loaded down with all their combat gear. There were probably thirty men in each landing craft. About 150 yards before one of the craft hit the beach, it was knocked sideways by a wave. Three of the men went into the water. One disappeared immediately. The other two struggled toward the shore near where we were standing. To our right was an LCM (landing craft mechanized). Cables had been placed from the boat to two

Caterpillar tractors to hold the LCM in position. The motors of the LCM were revved high to assist in the alignment. An LCM held three or four two-and-a-half-ton trucks and possibly a hundred men. The deck of the craft was very close to the water line. I was standing by a sergeant. The two of us took off our shoes, pants, and fatigue tops and started into the water to help the two struggling men. Before we got to them, one disappeared. We were both exhausted by the time we got to the remaining man. I marvel that we had remaining strength to help at all.

About that time we noticed that we were being pulled toward the side of the LCM by the current generated by the boat's propeller. Then stronger powers than ours took over. The revved up engine pulled the water and us toward the LCM. We were at the side of the boat. I indicated (somehow) to the sergeant that I would lift the man's arm up, and he would push him over the side of the craft. As I attempted to do that, I lost my footing and the current pulled me under the boat. I was in trouble. I grabbed a rock about three times the size of a football that was buried in the sand. That was useless. The next few moments were and are the most remarkable of my life. That current pulled me right up to the propeller blades. In that very small fraction of time before what should have been certain death, a great many things passed through my mind. Among other things I remembered my grandmother McMullin and the promises I had received in the temple. And, in that same small fraction of a second, I prayed. Then it felt like I was given fantastic power. I took hold of the barnacles on the bottom of the boat and pulled myself toward the point where I had entered. I had to be out of air. Then, another remarkable thing happened. As I came out of the water, some power lifted me into the air and actually held me in the air for a short time. While I was suspended in the air, I heard, "And I will give my angels charge concerning thee." Then I went back into the water, made my way over the side of the boat, and stepped over the outstretched body of the young man we had helped. . . . I walked down the front end of the boat onto the beach. Quite a few men were drowned that day. . . . My strength was nearly gone. I asked to be taken to the hospital. . . . I do know that my prayers on that dark beach were answered that day. And fear was gone.

* * * * *

I should write again about Sergeant Grant Fredrickson. He was the one at the testimony meeting back in New Guinea. Grant was a returned missionary, an infantryman, and a friend. As far as I know, he kept the commandments. While near Manila, I got in the jeep with Corporal Connelle, my driver, to go over and get the daily report from the Graves Registration Squad. Suddenly, it hit me. I remember throwing my leg into the seat, hopping in, and turning to the corporal with, "I don't know why, but I know that Sergeant Fredrickson is over on the floor this evening." At that time the Graves Registration Squad prepared the bodies on the cement floor of a house with a basement. We walked into the upper part of the house. The sergeant handed me the papers for the day. The third one down was Grant. There were probably a few tears. He was already wrapped in a shelter half, tied securely with communication wire. I just couldn't bring myself to untie that package.

A day or two later, Sergeant Swain, Lieutenant Woolf, and I went to his grave and dedicated it. Things were serene. Someone remarked, "It just seems like you can hear him saying, 'Thanks, brethren.'"

GEORGE L. NAYLOR

The following excerpts are from letters that George wrote to his wife, Billie. His love for his wife is apparent even in the midst of seasickness. The last excerpt expresses the feelings he had during his discharge from the United States Army, and his anticipation of seeing his wife.

My darling Billie:

Some of the officers on board say that seasickness is 99 percent imagination. Since I'm not a physician, I won't contradict that; but if it is true, I am cursed with a huge and utterly uncontrollable imagination. The past three days have been horribly miserable ones for me, and all because of seasickness. Every time I got in an upright position, I started vomiting. I have not eaten anything whatever, and my head has ached continuously; so you see what an imagination I must have. Since all I could do these last three days is lie quietly in my bunk and think, I've thought continuously of you and home. I cannot explain how recalling pleasant memories of you helped to alleviate the pain, but it did so very much. I thought of all the delightful times we've had together there at home, and I can tell you that I realize now as never before what a mansion of beautiful memories our home is. I sometimes

George L. Naylor in Tokyo, Japan, December 1945.

wonder that I had the courage to volunteer, knowing all the time how I would miss you. I feel just as I did that summer in Washington—that nothing on earth matters if I can get back to you and make you happy.

* * * * *

George L. Naylor and brother, Joel, in Tokyo, Japan, December 1945.

My darling Billie:

The atmosphere here at Fort Beale has brought back to my mind the unhappy nights I spent at Fort Douglas just after entering the service and those spent at Ford Ord just before going overseas, and the recollection of that unpleasant past has me down in the dumps. The one thing that keeps me from becoming despondent is the realization that this is all a thing of the past for us. As I sit here writing you, I find myself becoming more and more cheered by our situation. As I ponder it, I cannot help but thank God for the fact that my most fervent prayer of those dark hours has been answered. The prayer that during our hours of separation neither of us should become the victim of the many subtle temptations that so often cause married people in our same circumstances to violate their moral obligations to each other. On our boat headed for the Orient, rough men aboard boasted of the immoral things they were going to do with the Japanese women if they got to Japan. All I could do was to pray that I would not do those things. Now, I am so very thankful that the Almighty answered that prayer. I had an unquestioning faith that you would remain supremely faithful, and now that I have returned to you and have seen and heard the many evidences of the exemplary moral strength you have displayed during our separation, I know that I should want to die if I had been unfaithful to you. It is the most choice possible blessing that we are now able to reunite with renewed and strengthened faith in each other. Many of the people who were separated by war are not enjoying that priceless blessing. Talking with you tonight was swell. Surely hope these eight-day estimates (estimated time required to get discharged at Fort Beale) are all wrong.

JAMES R. NIELSEN

James served in the Navy aboard the USS Cape Ann. *The following incident occurred when he was anchored at the Palau Islands en route to the Philippines.*

I was the only one of the crew that wouldn't take weekly rations of one bottle of beer and a carton of cigarettes. Many of them wanted me to sell my rations to them, but I replied, "If that stuff is poison to my body, it is also poison to yours." I became marked as being very weird and unpopular with them.

Our ship was near the middle of the convoy and could not go any faster than the slowest ship of the convoy, which was five knots per hour. In the mess hall over the radio we heard the famous Tokyo Rose (a female propagandist employed by Japan), tell us that there was a fifty-ship convoy heading for the Philippines and that their imperial submarine fleet would send calling cards before we arrived. Our navy escorts consisted of a cruiser in front and two destroyers on each side.

On the second day as I was on lookout, I noticed the two rear destroyers head for the four o'clock area of the convoy. I reported it, and shortly thereafter their depth charges began to rock the convoy. The first explosion was so loud I expected to see one of our number go down. This went on for a few hours. The destroyers successfully fought off the enemy without any casualties to them or us. Our ship left the convoy at Leyte Island and headed up the west side of the Philippine Islands to the Lingayan Gulf which was nearest to Clark Air Base.

WAYNE A. OMER

A captain in the Marine Air Corps, Wayne had the distinction of watching President Roosevelt enter the nation's capitol to deliver his famous "day of infamy" speech following the bombing of Pearl Harbor. While he was in New Hebrides, he was assigned to a hut next to the famed aviator Charles Lindbergh.

At Turtle Bay, I noticed a sign nailed to a coconut tree which said, "LDS Meetings—Palacula Bay—Sundays 10 A.M." I inquired around and soon found two more LDS marines, and we all found a way to the meeting. We usually had twenty to forty men to church. I never saw any women there. Transportation to church was a problem, but it was

Captain Wayne Omer in cockpit of his plane, 1945.

solved by a Seabee (navy construction battalion) officer by the name of Paul Gilgen who sent his jeep for us each Sunday morning. Paul's home was in Ogden, Utah, and we became lifelong friends. I volunteered to be the branch chorister, and we took turns giving talks and lessons.

Another fellow I met at the branch meetings was Joe DeHaun who was an army parachute rigger. Joe's parents at that time were living in Holladay and my father, Gideon, was their bishop. Small world. Anyway, Joe was a neat guy. His job was servicing planes coming to and from the island. Joe would often find gear and equipment left behind on the planes. He asked me if I could use a small Coleman stove and an unclaimed parachute. I replied an emphatic, "Yes." (We had to sign for our own parachutes—to lose one carelessly was a court-martial offense.)

* * * * *

Wayne Omer among group of men attending sacrament meeting on the island of Espiritu Santo, New Hebrides, in early 1944. Although the personnel changed a lot from week to week, good organized meetings were held under the leadersip of Lt. Commander Felstrom.

On my second trip into Guadalcanal, the hydraulic system of my plane exploded in the cockpit just as I was preparing to land. All the controls and instruments were covered with hot pink oil and it was slippery. I had to make a no-flap landing with my windshield fogged up with oil, but happily the wheels were down and locked. With no flaps to slow me down I ran out of runway, but I managed to stop just as I was going into the bushes at the edge of the jungle. Close—but I made it. I called the tower and told them to come get the darn plane.

TERENCE O'ROUARK

Terence served as a captain in the Army Corps of Engineers during the war. He was a assigned to a plant in the Manhattan Engineer District, Oak Ridge, Tennessee. This plant produced key materials used in the atomic bomb.

I had arrived at Oak Ridge on January 13, 1943, and on January 27, witnessed the first production of U-235. U-235 is the fissionable isotope (material) which constitutes .7 percent of the natural uranium metal and is extracted by electromagnetic separation. A few weeks later I was directed to go to the chemical processing plant to pick up a small vial of U-235 for delivery to Los Alamos, New Mexico. This vial was packed in a six-inch cubed wooden box and was the entire production of U-235 of the United States and probably worldwide. Such experiences are not often afforded to twenty-one-year-old lieutenants. Needless to say the enormity of the incident was overwhelming.

The Manhattan Project

Early in the war, a German scientist discovered that splitting an atom unleashed great power. Due to the fact that many of the brightest researchers were German Jews who had escaped their homeland, American efforts toward harnessing the potential of the atom were greatly enhanced. Mindful that such power could be used to create a weapon of unthinkable power, leading scientific minds soon gathered at a facility in Oak Ridge, Tennessee, and began development of the atomic bomb.

The culmination of this research came on July 16, 1945, in southern New Mexico. At shortly after 5:30 A.M., the first nuclear explosion rocked the world . . . and changed it forever.

BOYD K. PACKER

Boyd enlisted in the United States Army Air Force in the spring of 1943. He was trained to fly bombers and was assigned as a pilot in the Pacific. Boyd was stationed with the American occupation forces in Japan for nearly a year. During that time, he was instrumental in baptizing the first Japanese family that joined the Church after the war.

Boyd K. Packer's brother, Colonel Leon C. Packer, was a much decorated pilot who became a brigadier general in the Air Force. Before Boyd left for the war in the Pacific, he visited with his brother in Washington D.C. He asked his brother how he kept himself pulled together in dangerous situations. His brother replied that he had a hymn that he would sing to himself, and the hymn would sustain him and help him stay on course. In the following account, Boyd shares a time when his brother's advice helped him through a dangerous situation.

In the spring of 1945 I was able to test that lesson Leon had taught me those months before. The war in the Pacific ended before we reached the Philippines, and we were ordered to Japan. One day we flew out of Atsugi airfield near Yokohama in a B-17 bomber bound for Guam to pick up a beacon light. After nine hours in the air, we let down through the clouds to find ourselves hopelessly lost. Our radio was out. We were, as it turned out, in a typhoon. Flying just above the ocean, we began a search pattern. In that desperate situation, I remembered the words of my brother. I learned that you can pray and even sing without making a sound. After some time we pulled up over a line of rocks jutting out of the water. Could they be part of the chain of the Mariana Islands? We followed them. Soon Tinian Island loomed ahead, and we landed with literally seconds of fuel in the tank. As we headed down the runway, the engines one by one stopped.

The following story is authored by biographer Lucile Tate and occurred near Okinawa.

On October 6, 1945, while awaiting orders and arrangements for transportation to Japan, Boyd and a few others went to Nara, south of Okinawa, for a conference of LDS servicemen. Later that evening they returned to the north end of Okinawa, expecting to take a boat back to their island. They learned, however, that all ships had been ordered to port because a hurricane was approaching. Boyd and his companions finally persuaded the commander of a PT boat to take them back to Ie Shima.

All bombers and other aircraft had been ordered to Saipan, Guam, or other islands that were out of the path of the storm. Finally landing, Boyd and his companions took shelter on the forty-foot coral cliff in tents that were fastened to it with every piece of metal they could find.

All that night and all day Monday the wind blew fiercely against the tents. Rain poured through the roofs and walls in a torrent. Waves from the sea ascended the cliff to within feet of them. On Tuesday the eye of the hurricane passed over and calm returned for a short time, then it hit again. The mess hall, built of eight-by-eight timbers set in concrete, was shorn off and blown away. Ships at sea were lost and many in port were wrecked and washed ashore. Cold and wet, shaken and sober, Boyd and his companions were safe. He and a few others held study classes, and on Sunday they held a simple sacrament service. "It was then," he says, "that the Book of Mormon became a part of my very soul."

J. DUFFY PALMER

A sergeant in the United States Marine Corps, Duffy was married at the time he enlisted in the service. Later during the battle for Iwo Jima, he was seriously wounded.

When we first went into boot camp we were issued dog tags. They had our names, serial numbers, and our religions on them. The problem was that when they gave us our tags they did not have our religion on them. They had a *P* on them for Protestant. We asked to have them changed, but they would not do it. I took mine and scratched out the *P* and scratched an *M* on. I did not know if people seeing them thought I was a Methodist or what, but to me that *M* stood for Mormon, and I felt better wearing them.

When we got ready to go overseas, I wanted my dog tags to read the right way. I could not get anyone to listen to me. I did have one advantage, both my company commander, Captain King, and the battalion commander, Major Antonelly, were friendly to me. The were both strong Catholics. I taught boxing and judo. Both of them had an interest in that and came out to watch and to participate. At least, Major Antonelly participated. He was an Annapolis wrestler and liked the rough and tumble.

When we were aboard ship and heading into action I again worked on the Navy to issue us proper dog tags. I was always rebuffed with the statement: "Mormons are Protestants." Talk as I might, I could not convince them otherwise.

One day I had my Irish temper up a little and went to the stateroom of the above stated officers. An orderly answered the door, and I told him I wanted to speak to Captain King and Major Antonelly. His curt response was, "That is a pretty big order for one sergeant—a captain and a major all at once." I told him to just ask the officers and see what they would tell him. He did. Soon both of these officers were in the room and asked me to sit down and tell them what it was that I wanted to talk to them about.

I showed them my scratched-up dog tags. I told them I wanted mine marked properly. I explained that I had scratched up the tags to show *M* for Mormon and that it was not right that I should have to go into battle with the wrong tags. They said, "Mormons are Protestants."

I assured them I was not a Protestant and that we as a church protested many of the things the Catholics stood for and that we were not now, nor had we ever been Catholic. I told them that we had not broken off the Catholic Church to become Protestant. I explained the organization of the Mormon Church—that we were a separate and distinct religion. I said that Jesus Christ was the head and that the Church was really named The Church of Jesus Christ of Latter-day Saints. They were still not willing to budge. Finally I asked them, "How would you like to go into battle with *J* or *H* on your tags?"

They replied, "Why would you ask that? We are not Jews or Hebrews?"

I responded, "No, and I am not a Protestant! I am a member of the Church of Jesus Christ of Latter-day Saints, commonly called Mormons!"

They replied, "Okay Sergeant, what do you and your brother want on your dog tags?" We had won! We went into battle with *LDS* on our tags.

*   *   *   *   *

A memory that is still so plain in my mind is the time the litter bearers were carrying me on the stretcher to the ship for evacuation. I came to and looked out as we jogged along and saw the flag of the United States of America still flying on Mount Suribachi. What a beautiful sight to my dazed, troubled, and worried mind. When I saw Old Glory flying high, I was thrilled. I wondered at that time if I would ever see the flag again. I wish every American could feel what I felt at that time for the flag and our country. I still have those feelings, and I am offended when the flag is not treated with great respect. How can any American mutilate, burn or offend that great symbol of liberty!

I do not remember the trip to the hospital ship. The first thing I remember was that I was in a ship. A doctor was dressing my wounds and telling me that I was not in good condition. That was something I was sure of, and he did not need to tell me that. He shoved gauze and other material into the large exit wound and dressed the neck entrance wound. There were ten to fifteen other wounded men in the same compartment. After the wounds were patched up and plasma was being pumped into my arms (the bleeding had not stopped), the doctor came over to me and handed me a glass of brown liquid. He said, "Here, drink this. It will keep you from going into shock." I asked him what the substance was. I was told that it was rum.

I said to the doctor, "I don't need it."

He said, "You are near death. If you go into shock we don't have a chance to save you. This will help you not to go into shock."

I then made a statement that I should not have made, I guess. I stated emphatically, "I don't need the rum. The Lord has seen me this far. He will see me the rest of the way. I don't want the rum!"

The doctor's reaction was strange. He slammed the glass of rum down and screamed, "All my life I have heard of big tough marines. They fight all the wars. The Army and the Navy do nothing, just the Marines. They always take all the credit. Now we have one of the toughest of all, not only is he a big tough marine sergeant, but he is favored of the Lord! You others have taken rum. He doesn't need it, God is going to take care of him! The Lord doesn't love you others, for you took rum!" He raved on and on and said he would not be responsible for me. My mind and my heart knew that I made the right decision. I prayed for relief from the screaming doctor.

I do not know how long he raved. I was again not conscious and did not know anything until the next morning. When daylight came, we found that six of those who had taken the rum had died. If I had taken some of it I feel sure that I would have been the seventh casualty. I knew that the Lord and His promises were absolutely true, I had a knowledge of that, and it was, and is a great blessing to me.

LLOYD R. PARTRIDGE

A first lieutenant in the Army Air Corps, Lloyd participated in his training for the service at Eglin Field along with the famed Colonel Jimmie Doolittle group. The following incidents took place during the Philippine campaign.

(Below) Lloyd R. Partridge, 1944.

(Far Below) Servicemen on Wake Island. Back Row: Bob Pew, Youker, Lloyd Partridge, Woodring. Kneeling in front: John Cutshall.

I had many experiences at Leyte, such as the time I had to land at Dulag on a small strip about twenty miles south of Tacloban. Our strip had been bombed out while I was on an intruder mission. We had no strip lights to land by, just our own landing lights. As I landed, I was well on the strip but just a little bit off center line. My left wing extended too far to the left and hit the guns on a P-38 which was parked on the side of the strip. The jar started the guns firing. The slugs from the guns filled my left engine, and the collision tore three feet off the left wing. Again, the Lord was looking after us since we were not injured, at least nothing but our pride.

Another night I was on an intruder mission headed for the island of Cebu when my right engine caught fire over Oarmoc Bay. That area was still occupied by the Japanese. I tried everything in the books to get the fire out and finally decided that I would have to bail out over enemy territory. To do that, I first had to jettison the wing tanks which I was carrying. The jettison mechanism malfunctioned, so there I was with a fire in the engine, a hung tank, and the necessity of going out the gunner's window, under the wing and down. Naturally, with the tank still on (between the engine and the fuselage), that was impossible, so, as a last resort, I headed back toward Tacloban. After another five or ten minutes, the fire burned itself out, and we proceeded back to base with no more problems except the single-engine landing and that was no problem with the P-61. We were prevented from bailing out into enemy territory and probably being captured by the enemy. That malfunction should not have occurred, but did.

L. TOM PERRY

Six weeks after Tom returned from his mission, he determined that he would volunteer for the Marine Corps. He was with the first occupation troops that entered Japan.

Coming off a mission, I wanted to be certain I didn't get out of the great environment of being on a mission, and that I had a chance to be with the LDS men.

I'll never forget the first Sunday that I was in boot camp in San Diego, seated in the little group church service that we were having, and in walked that first missionary companion of mine, a direct answer to prayer.

We had sacrament meeting on hillsides, in foxholes, in tents, and later, we built our own chapel. What a comfort that was.

* * * * *

We went out and fought with generals and colonels to get pieces of material so that we could construct our own LDS chapel on the island of Saipan, just about the time the war was ending. After our dedication at Saipan of our lovely chapel, many of us moved out the next day aboard a ship for occupation duty in Japan. We had constructed the chapel, completed it and had our dedicatory service on Monday night, and the next day we went down and boarded ship and went into occupation, never to see the chapel again.

After we'd been in Japan a few months I remember receiving a letter from a Mormon chaplain who had been assigned to the island of Saipan, stationed where the servicemen were coming from the islands of the Pacific to be processed for returning home. His base of operations was set up just a short distance from this chapel, and all the servicemen coming back from the Pacific had an opportunity of having church service on their way home. He thanked us for our efforts in building that chapel.

L. Tom Perry leads the music during dedication of the Saipan chapel.

Servicemen involved in the building and dedication of the Saipan chapel. L. Tom Perry is fourth from the left on the back row, directly under the light-bulb.

I was among the first wave of Marines to go ashore in Japan after the signing of the peace treaty following World War II. Entering the devastated city of Nagasaki was one of the saddest experiences of my life. A large part of the city had been totally destroyed. Some of the dead had not yet been buried. As occupation troops, we set up headquarters and went to work.

The situation was very bleak, and a few of us wanted to give more. We went to our division chaplain and requested permission to help rebuild the Christian churches. Because of government restrictions during the war, these churches had almost ceased to function. Their few buildings were badly damaged. A group of us volunteered to repair and replaster these chapels during our off-duty time so they would be available for the holding of Christian services again.

We had no command of the language. All we could accomplish was the physical labor of repairing the buildings. We found the ministers who had been unable to serve during the war years and encouraged them to return to their pulpits. We had a tremendous experience with these people as they again experienced the freedom to practice their Christian beliefs.

An event occurred as we were leaving Nagasaki to return home that I will always remember. As we were boarding the train that would take us to our ships to return home, we were teased by a lot of the other marines. They had their girlfriends with them saying good-bye to them. They laughed at us and indicated that we had missed the fun of being in Japan. We had just wasted our time laboring and plastering walls.

Just as they were at the height of their teasing, up over a little rise near the train station came about two hundred of these great Japanese Christians from the churches we had repaired, singing "Onward, Christian Soldiers." They came down and showered us with gifts. Then they all lined up along the railroad track, and as the train started down the tracks, we reached out and just touched their fingers as we left. We couldn't speak; our emotions were too strong. But we were grateful that we could help in some small way in reestablishing Christianity in a nation after the war.

EULA L. PETERSON

"Hedy" cared for sick and injured servicemen as part of her responsibilities as a nurse in the Navy. One of the highlights of her service was seeing Mrs. Eleanor Roosevelt during a tour she made of the hospital Hedy was stationed at.

Each base to which I was assigned always had a chapel or church on its premises. There was also a chaplain available. I am sorry to say I never inquired if there were any members of the Church on the bases except for when I was at the Admiralty Islands. I knew there were a few LDS members that met when they could, but I realized I would be the only girl and being rather shy, I decided not to attend.

We were allowed to attend church on Easter no matter what shift we were on, and I always attended. Being a nurse, I had to work on Sundays, and I had got out of the habit of going to church. I had been paying my tithing since I graduated from nursing school and prayed every day. I have always been very spiritual. The first roommate I had in the Navy was LDS. I never ran across another nurse that was LDS, but they all knew I belonged to the Church of Jesus Christ of Latter-day Saints as I let them know I did not drink, smoke, or drink coffee because of my religion.

Eula Louise "Hedy" Welker (Peterson) pictured in her nurse uniform.

* * * * *

It was at Mare Island where I learned the hospital and navy policies. I have forgotten the name of my chief nurse while there, but she received her orders to become chief nurse over all of the nurses in the Navy just before or after I left Mare Island. While on the island, I spent three months on an

orthopedic ward caring for patients who fought at Guadalcanal. Most of those patients had limbs missing. It made me heartsick to see all those young men who would go through life with that disability. I have pictures of several of them.

We had a patient who had his right leg amputated. His artificial leg had arrived but he refused to put it on. He was very depressed. A week went by and no one had been able to talk him into doing anything about it. This one Monday morning I talked to a couple of the corpsmen, suggesting that they hold the patient, and I would put the artificial leg on, and we would make him get up and walk. It was agreed and that is what we did. He was very angry with us, and I don't think he ever forgave me for doing it, but from that day on he went everywhere on his artificial leg.

EMIL M. PETTERBORG

An aviator in the Navy, Emil had several harrowing experiences during his assignments. One of Emil's assignments was on Attu Island in the Aleutian chain where he was assigned to Patrol Bombing Squad 136.

I would like to mention a couple of missions that are very interesting. Before we were sent on a bombing mission to the Kurile Islands, a weather plane would go ahead and check the weather over the target. If the weather was clear, the weather plane would radio back to the base that it was all right to send out the bombers. The weather plane had both bomb bays converted to bomb bay tanks so it could not carry any bombs, however all of the aircraft had five .50-caliber guns in the nose. I was assigned as a copilot on one of those weather missions. All went well and the weather was clear. We radioed back that the weather was clear. Then the pilot decided to go in and strafe the Japanese air base as long as we were there. He started in, and I reminded him that the two bomb bay tanks were empty, and they had not been purged. We then turned around and went back out to sea and purged the tanks.

After we went in and shot up the airfield, we returned to Attu. When they tried to refuel the aircraft, the gasoline spilled on the ground. We had taken a shell right between the two bomb bay tanks. Had we not purged the tanks I would not be writing this story. I had never thought of purging tanks before and had never done it. Did we receive help from above?

* * * * *

One other mission I will never forget was a short time later. We were assigned to bomb the loading docks in Paramushir the northern most island in the Kurile chain. Because of the long distance from Attu, all bombing missions were by individual aircraft since we didn't want to wait to join up with other aircraft and lose precious fuel.

As we approached our target, we saw through the broken clouds a Japanese tanker. Believing this to be a better target than the loading docks we decided to bomb it. As we started to turn to make a better approach, we saw another one straight ahead of us. We dropped down, and made a low pass over the tanker and dropped our bombs. At that moment we were hit—to this day I don't know whether we were hit by their guns or from the result of the bomb hitting the tanker since we were so low over the ship. At any rate the damage to our aircraft was very bad. The fuel system on the starboard engine was dumping fuel faster than the fuel transfer pumps could transfer it to the forward main. The oil system on the port engine was dumping oil, and without oil pressure, the propeller, which was kept in pitch by the oil pressure, caused the propeller to windmill, which was like having a flat disk the diameter of the propeller pushing through the air.

While trying to keep the aircraft in the air, we had a Japanese Zero flying formation on us about a hundred yards off our starboard side and another one above us on our tail. We thought it was the end when all of a sudden we saw a cloud bank directly ahead of us. As we entered the clouds, the pilot got vertigo and got us in what is called a graveyard spiral. After three or four rotations toward the sea, I was able to overpower him and get the aircraft under control. We came out of the clouds and because of our several rotations in the cloud, the Japanese Zeros were nowhere to be found.

We could now concentrate on the aircraft. We were able to take fuel from the individual tanks, bypassing the forward main that was dumping fuel, and thereby restoring the starboard engine to normal. The aircraft had a separate auxiliary oil tank in the rear of the aircraft, and the crew was able to pump oil into the port engine and this brought the port propeller into pitch so we now had a normal flight as long as the oil and fuel lasted.

With the amount of fuel and oil we had, we knew that we would never be able to reach Attu. Our only hope was to make it to the Russian Kamchatka Peninsula, not too many miles to the northwest. After throwing everything overboard, including the parachutes (parachutes over water would give us only a few minutes in that cold water), we were happy to see that peninsula ahead. Because we had thrown everything overboard, the aircraft was very nose heavy. We brought the aircraft into a grassy area, but with the nose of the aircraft so heavy, it immediately plowed a furrow several hundred feet with the tail sticking up in the air. As soon as the aircraft came to a stop we all exited as quickly as we could because we didn't know whether it would burn or blow.

Immediately out of the woods came the Russians with guns drawn. They forced us to sit down about a hundred yards from the aircraft. We never got a chance to see what damage the aircraft took when we dropped the bombs. We could not speak Russian, and the Russians could not speak English so we had to use some kind of sign language. They finally found a Russian who could speak some English.

We were taken to a small village, and we stayed there about a week, and then they decided to fly us to Tashkent. This was an enclosure where they had kept one of the Doolittle crews that bombed Tokyo. It took five days of flying to get us to Tashkent. The last stop before we got there was a stop at Alma Atta. That night someone stole my pants and flight jacket, so all I had was my light flight suit. (Not good for a Russian winter.) After we arrived at Tashkent, they were able to find me a pair of pants from an English commando. They weren't my size since I am six-foot-four.

By international law we were to be kept for the duration of the war because Russia and Japan were not at war with each other; however, before we arrived at Tashkent, the Russians had smuggled the Doolittle crew out of Russia.

After we had been in Tashkent for about six months, the Russians decided to smuggle us out of the country, too. We were put on a train headed for Tehran, Iran. After two days, the train pulled off on a siding and left our train car on the siding and the train left. We sat there two days and then another train came and hauled us back to Tashkent. We learned later that one of the Doolittle crew members talked to Drew Pearson, the radio commentator, who told the story of their smuggled trip out of Russia, and the Russians heard it and hauled us back to Tashkent. You could guess what we would have done to that crew member if we could have got a hold of him. In any event we were back in Tashkent for another month and a half before the Russians tried again. This time all went well.

REED G. PROBST

The following is from the Silver Star citation given to Reed, a commissioned Latter-day Saint chaplain. The citation illustrates the gallantry which many chaplains displayed while fulfilling their duties.

Chaplain (Captain) Reed G. Probst, Corps of Chaplains, United States Army. For gallantry in action at Biak Island on June 8, 1944. With severe artillery fire bursting all around him, Chaplain Probst stood in the open without protection and calmly conducted, in a normal manner, funeral services for soldiers killed in action. While the area around the beachhead was smothered with fire, Chaplain Probst moved about without regard for his safety giving aid and assistance to the wounded. Throughout the battle he never stopped his work among the dead and wounded except when there were none to care for. This inspiring display of courage won him the admiration and respect of the officers and enlisted men of the regiment in which he serves.

EDWIN V. RAWLEY

In a rare blend of tragedy and love, Edwin met his future bride while convalescing from a near fatal accident that occurred during training in California. Edwin was a first lieutenant and served as a navigator in the Army Air Corps.

In February 1944 I was the navigator on a B-24 bomber that crashed at March Field in Riverside, California. I was trapped under the burning wreckage, but I was able to wriggle

Front Lines *newsletters.*

on my back to a rupture in the side of the aircraft where I was pulled out by two infantrymen. I was taken to the station hospital with second- and third-degree burns. I was in shock. The burns were dressed, and my left hand was amputated. When I was ready for transfer to a plastic surgery center, I was sent to Bushnell General Hospital in Brigham City, Utah. Normally, wounded servicemen were set to the center nearest their homes, which, for me, would have been Walter Reed Hospital in Washington, D.C., but in my condition, I wouldn't have survived the trip. At Bushnell, my other hand was amputated. I underwent thirteen skin-graft operations, and my spirits were very low.

Then, in July, the Army initiated a cadet nurse program to train student nurses for positions in the Army Nurse Corps. My whole outlook on life abruptly changed one morning when two nurses entered my room—a major, the hospital's chief nurse, and a cadet. "Lieutenant Rawley, this is Miss Kay," the major said. "She's going to be taking care of you." There stood a woman who sparked more interest in me than any girl I'd ever seen. She was tall and slim, with lovely dark hair and sparkling green eyes. She had a sprinkling of freckles across her nose and a cute, crooked smile that lit up her face. I forgot the loss of my hands as I watched her go about her chores. I used every excuse I could invent to increase her visits to my room. We became good friends. But, eventually, she finished her training, left Bushnell, and became a lieutenant in the Army Nurse Corps. We kept in touch.

When I was ready to be released from the hospital, I was asked by the Air Force to return to duty as a hospital liaison officer, traveling to military hospitals to encourage new amputees. I was permitted to set my own itinerary, so wherever Lieutenant Kay was stationed, I just happened to show up.

Our courtship continued, and we were married on June 26, 1946, in a military wedding in Salt Lake City, Utah. The chief nurse at Bushnell didn't know how right she was when she said that Miss Kay was going to be taking care of me. Because I was sent to Bushnell, I found my wonderful eternal companion, who inspired me to obtain B.S. and M.S. degrees in wildlife management and complete a thirty-four-year career with Utah's Division of Wildlife Resources.

J. MURRAY RAWSON

Murray fought with the Fourth Marine Division. He was assigned to supervise the loading of thirteen ships for the invasion of Iwo Jima. At the time of his involvement in Iwo Jima, Murray was in a position to meet and interact with key persons involved with raising the American flag over Mount Suribachi.

When I woke up the next morning, what woke me up was the PA system on the boat saying that it was Sunday morning and the Mormon Church services were at 9:00 A.M. I looked at my watch, and it was 8:40 A.M. We were aboard a big aircraft carrier. I thought to myself, "I don't need to go to this meeting. I'm just going to stay here." Three times they made that broadcast. The third time I got up, put on my clothes, and went down to the pilots ready room. Sitting there on some chairs were four or five men. They were all sailors, I guess. I didn't know of any marines that were there, except me. One boy was a sailor. He asked, "Are you an elder?"

I said, "Yes, I am an elder."

He said, "I've been baptized, but I don't hold the priesthood, and we want to have the sacrament." They had sacrament trays there. It astounded me. They were just like the ones we had at home. They had everything there. He asked me if I would come and sit by him and offer those prayers. When I sat by him, his face was kind of familiar, but it didn't mean much to me. I asked him, "How come you don't hold the priesthood? Are you old enough? Are you worthy?"

He said, "Yes, I am worthy. I was baptized in Honolulu."

I asked, "Who baptized you?"

"I can't remember his last name, but his first name was Murray."

When we were on the island of Maui, once a week we got a day off in the Marine Corps besides Sunday. Every time we did, I would go from Maui over to Honolulu. I usually went to church, but I didn't do that every Sunday. . . . Once I had gone to the mission headquarters. I had found out where the mission president's office was. I went to see him. I told him who I was. He had asked me, "You don't happen to be a returned missionary, do you?"

I said, "Yes, I do." I had an ID. I showed that to him.

He said, "I've got a boy here who wants to be baptized. I don't have any missionaries." (It was during the war, and all the missionaries had been called home.) "Would you baptize him?"

I said, "Sure." I baptized him in the pool right behind the temple in Honolulu. I baptized him and left.

The sailor who asked me to bless the sacrament was the boy I had baptized a few months earlier. I blessed the sacrament, and we had our meeting there and bore our testimonies.

(Below) R. Herbert Reinhold.

(Far below) Marine Corps Certificate indicating the circumstances surrounding Herbert Reinhold's death.

Herbert Reinhold . . . Killed in Pacific action.

R. HERBERT REINHOLD

Herbert was born in Annaberg, Saxony, Germany. He was an American marine and was stationed aboard the USS Arizona. *He died when his ship was sunk at Pearl Harbor. The following is a letter he sent his parents prior to the awful event.*

Dear Mother and Dad:

Thanks for the nice Easter card. I just got it yesterday because it had to go to Honolulu. I guess you are wondering where I am aren't you? Well I am aboard the battleship USS *Arizona*. I like it here. We are in Pearl Harbor right now. I got a letter from Jack B., and he gave me his address so the first liberty I have I'll look him up. Boy, is this ship big. There are fourteen hundred sailors and eighty marines aboard. They are going to get another four hundred sailors so you can imagine how big the ship is.

I'm glad you were able to draw out the money. How is Eric doing? He hasn't written me lately. Tell him to write. Give my regards and best wishes to all the family. You'll have to pardon my writing but I'm writing this on my knee, and I'm in a hurry because I've a four-hour guard coming up.

Write me soon. I'll write again when I've more time.

Love to all,
Herb.

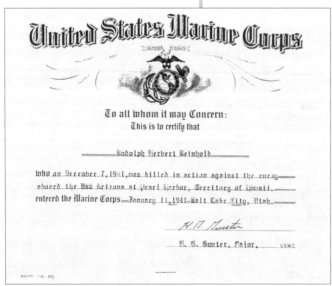

VERNON B. ROMNEY

Vernon served as a corporal in the United States Army and saw action at Leyte Gulf and Okinawa. In one of his assignments he served as an assistant to a Protestant chaplain. He later became the attorney general of Utah.

By October 19, 1944, I was anxious to get on with the war. I wrote, "There was an atmosphere of confusion aboard today. I went through the motions, but kept wondering about tomorrow."

A major read a fight talk written by General Bradley. It said the latest reports showed some eighteen thousand of the enemy on Leyte and that nine thousand were in our own area. Then we all went to religious services. A chaplain read the 23rd Psalm. We sang "America" and read the Lord's Prayer together. After church, Al Weipert, Roy Miles, a fellow named Erickson, and I sat in a little huddle. We talked about everything else, but we were absorbed in thinking about what would happen in the morning.

At last, it was Friday, October 20, 1944—D-Day. I got up at 3:00 A.M. with a great burst of anticipation. I ate a huge breakfast because I wasn't sure when I'd get another one. The general quarters' alarm sounded at 5:00 A.M., and everybody went up on deck.

Immediately we saw the war. A Zero flew over at low altitude, and our machine gun and 30-millimeter knocked it out of the sky. Seeing it flame and drop into the ocean was a big thrill for me. And it was good for my confidence.

The main event began immediately with battleships pounding the island from about thirteen miles away. I kept thinking what a Fourth of July celebration it would make. Then the cruisers and destroyers moved in. Planes flew over in great waves. By then it had become a fierce and terrible bombardment. I had never heard or seen anything like it.

We began to see explosions on land about three miles away. But soon the whole sky was filled with smoke and all we could make out was a vague outline of the beach and the jungle. A battleship kept pumping, and every once in awhile it would send a tracer round. We could see the whole trajectory. It was a beautiful sight. It was terrifying. But it was thrilling, too. That was one tough war machine in operation. I remember wishing Dad could see and hear it. I wondered if I would be able to describe to it to him. My next thought was, "How can anybody on shore live through this awful onslaught?"

At 9:58 A.M., the assault wave crossed the line of departure. It was a huge armada of alligators, VPs, LCMs, and ducks. My eyes filled with tears of pride as I saw them go. I prayed for all the brave men on their way in. We learned soon that the initial landing had gone well, although some men had been killed by enemy fire, and others had drowned in the surf. The radio reported that the infantry was having a hard time taking Hill 120. So a wave of bombers went over, and that was that.

Now it was our turn. At 3:30 P.M. Erickson, Miles, Boyle, and I went over the side and down the net, along with sixteen other communications people. We cruised around in our duck for half an hour, went alongside our navy guide ship, changed course again, and slammed into the beach. I stepped on Philippine sand at 4:35 P.M. The beach was absolutely battered. It was pulp. Craters and chunks of palm trees were everywhere. The shoreline was strewn with abandoned equipment and packing boxes.

Soon we were exhausted from wading through the salt water with our packs, rifles, and radio gear so we sat down for a few minutes to rest. Just then a sniper took a shot in my direction, and I hit the dirt. We crawled to a less exposed position and began digging in with our shovels so we could hide our radios. But it was hard going, what with stray bullets still skimming the ground, and heavy rain.

I saw Marsden Durham (an LDS chaplain) walking by. He looked healthy, but tired. I learned later that after he had gone only a few hundred yards past me, he was pinned down by mortar fire for more than two hours. Several of his men had already been killed.

It was dark by now, and Al Weipert and I dug in together and waited. I slept a few hours with a knife in my hand. But Al stayed awake all night. Early in the morning we heard a lot of small arms fire and heard rockets flying overhead in both directions. We learned that just a few feet away a tough GI had killed a Japanese with a knife, and then shot him with his own gun to make sure. I saw the first of the dead, an American soldier and five enemy soldiers with holes in their heads, all in one truck. I saw Marsden again. We wished each other luck.

Saturday afternoon the enemy fired heavy mortar rounds at the LSTs (landing ship tanks), that had been beached. The fire was just beyond us. I didn't feel too secure at that point. But things were calmer by evening. Sunday morning a

Catholic chaplain held Mass on the beach in full regalia. I thought that took guts.

We were starting to get newer reports from ships in the harbor. We learned that General MacArthur had come back to the Philippines with some 250,000 men and the old Manila government was intact. The Allied forces claimed to have destroyed eighty-two Japanese planes and ships.

HYRUM J. SANDBERG

A participant in the terrible Bataan Death March, Hyrum endured deplorable conditions as a prisoner of the Japanese for three and one-half years. He attained the rank of staff sergeant.

When the end of the fighting seemed close, I got orders to destroy my truck and help blow up ordnance warehouses. Our lines broke several times. The defense was a losing battle and on or about April 6, 1942, Major General King surrendered the total American and Philippine forces.

We started marching. I was in the first hundred or so of the groups. I kept my helmet to use as a washbasin or to keep the hot sun from baking down on my head. We were marching along. With each group of fifty we were five abreast marching. There were maybe two Japanese guards on either side. Sometimes there would only be one guard on either side, but they always had their bayonets on their rifles to guard against anyone escaping.

It was in the evening when we started marching. We marched along until about nine o'clock. I know we had been marching for a couple of hours or more when the guards finally let us sit down alongside the road and rest for a while. I got down in a kind of a ditch and looked up, and it was a real nice night, and I thought, "It's peaceful up there, but it sure is not peaceful down here where we are." It was a funny feeling to know that it was all over with.

We rested there for about a half an hour. . . . We marched that evening until the next morning when we came into a little

Hyrum J. Sandberg.

town. There was a schoolhouse, and we stopped there. They had a little kitchen set up with pots of steamed rice, and they gave us some rice. We had plenty of water at the schoolhouse. We were there for an hour and rested up pretty well, and then they started us walking and marching again.

We passed one town by the name of Marvellas down on the very tip of the peninsula, and I remembered a little submarine base that we had had there. It had been bombed out and there was nothing much left of the little town. We marched on through, and we were hoping to get some water because we had run out. Finally, they let us stop at a spring of water for a short rest. It was there that one of the guards spotted my class ring, my gold ring, and he took it off my finger. I still had my helmet, and he banged me on the head with the butt of his rifle. He said, "No, you can't keep your helmet." So he took it off and threw it down.

I remember stopping at that spring. It seemed like everybody wanted the water. We could only get one or two canteens under the well at the same time. So consequently, there weren't too many who got very much of the water.

During the march, we came to a free-flowing well. Officers and enlisted men fought each other to get their canteens filled up. That way no one got any water. It showed that no one was in charge, and the officers had no authority. But along the way we passed sugarcane fields and if there wasn't a guard along, we slipped out and grabbed two or three stalks of sugar cane. That helped a lot—made it so we weren't so hungry or thirsty. . . .

Men were feeling the strain of the long march and some dropped out and sat down. The guards would get them back in line but they didn't last long. The guards took the stragglers and bunched them together and took them out. What happened to them I don't know. Most of the time the stronger men helped the weak along the way. The big heavy men and older men seemed to have the hardest time making the march. Those who had malaria or dysentery dropped out first.

A fellow prisoner had his front two gold teeth knocked out by a Japanese rifle butt so the guard could have the gold. Finally, we were told to stop and count off. We lined up and passed by a truck that had some rice, fish, and soup for us. I remember how I liked the fish. The third day we marched until 6:00 P.M. and then we were allowed to rest. The march then went on through the night. A Japanese guard bayoneted and killed an American GI who was about fifty feet ahead of me. He had sat down and was cutting off the tops of his boots which were probably chaffing his legs and were too hot to wear. The Japanese placed a high value on everything and didn't waste anything. The guard probably thought it was wasteful to cut up boots like that.

R. PHIL SHUMWAY

Phil was an Army Air Corps pilot whose new P-38 had to be ditched on its first flight from New Caledonia to Guadalcanal. Phil survived for nine days on a small raft with no appreciable rations. The following is an account of the last days until his rescue.

During the time that I lay with nothing to do, I had a great deal of time to ponder the very basics of life. At that time I had absolutely no fear of death. I realized that the chances of my rescue were very, very slim indeed. However, I had become somewhat conditioned to this, having lost large numbers of my companions to the air battles in which we had engaged for the past year. I thought, even with some longing and anticipation, that I would shortly see my own mother and father who had preceded this time of death by seven years in the case of my father and fourteen years in the case of my mother. I wondered about the next phase of my existence. I had lived in such a way that I had not transgressed the laws of God. I held no fear of the things that were to come. My greatest sadness, however, was the fact that I would leave behind my wife of so short a time. Having been sealed in the temple to her, realizing that she was still but a girl, I had great sadness at the prospects of life for her. I prayed constantly to the Lord in a different way than I had ever known before. I seemed to talk and to visit and received a great peace. I do not have any recollections, and I am sure

Phil Shumway standing next to the raft that preserved his life for nine days at sea after his new P-38 went down.

this is correct, of feeling anything but a peaceful feeling. Anxiety, yes, hope that a miracle could happen, but no hysteria. I was always grateful for the peace which I was able to feel.

The afternoon of the eighth day found me on a sea as smooth as glass. Not a ripple showed as far as I could see on the horizon. Not one visible evidence of human life—no islands. I was completely by myself. About five o'clock in the afternoon, just before sundown, I saw coming over the horizon a convoy of ships. From my training, I could determine they were American ships even though I was in water wherein both friendly and enemy ships sailed.

I had often been assigned to cover convoys against attack from the enemy, and I knew the pattern of their travel. Consequently, I was somewhat frustrated, realizing they did not steer a straight course. . . . I watched them as they came toward me, and I watched again as they turned away. They were going at a rather slow speed, being laden with cargo, and I watched them as the twilight came. The wind came up and whipped the waves and made considerable sound as the water was whipped about by the ships.

It became evident to me that the convoy could come very close to me. In fact, it did. I watched in the dusk as those ships pulled beside me—some on one side, some on the other. One huge Liberty ship came so close that it almost ran over me. By that time I had stood in my little raft with the yellow, canvas bucket. I had tried to limber my vocal cords to where I could make a sound, and I did scream at the top of my lungs to the best of my ability—announcing to all that there was a man overboard. I could see no life whatsoever on board the ships. I continued to scream "man overboard" until the grey shadows of those ships slipped on into the night. That was the worst experience of my life. To have had ships come so close to almost overrun me and then to have them slip away was almost more than I could stand. I was in very poor physical condition. The wounds from the crash had infected my body. I was feverish and I had sores over my entire body. I had not eaten for nine days and was completely dehydrated. My spirits were then at the bottom. I considered it was time to jump overboard and end the suffering which had begun to creep upon me. But, that was only a fleeting thought and I realized that where I still had life, I had hope. I lay back down in my boat. By then I was very cold and wet from the spray. My sores stuck to the boat. I was feverish and I spent a terrible night.

When morning came, I was excited to see that I was in sight of an island—which one, I did not know. I was close enough that I could almost make out trees on the beach, and I realized that I had again, or supposed I had again, been given an opportunity for rescue. I knew, however, that in my weakened condition it was my last opportunity. I thus determined that I would slip from my boat and attempt with all of my strength to gain the island. I offered a prayer that I would have strength to do it, and then did slip from my boat and head toward the island. Possibly my resolve was not complete because I still pushed my little boat in front of me.

I had been thus engaged for about two hours, not seeming to make much progress toward it, when I saw two fighter planes circling some ways off. They circled then headed for the beach and searched the beach. What I did not realize was that my cries the night before had been heard by the crews of the ship. They could not stop, however, since that was not done in enemy waters, but they had signaled my position and there were search craft in the area. A little later, I saw several miles away, a coast guard trawler also running a search pattern. The fighter craft did not come close to me, but continued to search the beaches. In a little while a large PB2Y, known to us as a "Dumbo" search craft, came over the horizon.

At this point I got back into my boat, got my little canvas bucket and stood and began to wave, even though they were far off. They came directly toward me, some thousand feet high. As they came over, I waved vigorously, but again had my hopes dimmed as they went on over. However, they had not gone far until I saw them tip up on one wing, make a 180-degree turn and come plummeting toward me. I realized that I had been sighted.

The search crew came by waving to me and pulled up and gained altitude and dropped smoke bombs around to mark my position. Then came my friends, the fighter pilots. To keep my hopes up and to signal my rescue they buzzed me, almost taking my hat from my head. They stayed with me, as did the "Dumbo," until a little coast guard cutter came bouncing over the waves at top speed. The boat pulled along beside me. I took my little boat and watched as the big sailors came down the rope ladder and grasped my hand.

To that time I had felt self-reliant and had strength. When I felt the grip of my rescuers, I completely lost control and consciousness.

JAY SLAUGHTER

Jay reported activities of a different sort during his time in the military. Jay served in the Navy as a musician to entertain the men and women in uniform. After the war, he spent thirty years as the band director at Ricks College.

(Below) "The Avengers" performing as part of a weekly radio NBC broadcast which originated from Glenview, Illinois Naval Air Station, 1944–1946. They played every Saturday morning at 11:30. Playing in the band put Jay Slaughter in contact with renowned artists of the time, including Dizzy Gillespie, Bing Crosby, and others.

There was a rule in the Navy—if there were services of your faith on the shore, they had to get you to your service. So here I was, Jay Slaughter, in the captain's gig. A captain's gig is a boat. And regardless of the weather, every Sunday morning I went to church. Now I didn't go to church because I was so religious that I had to get the sacrament. No, I had a buddy, and it was a way to get a little time off. So there I'd sit on the captain's gig all alone with three or four guys swearing at me because they had to take this one dinky sailor clear to shore, and sometimes the waves were terrible. So I did that for, oh,

(Opposite page) Jay Slaughter with fellow band members. Jay is the third one from the left on the front row. He played the trumpet.

six or seven months. And pretty soon, I decided that I'd read the Book of Mormon. And the guys in the band, of course, would make fun of me, reading the Book of Mormon. But I'm the kind of guy that gets worse with a little antagonism.

Yeah, that's how I gained my testimony. I can't read the Book of Mormon? The heck I can. So I read it, the Doctrine and Covenants, the Pearl of Great Price, and I gained a testimony.

DOYLE G. SMITH

As a quartermaster in the United States Navy, Doyle was responsible for the navigation of his ship. He was stationed aboard the USS Hamul, *a destroyer tender.*

We had approximately one thousand men on board our ship. I have no idea how many were LDS, but we only had four that attended the sacrament service in the chaplain's office every Sunday morning. I don't remember any of the names, but one was head and shoulders above the rest of us in spirituality, and he took charge every Sunday. We took turns blessing the sacrament, but it was sort of a combination Sunday School and sacrament meeting, and he gave a lesson every week. One Sunday the chaplain came to us and said there were thirteen Presbyterians who had come from another ship to join in services, but unfortunately their services were over. He asked if we would mind if they joined our group. Would we mind! We went from our four to seventeen in one fell swoop. That was neat. It would be interesting to know if any of those thirteen ever joined the Church.

Of the four fellows, we never had contact or saw each other during the week except for one special occasion. I had been standing watch on a cold, miserable night and when I went to breakfast, the coffee smelled so good that I decided it might warm me up and be okay this once. That was unusual because I do not like coffee. I got my breakfast and sat down to eat, when somebody came and sat by me to chat while we ate. It was the leader from our group of four. I'm sure he wondered, but I never drank the coffee, and I am firmly convinced the Lord was saying, "Son, I don't think you need that."

ALMA B. SONNE

Alma served in the Fifth Marine Division as a rifle platoon leader. His platoon was in the initial assault wave at Iwo Jima, and only eight of its forty-five members survived the operation.

A hand gently tapped me on the shoulder, and I heard a voice say, "Lieutenant, it's 3:30." I awoke and remembered that this was the fateful day. I was going to die. All the training problems we had gone through the past three months had confirmed this. Every time we had simulated a military landing on the island, as yet unnamed, I had been declared a casualty. But the fun and games were now over. This day was the real thing, and I felt that my days were numbered.

After a hearty breakfast of steak and eggs, I walked out on the deck of the LST (landing ship tank) from where we were to debark to make our beach landing. I visited my platoon area where all the men were watching the ceaseless bombing of Iwo Jima, and with the dawn just approaching, the island took on a sinister look of a vicious monster raising his ugly head out of the black water. One of the men commented that he doubted anybody could survive the intense bombing over such a small area. The bombing had been going on for ten days. With the daily bombings from the B-29s, it looked as if the landing would be fairly easy. But, Colonel Jackson B. Butterfield, our battalion commander, had said differently. He had indicated that before the operation was over, half of us would be dead.

Alma B. Sonne.

* * * * *

I can testify that my life was spared because of the faith and prayers of my family—especially my father. When I returned home, he told me that when he learned of my involvement in the Iwo Jima operation, he would go to the vaults in the basement of the bank where he worked, sometimes a dozen times a day, and pray for my survival. He was a man of faith who knew that the Lord would answer his prayers. That is the only reason I believe that my life was spared. There were many men better than I, who, had they lived, would have done more for humanity. So I can only say that it was through that tremendous faith of my father and my family that I lived.

BUDDY SPEARS

The following is a letter written by Buddy to President Samuel O. Bennion of the First Council of the Seventy. The letter was written from "somewhere in the southwest Pacific."

We made sacrament cups from 20-millimeter shells cut off to about an inch in length. The tray for them is of oak wood with a polished brass handle. Bread trays, and a bowl to wash our hands before ministering, we made from aluminum casings in which 5-inch shells are stored. The crowning feature is a pitcher of brass, made from a 40-millimeter shell. We hammered out a spout in the front and welded out a handle. It holds just enough to fill our twenty cups. We are quite proud of the set and feel that it adds much to our meetings. We hope to increase our attendance soon to the point where we will be using all the cups in every meeting.

RAY N. TAYLOR

The following letter was published in the Church News: L.D.S. Service Men's Edition *on February 15, 1945.*

We are learning visual communication by flashing light and semaphore flags. Each day we pair off and send messages to one another.

For want of a test message to send, I began fumbling around in my pockets to see if I had any printed material.

I found a copy of the little *Church News* sent to the servicemen each month, and I started transmitting President Heber J. Grant's address to the servicemen.

Unknown to me, the instructor, a "salty" old chief, was standing off reading the message. He soon came around to me and started asking questions concerning the teachings of the Church. Now nearly every day he comes around to me and we have a short conversation—generally concerning religion.

A. THEODORE TUTTLE

This future General Authority was involved in the invasion of Iwo Jima and in the raising of the American flag at Mount Suribachi. The following is his account of the flag raising and a couple of letters that Ted sent to his wife, Marné.

A. Theodore Tuttle.

On D-Day we watched the naval bombardment of the island the last four of five hours from our ship and later from the LST (landing ship tank), we were changed to. It seemed no more than a practice problem and sailing around in the rendezvous area, we could see the whole drama before us. I had a feeling of expectancy of something big yet undesirable, this being my first actual battle where an enemy would be shooting at me; yet I wasn't nervous physically.

All I could see was smoke and exploding bombs. Hard to imagine that there could be anything alive on that island. There were no shells coming our way, and it looked as though it was all in our favor.

A 90-millimeter mortar hit our alligator (amphibious tractor) and tore off or bent the track. The right track still functioning pulled us a little farther, but we were still in the water. We had trouble in getting the ramp down in the rear of the boat and so we were just going over the sides when it dropped down. I stepped out in about three feet of water, turned around the side of the boat and started for the shore just as a huge breaker hit me and sent me down under the weight of my pack, etc.

The beach was loose, volcanic ash sand and it was like trying to run uphill through a wheat bin with a fifty-pound pack and other gear on my back. I struggled ahead and though it was difficult to walk, I finally gained a more suitable position by jumping in one shell hole after another whenever there wasn't too much mortar and machine gun fire. There were men all along the beach doing the same thing. . . .

A. Theodore Tuttle with his son, David, and wife, Marné, shortly after the war in February 1946.

D-plus four we had practically all the resistance settled. Lieutenant Shrier took his platoon up the hill. In his backpack he had a small American flag, I will never forget the cheer Colonel Johnson gave when he saw Old Glory raised on that hill. He lifted his hat and cheered, and we all joined in with him. It was a small flag, not easily seen. The colonel turned to me and said, "Tuttle go down to the ship and get a large battle flag."

I made my way to one of the ships, went aboard, and asked an ensign for a large battle flag. Since I had no identification or

insignia showing, he wondered who I was. I said, "If you want to be able to see a flag on top of that mountain you will bring me one." When he went for it, I found the galley and filled my jacket with apples and sandwiches. One can imagine I was immediately popular with the men on my return. . . . In a few minutes I returned with a large battle flag.

On returning to the field I asked the colonel whether I should take the flag up. He said yes, and I started up when he called me back and said, "No, I will send it with a runner who is taking fresh batteries up for the walkie-talkies." I gave the flag to Corporal Gagnon. He was one of the men who helped to raise it on Mount Suribachi. Joe Rosenthal was on hand to take a picture which became famous. . . .

After the island of Iwo Jima was secured and as we were sailing on to Kwajalein, we received a radio message, read by the communications officer, to the effect that if there were any survivors of the flag-raising picture they were to get off and go to Washington. Consequently, they were taken off and returned to the States to help sell war bonds. I discovered no atheists in foxholes.

* * * * *

Hilo, Hawaii, Camp Tarawa, October 7, 1944.

My darling Marné:

I am divinely happy tonight. I am grateful for the many blessings I have had and now enjoy. Two main reasons for my extraordinary joy: A letter from you today—of the first and fourth, and, a meeting from which I just returned where Chaplain Boud was present and where I was set apart as group leader in the Fifth Marine Division. A great honor and the greatest opportunity and responsibility I have ever had in my life.

I am naturally happy, but I also realize the great responsibility which is placed on my shoulders—however, I am starting out full of faith and confidence in this movement. God helping and guiding, we surely cannot fail. So you see, my wonderful darling why I am so thrilled and happy. God grant that I might always be so, because of righteous works and endeavors. . . .

Will write more tomorrow, my wonderful one—I love you dearly.

Ted.

(Opposite page) Raising the flag on Mount Suribachi, Iwo Jima. A. Theodore Tuttle retrieved from his ship the flag that was raised here, which was actually the second flag raised on February 23, 1945. The first flag raised was much smaller and was not visible from a distance. Joe Rosenthal's famous photo was taken using the Tuttle flag. Later, this image served as the inspiration for the U.S. Marine Memorial in Arlington National Cemetery in Arlington, Virginia.

(Below) Discharge certificate for A. Theodore Tuttle.

Officer candidates platoon 596, Oct. 1943. The photo was taken in San Diego, California.

Marné:

I've given considerable thought to your query, "Can we be satisfied with the rationalizing of saying he was needed more in heaven than on earth," with respect to Burke's death. Well, that is a difficult question. No one really knows, I guess, but in the light of the gospel we have, it seems more reasonable to suppose that his life's mission was completed and there was more need for him there than here. As to why a good man should be taken we can only conjecture, but this seems to be the best reason: that he is needed to preach the gospel by both example and precept to all these other men who are getting killed. That is a moot question. But the real answer lies in the Lord's statement that a man is saved whether he lives or dies if he is living righteously and a separation from this life a few years sooner really makes very little difference. Although it's hard to take. . . .

All my love to you, my precious wife.

I love you.
Ted.

ROBERT J. VON BOSE

Robert served as a corporal in the United States Army Air Corps. He was one of many servicemen who was introduced to the Church during the war by Latter-day Saint associates.

I was a junior in the School of Engineering at the University of Texas at the time of the attack on Pearl Harbor. I left school in January 1942, entered service on May 5, and became a pilot trainee until I was washed-out on a disciplinary action. I then became an aircraft-engines mechanic until a severe shortage of meteorologists brought my transfer to the

Weather Observer due to my college physics background. In late spring of 1944 I went to Kearns, Utah, for overseas orientation before being sent to the South Pacific.

I was content to spend my spare time at Kearns reading in the barracks (I was tackling *War and Peace* at the time), until a friend badgered me into going to a dance in Salt Lake City. We had just entered the foyer when two young ladies entered, introduced themselves, and went upstairs to the dance floor. We followed shortly. One of the ladies was not on the dance floor; she was in a side room at a pool table all alone. She beat me at pool but seemed to be enjoying our conversation as much as I. Her name was Patricia Williams. I not only took her home that night, but dated her several times. One evening we attended a Tabernacle Choir broadcast. Pat had recently graduated from nurses training at Salt Lake General Hospital and was staying at the home of a uncle until her grades were posted.

Pat knew I was subject to shipping out without notice and every date was contingent on my still being at Kearns. She was not ready when I went to pick her up one night. I sat down and picked up a book from the end table and started to thumb through it. Her uncle came into the room, saw what I was reading, and took the Doctrine and Covenants from my hand. Handing me the Book of Mormon, he said, "You should read this first to better understand the other."

Pat entered, took the book, put her name and home address in the front and said, "It's yours."

The next day I was gone. I read the book on a troop ship between Pittsburg, California, and Hollandia, New Guinea. We arrived on the island of Moratai. A few weeks later I asked the chaplain of the 321st Service Squadron, to which we were attached for rations and quarters, where Mormon services were held. He said there were none he knew of, but that men inquiring about religious services were so rare he would certainly remember to inform me if he heard of any. About five months later he hailed by the mess hall. A Mormon meeting had been scheduled. I arrived a little early and sat down on the back log of the rows of logs that served as a chapel. At five minutes after the assigned hour, no one had shown up. I started to leave when a jeep with two officers drove up, and they sat on the front log without a word. A minute later a jeep arrived driven by Sergeant Dean Grover of Spanish Fork, Utah. The meeting was canceled for lack of interest, but Grover agreed to discuss some of my doctrinal questions. We managed to get together even though his job of developing reconnaissance film whenever it came in, and my job of covering weather on bombing missions on short notice, made all our meetings hit or miss. One meeting was especially memorable.

Grover had put the plan of salvation showing premortality, mortality, death, judgement, and the degrees of glory on a chalk board. I was following his presentation but, at the same time, doing a lot of thinking about how that answered some questions left open in the Bible. A voice then spoke so clearly that I turned to see who else was with us. No one was there, and Grover didn't seem to hear it. The message was unequivocal, "That's the way it really is!" Suddenly I was an LDS convert with a testimony and my only options were to obey or not to obey. I didn't tell Grover about the voice. He explained that baptism would have to wait until an authority in the Church could approve it.

JAMES D. WETTSTEIN

James served in the Army Air Corps. He was stationed at Hickam Field during the attack on Pearl Harbor, December 7, 1941.

Sunday, December 7, came all too soon for me. I was half asleep about seven in the morning when a heavy explosion from the direction of Pearl Harbor jolted most of us awake. I sat up in bed and looked out the west window (we were on the second floor), and saw a plane dive across the window with a torpedo slung under the fuselage. My first inclination was that the darn Navy was at it again. They always had to do something like that on Sunday mornings. I saw the torpedo released and fall below the level of the trees and buildings between Pearl Harbor and me. In a few moments a geyser of water shot up two or three hundred feet into the air, and I knew that was no practice torpedo. Another heavy explosion jolted us.

Jumping out of bed, I threw a blanket over my shoulders and ran downstairs to see what else was going on. By then, planes were flying all over Hickam Field. One came down the road from the side of our barracks and banked around the front at about roof level. As it banked, we could see the big red balls on the wings and side of the fuselage. The pilot was looking out the top of the canopy. Because of the plane's attitude, we could see only teeth and goggles. The pilot was grinning from ear to ear. It didn't take but a moment to figure who was bombing us.

Now the planes were all over the field, bombing and strafing everything that moved. The bombers started with the fire station where the alert siren was located, then the depot at the south end of the field, and worked their way up Hangar Row, taking out every hangar that had planes or equipment in them. Some of the planes had been moved around that morning. (Makes me wonder how the enemy got their intelligence just before the raid.)

During a lull in the attack, I ran upstairs to get a pair of coveralls and shoes. I came down and jumped into a trench that ran in front of the barracks where they were installing some sewer lines. I put on my clothes and decided to go over to the operations building since I didn't yet know where I was going to work, and I knew some of our people worked over there. I ran as fast as I could and, upon arriving, went up to the control room where I got a good look at what was going on out on the flying field. Several B-17s, in from the States, were trying to land while being strafed by the Japanese fighters. They all got down, but were all shot up.

One gunner had managed to get a .50-caliber machine gun from an armament room and installed it on the waist mount of his disabled plane and managed to shoot one plane as it made a pass down the field. The plane hit the runway and bounced into the air. It then started smoking and dropping toward Fort Kamehameha on the south beach where it crashed into the porch of a building over there. Unfortunately, five or six men saw it coming, and trying to escape from the building, ran onto the porch at the same time. None survived.

I couldn't be of any help to the guys in the control room, so I went down and stayed by the east door of the building. I was not alone. Several other men were there with me. One of them lay out on the grass under a small tree. The ships at Pearl Harbor were putting up 5-inch antiaircraft shells. We told him, "What goes up must come down." He said it didn't bother him. Shortly a 3-inch piece of shrapnel whistled down and sliced him down through the armpit. On the way to the hospital I think he got the message.

Program for LDS conference held in Japan, Nov. 11, 1945. This conference was organized several months after the war concluded.

Shortly thereafter, a plane came over the hangars to the north of us and opened fire on the end of the building where we were standing. Fortunately, I saw it and yelled a warning. We all ducked behind the walls of the doorway and were not hit.

When one is under attack and armed it is one thing, but when one is unarmed it is the most helpless feeling in the world. That was how I felt about an hour into the raid, so I decided to go to an armament room two sets of hangars south of the operations building to pick up a weapon and some ammunition.

When I got there the sergeant was passing out receipt forms and wanting everyone to fill them out and sign away his life. I said, "Hey, Sarge, there's a war going on, we need weapons now!"

He said, "I guess you're right, help yourselves." I took a .45-caliber pistol and ran out into the hangar closest to the flight line. Three men were gathered around some boxes of ammunition counting out the rounds, and they asked me to help them. I said I had to get back to my duty post and picked up a box of fifty rounds. I started to run toward the next hangar, and when I got halfway between the two, a bomb came through the roof of the hangar where the three men were counting ammunition. The blast carried me into a hangar, but didn't hurt me because the blast went over my head. Only the shock wave hit me. The three men were killed instantly.

I got pretty thirsty after several hours. When the attack started the enemy bombed the water main on Hangar Avenue by the fire station, so we were without water. There was a Coke machine in the building which the ranking officer ordered opened and drinks were passed out to everyone. I have never tasted anything so good. I was so dry I had to be primed to spit.

During the lull, some major came down the hall wringing his hands and crying that the Japanese had landed tanks on one of the shores of Oahu and that we would soon be overrun. That rumor was soon squelched, and we all tried to get some order to things before nightfall.

BERT M. WHEATLEY

Bert was an Army sergeant who served in military hospitals in the States and in the China-Burma-India theater. The following event occurred at Borden General Hospital in Chickasha, Oklahoma.

Each morning as new patients came in, I'd check to see if there were any from Utah or eastern Idaho. One soldier I remember was from east of Idaho Falls. After breakfast was served and I had a break, I visited his ward and found his father and mother there as well. Their son was unconscious, and they were glad I'd come. They asked if I could get another priesthood holder to come and give him a blessing. We, at this time had a Lamar Olsen, a patient. I had him come, and one of us anointed the unconscious soldier with consecrated oil and the other gave the blessing. The soldier immediately came out of the coma. His mother and dad were thankful. The next morning we called, and he was in a coma again. Again, we gave him a blessing, and he came out of it. It seemed he was fine for a few hours and then he would slip into unconsciousness again. On the fourth morning, his mother said it must be faith that was keeping him on earth. She asked us to give him another blessing, and in that blessing to dedicate him to the Lord. She couldn't stand to see his suffering. She said if her son was supposed to get well, he would, and if not, the Lord would take him home. We did what she wished, and a half hour later, he was called home.

(Top) Bert M. Wheatley.

(Bottom) Taking a rest on a flying anthill. Bert is the one on the left wearing the cap.

CARROL N. WHITE

Carrol served as a gunner's mate in the United States Navy. He was stationed aboard the USS Laurens, *an attack transport, that participated in the Luzon and Okinawa invasions.*

I was fortunate to get to go home a few days on leave. While there I met my future wife. We had just started on our first date when she told me that she was a Mormon and she would always be. I knew after our first date that we would be married someday. I didn't know anything about Mormons except that they came to Salt Lake City, and Brigham Young was their leader. The day after we met was a sad day as I had to go back to my ship. Our new orders were to go back out to the South Pacific and bring all the servicemen home. A few days out of San Francisco, on a Sunday, there was an announcement that there would be a Mormon Church service. I had never been to a Mormon Church service, so I decided to attend.

The opening hymn was, "We Thank Thee, O God, for a Prophet." What a strange hymn. I'd never heard it before and didn't know its significance until later. One of the speakers spoke of eternal marriage. I'd never heard that concept before, but it sounded wonderful. One spoke of the Word of Wisdom. He said alcohol, tobacco, tea, and coffee were not good for man. I had tried smoking a time or two, but couldn't stand the stink. I hated the taste of alcohol, and the only way that I could drink coffee was to dilute it with half cream and sugar. Perhaps, I was already a Mormon and didn't know it.

(Top) Carrol N. White on Christmas day in Buckner Bay.

(Bottom) Carrol N. White (farthest right) with other crew members.

There were some returned missionaries in the crew. One of them gave me a small brown military copy of the Book of Mormon, which I still have. One day I was reading that Book of Mormon up on the bow of the ship when Father Wagner, the ship's chaplain, came by and asked what I was reading. I handed it up to him. He looked at it briefly and handed it back. He said, "You'd better stick with the Methodists." I'm sure glad that I didn't follow his advice. Those Mormons on the ship were not only good sailors, they were excellent missionaries who taught me the gospel. I thank them.

* * * * *

For me the most terrifying incident during the war didn't happen in actual combat. I think most of the crew will agree it was the time we encountered a typhoon. It was in the middle of the night when the storm was at its worst. The mountainous waves were twice as high as the ship and we were being tossed around like we were in a washing machine. I was standing watch on the bridge. The captain and other officers were on the bridge. I could tell that they were concerned about the ship's safety.

Carrol N. White's ship, an attack transport ship, APA 153.

Suddenly it felt as though the ship had run aground or struck a reef. It began to shudder and shake and list to starboard. There was a terrible sound of banging and crashing below decks. I was standing on the post side of the bridge leaning against the bulkhead. The list became so great that I lost my balance and went sliding across the deck. I knocked down the captain and other officers, and we all ended up on top of each other on the starboard side of the bridge.

I don't know how long the ship stayed in that listed position, but it seemed like an eternity. Then ever so slowly the ship began to right itself until we were back on an even keel. As we got to our feet, we looked at each other. No one said a word. We were all scared to death. I'm sure we were as white as a sheet. We knew that if the ship had capsized, none of the crew would have survived. There was a lot of damage to the ship's equipment, but none that kept the ship from operating. Many of the crew were thrown from their bunks and had bumps and bruises but nothing serious. We found out the next day that it was really a miracle that the ship didn't turn over. The ship's vital specifications stated that the ship should never be subjected to more than a thirty-eight-degree list or it would capsize. Most of the crew, including myself, credit divine intervention that stormy night that saved us all from a watery grave. I have always been thankful to have survived the war. My three best friends gave their lives for our country.

BILLY J. WILHITE

Billy joined the Navy in 1940 and served as an electrician's mate. He was stationed aboard the USS McCall. *Following the war, he served for thirty years in the Civil Service for the Navy.*

Billy J. Wilhite. This photo was taken in Nov. 1943, just after he and his bride were married in the Mesa, Arizona, Temple.

I arrived back aboard my ship, the *McCall*, on a Friday evening. Early Saturday morning, we got underway as part of the USS *Enterprise* carrier task force. There was the carrier in the middle, with one heavy cruiser and two light cruisers around the carrier. On the outer circle were nine destroyers, the *McCall* being one of them. We took some aircraft out to Wake Island, and then turned around and headed back to Pearl Harbor. We did all that without taking on any additional fuel. We were only going to be gone one week. A storm slowed us down, and we did not get back to Pearl Harbor as scheduled. We were scheduled to arrive Sunday morning, December 7, 1941. The Japanese knew we were expected back on Sunday morning.

This Sunday morning, I had stood the 4:00 A.M. to 8:00 A.M. watch in the IC room. I was relieved earlier than 8:00 A.M. for breakfast. After breakfast, it was Sunday routine. There was a small compartment above the crews' head and alongside the emergency radio shack, known as the "movie shack." That was where we stored the projector, and its amplifier was installed there. We also had a radio which we could tune in to public radio. One of the electricians turned the radio on, and we played it on the large loudspeaker on the fantail. He tuned in to a station in Honolulu. It was telling about airplanes coming over and dropping bombs, and this ship and that ship being sunk. They were identified by name. We looked at each other and wondered what was going on. It was Sunday, and we didn't have drills like that on Sunday. About that time, general quarters sounded. The men headed for their stations very quickly. I went to the after steering room and relieved the man there, who then went to his station on the bridge. The machinist's mate was soon there. I put on the headphones for communication with the bridge. We made sure the hatch to the crews' quarters was dogged down good and watertight. The smaller emergency escape hatch was always closed, but we checked it anyway. I can remember hearing our commanding officer being on the phone and saying these words: "Hostilities with Japan commenced with air attack upon Pearl. We are at war!" The carrier sent planes in to see what was going on. Our fellows on the mainland there were quite trigger-happy by then and were shooting at anything that moved. That included the planes from the *Enterprise*. None were damaged.

During the time we were at general quarters, we wondered whether we could go through the emergency escape hatch with our kapok life jackets on. After we were released from GQ, we tried it, and we made it. If we had to, we could do it.

During the rest of the day, I can remember that the electricians not on watch were checking and repairing all the headset telephones used throughout the ship. There was a strap over the head with a unit over each ear, so we could hear from both of them. There was a strap around the neck which supported the microphone on our chests, which we could adjust to be close to the mouth. We had to press a button on it to be able to transmit. Both the earpieces and the mouth piece could act as transmitter or receiver. By having to press a button to talk, it kept out all other noises. Those units worked with only one earpiece working. But now, everybody wanted them to work 100 percent. . . . We checked and repaired as needed all of them.

When we did go into Pearl Harbor, we made a circle around Ford Island before we went to the fuel docks for fuel. I saw ships sitting in the mud, sunk alongside the piers, and aircraft burned on the runways and near the hangars.

CLYDE E. WILLIAMS

Clyde was a pilot in the United States Army Air Corps and was stationed in China through much of the war. In 1946 he was assigned to the Twenty-first Troop Carrier Squadron. It was in this assignment that he made the following Iwo Jima flight.

I made many flights to Iwo Jima, one almost turned out to be my Waterloo. While taking off in a thirty-five-mile an hour crosswind from the right, the left engine quit just before the wheels left the ground. With insufficient flying speed, plus the pull of the right engine and the crosswind, I was unable to control the flight of the plane.

We headed straight for a cliff. I know from experience what can go through a person's mind when he is expecting to die. I could see no way in this world to get over that cliff. . . . Someway, somehow, beyond my understanding, we partially cleared the cliff with only the tail section hitting which broke off at the bulkhead to the rear of the cabin. Also the aileron scraped and was torn from the left wing as it cleared the cliff. We then flew for about 150 feet and scraped again as we went over another small cliff tearing off the undercarriage. The plane was now on the ground, but was spun around and chewed up by lava rock. We came to rest on the edge of the cliff with part of the plane hanging over. The airplane was on fire and burning, the wings were broken off, the engines were broken off, and the bottom of the plane was ground off up to the floor of the cabin and the cockpit, but luckily for us, both were still intact, protecting us from disaster.

A little humor at this point. The crew chief, who was only twenty years old, said the escape hatch to the rear of the pilot seat was jammed as he tried to climb over me to get out through the window on my side. I opened the window for him, but with his eagerness to escape, he left by way of the window on the copilot's side. I then got up and went to the escape hatch and turned the handle. The hatch opened with no problem at all and the hatch fell out so that we were able to escape through it.

There were thirty-two people on board, none were seriously injured, and I came out unharmed. That had to be the worst airplane crash that I have ever heard of without someone being killed. How did I get out of it? God was my copilot.

NEIL W. WIRICK

Neil was a member of Air Group 27 while stationed aboard the USS Princeton. *He had to abandon ship when the* Princeton *was damaged by Japanese land-based planes.*

On the morning October 24, 1944, during general quarters, some of us in Torpedo Squadron 27 were scheduled for takeoff as soon as fighter planes from Fighting Squadron 27 landed. They had been sent out to intercept a large bunch of Japanese planes heading for our battle group. I was dressed in my flight gear and started out to the hangar deck to check my plane. As I went down the catwalk, a voice said, "Go Back."

I thought, "Why? I'm ready. I have everything I need." I took another step and the voice again told me to go back. I wondered what was going on in my head, but I went back into the after ready room where the squadron spent most of their time. After closing the hatch and standing inside a bit, I began feeling a bit foolish. I started to leave, but it felt as if a hand was placed against my chest, and I was stopped. At that moment, the 40-millimeter guns on the ship started firing, then the 20-millimeters began. I knew we were under attack by a plane or planes very close. Then I felt a thud, and the ship shuddered. I quickly went to the catwalk on the starboard side and saw pieces of plank and a sailor flying through the air. Smoke was detectable in the air. I hurried back to the after ready room and told the others, "We've been hit by a bomb."

If I had not been stopped by the voice and delayed, I would have been on the hangar deck when the bomb hit. The bomb had punctured a gas tank on a torpedo plane and started the planes and ammunition on fire. . . .

The time I spent in the water after abandoning ship also brought another confirming blessing showing me the goodness of our Father. There was a fairly large swell in the water. One moment I'd be up and could see ships in the distance and sailors or groups of men on life rafts, then I'd be down in the bottom of the swell and could see only a wall of water in front of me or the sky overhead. Then on the wall of water there was shown to me a vision of my parent's home in Blackfoot, Idaho. Dad had recently painted it. I even saw a nail in the wood that needed to be hit a few times with a hammer. Then it was gone—and I knew. I knew that I'd live to go home. Two months later I was in Blackfoot, Idaho, on survivor leave. I saw the house and nail as I saw it east of the Philippine Islands in the midmorning of October 24,1944.

ROBERT L. WRIGHT

A navy man, Robert entered the service while living in Los Angeles. He was in an armed guard unit where he served as a signalman. He was preparing for the invasion of Japan when the atomic bombs were dropped on Hiroshima and Nagasaki.

My last merchant ship was a Liberty cargo ship. We traveled through the Panama Canal and we crossed the Pacific to the island of Saipan. While crossing the Pacific, we went into serious gun drill practice, as we were certain that we were headed for an invasion of Japan. We practiced taking the 20-millimeter guns apart and putting them back together again for speed. The gun crew practiced firing those guns at a target being pulled behind an airplane. As a signalman, I had never had any experience firing one, but the lieutenant insisted that I had to take a turn in the event that one of the gun crew got injured. So I strapped myself into the shoulder harness and proceeded to shoot the target down. I was feeling pretty good about myself, but the gun crew and the lieutenant were quite upset. No one had told me that I was not to actually hit the target.

The next day they practiced firing the 5-inch gun on the stern of the ship. Probably because of my goof the previous day, the lieutenant ordered me to stand in front of the powder magazine, with my back to the gun, and hand the gun crew a powder bag after each firing. After six firings I was relieved of my position, but my nerves were a wreck. The concussion after each firing reverberated around the gun turret.

From Saipan we moved to Guam harbor where there were many more ships anchored preparing for the invasion of Japan. It was only a few days after the bombs were dropped that we were informed that Japan had surrendered and the war was over. All of the men in the harbor began stringing all of the signal flags from the masts of their ships. The entire crew helped me rig our flags from one end of the ship to the other. It was a very happy and joyous occasion to see all of the ships in the harbor rigged out like that and realize the occasion.

JOHN O. YOUNG

"J.O." was a young civilian working on Wake Island before the war began. Shortly after the attack on Pearl Harbor, Wake Island was attacked, and he fought alongside the American troops. When Wake fell into Japanese hands, J.O. became a POW.

The morning of the last attack, December 23, 1941, as dawn broke, the American flag was flying over the compound. Not much later the white surrender flag was flying, and later in the morning the Rising Sun was hoisted. A couple of days later, I was on a work detail, and we were marched by the Japanese officers' office. Wadded up in a fishnet, our American flag was being used as a doorstop. One cannot imagine what a horrible and helpless feeling it was to see our flag so desecrated. One thing we found out at once was that when Old Glory did not fly there was no freedom.

* * * * *

There were a number of us in the POW camp who were members of the Church of Jesus Christ of Latter-day Saints, but there was not a Book of Mormon among us. The only time we saw one in Osaka was when an army captain was brought in. He had a triple combination which he guarded most carefully. Forest Packard was the group leader on Wake, but had no papers to prove it, so the Japanese would not recognize us as a group. We would meet in the evening once in a while to study from the Bible and have prayer. Oscar Ray and I sat out on the sunny side of the barracks, and he taught me section 121:33-46 from the Doctrine and Covenants which he had memorized. He was quite a scriptorian, and also learned Japanese quite well.

* * * * *

The following is a letter written by John to his parents from a Japanese prison camp in Shanghai.

Dear Folks:

We are all living for that wonderful day when we meet again. There are several of us Mormons that meet each night for evening prayer. It helps a lot.

I can't tell you all how much I love you or how much I think of you. But I have to just keep hoping and praying that this war will terminate soon—so long until then.

Your son,
J.O. Young Jr.

(Below) Cleve and Clyde Swenson with other men in their unit. These twin brothers from Spanish Fork, Utah, served side-by-side in the Army. They were assigned to an Intelligence and Reconnaissance platoon, which was stationed in the Philippines. After the war ended, Cleve and Clyde served with the occupation forces in Japan. Clyde is second from the left on the bottom row, and Cleve is third from the left on the same row.

(Above) The Good Conduct Medal is awarded on a selective basis to a soldier who distinguishes himself by exemplary behavior, efficiency, and fidelity. The obverse of the medal depicts an eagle standing on a sword and book . The eagle represents superiority and vigilance, the sword denotes loyalty, and the book represents ability and knowledge. The symbols are encircled by the words efficiency, honor, *and* fidelity—*virtues displayed by the recipient. The reverse depicts a lone star and the words* for good conduct *encircled by a wreath of laurel and oak leaves. The star represents merit, while the wreath denotes strength and reward. Many Latter-day Saint servicemen received this recognition.*

(Below) Group picture of LDS servicemen from various ships. The meeting was convened by Chaplain A. Gifford Jackson, April 1945. Mog Mog Islet, Ulithi (Western Pacific).

(Below) Latter-day Saints gathered in front of the Oahu Stake Tabernacle in Honolulu, Hawaii. Following the formation of the Japanese Mission in Hawaii in 1937, hundreds of Japanese-Americans were converted to the gospel. During the war, members of the Japanese Mission organized a victory drive, and raised funds to purchase 6,000 books, a "talkie movie" projector, and other items to make conditions more desirable for U.S. soldiers stationed in Hawaii. After the war, many of the Japanese-American Saints were instrumental in opening doors and proclaiming the gospel in Japan and the South Pacific islands (1999–2000 Deseret News Church Almanac, p. 194. Jay C. Jensen, "LDS Japanese Aid U.S. Soldiers: Members on Hawaii Have Drive," The Deseret News, Church Edition, November 28, 1942, 1, 6).

(Above Row of Photos) Crash of an FR-1 Fireball aircraft upon return from action. The pilot was picked up by the ship's destroyer escort, and then returned aboard in a basket and line (second to last image). The last image shows Kenneth C. Madsen (far right in photo) with shipmates loading guns (40MM ammunition).

(Right) Kenneth C. Madsen (on right) and fellow sailor. Kenneth was a petty officer aboard the USS Badoeng *Strait.*

(Above) P40 Class, May 27, 1943. Harley R. Moulton is the fifth from the left on the second row.

(Left) Sgt. Harley R. Moulton served in the 9th Fighter Squadron, and spent time on Okinawa. Harley's responsibilities included maintenance of the P-40 aircraft. After the war, Sgt. Moulton participated in the occupation of Japan until November of 1945 when he returned to the United States. He arrived home in Jackson Hole Valley, Wyoming, on Christmas Eve.

SOURCE CITATIONS

The name of each individual quoted in the book is listed below with a citation of the original source of the account. While most of the material in this book will be preserved in the Saints at War Archive located in the L. Tom Perry Special Collections of the Harold B. Lee Library at Brigham Young University, some items have been previously published in other sources. For these special cases, a specific reference is provided. The accounts that were not previously published are identified as "SAW," indicating that the original source is in the Saints at War Collection; the page number that follows indicates where the account can be found in the manuscript. When pages have not been numbered, the citation reads n.p., indicating a lack of pagination. "Spec. Coll." is an abbreviation denoting BYU Special Collections; and *CN* denotes *The Church News*.

The book contains only a few of the many veteran accounts contained in the Saints at War Archive. The collection will be open to the public, and all are invited to examine the many other wonderful accounts of faith and courage placed in the archive by veterans and their families.

FULL NAME	PREFERRED	SOURCE
Abbott, N. Keith	Keith	SAW, n.p.
Acomb, Allan M.	Allan	SAW, 69-72
Ahlstrom, Paul W.	Paul	SAW, 281
Alleman, James K.	James	SAW, 26-29
Anderson, George R.	George	SAW, n.p.
Anderson, Lars	Lars	SAW, 5-6
Anderson, Mays W.	Mays	SAW, 1-2, 4
Arnett, Charles W.	Charles	SAW, n.p.
Backman, Robert L.	Robert	SAW, L. Aldin Porter contribution
Bailey, Rosalie S.	Rosalie	SAW, n.p.
Banks, W. Fred	Fred	SAW, 20-23
Banks, Joseph	Joseph	SAW, 119-121
Barnes, Richard W.	Richard	SAW, n.p.
Barney, Melvin D.	Melvin	SAW, 4-5
Barnhill Sr., Marion F.	Marion	SAW, n.p.
Bartlett Jr., Robert E.	Robert	SAW, 3-4
Baugh, Francis H.	Francis	SAW, n.p.
Bascom, Raymon O.	Raymon	SAW, 2-4
Beach, Roy C.	Roy	SAW, 18
Beebe, Fred G.	Fred	SAW, 97-98
Beeler, Alfred W.	Bill	SAW, 1, 3-4, 6
Bennion, Mervyn S.	Mervyn	Spec. Coll., 16–18
Berges, Herman H.	Herman	SAW, 2-5
Bingham, VerNon A.	VerNon	SAW, n.p.
Binkerd, Jack E.	Jack	SAW, n.p.
Bitter, Grant B.	Grant	SAW, 2-3
Black, H. Reed	Reed	SAW, n.p.
Black, William B.	William	SAW, n.p.
Bloomfield, Don C.	Don	SAW, n.p.
Boettcher, Hans Max	Hans	SAW, n.p.
Borup, Theron W.	Theron	SAW, 68-69
Boud, John W.	John	SAW, 47-49
Bradfield, Floyd	Floyd	SAW, n.p.
Bright, Hobart	Hobart	SAW, n.p.
Brimhall, Don S.	Don	SAW, 15-17
Brown, George E.	George	SAW, 3
Bruce, Wallace	Wallace	SAW, n.p.
Buckner, E. LaMar	LaMar	SAW, 203–204
Bullock, J. Robert	Robert	SAW, 3-4 Hinckley Institute Interview, U of U, 3–4
Bush, Don E.	Don	*Ten Who Were One,* 61–62, 92–95
Cahoon, Douglas R.	Doug	SAW, 99, 103, 105, 108, 114
Call, Lewis	Lewis	SAW, 6

Full Name	Preferred	Source
Call, Orland	Orland	SAW, 5-6, 11-12
Carlson, E. James	James	SAW, 2-5
Catmull, A. Earl	Earl	SAW, 3-6
Chapman, Arthur O.	Arthur	SAW, n.p.
Christensen, Allen C.	Ace	SAW, 3-5
Clark, Marvin M.	Marvin	SAW, 16
Cline, Victor B.	Victor	SAW, n.p.
Cole, Walter N.	Wally	SAW, n.p.
Cooper, Warren L.	Warren	SAW, 3-4
Curtis, Reuben E.	Reuben	Spec. Coll., oral interview
Curtis, Theodore E.	Theodore	"With LDS Servicemen and Their Chap," *CN,* May 27, 1944, 8
Dahl, John H.	John	SAW, 11
Daleboht, Martin J.	Martin	SAW, n.p.
Dalton, Lee T.	Lee	SAW, 3
Davis, Earl C.	Earl	SAW, 6-8
Davis, F. Keith	Keith	SAW, 5
Davis, William H.	William	SAW, 3 handwritten account, 3–4; Chapters 2, 3
Despain, Parley W.	Parley	SAW, 6
Doman, Albert H.	Albert	SAW, n.p.
Dunford, Alma R.	Alma	SAW, n.p.
Durham, L. Marsden	Marsden	*CN,* Mar. 3, 1945, 9
Earl, Ken O.	Ken	SAW, 34
East, Franklin T.	Franklin	SAW, n.p.
Ellsworth, Reid F.	Reid	SAW, 30-31, 34-35
Fairbourn, Clyde L.	Clyde	SAW, 53-56, 61-62
Fenn, Golden L.	Golden	SAW, 23-24
Fife, A. Louis	Louis	SAW, 6
Fife, Leland J.	Leland	SAW, 1-4
Fink, Hyrum	Hyrum	*CN: LDS Service Men's Ed.,* May 15, 1944, 9
Fischer, Wilford A.	Wilford	*SAW,* 112-118
Forsyth, Glenn	Glenn	SAW, 13-14
Foster, Charles F.	Charles	SAW, 2
Frogley, H. Ronald	Ronald	SAW, n.p.
Frost, Herbert H.	Herbert	SAW, 26a
Gagon, Edwin B.	Edwin	SAW, 4, 7, 21
Garr, Glen J.	Glen	SAW, 7, 18
Gerrard, Ken A.	Ken	SAW, n.p.
Gibson, Arvin S.	Arvin	SAW, 12-13, 16–17
Gilgen, Chester M.	Chester	SAW, n.p.
Gold, Wayne B.	Wayne	SAW, n.p.
Golding, George E.	George	SAW, 33-34
Graham, Melvin C.	Melvin	SAW, n.p.
Grant, H. Lyle	Lyle	SAW, 17-20
Greenwood, Rex	Rex	SAW, 7, 10
Guymon, Wayne	Wayne	SAW, n.p.
Hadley, Vard L.	Vard	SAW, n.p.
Haight, David B.	David	*CN,* Mar. 20, 1976, 4–5
Hall, Benner A.	Benner	SAW, n.p.
Hall, Donald E.	Donald	SAW, 4
Hancock, Leonard L.	Leonard	SAW, 78
Hanks, Morgan	Morgan	SAW, n.p.
Hansen, George Scott	Scott	SAW, 86
Hardy, Douglas	Douglas	SAW, n.p.
Harrop, Raymond W.	Raymond	SAW, n.p.

FULL NAME	PREFERRED	SOURCE
Hatch, Myran	Myran	*CN: LDS Service Men's Ed.,* Feb. 15, 1945, 7
Haupt, Floyd E.	Floyd	SAW, 3, 6-7
Haynie, Donald L.	Donald	SAW, 2
Hegyessy, Harold M.	Harold	SAW, 110-115
Hemingway, Robert D.	Robert	SAW, 10-12
Hilbert, Horst K.	Horst	SAW, 7
Hillier, Robert B.	Robert	SAW, 43-44, 49
Innis, Gordon W. M.	Gordon	SAW, 13
Johnson, Blaine H.	Blaine	SAW, n.p., SAW, 74-75
Jones, H. Wendell	Wendell	SAW, 14-17, 19
Jones, Jack R.	Jack	SAW, n.p.
Jones, M. Glen	Glen	SAW, n.p.
Jordan, D. Reed	Reed	SAW, n.p.
LaPine, Glenn	Glenn	SAW, 3-4 Hinckley Institute Interview, U of U, 3–4
Larson, John A.	John	SAW, n.p.
Layton, Alan W.	Alan	SAW, 47, 50
Leavitt, Gerald N.	Gerald	SAW, n.p.
Lewis, Boyd & Loyd	Boyd & Loyd	*The Herald Journal–Logan Ed.,* Feb. 19, 1995, 25–26
Lewis, Doran C.	Doran	SAW, 7-8
Lofgren, David E.	David	SAW, n.p.
Marshall, Jack	Jack	SAW, 25-26
Massey, Enid	Enid	SAW, n.p.
Massey, Norval G.	Bun	SAW, n.p.
Maxwell, Neal A.	Neal	*Ensign,* Feb. 2001, 14
Maynes, Alden D.	Alden	SAW, n.p.
McMullin, Basil D.	Basil	SAW, 4
Mecham, Arlin L.	Arlin	SAW, 40-41
Meservy, Royal R.	Royal	SAW, n.p.
Miller, Lloyd	Lloyd	SAW, 3,4,15-16
Millet, Paul A.	Paul	SAW, 2
Mills, Richard S.	Richard	SAW, 5
Monson, Thomas S.	Thomas	*The Improvement Era,* Nov. 1966, 101
Moore, Oakley	Oakley	SAW, n.p.
Morgan Jr., Edmond	Edmond	SAW, 10-12, 15
Moulton, J. Heber	Heber	SAW, 8, 17–18, 19–21, 29
Murdock, Quentin C.	Quentin	SAW, n.p.
Naylor, George L.	George	SAW, 152, 168, 222
Nielson, James R.	James	SAW, n.p.
Nilsen, Reed E.	Reed	SAW, 3
Nishimoto, Arthur K.	Arthur	SAW, 7, 10
Omer, Wayne A.	Wayne	SAW, 17, 18, 20
O'Rouark, Terence	Terence	SAW, 6
Ottley, Wayne W.	Wayne	SAW, 16
Packer, Boyd K.	Boyd	*Ensign,* Nov. 1999, 23–24; *Boyd K. Packer: A Watchman on the Tower,* 59
Palmer, J. Duffy	Duffy	SAW, 8-10, 47-49
Partridge, Lloyd R.	Lloyd	SAW, 38
Perry, L. Tom	Tom	*Ensign,* Apr. 2001, 10–11, *CN,* Apr. 27, 1974, 3; *CN,* Aug. 19, 1944, 16
Peterson, Eula L.	Eula "Hedy"	SAW, n.p.
Petterborg, Emil M.	Emil	SAW, n.p.
Probst, Reed G.	Reed	*CN*
Rahde, Heinz	Heinz	*New Era,* Jan. 1986, 36-39
Rappleye, Foster D.	Foster	SAW, n.p.
Rawley, Edwin V.	Edwin	*Good Housekeeping,* Feb. 1997, 78

Full Name	Preferred	Source
Rawson, J. Murray	Murray	Spec. Coll.
Reinhold, R. Herbert	Herbert	SAW, n.p.
Rice, William	Bill	SAW, 5-6 Hinckley Institute Interview, U of U, 5–6
Rigby, Alden P.	Alden	SAW, 69, 84-85, 91
Ririe, David	David	SAW, 16, 22
Romney, Vernon B.	Vernon	SAW, 51-53
Russell, John D.	John	SAW, n.p.
Rynearson, Calvin	Calvin	SAW, 4
Sandburg, Hyrum J.	Hyrum	SAW, 4-5
Schubert, Kenneth W.	Ken	SAW, 8-10
Schwiermann, Artur	Artur	SAW, 23
Shallbetter, Raymond J.	Raymond	SAW, 12
Sharp, Bernell	Bernell	SAW, 2-3
Shumway, R. Phil	Phil	Spec. Coll., 286–287
Simpson, Eldin	Eldin	SAW, 54-55
Sleight, Lynn G.	Lynn	SAW, n.p.
Slaughter, Jay	Jay	SAW, 8-9
Sloan, Hugh C.	Hugh	SAW, n.p.
Smith, A. Marion	Marion	SAW, n.p.
Smith, Doyle G.	Doyle	SAW, n.p.
Smith, Louis	Louis	SAW, n.p.
Smith, Stanley G.	Stanley	SAW, n.p.
Smith, Willard Deloy	Deloy	SAW, 115-116
Sonne, Alma B.	Alma	SAW, 1
Spears, Buddy	Buddy	CN, May 13, 1944, 8
Stephenson, Glen H.	Glen	SAW, 2
Stewart, Walter	Walter	SAW, 248-250
Stradling, John S.	John	SAW, 256, 274, 276, 294
Stratford, Ray	Ray	SAW, n.p.
Taylor, Ed Martin	Bud	SAW, news clipping
Taylor, Jack	Jack	SAW, n.p.
Taylor, Ray N.	Ray	CN: LDS Service Men's Ed., Feb. 15, 1945, 7
Tingey, Wynn	Wynn	Minidoka County News, Feb. 7, 2001, 1
Tipton, Vernon	Vernon	SAW, 5
Tsuya, Roy I.	Roy	SAW, n.p.
Turley, Grant M.	Grant	SAW, 121, 126, 135
Tuttle, A. Theodore	Ted	SAW, 1-3; letter file
Vlam, Pieter	Piet	SAW, 97-103
von Bose, Robert J.	Robert	SAW, 1-2
Walker, Elmo L.	Elmo	SAW, n.p.
Webb, LaVarr	LaVarr	SAW, 10-12
Wettstein, James D.	James	SAW, 9-11
Wheatley, Bert M.	Bert	SAW, n.p.
Wheeler, Jay E.	Jay	SAW, 28-29, 32
Whitaker, W. Dean	Dean	SAW, prologue
White, Carrol N.	Carrol	SAW, n.p.
Wilhite, Billy J.	Billy	SAW, 11-12
Williams, Clyde E.	Clyde	SAW, 18-19
Willis, Curtis	Curtis	SAW, 267-270
Willison, Keith R.	Keith	SAW, 1-3, 6
Wirick, Neil W.	Neil	SAW, 2
Wright, Robert L.	Robert	SAW, n.p.
Wright, Forest A.	Forest	SAW, 3
Wyrouck, Sam H.	Sam	SAW, n.p.
Yeates, Clyde K.	Clyde	The Deseret News, Dec. 22, 2000, A1
Young, John O.	"J.O."	CN, Mar. 18, 1944, 7

PHOTO CREDITS

FRONT MATTER:

p. vii   Forest A. Wright, courtesy of Lola Anderson Wright.

p. viii   James Ralph Jensen, courtesy of Georgia Jensen Blosil.

p. 2   Heber Partington, courtesy of Heber Partington.

p. 2   Burial site of Charles Stanley Bascom, courtesy of Lamona J. Newren.

p. 3   LDS group at Naka, Horisha, Japan, courtesy of Howard Norton.

THE CHURCH AND THE WAR:

p. 4   LDS Base Chapel on New Guinea, courtesy of Heber Partington.

p. 5   Serviceman baptism on beach at Saipan, courtesy of Gerald L. Erickson.

p. 6   Father and son, Fred Turley and Grant M. Turely, courtesy of Stan Turley.

p. 7   "The Church and the Present War" pamphlet, courtesy of Reed A. Benson.

p. 8   *Deseret News* article on First Presidency's message on war, courtesy of Reed A. Benson.

p. 9   Memorial service for Borgstrom sons, courtesy of LDS Church Archives.

p. 9   President Boyd K. Packer and first post-war Japanese converts, courtesy of Howard Norton.

p. 10   LDS servicemen visit outside a newly erected chapel in Italy, courtesy of Eldin and Irene Ricks.

p. 10   Servicemen's Conference in India, 1945, courtesy of Franklin Brough.

p. 11   Servicemen's Conference in Okinawa, 1945, courtesy of Grant Southam.

p. 11   Program for Servicemen's Conference in France, 1945, courtesy of Reed Benson.

p. 11   Servicemen's Conference in Italy, 1945, courtesy of Eldin and Irene Ricks.

p. 12   Program from Servicemen's Conference on New Britain, courtesy of Lyle G. Stewart.

p. 12   Servicemen register for LDS Conference in China, 1945, courtesy of LDS Church Archives.

p. 13   Chaplain Eldin Ricks, courtesy of Irene Ricks.

p. 13   Jeep decorated by LDS chaplains, courtesy of Claude Burtenshaw.

p. 15   USS *Joseph Smith*, courtesy of LDS Church Archives.

p. 16   Hugh B. Brown addressing conference of Latter-day Saints in Paris, courtesy of Paul Ahlstrom.

p. 16   LDS servicemen's editions of the *Church News*, courtesy of Don V. Tibbs and Reed Benson.

p. 16   Cover of LDS Armed Forces Church Directory, courtesy of Reed Benson.

p. 17   Servicemen studying the servicemen's edition of the scriptures, courtesy of Claude Burtenshaw.

p. 17   Servicemen's edition of the scriptures, courtesy of Reed Benson. Photo by Maren E. Ogden.

p. 18   Examples of V-Mail, courtesy of Irene Ricks.

p. 19   Funeral proceedings for Heber J. Grant, courtesy of LDS Church Archives.

p. 20   Elder Ezra Taft Benson with LDS German refugees in Germany, courtesy of LDS Church Archives.

p. 21   Dutch Saints load potatoes on truck bound for Germany, courtesy of LDS Church Archives.

p. 22   Budget ticket issued to LDS servicemen during war, courtesy of family of Walter Cole.

p. 23   *The Church News* (*L.D.S. Service Men's Edition*), Nov. 1944, courtesy of Don V. Tibbs.

THE EUROPEAN THEATER:

p. 26   European-African-Middle Easter (EAME) Campaign Medal, courtesy of Institute of Heraldry, Dept. of the Army, United States of America.

p. 27   Alvin R. Carlson with a little girl in Italy, courtesy of Karen L. Mathis.

p. 28   Northern Europe map, courtesy of The General Libraries, The University of Texas at Austin.

p. 29   Southern Approaches to Europe map, courtesy of The General Libraries, The University of Texas at Austin.

p. 30   B-17 with severe damage to rear section, courtesy of Ray Matheny.

p. 31   German armbands, courtesy of Ferrel W. Bybee. Photo by Maren E. Ogden.

p. 33   American landing party rescues other Allies during D-Day Invasion, courtesy of National Archives Still Pictures Branch.

p. 35   LDS group at Poix, France, courtesy of Halbert L. Iverson.

p. 36   Scene of destruction somewhere in Europe, courtesy of National Archives Still Pictures Branch.

p. 37   Tank with "duck feet" being tested in France, courtesy of the L. Tom Perry Special Collections, Harold B. Lee Library, Brigham Young University. Photo by Jay Heslop.

p. 38   Arnett's B-24 bomber crew, courtesy of Charles Arnett.

BIBLIOGRAPHY

EUROPEAN SOURCES:

Keegan, John. *The Second World War.* London: Century Hutchinson Ltd., 1989.

Lyons, Michael. *World War.* Upper Saddle River, New Jersey: Prentice Hall, 1999.

Parker, R.A.C. *The Second World War.* New York: Oxford University Press, 1997.

Reader's Digest. *Illustrated Story of World War II.* Pleasantville, New York, The Reader's Digest Association, Inc., 1969.

PACIFIC SOURCES:

Chambers, John Whiteclay ll, ed. *The Oxford Companion to American History.* New York: Oxford University Press, 1999.

Parrish, Thomas and S. L. A. Marshall, eds. *The Simon and Schuster Encolpedia of World War II.* New York: Cord Communications Corporation, 1978.

Shaw, Anthony. *World War ll Day by Day.* Osceola: MBI Publishing, 2000.

Van der Vat, Dan. *The Pacific Campaign: World War ll, the U.S.-Japanese Naval War, 1941-1945.* New York: Touchstone, 1991.

INDEX

THE SAINTS AT WAR ARCHIVE NEEDS YOU

The Saints at War Archive provides a unique opportunity for veterans and their family members to preserve the legacy of Latter-day Saint military service during times of war. The chief objective is to establish a permanent archive of written histories, oral histories, letters, journals, images, and other documents that will be maintained at the L. Tom Perry Special Collections Library at Brigham Young University. To date, hundreds of Latter-day Saint World War veterans and their families have contributed to the project.

Plans are in place to expand the collection to include veteran experiences of later conflicts of the twentieth century, including the Korean and Vietnam Wars. The project directors invite veterans and others involved in any of these conflicts to consider how they may contribute to this effort to preserve latter-day voices of war. Future generations of students, family members, and scholars will find this resource invaluable, as well as inspiring, as they study the experiences of Latter-day Saints during war.

Those interested may learn more about the project by visiting the Saints at War website or by contacting the project directors at Brigham Young University.

Saints at War Archive
375 Joseph Smith Building
Brigham Young University
Provo, Utah 84602

www.saintsatwar.org